T0357247

GOLDEN STATE

ALSO BY MICHAEL HILTZIK

*Iron Empires: Robber Barons, Railroads, and the
Making of Modern America*

*Big Science: Ernest Lawrence and the Invention That
Launched the Military-Industrial Complex*

The New Deal: A Modern History

Colossus: The Turbulent, Thrilling Saga of the Building of Hoover Dam

*The Plot Against Social Security: How the Bush Plan Is
Endangering Our Financial Future*

Dealers of Lightning: Xerox PARC and the Dawn of the Computer Age

A Death in Kenya: The Murder of Julie Ward

GOLDEN STATE

The MAKING *of* CALIFORNIA

MICHAEL HILTZIK

MARINER BOOKS
New York   Boston

HarperCollins books may be purchased for educational, business, or sales promotional use. For information, please email the Special Markets Department at SPsales@harper collins.com.

The Mariner flag design is a registered trademark of HarperCollins Publishers LLC.

FIRST EDITION

Designed by Emily Snyder
Map illustration © THEPALMER / Getty Images

Library of Congress Cataloging-in-Publication Data has been applied for.

ISBN 978-0-358-53934-6

24 25 26 27 28 LBC 5 4 3 2 1

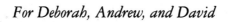

For Deborah, Andrew, and David

Nowhere else were we Americans more affected than here, in our lives and conduct, by the feeling that we stood in the position of conquerors in a new land.

—JOSIAH ROYCE, *California*

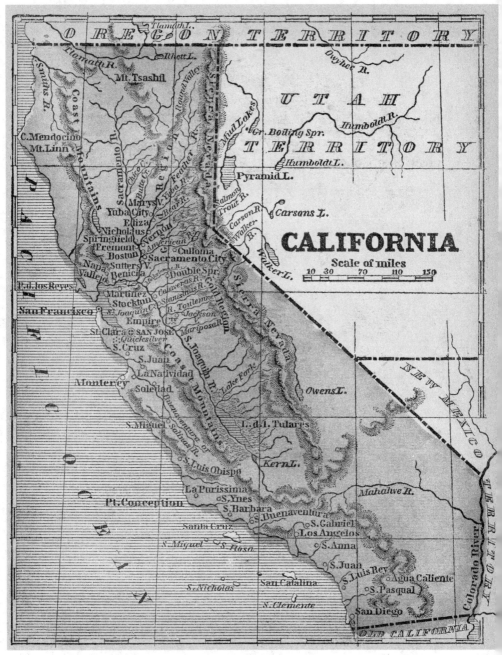

California in 1855, by cartographer Sidney E. Morse

CONTENTS

PROLOGUE

CALIFORNIA, LAND OF CONTRADICTIONS

L IKE MILLIONS OF immigrants before me, I came to California enthralled with the possibility of making a new life. Not that I was
discontented with the old one, exactly, only suffused with a feeling of stagnation. I had been born, raised, and educated in New York State and started
my career there and continued it in New England, so my horizons seemed
rather constrained.

California beckoned via a job offer from the *Los Angeles Times*. It was 1981.
I was single, in my late twenties. Visions of California's promise swirled in my
head: freethinkers, liberal politics, cultural and ethnic diversity, sun, surf—an
entirely novel landscape to engage mind and body. California values seemed
to have pervaded our nation's politics, our economics, our culture, every corner of our way of life. The Sierra Club had been born here; at Berkeley, the free
speech movement launched the era of college protest; new frontiers in science
and technology were being explored by young engineers on a Bay Area hillside. One of them, the brilliant computer scientist Alan Kay, had set forth a
credo for those seeking a glimpse of things to come: "The best way to predict
the future," he said, "is to *invent* it."

What better vantage point from which to witness the building of a new
world?

I found an apartment in a hip section of Long Beach, near the water, and
turned in my aging, corroded car for a new coupe (the salesman, helping
me transfer my belongings from my Ford Galaxie, discovered a bent and

battered snow shovel in the trunk and showed it around the lot like a paleo-lithic relic).

In an experience that millions before me had had, however, my concept of California as a paradise on earth did not survive its first encounter with reality. In late August, during my first weekend in town, I walked what my map showed to be three blocks to the water with a lawn chair and beach towel, only to discover that what looks on paper like an easy stroll can turn into a miles-long slog on foot. I expected to be dipping my toes into the clear waters of the Pacific, but the beach fronted on a murky bay fed by the Los Angeles River, a once-bucolic stream now imprisoned in a concrete channel and carrying the fetid runoff of thousands of square miles of paved-over terrain. The rainbow sheen of petroleum on the water's surface signaled that the vast ports of Long Beach and Los Angeles stood just beyond the breakwater. The mysterious islets just offshore bearing parti-colored towers surrounded by palms could be mistaken from a distance for amusement parks; in fact, they were oil platforms, their gaudy facades concealing derricks and pumps operating twenty-four hours a day.

I had been misled into thinking of California as a place of unalloyed cosmopolitanism. Instead, I landed in a community built by midwestern transplants that had acquired the nickname "Iowa by the Sea." Neighboring Orange County, where I was assigned as a business reporter, was a hotbed of far-right politics nestled within California's coastal strip of blue.

A few weeks after my arrival, a press release from John G. Schmitz, a former Orange County congressman now holding a state senate seat, crossed my desk. Schmitz had been drummed out of the John Birch Society for being *too* conservative. "State Sen. John G. Schmitz survives the attack of the bull dykes," the document read, recounting how at a series of public hearings around the state for an antiabortion bill he was sponsoring, he had been con-fronted by "a sea of hard, Jewish and (arguably) female faces." A few months later, Schmitz, who had run for office on a family-values platform, was swept up in a scandal involving a mistress charged with child endangerment for her treatment of the infant they had had together. He lost the next election and never ran for office again.

Plainly, there was more to California than the bright, liberal image. That was always true. It still is.

Getting a grip on this vast, diverse state is challenging but necessary. California is often depicted as a place almost alien to the rest of the country.

According to a widely repeated line sometimes attributed (probably errone-ously) to Mark Twain, "America is built on a tilt and everything loose slides to California." Yet as of this writing, California is home to more than one in eight Americans. In a very real sense, it *is* America. To understand Califor-nia is to understand America; to understand America, one must understand California.

This is not a new concept. The reform-minded economist Henry George expressed it in 1880, explaining for his readers an outburst of anti-Chinese sentiment in San Francisco. "It is yet a mistake to regard California as a com-munity widely differing from more Eastern States," George wrote. "I am, in fact, inclined rather to look upon California as a typical American State, and San Francisco as a typical American city. It would be difficult to name any State that in resources, climate, and industries comes nearer to representing the whole Union."

Yet there is something exceptional about California that has commanded the attention of America and the world through the five centuries since European explorers first heard rumors of its riches and decided to see for themselves. California was the destination of all three of the great human migrations of American history: the Gold Rush of 1848–1849; the inflow to Southern California at the turn of the last century that transformed an unprepossessing, arid basin into the teeming Los Angeles metropolis; and the flight from the Dust Bowl in the 1930s. The first was driven by spec-ulation, the second by ballyhoo, and the third by destitution, but the mi-grants were all motivated by the common goal of starting over. "They who came to California," wrote Joan Didion, a child of Sacramento, quoting her own eighth-grade graduation speech, "were not the self-satisfied, happy and content people, but the adventurous, the restless, and the daring." Not all found what they were looking for, quite obviously. The doubts and worries that afflicted those who came west for a new life only to have their hopes dashed can be seen in the careworn expression on the face of Florence Owens Thompson, the "Migrant Mother" of the iconic Dorothea Lange photograph taken at a failed farm camp on the Nipomo Mesa, scarcely ten miles from the Pacific Ocean, the very end of the road.

Still, the gravitational attraction of the place for those in search of new lives and loves has never faded. In our own times it can be detected in pop-ular songs and poems. Tony Bennett's lover calls him to reclaim his heart in San Francisco; Joni Mitchell sings of leaving the cold and settled ways of Paris to come home to California. The Mamas and the Papas dream of escaping gray skies and brown leaves to be safe and warm in LA; the Beach Boys wish they could transform all the girls they meet into California girls.

From lyrics and verses, one might think the draw is chiefly the sun. For Neil Young, the California sunset offered "all the colors in the sky." The poet Vachel Lindsay counted "ten gold suns in California / When all other lands have one." Lindsay also wrote, however, of seeking California's "spiritual gold." And truly, California is one of the few places on earth that can be thought of as both a geographical location and a state of mind. It is the latter aspect that has beckoned multitudes. Many come not to partake of its natural riches, though these are plentiful, but to carry forward their personal quests for a fresh environment mentally, intellectually, spiritually.

Taking California's measure may not be as straightforward a task as it sounds, for California has consistently been the most misunderstood state in the union.

"There has always been something about it that has incited hyperbole, that has made for exaggeration," wrote Carey McWilliams, among the foremost chroniclers of California's historical pageant. (He titled his 1949 one-volume history of the state *California: The Great Exception*, though he was not entirely clear about what it was an exception *to*.) McWilliams might better have labeled California "the great contradiction," for its path to global influence and power has been paved with boom-and-bust economics, social friction, and leadership in progressive and reactionary politics alike.

McWilliams divided those who had written about California into two categories: "The skeptics who, in retrospect, have been made to look ludicrously gullible; and the liars and boasters who have been confounded by the fulfillment of their dizziest predictions." Up to the present day, reportage about California has fallen neatly into one of those categories—either proclaiming a new stage in the "California dream" or anticipating the dream's ultimate demise.

The tug-of-war between California's enthusiasts and detractors is older than its statehood, which came in 1850. The Gold Rush of 1849 instilled in a vast migratory swarm of "Argonauts," as the newcomers were known, visions of fortunes to be made in the valleys and riverbeds of California. With them came the doubters. One was an adventurer from North Carolina, Hinton R. Helper, who arrived in the teeth of the Gold Rush with a skeptical chip on his shoulder and promptly condemned in messages to his friends at home the state's "rottenness and its corruption, its squalor and its misery, its crime and its shame, its gold and its dross." He was not wrong, exactly, merely hyperbolic.

To Henry David Thoreau, there was something disreputable in the grasping for wealth that defined the allure of the distant state. "The rush to California . . . and the attitude, not merely of merchants, but of philosophers and prophets, so called, in relation to it, reflect the greatest disgrace on mankind. . . . The hog that gets his living by rooting, stirring up the soil so, would be ashamed of such company."

Horace Greeley, to whom is attributed, perhaps apocryphally, the advice to young men to "Go west," returned to New York from his sole visit to California (in 1859) of two minds about the place. He wrote fervently of the land's natural fruitfulness: "The fig-tree grows in these valleys side by side with the apple . . . the olive grows finely . . . and I believe the orange and lemon as well. But the grape bids fair to become a staple throughout the state." But he also warned his readers that opportunity in California was almost tapped out. "No more merchants or clerks are wanted; and of those who come hereafter, nine-tenths will go back disappointed or impoverished, or stay here paupers." Greeley judged "the master-scourge of this state" to be "the deplorable confusion and uncertainty of land titles," dating from the era of Mexican governance prior to US annexation in 1848. He was correct about the land disputes, which would cast a shadow over the state's development for many years. But he was wrong about the boundaries of opportunity, as would be attested to by the millions who established families and careers, if not fabulous fortunes, in the decades ahead, when the state's population grew from the 380,000 residents of Greeley's time to 1.5 million in 1900 and nearly 40 million at this writing.

Mark Twain soaked up the spirit of the land during a sojourn in the 1860s while the vestiges of the Gold Rush were still at hand. He was appalled at the condition in which the prospectors left the landscape, writing in *Roughing It* (1872) of "its grassy slopes and levels torn and guttered and disfigured by the avaricious spoilers" and lamenting the sight of what were once "streets crowded and rife with business" reduced after the exhaustion of the gold mines to "nothing . . . but a lifeless, homeless solitude."

While it lasted, however, the era brought to California "a splendid population" of "stalwart, muscular, dauntless young braves," Twain wrote. "It was that population that gave to California a name for getting up astounding enterprises and rushing them through with a magnificent dash and daring and a recklessness of cost or consequences, which she bears unto this day—and when she projects a new surprise, the grave world smiles as usual, and says, 'Well, that is California all over.'"

Californians have always shown the determination to create their own destinies. Much of the loose material in the putative Twain quip became transformed in California's environment into something greater—and often something transformative for the outside world.

Unwilling to wait for Congress to decide whether to admit the territory as a free or slave state, California's white settlers took matters into their own hands by writing their own constitution in 1849, a year before admission to the union. On their own initiative, they allowed "neither slavery, nor involuntary servitude." At the turn of the last century, California stood in the vanguard of progressive politics, as personified by Hiram Johnson, who during his governorship (1911–1917) established its tradition of ballot-box legislating through initiatives, referendums, and recalls. His goal was the restoration of the public's political power, which had been ceded to corporate interests. In the 1930s the state became a hotbed of utopian social and political thought. The socialist writer Upton Sinclair ran for governor in 1934 on a platform he labeled EPIC, for "End Poverty in California"; he might have won if not for a conservative smear campaign featuring, among other fakeries, repurposed Hollywood film clips that purportedly showed hordes of hobos and tramps flowing over the border to take advantage of Sinclair's handouts. Around the same time, a Long Beach physician named Francis Everett Townsend proposed a plan to end poverty among seniors by paying two hundred dollars a month to every American sixty and older. The Townsend plan did not make sense economically, but it did help ensure the enactment of Social Security in 1935. By this time, an evangelist preacher named Aimee Semple McPherson—guided west by divine instruction, or so she said—had established a temple from which she proclaimed a heaven on earth; she pioneered the use of the new technology of radio to send her message around the world, garnering international fame.

Today, in the first decades of the twenty-first century, California's prodigious influence on national and global economics and politics is settled fact. Its gross domestic product is estimated to be more than $3.5 trillion; if it were a country, it would rank fifth globally, behind the United States, China,

Japan, and Germany and ahead of India, Britain, France, and Italy. Following the 2020 US census, California lost a congressional seat, an unprecedented development in the modern era, but its delegation of fifty-two representatives was still almost half again as large as that of the runner-up, Texas, with thirty-eight.

The state's size and wealth has produced what economists call the *California effect*. The term was coined in 1995 by political scientist David Vogel of the University of California to describe how the state's size, influence, and position "on the cutting edge of environmental regulation . . . helped drive many American environmental regulations upward." Like a giant planet gathering moons to its orbit by the sheer force of gravity, California prompted other states to apply its standards for automobile and industrial emissions. The term came to signify the state's ability to project more than merely its environmental values onto the nation at large. The California effect placed the state in the forefront of movements such as women's suffrage, religious evangelism, citizen legislating, progressivism, conservatism, environmentalism, and conservationism. Its political, economic, and social values did not flow in one direction. Many of the ideas, forces, innovations, and inventions that have transformed life in America originated in California, but even those that originated elsewhere were often put through a California filter before being sent back out again, validated by the state's outsize influence.

Not everything out of California has been positively inspirational or as inspirational as it might have seemed on the surface. California's 1849 constitution may have outlawed slavery, but it granted the right to vote to white male citizens alone, denying it to Black, Chinese, and Japanese men and to all women. The following year, legislation barred Black people and Indigenous Americans from giving testimony at trial against "any white person," a restriction extended to Chinese residents in 1854.

Racial discrimination and violence run deeply through California history. When, following the completion of the transcontinental railroad, Chinese laborers began to chart their own economic path, they became targets of resentment and discrimination by union leaders and political demagogues. Laws constraining Chinese employment, landownership, and freedom of movement appeared, along with mob violence. The anti-Chinese politics of California imposed its weight on federal policy, culminating in the Chinese

Exclusion Act of 1882 and the laws that succeeded it, effectively quashing all Chinese immigration.

The anti-Chinese agitators then turned their sights on the Japanese. Anti-Japanese prejudice led to the unpardonable policy of incarceration the United States inflicted on Japanese residents, including American citizens of Japanese ancestry, during World War II. Among the outstanding ironies of California politics was that Earl Warren, the popular progressive governor who as chief justice of the United States drafted that landmark of court-ordered desegregation *Brown v. Board of Education of Topeka*, was a most uncompromising advocate of the transportation of 110,000 Japanese residents of California to concentration camps.

DESPITE ALL THE recurring hand-wringing about the fate of the California dream, there has always been something mystical and magnetic about the state beyond the quest for material wealth from gold (starting in 1848) and oil (a couple of decades later). People are enthralled by its physical beauty, comprising towering sequoias, Big Sur, and the inspirational Yosemite Valley. Its multifarious climate encompasses a coastal zone of Mediterranean temperance as well as inland deserts and snow-capped mountain ridges. Its harbors are among the finest on either coast. And its seemingly endless hectares of arable or irrigable land can support everything from Greeley's apples, oranges, olives, lemons, and grapes to almonds, pistachios, cotton, and vast expanses of alfalfa.

California offered opportunity to those who felt their ambitions constrained by the stagnating institutions of the East Coast. Among them was Ernest Orlando Lawrence, who in 1928 had been waiting his turn for advancement in the physics department at Yale when the University of California came calling with the promise that he could take charge of his own career. He was twenty-seven. Within three years he had invented the cyclotron, an atom smasher that transformed the study of physics and placed California at the center of a scientific revolution.

Forty years later, Xerox Corporation, fat with profits from its monopoly on office copiers but fearful that new technologies might render its products obsolete, built a laboratory to "invent the future" in California as far as one could get in distance and spirit from the convention-bound headquarters in Rochester, New York, and staffed it with the smartest young scientists and engineers it could find. There they invented the personal computer. The peninsula south of San Francisco where they worked soon became known as Silicon Valley; its confluence of intellect, money, and marketing produced innovations and wealth on an unimaginable scale—a seedbed emulated by localities across the country and the world but never equaled.

MY FIRST SOJOURN in California was brief, scarcely two years, after which the *Los Angeles Times* sent me back to New York to cover the financial industry and then on assignments abroad. When I returned in the mid-1990s, I came with a family. California was different from the state I remembered, yet somehow the same. It was still an economic powerhouse, though the aerospace industry that had fueled its growth through the postwar years had suffered a grievous collapse and been supplanted by the uniquely innovative culture of the computer industry in Silicon Valley.

A state that had been a stronghold for Republicans at the national level was turning toward the Democrats—in 1992, Bill Clinton became the first Democratic presidential candidate to carry the state since Lyndon Johnson's 1964 landslide. The transformation did not proceed along a straight line. In 1994, the voters passed Proposition 187, which denied public services to undocumented immigrants but was written broadly enough to encourage police to question and detain almost anyone they suspected of being an undocumented immigrant, mostly because of the color of their skin. The measure was overturned by the state's supreme court, but the wheel kept turning. The proposition proved to be the last gasp, even the death rattle, of California's anti-diversity Republican Party, which launched itself down a path of statewide political irrelevance. Orange County, that hive of reactionary Republicanism in the 1980s, was turning distinctly blue; in 2018, every one of its seven congressional seats went to the Democrats.

Yet the vaulting self-confidence of 1980s California had begun to fade. The era of limitations was upon the state, proclaimed by its scholarly governor Edmund Gerald "Jerry" Brown Jr. The growing population strained public services, provoked a crisis in housing, and encroached on the hills and forests, turning wildfires into an economic threat. Increasingly frequent droughts produced water shortages and led to rationing. Global warming is destined to force a drastic reconsideration of water rights that have been in effect since the eighteenth century and threatens to reverse advances in environmental policies that have been among the state's proudest achievements.

California's solution to these challenges—still a work in progress—will test the "California effect" for decades to come.

TO THE QUESTION of what made California, we must look not only to its people but to nature.

Any relief map of California—even a view of the state through an airliner window—testifies to the extraordinary violence of its geological history, leaving what Josiah Royce, one of the state's pioneering historians, described as "a country full of tell-tale landscapes, that show at a glance the general topographical structure of the whole land." Over the course of nearly two billion years, the geological record reflected the clash of gargantuan plates of rock and flows of magma in the subterranean depths. In these collisions, up-thrusts, sideswipes, foldings, and metamorphoses, gigantic blocks of granite were heaved toward the sky, pitched onto their sides, upended, turned ninety degrees; vast inland seas were filled and drained and filled again in epochal rhythms. The entire coastal landmass west of the over-seven-hundred-mile-long San Andreas Fault was once the west coast of mainland Mexico, but it crept inexorably north and became reattached to the continent, creating the California we recognize today.

In California, geology and geography are destiny. Wrote Royce: "Nowhere else were we Americans more affected than here, in our lives and conduct, by the feeling that we stood in the position of conquerors in a new land."

In California, geology and geography are also prologue. In the 1830s, the settlers who were lured west by reports of a salubrious climate and the promise of almost effortless wealth discovered upon their arrival that making the landscape serve them required a makeover on a Promethean scale. The newcomers stripped valleys of their grasses and trees and replanted them with alien fruits and vegetables. They dredged and redirected and corralled riverbeds, expanded shorelines with landfill, regraded mountain passes, and drove tunnels through the mountains. Every variety of human creativity was mustered to counteract the territory's sunbaked aridity and relocate water from where it was abundant to where it was scarce. "In general, Californians have not been pleased with the natural distribution of water," observed ecologist Allan A. Schoenherr. Given the choice between moving people to where the water is or moving the water to the people, Californians have almost invariably done the latter, in the process creating the most elaborate aqueduct system in the world.

One can try to define California through numbers, some of which give a clue to its gravitational pull: The state is 163,696 square miles, making it the third largest in the United States; its population is the largest of any state by a 35 percent margin. California possesses the widest range of elevation in the United States, from the 14,496-foot Mount Whitney, the highest peak in the lower 48 states, to Death Valley, which, at 280 feet below sea level, is the lowest point in North America, the two landmarks less than ninety miles apart as the crow flies.

Yet the raw statistics by themselves cannot provide an adequate picture of the diversity of the land, which encompasses some of the richest farmland in the country and some of its most desolate moonscapes. It is not just outsiders who have concluded, now and then, that California is too big and too variegated to be just one state; that has occurred to Californians too, now and then, when the interests of northerners and southerners or rural folk and city dwellers appear to diverge so completely that it can be hard to conceive of the groups as members of the same species.

For all its variety, the geology of California can be slotted into three major categories: mountains, valleys, and deserts.

The Sierra Nevada and the Coast Ranges are the state's most conspicuous terrestrial features, mountain ridges running roughly parallel to the coastline on a northwest–southeast axis roughly eighty to one hundred miles apart. The Sierra Nevada, four hundred miles long and fifty miles wide and named by the Spaniards for its toothed ridgeline and year-round crown of snow, runs along much of the state's eastern border and offers some of its most spectacular natural vistas, including the glacier-sculpted Yosemite Valley and the serrated ridge of the Kaweah Peaks, the vestige of a string of primordial volcanoes. The Sierra Nevada is a gigantic mass of granite turned on its side by tectonic forces; its western slope is, in geologic terms, the top of the primordial granite block tipped over. The range's volcanic origin is revealed not only in its gray, coarse-grained granite but in its red and black outcroppings. (The state's most notable active volcano, Lassen Peak, in the far northeastern corner where the Sierras shade into the Cascade Range, staged its most violent eruption of modern times in 1917.)

The Sierras are the youngest features of the California terrain, in some places displaying signs of glacial activity dating back only sixty thousand years. That accounts for much of the natural drama of the landscape, for glacial advances and retreats are vividly evident in its cirques (semicircular, amphitheater-like basins), arêtes (razor-thin ridges), pyramid-shaped peaks known as horns, and fields of rubble known as moraines.

The Coast Ranges lie to the Sierras' west, running along the fault lines where the Pacific Plate sinks under the North American Plate. The Coast Ranges compete with the Sierras for California's most spectacular natural scenery. Here one finds Big Sur, a rugged stretch of cliffs sustaining a relentless pounding from the angry sea that the Australian landscape artist Francis McComas aptly called "the greatest meeting of land and water in the world."

The two north–south mountain ranges converge near the latitude of Santa Barbara at the western end of the Transverse Ranges, which cross the state on an east–west axis. These ranges—the Santa Monica, San Gabriel, and San Bernardino—once ran in the same north–south direction as the Coast and Sierra Nevada ranges but were rotated by geological forces about ninety degrees clockwise, like a swinging door hinged at the San Andreas Fault. The Transverse Ranges are among the oldest geologic formations in California, with bands of gneiss, a metamorphic rock formed by intense heat and pressure on igneous and sedimentary rocks, thought to be as much as 1.7 billion years old. Nestled south of the Transverse Ranges is the most heavily populated region of California, an area less than one-sixth of the state's territory but home to more than half its residents.

The Coast Ranges and Sierra Nevada cradle the state's sprawling Central Valley, ranked among the richest tracts of agricultural land in America. The valley is shaped like an elongated bowl, 430 miles long and 75 miles wide, lying as much as 400 feet above sea level at either end and below sea level in the center. More than any other part of the state, the valley displays the imprint of human activity. It was once carpeted with grassland that erupted with wildflowers at the coming of rain—blue lupins and poppies celebrated for their audacious coloration by John Steinbeck, a native of the region, in his masterpiece *East of Eden*: "If pure gold were liquid and could raise a cream, that golden cream might be like the color of the poppies." More than one hundred forty-five million years ago, the waters drained out of what was then a vast wetland, leaving behind a layer of marine sediment thirty thousand feet deep that was then covered over by alluvial deposits washed down from the mountains. Much of this natural glory has been eradicated by overgrazing, which began back in the pre-statehood period and reached a climax after the Gold Rush, when three million cattle and nine million sheep raised to feed the prospectors gnawed the land bare and packed the soil hard with their hooves.

Three deserts lie along the state's eastern border. North to south, they are the Great Basin, the Mojave, and the Colorado. The first of these is a small slice of a much larger desert reaching into Oregon, Nevada, and Utah, an expanse of brackish pools and dry lake beds in its lower elevations and an otherworldly volcanic plain, the Modoc Plateau, in the state's northeastern corner.

Within the V formed by the western edge of the Sierras and the northern slopes of the Transverse Ranges, chiefly the San Gabriel and San Bernardino Mountains—or, if one prefers, between the Garlock Fault on its north and the San Andreas on its south—lies the Mojave Desert. The Mojave extends all the way to the Colorado River, which defines the California-Arizona border. The Mojave, known as the high desert for its 3,500-foot elevation, is treasured by enthusiasts of the California outdoors for the breathtaking scenery of its three sprawling national parks: Joshua Tree, Death Valley, and the Mojave National Preserve.

Southwest of the Mojave lies the Colorado Desert, which includes an elongated trough known as the Salton Sink, the deepest part of which is the Salton Sea. This mineral-rich body of water did not exist in its modern form until 1905, when the sink was inundated by spillover from the Colorado River after an incompetent attempt at building a canal to carry its water west. In prehistoric times, the sink and much of the surrounding territory was covered by an immense inland sea stretching south from the Coachella Valley to beyond the Mexican border. The sea was dubbed (in the modern era) Lake Cahuilla, after the local American Indian tribes; the fossilized evidence of its past can still be excavated miles from the shores of the Salton Sea.

These three categories of topography have interacted with one another for millennia, producing California's immeasurably varied climate.

Air cooled by a sea current flowing south from Alaska is trapped by the Coast Ranges and condensed into the fog common along the Northern California coast. That may have had much to do with the repeated failure of sixteenth-century mariners to spot the inlet—later dubbed the Golden Gate—that opened onto the peerless harbor of San Francisco Bay, as they cruised along the coast. The fog nourishes the towering forests of redwoods, California's state tree.

The region inland of the Coast Ranges is sheltered from precipitation by the mountains' rain shadow, which produces near-desert conditions in much of the Central Valley. A similar phenomenon occurs at the Sierra Nevada, the western slope of which receives abundant precipitation and the sheltered eastern slope much less. The rains flow down through the canyons of the Sierras in a filigree of streams collecting in two major rivers: the San Joaquin, which flows north, and the Sacramento, which flows south. They meet in a quilt-like delta feeding into San Francisco Bay and thence the water flows out to the ocean via the Golden Gate—that is, whatever water has not been impounded behind dams for irrigation or sent south to sustain the voracious water users of Southern California.

A mapmaker's perspective shows how topography has dictated settlement of California from the pre-statehood period to modern times. Most of the state's population is crammed into the flattened terrain between the Coast Ranges and the sea, with the uncanny metropolis of Los Angeles spreading out toward and into the foothills to its north and down the coast toward San Diego to the south.

This is the record of how humankind brought an alien landscape to heel. Yet from time to time, nature flicks its dragon tail to remind Californians that they cannot truly conquer this land; they can only occupy it, subject to what the environmentalist Marc Reisner called an "uneasy truce." Almost the entire state is crosshatched by faults, which produce the earthquakes that have been a defining characteristic of the region for much longer than there have been humans to feel the shocks and tremors. The quakes often reveal nature's capacity for surprise: One of the largest in the state's recorded history occurred in 1952 near the town of Tehachapi, at the southern end of the Sierra Nevadas, on a thirty-four-mile fault that had been inactive for millennia. Twelve people died. The San Andreas is the best-known fault, running from the Gulf of California to just north of San Francisco, where it cleaves an enormous wedge of land away from the mainland (creating the fingerlike Tomales Bay) and enters the Pacific. The fault scarified the land through its innumerable seizures in geologic time and human memory, notably the great 1906 earthquake that leveled much of San Francisco.

Under the northern Coast Range, about seventy miles north of San Francisco, a huge magma-filled chamber four miles beneath the surface gives evidence of the still lively tectonic activity underground. The region is known as the Geysers, an area of hot springs and thermal pools exploited by local tribes for thousands of years in the past and today by a complex of eighteen geothermal power plants; it is the largest geothermal field in the world and the source of about 20 percent of California's renewable energy.

Human efforts to engineer changes in the California environment have never ceased; some have been aimed at fixing problems created by the humans themselves. The canal-building mishap that inundated the Salton Sink and threatened the agricultural survival of Imperial Valley necessitated a three-year, multimillion-dollar battle to force the Colorado River back between its banks, followed by further canal-building and ultimately the construction of Hoover Dam. The dam provided the water and electricity that fostered the explosive growth of Southern California, which brought further problems of air and water pollution. The encroachment of agriculture, the use of DDT, and the killing of wild birds reduced to single digits the population of California condors, magnificent carrion-eaters that had thrived in their California habitat for forty thousand years. A program was launched to save the species from extinction by captive breeding, and the last wild bird was taken in 1987. Eventually, a genetically diverse population was returned to the wild, where more than three hundred birds now live.

I conceived this book as an examination of all that California has taught the rest of America and the world. This was during the Trump administration. California values, at least as they represented progressive policies, had seldom been so vibrantly on display. California's attorney general at the time, Xavier Becerra, would ultimately file 122 lawsuits against the administration, including nine on Trump's last day in office. The state worked to build a legal bulwark against the full spectrum of Trump policymaking, including his efforts to undermine the Affordable Care Act and the Endangered Species Act and to roll back emission regulations. California was on the winning side of the vast majority of these cases at the trial and appellate levels of federal courts.

The story turned out to be vastly deeper and more complex than I anticipated and, gratifyingly, more fascinating. Many California values as they developed over the centuries might have been less uplifting than its liberal campaign against the Trump White House, but they were profoundly influential nonetheless.

From the coming of the Spanish conquistadores in the sixteenth century to the flowering of high technology in the twentieth and twenty-first, California has held the imagination of the outside world in thrall, offering inspiration, instruction, and admonition. To understand how that came about and why it continues to be, we must start at the beginning.

PART I

The QUEST for EL DORADO

1

A TERRESTRIAL PARADISE

CALIFORNIA ENTERED EUROPEAN consciousness wreathed in dreams and fables.

One dream grew from the faith in a shortcut between the Atlantic Ocean and the Pacific through the great landmass of the Americas, the better to reach the East Indies, as Christopher Columbus had hoped, and later as a direct route from Spain to the Philippines. The Spaniards called this the Strait of Anián, the British the Northwest Passage.

Another dream was of fantastic riches to be found in a mythical land. The explorer Francisco Vázquez de Coronado chased rumors of such a place, called Quivira, on expeditions east from the Colorado River. Other tales were of the Seven Cities of Cibola, where the inhabitants lived in palaces of gold with walls bedecked with precious stones.

In time the entire region would become known as El Dorado. The Spanish term originally denoted "the gilded man"—based on the legend of a chieftain who covered himself in gold dust at the dawn of every day. Ultimately, the term became a metaphor for the glimmering objective haunting the conquistadores' dreams. Early conquests in the New World—of the Incans in Peru by Francisco Pizarro and of the Aztec Empire in Mexico by Hernán Cortés—seemed to validate these expectations, for the gold sent from there to Spain fattened its treasury and financed further explorations while whetting the appetite for new discoveries that would put the others to shame. But ultimately these dreams were dashed, as Coronado learned in 1541, when he located the fabled Quivira on the plains of present-day Kansas but found it to be only a settlement of farmers living in thatched huts and strolling about almost entirely naked.

The lands of El Dorado seemed perpetually to beckon from just beyond the next mountain ridge. The unsuccessful quest did lead the Spaniards, however, to discover California, which would turn out to be as close to a real-life El Dorado as they could have imagined.

THE ORIGIN OF the name *California* has been the subject of learned speculation for the better part of four hundred years. Its etymology is elusive; Jesuit missionaries in the eighteenth century suggested that it was drawn from the classical languages—*calida fornax*, Latin for "hot furnace," alluding to the hot climate, though as the historian Hubert Howe Bancroft observed, the climate is no warmer and often cooler than the Mediterranean climes from which the explorers hailed. The Jesuits also surmised that the name might have been a corruption of some phrase the explorers heard from the lips of Indigenous Americans they encountered, although in 1758, Miguel Venegas, a Jesuit historian of California, admitted that "in none of the various dialects of the natives could the missionaries find the least traces of such a name being given by them to the country." Speculation about a Greek derivation relies on the root *kalli* or *kala,* giving us, for example, *kala phor nea,* which could mean "beautiful woman," or some other similar formulation meaning "fertile land" or "new country."

The most enduring, or perhaps uncomplicated, derivation was proposed by the historian Edward Everett Hale, best known as the author of the short story "The Man Without a Country." In 1862, Hale reported that he had excavated the name California from a knightly saga published in Spain in 1510 titled *Las Sergas de Esplandián,* or *The Exploits of Esplandián.* This was a sequel to a popular series of chivalrous romances—"worthless" and "deservedly forgotten," scoffed Hale—about a hero known as Amadís de Gaula, or Amadís of Gaul. (The author of *Esplandián,* Garci Rodríguez de Montalvo, had translated the previous volumes from the Portuguese to Spanish.)

What caught Hale's eye was an episode in which Esplandián defends the city of Constantinople from the Turks. Allied with the attackers is an Amazon queen who is taken prisoner in battle by Amadís, falls in love with

Esplandián in captivity, converts to Christianity, and joins in the city's defense. The queen's name is Calafia, and the land over which she reigns is California.

Montalvo surely understood his market, for his description of Calafia and her land was tailored to appeal to a fantasy-besotted readership.

> Know ye that at the right hand of the Indies there is an island named California, very close to that part of the Terrestrial Paradise, which was inhabited by black women, without a single man among them. . . . They were robust of body, with strong and passionate hearts and great virtues. . . . The island everywhere abounds with gold and precious stones: and upon it no other metal was found.

All the necessary connections between the story of Calafia and the dreams and desires of the Spanish explorers are in place. In this period they supposed themselves to be east of the Indies—that is, at the Indies' right hand; they believed that the region they were exploring was an island; and the storied abundance of gold speaks for itself. Amazon women too were a durable feature of European myth and legend.

Whether Cortés or his crews were sufficiently conversant with *The Exploits of Esplandián* to apply a name from the romance to a feature of the landscape has been debated ever since Hale made his claim. Montalvo's translations of the first books of Amadís de Gaula prior to 1508 and the publication of *Esplandián* in 1510 gave the saga three decades to work its way into Spanish culture even among unlettered seamen before the name California appeared for the first time in a journal of a Spanish exploratory voyage and five decades before it appeared on a map. Montalvo's works became so popular that they made an appearance in *Don Quixote* as examples of the chivalric fictions that two of the don's neighbors, a priest and a barber, consign to a bonfire to break him of his troubling obsession with knightly gests. (They spare the Amadís volumes from the flames, but not *Esplandián*.) The first part of *Don Quixote*, in which this episode takes place, was not published until 1605, however, so how the name California made it into the journals and onto the maps remains unclear. Some commentators, including Bancroft, speculated that it was used sarcastically, as if the dreariness of the land mocked the expectations of a "terrestrial paradise." But the Spanish were not normally given to wearing their disenchantments on their sleeves, much less inscribing them on their maps.

THE SPANISH EXPLORATION of Alta California (Upper California)—roughly, the territory above the mouth of the Colorado River, where it empties into the Gulf of California, and stretching some nine hundred miles north to present-day Cape Mendocino and east toward the Rocky Mountains—spanned more than sixty years. The intensity of interest by the Spanish crown and its viceroyalties in Mexico waxed and waned in concert with the credibility of reports of golden cities and mines or other deposits of riches in the region. Cortés, after subjugating the Aztec Empire of Montezuma in 1521 following a brilliantly commanded invasion of the Mexican interior from Veracruz on the east coast—assisted by smallpox, a disease endemic among the Spaniards but for which the indigenous Mexicans had no immunity—proceeded from the conquered Aztec capital of Tenochtitlán to the west coast to establish a staging post for further explorations and, he hoped, conquests.

The explorers failed to find the gold mines or the strait they sought, but they did come in contact with many of the more than one hundred indigenous tribes inhabiting the region. These encounters sometimes erupted in attacks on the landing parties, always instigated by the Indians, according to the surviving written reports (invariably those of the Spaniards). On the whole, however, the meetings were untroubled, typically concluding with an exchange of gifts and sometimes with an escort of the departing ships by fleets of canoes. Visiting explorers were especially impressed by the Chumash of the Santa Barbara Channel due to their evident industriousness and the geometric layouts of their dwellings and towns. The last of the explorers, Sebastián Vizcaíno, wrote admiringly to his monarch King Felipe III of the Indians he met upon landing at what he dubbed the Bay of Monterey; he called them "meek, gentle, quiet, and quite amenable to conversion to Catholicism and to becoming subjects of Your Majesty." The sealskin hides they wore for clothing, he noted, were tanned and dressed "better than how it is done in Castile." As for their skill as mariners, "they go out into the ocean with fourteen oarsmen and they can sail with ease even during a strong storm."

Hernán Cortés was a grim, gray-faced aristocrat who engaged in ceaseless conflict with his fellow Spanish commanders in the New World and with Spanish courtiers in Madrid, whom he accused resentfully of underappreciating the wealth he had delivered into their coffers. These disagreements required him to voyage home on more than one occasion to plead his case and also inspired him to commission new expeditions to find gold and the Strait of Anián. One such expedition, from 1533 to 1534, was led by a Cortés relative named Diego de Becerra. He never made landfall himself; he was slain en route in a mutiny led by his pilot, Fortún Jiménez, who subsequently brought the ship to a bay in what he assumed to be the east coast of an island. It was, in fact, the Baja California peninsula. The conception of California as an island would persist in Europe for more than a century, even after further Spanish explorations proved it to be false.

JIMÉNEZ IS GENERALLY accorded the distinction of leading the first European party that set foot in California, though his sojourn was brief: He and twenty crewmen were killed by natives of the region as they landed. From his contemporaries' standpoint, what was more important was the story that two survivors brought home of beaches paved with pearls—confirmation to the Spanish of the wealth lurking beyond the horizon. (A later account explained that Baja Indians dredged up oysters from shallow coastal waters, placed them in bonfires to open them, and—interested only in the meat— discarded the blackened pearls on the beach "as if they were stones of no value.")

Cortés himself crossed to the new land in 1535, christened the "island" Santa Cruz, and attempted to establish a colony there. Barren and far from supply sources, the location was a difficult one to settle. Cortés had already decided to abandon the colony and perhaps had given up any thought of continuing his expeditions westward when an electrifying piece of news arrived. It was brought to Mexico by one Álvar Núñez Cabeza de Vaca, a crew member of the most ill-starred Spanish expedition of the time, a group that had headed west from Florida in 1528 and came apart almost immediately due to storms, attacks by indigenous warriors, starvation, and disease. Cabeza de Vaca, who had wandered across the southwest for more than six years, some of them spent in Indian captivity, was one of only four survivors of a landing party that had numbered six hundred when they left Spain. He gabbled of having heard firsthand reports of Quivira and the Seven Cities of Gold, which got the blood of Cortés boiling anew.

In 1539, Cortés equipped an expedition to be commanded by Francisco de Ulloa. One of Ulloa's three vessels was wrecked on the way up the eastern coast of the new land, but the other two reached the mouth of the Colorado, turned south, rounded present-day Cabo San Lucas, and headed up the west coast, establishing that the territory they were skirting was a peninsula, not an island. After he got about halfway up the peninsula, Ulloa sent one ship home to report and continued north on the other. Nothing is definitively known about the rest of his voyage, though there are disputed reports that he eventually returned to Spain. He might have been the first white man to reach the coast of today's state of California by sea, or he might not. Given the absence of confirmation of Ulloa's landfall, credit for that accomplishment has generally fallen to another mariner, Juan Rodríguez Cabrillo.

Cabrillo was a Portuguese navigator in Spanish service. His three-ship flotilla was outfitted in 1542 by Antonio de Mendoza, the Spanish viceroy in Mexico. Cortés had returned to Spain in 1539 on yet another voyage of self-justification; he would die in Spain in 1547, never having returned to the New World. Mendoza enthusiastically took up Cortés's determination to find gold and the Strait of Anián, sending an expedition north along the Colorado to hunt for the fabled cities of gold, and Cabrillo westward to search for the route to the Indies.

Cabrillo's route and landfalls are not entirely known, partly because accounts of his voyage are abridged or translated copies of originals that have been lost and partly because Spanish latitude readings are dubious. It is widely accepted, however, that on September 28, 1542, three months after he sailed from the Mexican port of Navidad, he entered a landlocked harbor he christened San Miguel, today's San Diego. On this basis, Cabrillo has been judged the first European to set foot on the Alta California coast.

About ten days later, Cabrillo reached Santa Catalina Island and traded gifts with the indigenous people who came out to meet the Spanish ships by canoe; the following day, he sailed into San Pedro Bay, which Cabrillo dubbed Bahía de los Fumos ("Bay of Smoke"), signifying that it was wreathed in what modern residents call smog, a product of Indian fires and the temperature inversion that traps the smoke near the ground. He proceeded north into Santa Monica Bay and presently to Point Conception, north of today's Santa Barbara. From there he discovered two of the Channel Islands: San Miguel, which he named La Posesion, and San Lucas. Cabrillo continued on, paralleling what are now called the Santa Lucia Mountains, a coastal range he would name the Sierras Nevadas due to their crown of snow (not to be confused with the more imposing range well to the east).

Cabrillo is assumed to have reached as far as today's Point Reyes; he spotted Monterey Bay along the way but failed to notice—whether because it was shrouded in fog or because his ships were too far out to sea to spot it—the Golden Gate, the inlet to San Francisco Bay, the finest harbor on his route. Then he once more headed south, explored Monterey Bay, and returned to San Miguel Island on November 23. By then he was deathly ill; a broken leg he had suffered during his first stop at San Miguel had turned gangrenous. He died on January 3 after instructing his second in command to resume the exploration north. The expedition made it to present-day Oregon and returned to Navidad on April 14, having conducted the most far-reaching exploration of the California coast yet. They brought along two boys from the Ipai (Kumeyaay) Tribe whom they planned to train as interpreters in what may be the first recorded kidnapping of Indian children by Europeans in California; if so, it marks the introduction of a dismal tradition in the relationship between whites and Indians.

The boldness of Cabrillo's voyage cannot be overestimated, conducted as it was by "two small vessels . . . on an unknown coast and in the dead of winter when the North Pacific is unusually stormy" by a crew suffering from sickness and starvation. Still, the difficulties faced by Cabrillo and his men, their failure to find an entrance to the Strait of Anián, and Coronado's failure to find the lost cities of gold cured the Spaniards of their coastal wanderlust, at least for a time. After the Spanish conquest of the Philippines, in 1565, two expeditions set off from those islands to explore the California coast, one in 1584 and one in 1585, but they made no significant discoveries after punishing eastbound voyages (one ending in a shipwreck at Point Reyes). Finding a short route from the Philippines to Spain was the top priority, as the trading vessels often completed their journeys with most of their crews having perished at sea or afflicted with scurvy, the vitamin C deficiency that turned them into sallow, toothless, enfeebled wraiths.

In the meantime came the Englishman Francis Drake, who is reported to have made landfall in California during his 1577–1580 voyage circumnavigating the globe. Drake was a notorious freebooter, dubbed by his foreign contemporaries "chief of the pirates," and one of the outstanding fabulists of maritime history. That makes his role in the discovery of California uncertain, with some modern historians doubting that he ever visited Alta California at all.

What is known is that Drake crossed through the Strait of Magellan in

1578, then sailed up the west coast of South and Central America, sacking Spanish settlements along the way and loading up on loot seized from captured Spanish galleons. His original fleet of six ships was reduced to one by storms, mutiny, and other mishaps. The survivor, the *Golden Hind,* was so overladen with booty and dilapidated by its encounters with the elements that it was forced to put in to a harbor for a six-week overhaul. The question that has absorbed historians ever since is where? Attention has focused on two possibilities: Bodega Bay and Drake's Bay on the leeward side of Point Reyes, both north of San Francisco. If one takes the historical reports of Drake's voyage as fact, it appears that, like Cabrillo, he unwittingly sailed past the Golden Gate.

Both possible candidates for Drake's landfall present problems. Drake is said to have dubbed his landfall Nova Albion—New Albion—and to have left a hammered-brass plate onshore claiming the spot for Queen Elizabeth I. A map purportedly tracing Drake's voyage and published between 1589 and 1592 with an inset displaying the port of New Albion is of no help, since it fails to specify the port's location on the coast and in any event bears suspicious similarities to maps of the semicircular harbor of Acapulco, which the Spanish settled in the 1520s.

Accounts and artifacts associated with Drake's California landfall have been rich with misinformation and hoaxes. A brass plate that surfaced as a chance find in Northern California in the 1930s was given prominent display in the Bancroft Library of the University of California but was exposed in 1979 as a modern forgery. After Drake's return to England in 1580—when he was knighted by Queen Elizabeth—official reports of his voyage were suppressed and eventually issued in highly edited forms ten years or more after the fact. Unofficial reports, including one given by Drake's son and crew member John after he was captured by the Spanish in 1584, are contradictory and inconsistent, leading to modern speculation that Drake may have sailed no farther north than Monterey or even past the southern tip of Baja California. All that can be said for sure is that his claims inspired England's further interest in the California coast, which would in turn help trigger American interest in the region some two hundred years on.

SPAIN DID NOT resume coastal exploration until six decades after Cabrillo's voyage. This time the task was placed in the hands of Sebastián Vizcaíno, a merchant and mariner. Vizcaíno was a prideful character but one in bad odor with the viceroy, the Conde de Monterrey, who was irked that he had failed to fulfill a contract to establish settlements on the east coast of the peninsula. The Spanish administration still wished to find a port of call on the California coast for ships completing their exhausting journeys east from the Philippines, so the viceroy imposed the task on Vizcaíno, perhaps to give him a chance to expiate his earlier failure.

Vizcaíno's expedition was the best-manned and best-equipped of the Spanish era, with three ships, three hundred soldiers and sailors, and three Carmelite friars, one of whom had served as a cartographer and pilot before taking his vows. Vizcaíno set out from Acapulco on May 5, 1602. He would leave his mark on history largely through the names he bestowed on his landfalls, often discarding Cabrillo's choices; he defended himself by pleading that his geographical observations were so much more accurate than his predecessor's that he could not be sure he had stopped at the same places. In the event, he renamed Cabrillo's San Miguel after his own flagship, the *San Diego*; Cabrillo's Sierras Nevadas became the Santa Lucia Range; and Cabrillo's islands of San Salvador and Posesion were dubbed Santa Catalina and San Miguel—all names that survive to this day. He also christened the Santa Barbara Channel and Point Reyes and found and named Monterey Bay (thus flattering the viceroy), praising it as "the best port that could be desired" due to its shelter from the wind, abundant fresh water, and pines and oaks for ship repairs near the shore. Given Monterey's subsequent importance as a port, settlement, and capital, discovering the bay was surely Vizcaíno's greatest achievement.

Still, he ran into some of the same difficulties experienced by earlier Spanish explorers—storms, scurvy, and a desperate shortage of provisions. Vizcaíno sent the sick men home on one of his ships, although twenty-five men died on the way, and continued north; he reached Drake's Bay on January 9—having sailed unawares past the Golden Gate and San Francisco Bay—and appears to have gotten as far as Cape Mendocino before turning back.

For the time being, Spanish interest in the California coast was spent. The Spanish would make no further inroads or explorations in Alta California for 167 years. When they returned, they came as evangelists, as though to transform Vizcaíno's observation to King Felipe III into a foretelling. This phase of Spanish relations with the indigenous population of California would, however, prove far more troubling than the first.

AFTER THE CONQUISTADOR era, the goal of the Spanish in Mexico and California evolved from material to spiritual—in essence, to "civilize" the Indians by Christianizing them. This was bound to be an expensive endeavor, so the Spanish crown outsourced it to the Society of Jesus; the Jesuits, an increasingly powerful and rich force in Europe, were expected to pay for the effort themselves.

The Jesuits began establishing missions on the Mexican mainland in the 1670s, pushing north as far as Sonora. They then transferred their attention to Baja California, which they placed under the supervision of two highly educated missionaries, Eusebio Francisco Kino and Juan Maria de Salvatierra, the former a native of the Tyrolean Alps who had taught mathematics at a Bavarian university, and the latter an experienced administrator and fundraiser. Kino and Salvatierra established their first mission in Baja at Loreto, north of the harbor of La Paz, in 1697. The Jesuits would found seventeen more in Baja, mostly along the eastern coast, until 1767, when Spain's King Carlos III expelled the order from Mexico and California.

The Jesuits' sudden fall from grace resulted from growing resentment among the Bourbon monarchs of Western Europe, who rejected the order's influence over education and its sedulous loyalty to the papacy. After evicting the Jesuits from the New World, the Spanish crown took over the effort of colonizing Alta California. The crown exerted control over the indigenous population with ever-increasing energy, not least because Spain had grown wary of competition in the California coastal region from Great Britain, the Netherlands, and Russia. José de Gálvez, whom the Spanish appointed inspector general over the Mexican domain dubbed New Spain, and his deputy Gaspar de Portolá turned the task of evangelizing the Indians over to the Franciscan order, which maintained a missionary training school in Mexico City. The first band of Franciscan missionaries to cross to Baja, reaching Loreto on April 1, 1768, was led by Junípero Serra, a Majorca-born former professor of philosophy. His name would become deeply inscribed in California history, for good and for ill.

At forty-eight, Gálvez became the driving spirit of the effort to occupy Alta California, a task he dubbed the "Sacred Expedition." Gálvez, born in 1720 on the southern coast of Spain, came from a family of low-ranking nobles with little in the way of worldly goods. The experience of forcing his way up through the Spanish ranks from a genteel poverty to the post of a colonial administrator produced a dictatorial, venal, and vindictive personality adept at currying favor with his superiors and intolerant of subordinates who failed to measure up to his expectations. These qualities served him well as inspector general on the frontier and helped explain his determination to push Spanish dominion north almost by brute force.

Gálvez's plan was ambitious and audacious. Four parties, two hundred twenty-five men in all, would strike out for San Diego and Monterey, two by sea and two by land, to secure what was assumed to be the entire coast of Alta California. All were to rendezvous at San Diego before continuing on. The entire project was under the direct command of Portolá, who would travel with the second overland party.

The first vessel to head out was the *San Carlos*, which left La Paz on January 9, 1769. Almost as soon as it rounded Cabo San Lucas, a storm drove it well out to sea; it would not arrive in San Diego until April 29, a voyage of nearly four months. The *San Carlos* was beaten to the destination by the *San Antonio*, which left Cabo San Lucas on February 15 and made landfall on April 11.

The first land expedition left Loreto on March 24 with twenty-five soldiers, forty-two Christianized Indians, three muleteers, and one hundred eighty-eight mules and horses; they reached San Diego on May 14. The second land expedition, with forty-four Indians, Portolá at its head, and Serra in the party, left May 15 and reached San Diego on July 1. Thirty Indians from each party deserted or died en route.

In San Diego, the land expeditions found the seaborne travelers to be in a sorry condition. The seamen were racked with scurvy. All but two of the twenty-six crew members of the *San Carlos* had died of the illness; all but two of the crew of the *San Antonio* were sick. A third ship, the *San Jose*, had sailed for San Diego from Loreto on June 16 but never arrived. It was assumed to have sunk with all on board.

Of the roughly three hundred men who had left Baja for San Diego— including an indeterminate number on the *San Jose*—at least seventy-five had lost their lives and almost as many had deserted along the way. Portolá sent the *San Antonio* back to Baja for supplies and a fresh crew—as only eight of the ship's original twenty-eight sailors were in a condition to sail—and to report on the expedition's progress. He continued on to Monterey, necessarily by land. He left San Diego on June 14 with what was, according to his recollections, "a small company of persons, or rather say skeletons, who had been spared by scurvy, hunger, and thirst." At their head were thirty-four soldiers armed with lances, broadswords, and muskets and wearing reinforced deerskin jackets and carrying shields to defend against Indian arrows. They expected their trek to take at least four weeks, since they were passing through "unknown lands and on unused paths," with their target destination the bay and port of Monterey described in Vizcaíno's records 167 years earlier. In fact it took four and a half months. The travelers faced "excessive heat and intense cold" and stopped every four days to rest and reconnoiter as they made their way through an "ungracious country" with "no object to greet either the hand or the eye save rocks, brushwood, and rugged mountains covered with snow."

The expedition seldom traveled more than nine miles in a day, often as few as four. They followed a route that took them through points that many generations later became landmarks of developed California, including the future sites of downtown Los Angeles, the San Fernando Valley, and Santa Clarita. Early in the journey, as they crossed the Santa Ana River (today a concrete-lined drainage canal emptying into the sea off the Orange County coast), they felt four violent earthquakes that provoked aftershocks for another week; they named the river Jesus de los Temblores. The tribes they encountered were generally friendly and sometimes spoke of bearded men they had seen before and ships under sail offshore; they displayed European artifacts they had presumably acquired by trading with other tribes or directly with the crews of Cabrillo, Vizcaíno, or oceangoing ships from the Philippines.

On October 1 the travelers camped on a riverbank from which they could scan the broad sweep of the seashore. Although they were roughly at the latitude where Vizcaíno had placed Monterey Bay, they saw nothing that matched his description of it. They pressed north, at one point coming to a forest of "tall trees of reddish-colored wood of a species unknown to us," in the words of Juan Crespi, a Franciscan accompanying the overland trekkers; they named the trees after the color of the wood, *palo colorado*—the redwood, destined to reign as the iconic tree of the state of California.

Portolá sent a patrol to reconnoiter. On November 2 from a hilltop they spied Point Reyes far in the distance and, nearer at hand, a great inland sea. They meant to explore further but were blocked by an "estuary" and returned to camp. The truth, of course, was that Portolá had camped at Monterey but failed to recognize it, perhaps because he had approached by land and the perspective was different from what one would see from the water. The inland sea that the patrol had discovered was San Francisco Bay. The Golden Gate had finally given up its secret, though grudgingly, for the bay was mistaken by the patrol as the estuary that impeded their progress; the Spaniards still did not realize what they had found.

At camp, Portolá convened a meeting of his sick, exhausted, and crestfallen men. With little hope of being relieved by ships coming up the coast, they voted to return to San Diego. Captain Don Fernando de Rivera y Moncada, who had led the first overland party from Baja and thus had traveled some fifteen hundred miles searching in vain for Monterey, warned Portolá that if provisions ran out, the soldiers would mutiny. They arrived back at San Diego on January 24, having reduced their herd of mules by one a day for food, to find the garrison's morale at a low ebb. Fifty men had died of sickness and starvation, and the camp had been consistently harried by the Kumeyaay Tribe. As they bore the news that they had failed to find Monterey, they were received joylessly. "You come from Rome without having seen the Pope," Serra snapped.

Portolá calculated that if the *San Antonio* did not return, the remaining stores of maize and flour would sustain the seventy-four men in camp for twelve and a half weeks. That set the deadline at March 19, the feast of Saint Joseph. Providentially, on that very day the sails of the *San Antonio* were seen on the horizon, but then they disappeared. Assuming that the expedition had long since relocated to Monterey, Captain Juan Pérez had headed there, only to discover upon putting in at a Chumash settlement in the Santa Barbara Channel that the explorers had returned south. The *San Antonio* finally landed at San Diego on March 23. Almost the entire crew had died of scurvy, but as Portolá recounted, "we got very particular consolation out of the corn, flour and rice" the *San Antonio* brought.

Portolá staged another overland trek to Monterey and directed the *San Antonio* to meet him there. This time his company recognized the bay from Vizcaíno's description. That was confirmed by the *San Antonio* when it sailed in from the sea. Pérez carried news of the successful completion of the Sacred Expedition to Mexico City, arriving on August 10, 1770, to the pealing of church bells and a celebratory Mass. Monterey was established as the capital of Alta California and would remain so for the next three-quarters of a century, through Mexico's attaining of independence from Spain in 1821 and until the American occupation of the territory in 1846 and its formal acquisition by the United States in 1848.

THE SPANISH LAUNCHED their campaign to conquer Alta California in earnest in 1768 as a counterweight to the threatened colonization of the region by the British, Dutch, French, and Russians. In the trail of the Spanish military came Franciscan missionaries, whose goal was to introduce Catholicism to the heathen Indians by educating them in mission settlements. Serra, the founder of the Catholic mission system in California, viewed the Indians brought into the missions as children to be converted—forcibly if necessary. Physical chastisement was a common practice; in 1780, Governor Felipe de Neve objected that the treatment meted out by the Franciscans "renders the Indians' fate worse than that of slaves." Serra wrote him crisply in reply that the treatment was, after all, effective: "In the matter of correcting the Indians, when it appeared to us that punishment was deserved, they were flogged, or put in the stocks, according to the gravity of their offense. In consequence, they took pains to carry out their respective duties." The missionaries, Serra added, had merely adopted punishments that the military authorities introduced: "That spiritual fathers should punish their sons, the Indians, with blows appears to be as old as the conquest of these kingdoms."

In the half century following the arrival of the Spanish colonizers, the Indian population of Alta California fell by more than one-fourth, from an estimated 133,500 in 1770 to 100,000 in 1823. The best that could be said about the missionaries' role in the tragic decline was that it was unpremeditated. The Franciscans did not intend to shrink the ranks of their new adherents—*neóphitos*, or "neophytes," as they termed them—but that outcome was the inevitable consequence of their methods and the conditions at the missions. (Unconverted and recalcitrant Indians were known to the friars as *gentiles*, spelled the same in Spanish and English.)

Disease was the principal factor in the decline in the Indian population of California during the Spanish occupation. "From the first entrance of the Europeans into the new world, the aboriginal inhabitants suffered one sweeping epidemic after another, each segment of the population undergoing in turn a cycle of devastating pestilence followed by gradual immunization and recovery," observed Sherburne Friend Cook, the author of a pioneering study of the conflict between California Indians and white settlers. Cook reckoned that these sequential epidemics might have caused almost half the deaths during that period. Measles, smallpox, and cholera were among the diseases visited on the susceptible Native populations, their spread abetted by the missionaries' practice of crowding large numbers of Indians into communal lodgings. In their natural environment, the Indians lived in small groups, some smaller than one hundred persons, and out in the open, but some missions housed several thousand Indians in one place; they "ate together, worked together, and even slept together, in close quarters."

The worst scourge was syphilis, the "putrid and contagious disease" of which the first recorded appearance in Alta California coincided with the arrival of explorer Juan Bautista de Anza at Mission San Gabriel, outside present-day Los Angeles, in 1776. Once introduced, the disease spread rapidly via sexual relations between Spanish soldiers and Indian women. Not infrequently, the relationship was one of rape, to the point that in 1785, Pedro Fages, the Spanish governor, wrote to the military commanders to protest the "vicious license" of officers and men of the Spanish presidios and the "scandalous disorders which they commit with the gentile and Christian women" (that is, the unconverted and converted Indians).

Syphilis caused the deaths of many of its adult victims and left others with weakened constitutions, making them more susceptible to pneumonia, tuberculosis, and the other diseases becoming endemic in the Indian population. Miscarriages among infected women soared, as did cases of congenital syphilis among their babies, increasing the rate of infant mortality. For the Indians, syphilis was a multifaceted disaster.

Over time, the missionaries' ability to attract converts and keep them waned. Indians resented being forced to labor in the mission fields and bridled at the corporal punishments visited upon them by the Franciscan brothers for various offenses. Stock stealing, for example, was punished by flogging, typically up to twenty-five lashes. When the neophytes and gentiles displayed more resistance, the padres' response turned harsher. The offense of "fugitivism" appeared more often in records of mission discipline, and the mode of punishment intensified from flogging to imprisonment and thence to hard labor. Indians who fled the missions testified that they had been whipped for crying when their relatives died, had been forced to work while ill, and were placed on starvation rations if they refused to work.

The missionaries soon came to rely on soldiers to keep their neophytes under control, a development the military welcomed, for it enhanced its authority over the church. With the evolution of conversion from voluntary to compulsory, relations between the Indians and the missionaries deteriorated. The number of fugitives increased; Cook estimated that in 1817 alone, more than four thousand Indians fled the nineteen California missions. A rebellion in 1824 by the Chumash at three Santa Barbara missions at which soldiers had treated the Indians with notable brutality resulted in death sentences for seven neophytes and up to ten-year terms of imprisonment at hard labor for at least a dozen others. More than 450 indigenous people, or about half of the mission population, fled from the Mission of Santa Barbara during the uprising; only 163 were caught and returned.

Rule by the Spanish and Mexicans thus established a punitive tradition in white relations with the indigenous peoples of upper California. In the era of American colonization, especially after the Gold Rush, that tradition would produce a cataclysm.

2

THE AMERICANS ARRIVE

IF ONE WISHES to pinpoint the moment when Americans' eyes first turned to the possibility of annexing California, an ideal choice would be October 30, 1796.

On that day a Boston fur-trading frigate named the *Otter* first made port at Monterey, the capital of Spanish California. The *Otter* had lurked offshore in the mists and fog for several days, as if lost; finally, it lowered a launch, which capsized within view of the shore; its five American occupants were rescued by onlookers on land. On October 30, favorable winds finally allowed the *Otter* to enter the harbor, and Captain Ebenezer Dorr presented the local authorities with his passport, which bore the signature of President George Washington.

Dorr and his crew had set out to carry one thousand otter skins from the west coast of North America to China via the Sandwich Islands (Hawaii) but they had lost their way and run out of food and water. They were treated with all the hospitality the Spaniards were known for, although Dorr did not reciprocate in kind. In violation of an express prohibition from the locals, he stranded at the point of his gun ten crewmen he no longer needed on the voyage and did not wish to pay. The encounter awakened America to the virtues of bringing under its control a coastal port in Mexican California for provisioning and trading and augured for the resident Spaniards the unhappy consequences of America's expansionist impulses.

Despite Spanish laws forbidding trade with foreigners, contacts proliferated between American traders and Mexican citizens (those of Spanish extraction, known as Californians or Californios). But as Spain was some six thousand miles away, enforcement was almost impossible. Nor was it welcomed in California, especially as the trading became spectacularly lucrative for the parties on both sides. Otters were abundant in the waters between present-day San Diego and Oregon, and the locals were happy to collect the pelts and sell them to the American vessels that sailed the sea routes to China. On their return voyages from the Far East, the ships came laden with tea and silks that found ready markets in North American ports of call.

After Mexico achieved independence from Spain in 1821, American ships traded more openly with the Californios, who were no longer operating under even the theoretical burden of Spanish law. The Americans brought manufactured goods from the east coast and returned with cattle hides and tallow. New England whalers plying the Pacific also began putting in at California ports for repairs and provisions before setting off on the voyage home around Cape Horn. That period marked the start of permanent settlement by Americans, many of whom married into local families, became Mexican citizens, or otherwise assimilated into the newly independent land.

While this was happening, alarm bells were ringing in Washington over the interest in North America's west coast shown by Russia, Britain, and France. One of the earliest warnings came from Captain Robert Shaler, a veteran of the China trade, who wrote in 1804 of the rich flora and fauna of the California coastal region, its invigorating climate, and the paucity of the Spaniards' defensive arrangements. Given the lack of fortifications on the coast and the failure to raise or equip a defensive force, Shaler observed, San Francisco, Monterey, and Santa Barbara have "only the show of defence, and would fall an easy conquest to the smallest ship of war."

Shaler sounded the alarm about Russian intentions in particular. In 1805, the Russians' trapping and trading post at Sitka, Alaska, fell under the grip of starvation after the failure of two supply expeditions, and an envoy of the Russian-American Company, Count Nikolai Petrovich Rezanov, sailed to San Francisco on the three-masted schooner *Juno*. Rezanov's goal was to establish a trading relationship with the Spanish that would keep Sitka supplied. This he managed to achieve by seeking the hand of Doña Concepción, the fifteen-year-old daughter of the local commander, Don José Argüello.

The real-life star-crossed love affair of Rezanov and Doña Concepción inspired the first fictional romances set in Spanish California. Ordered by Don José to obtain the blessing of the pope in Rome, Rezanov set off but perished en route, dooming his betrothed to pine away for her missing lover in a convent for the rest of her life. The story has been mined as literary raw material for fiction, poetry, and even opera for more than two hundred years.

Russia expanded its presence on the West Coast over the next two decades. In 1812 the Russian-American Company established a colony in Sonoma, north of San Francisco, called Fort Ross. (The name derived not from a Scotch-English surname but from the Russian-language term *Rus*, denoting the Russian people.) The colony's apparent purpose was to serve as a headquarters for fur trading and as a supply depot for Sitka, but the US government increasingly suspected that Russia's extension of its coastal presence south toward San Francisco signaled other goals. In 1818, John Bartow Prevost, a representative of President James Monroe, reported on the threat Fort Ross posed to San Francisco, which he described as "wholly without defense and in the neighborhood of a feeble, diffused and disaffected population." In his December 1823 address to Congress outlining what became known as the Monroe Doctrine, the president specifically referred to the potential for conflict between the United States and imperial Russia "on the northwest coast of this continent" and stated that "as a principle in which the rights and interests of the United States are involved," the "American continents . . . are henceforth not to be considered as subjects for future colonization by any European powers."

The real bulwark against European colonization of the California coast would not be presidential doctrine but American colonization. This began in the 1830s, after American travelers began sending glowing reports of a California paradise to East Coast readers.

Among the earliest accounts was that of Kentuckian James O. Pattie, who in 1824, at the age of fifteen, had joined his father on a trapping expedition to California. "Those who traverse it, if they have any capability whatever of perceiving, and admiring the beautiful and sublime in scenery, must be constantly excited to wonder and praise," Pattie wrote in a memoir published a decade later. The inhabitants, however, drew Pattie's contempt, perhaps understandably—the Spanish authorities had imprisoned him and his father as spies under conditions that brought about the older man's death. They "are equally calculated to excite dislike, and even stronger feelings of disgust and hatred," Pattie wrote. "The priests are omnipotent. . . . Two thirds of the population are native Indians under the immediate charge of these spiritual rulers in the numerous missions. It is a well known fact, that

nothing is more entirely opposite to the nature of a savage, than labor. . . .
No bondage can be more complete than that under which they live." Pattie
established what would become a familiar model for depictions of California:
reverence for the countryside combined with disdain for its inhabitants.

Published in 1840, *Two Years Before the Mast*, Richard Henry Dana Jr.'s
classic chronicle of his voyage from Boston to the West Coast upon a hide-
and-tallow brig, gave the public a further glimpse of the contrast between
California's land and its people. Dana, who had joined the crew as a nineteen-
year-old on leave from Harvard, introduced his readers to

> a country embracing four or five hundred miles of sea-coast, with several
> good harbors; with fine forests in the north; the waters filled with fish, and
> the plains covered with thousands of herds of cattle; blessed with a climate,
> than which there can be no better in the world; free from all manner of dis-
> eases, whether epidemic or endemic; and with a soil in which corn yields
> from seventy to eighty fold.

But he branded the Californios "an idle, thriftless people, [who] can make
nothing for themselves. . . . The men are . . . proud, and extravagant, and
very much given to gaming; and the women have but little education, and
a good deal of beauty, and their morality, of course, is none of the best." He
concluded with an implicit invitation to Americans seeking their fortune:
"In the hands of an enterprising people, what a country this might be!"

The reports by trappers, adventurers, and intrepid tourists in California
fostered a wave of migration in the 1840s. From the Eastern Seaboard to what
was then the nation's western frontier—today the Midwest—Americans be-
guiled by the promise of limitless agricultural potential sold their homesteads and joined organized expeditions to the West Coast. John Bidwell, a
Missouri schoolteacher, met "a Frenchman named Roubideaux, who said he
had been to California," in November or December 1840. "His description
was in the superlative degree favorable, so much so that I resolved if possible
to see that wonderful land, and with others helped to get up a meeting . . .
and invited him to make a statement before it in regard to the country. . . .
Roubideaux described it as one of perennial spring and boundless fertility."

Bidwell and his fellow Missourians, who were living in a territory where
malaria was endemic, peppered the speaker with questions about the prevalence of "fever and ague" in the distant land. Roubideaux assured them that

"there was but one man in California that had ever had a chill there, and it was a matter of so much wonderment to the people of Monterey that they went eighteen miles into the country to see him shake." The following May, Bidwell led a party of forty-seven to California. Bidwell would ultimately make a fortune in his new home from ranching and gold prospecting and would serve California as a state senator and congressman.

The arrival of organized groups of immigrants caused no little alarm among the Californio leaders, who feared that the newcomers might be a fifth column dispatched by a US government angling to seize the territory by stealth. After all, Mexico's loss of Texas upon that region's declaration of independence in 1836 had been preceded by just such a wave of emigration from the eastern United States.

That said, the settlers of the 1840s seemed on the surface to be rather less unruly than the American migrants of an earlier day. During the 1830s, waves of freebooters had washed into Alta California, aiming to exploit Mexican California's unsettled political environment and the negligent enforcement of its laws. Many were "men of a turbulent and undesirable class, being for the most part deserters from vessels on the coast," the historian Hubert Bancroft judged, not unreasonably. Notable among them was Isaac Graham, a hunter from Tennessee whose distillery in the Sierra foothills attracted American roughnecks of every description. Graham assembled an ornery force from his clientele and placed it at the service of Don Bautista Alvarado, a landowner who was plotting to launch a revolt against the Mexican administration.

With the help of Graham, who hoped to profit by joining a newly independent regime on the ground floor, Alvarado besieged the Monterey headquarters of the incumbent governor of Alta California and managed to take him prisoner. The Mexican administration eventually settled the matter simply by appointing Alvarado governor, as his prisoner's successor.

To Alvarado's dismay, however, Graham's riflemen proved to be more ornery in victory than they had been as layabouts at the distillery. "I was insulted at every turn, by the drunken followers of Graham," Alvarado groused to Alfred Robinson, a businessman who later wrote a book about pre-statehood California society. "When walking in the garden," Alvarado complained, "they would come to its wall, and call upon me in terms of the greatest familiarity: 'Ho! Bautista, come here' . . . 'Bautista, here.'—'Bautista, there'—and Bautista every where."

After a few years of such rude treatment, Alvarado was thoroughly exasperated with Graham and not a little paranoid. When Graham circulated an invitation to a horse race among his American compatriots, Alvarado interpreted it as evidence of a seditious conspiracy and had him arrested along with about one hundred of his followers, confined them in chains aboard a prison ship, and convicted them at a sham trial. Eventually, with the connivance of American and British officials, they were acquitted at a second trial in Mexico and repatriated to California, where they filed claims for indemnity. The US government elevated the unpaid claims into an issue of US-Mexican relations and used them to justify increasing the US Navy's presence off the California coast. Ultimately the claims figured into the rationale for the United States to go to war with Mexico. Graham had not only advanced Alvarado's private revolution but also helped to create the very public and official state of belligerency that followed.

AS THE FLOW of settlers into Alta California mounted, so did Washington's interest in the annexation of the territory. John Tyler had been an expansionist president, but expansion policy became supercharged with the election of James K. Polk in 1844. Within months of his inauguration in March 1845, Polk advised his cabinet that the peaceful acquisition of California would be one of the four principal goals of his administration. (The other three were settling a dispute with Britain over the Oregon territory, cutting the tariff of 1842 to reduce its protectionist effect, and reviving the independent federal treasury that the Whigs had repealed under Tyler in 1840.) Four paths to annexation, not all of them peaceable, were evident. These were a direct purchase, for which Polk was prepared to pay as much as forty million dollars; a rebellion by native Californios, quietly aided and abetted by American settlers; a declaration of independence by American colonists once they reached sufficient numbers; and seizure as a spoil of war.

The impression persisted in America that Mexico's control over Alta California was so ineffectual that the region would inevitably drop into American hands like a windfall in an apple orchard. The government in Mexico City was exercising its authority over a territorial capital more than 2,200 miles away and a population that preferred to manage their own affairs with minimal interference—a resistance to outside supervision that exists among Californians to this day. Lieutenant Charles Wilkes, the leader of an American expedition exploring the Pacific Coast from 1838 to 1842, reported upon disembarking in Monterey "a total absence of all government in California and even its form and ceremonies thrown aside." Sir George Simpson, a director of the Hudson's Bay Company, put in at Monterey in 1842 and wrote that the fort had had insufficient gunpowder to salute his ship as it entered the harbor and had to borrow some for the purpose from the ship itself.

That same year, the Mexican government dispatched General Manuel Micheltorena to Monterey to take office as governor of Alta California and impose a modicum of administrative authority. He brought ninety soldiers, most of whom had been recruited from prisons in Baja California. Witnesses to the debarkation were appalled by the troops' squalor. "To me they presented a state of wretchedness and misery unequalled," Robinson reported. "Not one individual among them possessed a jacket or pantaloons; but naked, and like the savage Indians, they concealed their nudity with dirty, miserable blankets. . . . They appeared like convicts; and, indeed, the greater portion of them had been charged with the crime either of murder or theft. And these were the soldiers sent to subdue this happy country!" The local Californios disdained them as *cholos*, meaning "half-breeds" or "ruffians." Micheltorena lasted barely two years as governor; he was ousted in February 1845 in a rebellion organized chiefly by Californios who were discontented by the *cholos'* thievery and generally obnoxious behavior and by the governor's issuing generous land grants to Americans and Europeans living in the country, presumably in return for generous bribes.

Polk appeared to be sincere about acquiring California without shedding American blood; his references to the prospect of war sounded like saber-rattling meant to bring Mexico to the bargaining table. If war turned out to be necessary, Polk was serene about its course, expecting it to be a modest affair lasting perhaps ninety days and concluding with an annexation.

Several obstacles to Polk's intentions arose, however. One was the mind-set of the territory's American settlers, which was not conducive to the gradual and deliberate process of annexation he favored. At the beginning of the decade, there had been an inconsiderable four hundred or so American residents among the five thousand white inhabitants of the territory, the vast majority of whom were of Spanish extraction. But the Americans were the fastest-growing and most dynamic community in the region and wielded significant political influence in far-off Washington. In July 1845, a few months after Polk's inauguration, John A. Sutter, a transplanted Swiss native who would play multiple roles in California's pre-statehood history, predicted "thousands coming within the year" in a letter to Thomas O. Larkin, the preeminent American landowner in the territory. "Mexico cannot stem the stream," he wrote from New Helvetia, the fort and trading depot he had established in 1839 on the site of what later became Sacramento. Other reports forecast similarly voluminous inflows and offered observations about the likely impact of their numbers on the prospects of annexation if they were given even the slightest nudge from the US government. California is "destined ere long to be annexed to the United States," one southern newspaper told its readers in May 1845 in a typical press notice. "The large number of Americans already settled and immigrating there, give assurance of the result."

Polk's inaugural year, 1845, saw the coinage of the term *manifest destiny* to justify the expansion of America—that is, white America—across the continent. John L. O'Sullivan, editor of the *United States Magazine and Democratic Review*, originated the term in an essay urging the prompt annexation of Texas as "the fulfillment of our manifest destiny to overspread the continent allotted by Providence for the free development of our yearly multiplying millions." O'Sullivan was certain that California would follow Texas into the American fold because "imbecile and distracted, Mexico never can exert any real governmental authority over such a country." He foresaw the same result from emigration as the American settlers did: "A population will soon be in actual occupation of California, over which it will be idle for Mexico to dream of dominion. . . . Their right to independence will be the natural right of self-government belonging to any community strong enough to maintain it."

The Americans in California displayed palpable impatience for overt action by the US government on their behalf. "We only want the Flag of the U.S. and a good lot of Yankees, and you would soon see the immense natural riches of the Country developed and her commerce in a flourishing condition," Stephen Smith, the owner of a thriving Sonoma sawmill, wrote in December 1845 to John C. Calhoun, who, as Tyler's secretary of state, had presided over negotiations for the annexation of Texas and who had just been reelected to the Senate by South Carolina. "We hope and trust that . . . to protect the trade and the interests of our Citizens residing here with their property, at least one American Ship of War will be kept Cruising on the Coast."

Another obstacle to clear and consistent US government action on the

West Coast was the difficulty of long-range communications; Samuel F. B. Morse's electrical telegraph system connected Baltimore to Washington in 1844, but the West Coast would not be reached until 1861. Naval commanders cruising off the Pacific coast had standing orders to seize strategic installations upon the outbreak of war between the United States and Mexico or if they observed suspicious deployments of European naval vessels, but false, or at least unverified, reports of war were common. This had produced an embarrassing incident in 1842: Commodore Thomas ap Catesby Jones, commander of the US Pacific squadron, spotted three British men-of-war patrolling near the coast just as he received a note from a US consul in Mexico hinting that war was imminent. Jones sailed into Monterey Bay and seized Mexican vessels anchored in the harbor, then sent a detachment of men, marching six abreast and accompanied by a band playing "Yankee Doodle" and "The Star Spangled Banner," into the city. The Mexican garrison, outnumbered 160 to 54, surrendered without firing a shot. Jones promptly ordered the American flag raised over the Presidio, the city fortress.

Jones was mistaken about the outbreak of war, however. Upon entering the Presidio, his officers discovered written evidence that Mexico and the United States were still at peace. Jones promptly lowered the Stars and Stripes, set free the captured Mexicans, and issued a formal apology to Governor Micheltorena. His triumph had lasted barely a single day, but his foray did presage how America's war with Mexico, once it did erupt, would proceed in California—with the Californios outnumbered and outgunned by the American military in almost every encounter.

Polk's insatiable appetite for secrecy and intrigue was a further impediment to the bloodless acquisition of California. In diplomacy, secrecy is a valuable—indeed, often indispensable—tool, but it is also hazardous. While it is preserved, it can be interpreted as inaction; if breached, it can make any activity appear sinister. Both consequences of secrecy would undermine American policy on California.

The trouble started with Polk's choice of an envoy to reopen diplomatic relations, which Mexico had severed due to American support for Texas independence. He was William S. Parrott, who had been formally designated persona non grata by the Mexican government following a failed business deal. Nevertheless, Parrott was sent to seek Mexican president José Joaquín de Herrera's consent to the appointment of an American ambassador. When his secret assignment leaked out in Mexico, it became impossible for

Herrera's government to receive him, for that would look as if Herrera was colluding with the same people who had plotted to seize Texas.

Polk already had an ambassador waiting, John Slidell of Louisiana. Slidell's appointment was a secret, as was his assignment: to acquire California by purchase. Secretary of State James Buchanan's written instructions to Slidell attributed the imperative for acquisition to "designs upon California" by Britain and France, which "would be so fraught with danger to the best interests of the United States." But there was more to it. "The possession of the Bay and harbor of San Francisco is all important to the United States," Buchanan wrote—the advantages "so striking, that it would be a waste of time to enumerate them here. . . . Money would be no object when compared with the value of the acquisition."

He exaggerated, but not by much. Buchanan told Slidell that Polk was prepared to pay as much as twenty-five million dollars for Monterey and San Francisco, twenty million for San Francisco alone. (Of course, Polk had told his cabinet that he was actually prepared to go as high as forty million.) The United States would also pay the claims of American citizens against the Mexican government, possibly including the indemnities claimed by Graham and his followers, estimated at about five million dollars. Polk imagined that, given the Herrera presidency's parlous financial condition and its impotence in Alta California, Slidell's offer would be welcome.

Events overtook Slidell's mission. Herrera was deposed on January 2, 1846, by Mariano Paredes y Arrillaga, who was himself deposed eight months later in a coup that brought Antonio López de Santa Anna to power—after Polk arranged for Santa Anna's safe passage from his refuge in Cuba to Mexico. For a brief moment, Polk thought Santa Anna would return the favor by ceding California peacefully for thirty million dollars. His expectations were dashed, for Santa Anna instead marched on American troops commanded by Zachary Taylor (only to be routed at the Battle of Buena Vista). It had become clear that war was the only path to the annexation of California. This happened in no small part because while Polk was occupied with diplomatic intrigue, the American colonists in California had taken matters into their own hands.

3

THE BEAR FLAG REVOLT

L ATE ON THE afternoon of June 14, 1846, a ragtag company of armed ruffians raised a sheet of bleached white cotton painted with a red star and the stout figure of what was supposed to be a grizzly bear up a flagpole on the central square of Sonoma. Led by a stolid Massachusetts-born carpenter named William Brown Ide and a brawny, obstreperous bear trapper named Ezekiel Merritt, they had ridden for two days from New Helvetia in the expectation of taking this provincial Mexican citadel by stealth or, failing that, by storm.

Neither proved to be necessary. Rather than an armed camp, Sonoma, located about fifty miles north of San Francisco and fifty miles from the Pacific shore, turned out to be a tranquil and largely depopulated outpost of the Mexican empire. "A more peaceful burg than this stronghold of the *Frontera del Norte*," Bancroft observed, "it would be difficult to find." Sonoma's commandant, Mariano Guadalupe Vallejo, had sent the garrison soldiers home two years before. He now ruled in tranquility over a house facing the square that he shared with his wife and a daughter; they were the hub of a social circle that included Vallejo's brother, one doctor, and another daughter and her American husband living nearby.

The thirty-three Americans breached Sonoma's peace at daybreak, intent on founding the "California Republic." Their approach differed from that of most of the American settlers in Alta California and of the US government— their strategy was to keep a low profile and provide only tacit support to the

Mexican citizens in the region, the general expectation being that the Mexicans of Alta California—the Californios—would act on their own initiative to secede from Mexico and then seek annexation by the United States. Although the invaders did take the garrison of Sonoma without violence, their actions undermined the US government's goal of allowing an independent California to emerge organically and peacefully. Instead, they ensured that independence could not be achieved without the United States going to war.

So was launched the Bear Flag Revolt.

In this rump action—a foray by an indifferently organized and undisciplined force operating without official sanction—contemporaries and the earliest chroniclers of the period detected the seed of California exceptionalism, that self-reliance and individualism that later generations would take as their birthright. The qualities of the rebels that stand out today, in retrospect, are their self-delusion and opportunism.

The Bear Flag Revolt occurred at a time of increasing tension between the Mexican authorities and American immigrants and of rising discord within the Mexican community itself. Micheltorena's ouster in 1845 had aggravated the instability of Mexican rule due to the uneasy relationship between the contending claimants to the former governor's authority: Don Pío de Jesús Pico and José Castro. "Neither would have been chosen by the leading citizens . . . and neither would have selected the other as his associate," Bancroft observed. The men tried to stay out of each other's way; Pico established his seat as titular governor of Alta California in Los Angeles, and Castro presided as *comandante general* in Monterey, more than three hundred miles to the north.

Meanwhile, Americans by the hundreds continued pouring over the border with California. The Mexican authorities were certainly justified in fearing the prospect of further insurgency. Saber-rattling in the American press was growing ever louder. "There will soon be more Yankees than Mexicans there, and they will, most likely, establish a government of their own, entirely independent of Mexico," reported a widely circulated American newsweekly on June 7, 1845.

Into this combustible state of affairs, John Charles Frémont injected himself. One of the most controversial adventurers in the history of California and the West, he would make an unstable situation worse.

There was no question of Frémont's courage, tenacity, and resourcefulness as an explorer of America's interior wilderness, no grounds to doubt the reports of privations he and his men had suffered in their efforts to map the continent. In recounting his second expedition (of five), which brought him over the Sierra Nevadas in 1843, Frémont wrote of blinding snow, frost-bite, malnutrition, pack animals perishing from the elements, Indian guides vanishing in the dead of night, and men going insane in the labyrinthine mountain passes of the Sierras.

"The times were severe when stout men lost their minds from extrem-ity of suffering . . . and when mules and horses, ready to die of starvation, were killed for food," Frémont wrote in his memoirs. One demented crew member who had wandered off "into the woods without knowing where he was going" was brought back to camp alive, only to jump to his death in a freezing, foaming mountain torrent, imagining it to be a placid sum-mer stream. Frémont retained his own indomitable spirit in the face of these challenges: "All this gave the country a charm for me. It would have been dull work if it had been to plod over a safe country." These were the doughty adventures that would make Frémont a household name. Those who met the explorer in person were surprised to encounter not the Hercu-lean figure suggested by his published accounts but a man of small stature and cultured manners—in the words of the artist Alfred S. Waugh, "a pale in-tellectual looking young man, modest and unassuming, seemingly more accustomed to the refinements and luxuries of life, than to the toils and dangers of the wilderness. . . . Yet in his eye, you saw something which shewed contempt of danger and proclaimed him a man to be obeyed under all circumstances."

There was a less admirable side to Frémont, however. As a political figure and a military officer, he was timid, indecisive, vainglorious, dis-honest, even cowardly. The members of his expeditions admired him as a leader, but for those who came in contact with him in those other fields, familiarity bred doubt, disdain, and contempt. Nor was he above claiming accomplishments for himself that belonged to others. After the Mexican-American War, Frémont assumed the title of "Conqueror of California." This provoked William Ide to establish his own claim to that mantle by writing a book-length refutation.

The most acrid description of Frémont as a player in the California ac-quisition drama came from Bancroft, who considered Frémont's behavior thoroughly discreditable. Writing some four decades after the events but drawing from direct interviews with many of the participants, Bancroft described Frémont as a "fool," "insolent," "rash," "reckless," and "selfish and dishonorable." These judgments were wholly defensible, as was Bancroft's conclusion that Frémont's activities in connection with the Bear Flag attack were "ill-timed [and] ill-judged." More likely than not, he reckoned, they impeded rather than advanced the goal of peacefully transferring Alta California to US jurisdiction by forcing the government's hand before it was ready to negotiate an annexation with the Mexican government.

The key to Frémont's success as a public figure, which eventually led to a single six-month term as a US senator from the newly established state of California and the nomination as the first presidential candidate of the Republican Party (he lost the election to James Buchanan), was that he had married well. His wife, Jessie, was the redoubtable daughter of the fiercely expansionist senator Thomas Hart Benton of Missouri. She would stage-manage her husband's public career so adroitly that the Frémonts can properly be placed among the pioneering celebrities in American history and were certainly the first to emerge as national figures from the California wilderness. To this day, Frémont's name adorns nineteen counties, cities, and towns in fifteen states; eight mountains and other geographical features; and dozens of schools, school districts, and libraries across the Lower 48.

In January 1846, still playing the role of explorer, Frémont arrived in the harbor of a small settlement, Yerba Buena, the eastern shore of which was washed by the waters of a well-protected bay and overlooked by an island later called Alcatraz.* This tiny community soon rechristened itself San Francisco, under which name it would grow into a world-famous metropolis. Contemplating the narrow inlet through which he had just entered the bay, Frémont—as he would recall—thought of the name the ancients gave to the harbor of Byzantium (later Constantinople and today Istanbul): Chrysoceras, the "Golden Horn." He scribbled a label for the strait onto a map he delivered to the US Senate in 1848, and it stuck: the Golden Gate.

An American settler escorted Frémont from Yerba Buena 110 miles down the coast to Monterey and introduced him to the American consul. This was Thomas O. Larkin, a forty-four-year-old merchant with a stern demeanor and a thirst for wealth who had come west from his native Massachusetts in 1832 to make his fortune and had succeeded spectacularly.

---

* *Yerba buena* is Spanish for "good herb" and colloquially referred to mint or spearmint. *Alcatraz* derives from the Spanish for large seabirds such as gannets.

Larkin's method of doing business in Mexican California differed from that of his fellow Americans; their standard practice was to assimilate by converting to Catholicism, acquiring Mexican citizenship, and marrying a daughter of the local Mexican grandee. Larkin kept his Protestant faith and his American citizenship and married a wealthy American widow he had met aboard ship during his passage to California, yet within a few short years he had established himself in milling, lumbering, ranching, goods trading, and moneylending (among his debtors was Governor Micheltorena, whose ouster rendered the debt uncollectible). In 1834 Larkin erected the first two-story home in Monterey and made it the center of the city's social life.

Larkin also established himself as a reliable front man for the US government's policy of peaceable annexation. Adhering to the precept that the key to a nonmilitary acquisition was a healthy infusion of American colonists, he regaled eastern newspapers with alluring descriptions of California's landscape and life, using the pseudonym Paisano. In a sketch published on the first page of the *New York Herald* on June 12, 1845, Paisano reported: "We have neither the yellow fever nor the black vomit; no fevers and agues . . . Solomon, in all his glory, was not more happy than a Californian."

Upon assuming the presidency, James K. Polk formally deputized Larkin as a confidential government agent. Secretary of State Buchanan instructed him in a secret letter to persuade the Californios that affiliation with the United States, rather than Britain or France, would be in their financial and political interests and to counsel his American friends to sit tight and wait for events to take their natural—that is, peaceful—course.

Buchanan's orders were delivered by one Archibald H. Gillespie in yet another manifestation of Polk's taste for intrigue. During a White House meeting on the evening of October 30, 1845, Polk invested Gillespie, a Marine lieutenant, with "a secret mission" to Larkin. Gillespie committed Buchanan's written instructions to memory and destroyed the original document. Disguised as an invalid merchant traveling for his health, he carried an innocuous letter of introduction from Buchanan to Frémont and a packet of letters to Frémont from his wife and father-in-law.

Arriving at Monterey on April 17 after an arduous sea journey of nearly six months, Gillespie summoned Larkin aboard the ship to receive Buchanan's instructions. Frémont's activities already had upended the government's strategy. After his meeting with Larkin, he had proceeded to explore the territory around Monterey with his expedition members, most of whom were soldiers in the US Army. Larkin was unhappy about having an American military force traipsing about Alta California. He knew that the local authorities were even more uneasy, so he brought Frémont to a meeting with José Castro. Frémont recalled later that he assured the Mexican general that "I was engaged in surveying the nearest route from the United States to the Pacific Ocean," that "the object of the survey was geographical . . . that it was made in the interests of science and of commerce, and that the men composing the party were citizens and not soldiers." He told Castro that his sole purpose in coming to Monterey was to obtain supplies and that as soon as provisions were in hand, he and his men would head north to Oregon to continue the survey. After hearing this explanation, Castro gave Frémont permission to stay on briefly instead of ordering him to depart California at once.

Shortly after, Frémont broke his promise by moving south along the coast in the exact opposite direction of Oregon. Castro reacted promptly to what was at best an insult and at worst a provocation to war, ordering Frémont to "immediately retire beyond the limits of this department." Frémont responded with a verbal harangue to Castro's envoy about "General Castro's breach of good faith, and the rudeness with which he communicated it. . . . I peremptorily refused compliance to an order insulting to my government and myself." He retreated only as far as Gavilan Peak, about thirty-five miles northeast of Monterey but with a commanding view of the city's inland approaches. There he erected fortifications and raised the US flag at the summit.* Castro, meanwhile, mustered an armed force of more than one hundred men.

Larkin messaged Frémont that "your encamping so near Town has caused much excitement" and proposed that he move his camp "some greater distance" away to avoid provoking an attack. Frémont's behavior, he added, could "cause trouble hereafter to Resident Americans." Larkin could not have been comforted by Frémont's combative reply: "If we are unjustly attacked," he wrote, "we will fight to the extremity and refuse quarter, trusting to our country to avenge our death."

A few days later, however, Frémont broke camp and stole away. Gillespie finally made contact with him in Oregon on May 9. What Gillespie

---

* The peak is today known as Frémont Peak, the dominant feature of one of California's state parks.

told Frémont at that meeting cannot be conclusively determined because no written record exists and the recollections of both parties differ. But in an edition of his memoirs published in 1887, four decades later, Frémont implied that he was instructed to take a military stance to support the American government's quest for California:

> The information through Gillespie had absolved me from my duty as an explorer, and I was left to my duty as an officer of the American Army with the further authoritative knowledge that the Government intended to take California. . . . It had been made known to me now on the authority of the Secretary of the Navy that to obtain possession of California was the chief object of the President.

Whatever truly passed between the two men, the record shows that Frémont turned south, crossed back into California, and set up camp at Sutter's Fort, the stockade of New Helvetia. He claimed at the time that he did so because his advance northward was hindered by deep snow, hostile Indians, and dwindling supplies, but wrote later in his memoirs that he had acted deliberately to take California. "War with Mexico was inevitable. I resolved to move forward on the opportunity and return forthwith to the Sacramento Valley to bring to bear all the influences I could command. . . . This decision was the first step in the conquest of California."

Although Frémont's reappearance at New Helvetia placed him back among restive American settlers, he still was not ready to take matters into his own hands. Whether he hesitated out of nervousness, indecision, or the lack of official authorization to act, he avoided any overt encouragement of the local settlers, who by now were girding for their attack on Sonoma.

The attack party appealed to Frémont for help as they mustered at Sutter's Fort but were rebuffed. As Ide recollected, Frémont told them that he was "not at liberty to afford us the least aid or assistance; nor would he suffer any of his men to do so." Ide described Frémont as confident that he could "whip Castro, if he chose, but that he should not do so, unless first assaulted by him"; he told Ide he was determined to remain quietly at New Helvetia until he received enough provisions for a march out of California and back to US territory. Several of Frémont's men, including the legendary scout Kit Carson, asked to be discharged so they could join the settlers. Frémont turned them down.

It was already impossible to interrupt the sequence of events that Frémont's adventures had triggered. Rumors spread among the settlers that Castro was bent on taking his revenge on Frémont by punishing them. Ide circulated a proclamation purportedly by Castro (likely a forgery, possibly by Ide himself) ordering "all foreigners, whose residence in the country was less than one year, to leave the country, and their property and beasts of burden, without taking arms, on pain of death." But there was no reason to doubt that Frémont had infuriated Castro. Ide later wrote that Frémont, "after having provoked the assumed authorities of the country, left us [settlers] to experience the wrath and retaliatory vengeance his acts had engendered."

Still, despite Frémont's explicit refusal to help, the settlers were energized by his presence. Bancroft's conclusion that the Bear Flag attack would not have occurred if Frémont were not nearby may have arisen from his disdain for Frémont's character, but it is not unfounded.

THE ACTION NOW shifted to Sonoma. The noisy arrival of the rabble awakened Vallejo. When the general got out of bed and peered out his window, he was stunned to find his quarters surrounded by armed men who were "not wearing a uniform but . . . were armed and looked ferocious." Vallejo's wife urged him to flee by a rear door, but he told her that "such an act was undignified and that under no circumstances could I decide to abandon my young family." Instead, he donned his uniform, greeted the marauders from his front door, and invited several of them into his home to parley. From these men—Ezekiel Merritt; Robert Semple, a doctor attached to the group; and William Knight, who functioned as interpreter—Vallejo promptly discovered that they had no plan of action to follow their seizure of the garrison.

The invaders lounging about the square did not inspire confidence among the residents who emerged into the dawn to give them the once-over. Rosalia Leese, Vallejo's daughter, described them as "a large group of rough-looking men, some wearing on their heads caps made with the skins of coyotes or wolfs, some wearing slouched hats full of holes, some wearing straw hats as black as charcoal. . . . Several had no shirts, shoes were only to be seen on the feet of fifteen or twenty among the whole lot."

These armed men restlessly waited for news from inside the house. "The sun was climbing up the heavens an hour or more," Ide recalled, "and yet no man, nor voice, nor sound of violence came from the house to tell us of events within." At this point the incursion descended into farce. The Americans sent John Grigsby, an army officer who had accompanied the rebels, into the house to find out what was going on. When he failed to reemerge, they sent in Ide, who solved the mystery. Vallejo had brought out his finest spirits and plied his visitors liberally. "There sat Merrit [sic]—his head fallen," Ide recounted. "There sat Knight, no longer able to interpret; and there sat the new made Captain [Grigsby], as mute as the seat he sat upon. The bottles had well nigh vanquished the captors."

Semple, who evidently had remained sober, was engaged in writing articles of capitulation for Vallejo to sign. These allowed Vallejo and his compatriots to remain at Sonoma under guard once they pledged not to take up arms against the insurgents. In return, the safety of their families and property would be guaranteed. However, once the agreement was read aloud on the square, the scant discipline that had existed among the invading troops collapsed altogether. Some demanded that the prisoners be dispatched to Frémont in New Helvetia; others insisted on their right to plunder. Ide supervised the seizure of the meager arsenal—nine small cannons and about two hundred fifty antiquated muskets—and arranged to transfer the prisoners to Frémont's headquarters seventy-five miles to the east under a nine-man guard.

The other insurgents remained in Sonoma under Ide's supervision. Among their first acts was to hoist a flag of independence. Responsibility for its design fell to William L. Todd (a cousin of Mary Todd Lincoln, the future First Lady). In red paint or berry juice, he drew a five-pointed star, the silhouette of a stocky creature meant to be a grizzly bear, and the words *California Republic* on a rectangle of plain cotton cloth about three feet by five. Sewed onto its bottom edge was a strip of red flannel said to have been torn from the petticoat of a local settler. Vallejo later sneered that the fat creature "looked more like a pig than a bear."

On June 14, 1846, the Bear Flag was hoisted over the Sonoma town square and the California Republic declared. Although cleaned up and modernized, all the elements of that first crude California flag—the red star, the bear, the red stripe, and the words *California Republic*—still adorn the official flag of the state of California.

Two days later, Merritt rode into New Helvetia with the prisoners in tow. Frémont was anything but pleased to see them. At first he disavowed responsibility for the prisoners and consigned them to Sutter's custody. On reflection, however, he resolved that since the Bear Flaggers appeared to have succeeded with their foray into Sonoma, the time was ripe for him to turn their efforts to his own advantage—or, as he wrote in his memoirs, "I decided that it was for me rather to govern events than to be governed by them." With about ninety men, he headed west to Sonoma to take command from Ide and place his own force at the service of the US government, which was represented by warships stationed offshore at Monterey. Arriving in Sonoma on June 25, Frémont's group was not an especially awe-inspiring military formation. About one-third of the marchers were settlers attached helter-skelter to Frémont. "There were Americans, French, English, Swiss, Poles, Russians, Chilians, Germans, Greeks, Austrians, Pawnees, native Indians, etc.," reported an associate of Sutter's.

By then, the United States and Mexico were indeed at war. Following a series of American provocations, the US Congress declared war on May 13; Mexico responded with its own declaration on July 7. Frémont made contact in Monterey with Commodore Robert F. Stockton, commander of the Pacific squadron, who dubbed Frémont's party the California Battalion and sent it aboard a Navy ship to San Diego, which Frémont seized easily. For the first time, Frémont gained renown not as an explorer but as a military commander. President Polk, in his second annual message to Congress, delivered on December 8, 1846, made oblique reference to Frémont, reporting that "our squadron in the Pacific, with the cooperation of a gallant officer of the Army and a small force hastily collected in that distant country, has acquired bloodless possession of the Californias, and the American flag has been raised at every important point in that Province."

In California, the Mexican-American War was a largely desultory affair, more a series of isolated skirmishes between American forces and outnumbered Californios than a strategically and tactically consistent military operation. The defenders typically melted into the hills in the course of these encounters, leaving the Americans with an inflated sense of conquest even while being harried by guerrillas.

But not every confrontation ended with an American victory. A notable defeat occurred on December 6, 1846, in San Pascual, a town about thirty miles north of San Diego. A detachment of American troops under Brigadier General Stephen Watts Kearny had marched west from New Mexico to intercept what Kearny had been told was a squadron of Californio soldiers. Operating on faulty intelligence (from Kit Carson) regarding the size of the Californio force, Kearny left most of his brigade behind in Santa Fe and marched with only one hundred dragoons. His exhausted troops, their gunpowder soaking wet and useless, were ultimately forced into savage hand-to-hand combat with defenders armed with lances. Eighteen American men died in the battle and nineteen were wounded. Kearny retreated to high ground and was rescued five days later by reinforcements Commodore Stockton sent from San Diego.

The Battle of San Pascual had little effect on the war itself but did heighten the enmity between Stockton and Kearny, who were already at odds over which of them had military and civil authority over the California territory. Their disagreement would be only one manifestation of the confused and indifferent military governance imposed on California following its putative conquest by the United States. This had been signaled by the raising of the American flag over Monterey on July 7, 1846, although a peace treaty would not be signed until six months later.

While Congress dithered over granting California statehood, its inhabitants came under the rule of seven successive American military governors. The governors treated the native Californios indulgently, guaranteeing their safety and their properties as set forth in the terms of the Treaty of Cahuenga, which ended hostilities within California. This pact, reached on January 13, 1847, granted the Californios all the rights enjoyed by US citizens provided that they turned in their arms.

Relations among the American commanders did not reflect the same tranquility, for they squabbled constantly over their powers and prerogatives. The conflict between Stockton and Kearny derived partially from a clash of personalities but also from contradictory orders the two officers received from Washington. In truculent written exchanges, Stockton held that his establishment of civil government in upper California prior to Kearny's arrival gave him supreme authority, while Kearny claimed to hold explicit orders from President Polk to assume command. In the meantime Stockton appointed Frémont as his successor as governor. Accordingly, Frémont treated Kearny, indisputably his army superior, with nervy insolence. Kearny, perhaps aware that Stockton was soon to be replaced as commander of the Pacific fleet, chose to allow this unstable situation to continue, leaving the newly acquired territory without a functioning government. The smoke finally cleared on February 13 when Kearny was officially placed in charge. He promptly ordered Frémont to relinquish command and join him on a journey to Washington.

The two men headed east on May 31, stopping briefly in the High Sierra to bury the mummified remains of the Donner party, a band of emigrants from Illinois who had come to grief in a snowy mountain pass the previous winter. The last survivors of this now legendary disaster had left the site only a few weeks earlier; to this day, the site of their demise bears the name of Donner Pass. When the men reached Fort Leavenworth on the Missouri River, Kearny informed Frémont of the real reason for their trip: Frémont was to face court-martial in Washington for his insubordinate behavior toward the general. At his trial, which began on November 2, Frémont was found guilty on all charges and ordered discharged from the Army. President Polk, however, overruled the sentence and told Frémont to report for duty. Willful to the last, Frémont refused Polk's offer of clemency and demanded that his conviction be reversed. When this was denied, he resigned his commission and embarked on political pursuits. He would meet with only middling success, a disappointing coda to what had once promised to be a brilliant career.

During the long interregnum between the American conquest of California and its admission to the union, the colonists became increasingly discontented with Washington's neglectful treatment. Among the points of contention was the character and behavior of local administrative officials. Known as alcaldes, they were appointed by the military governors and given little guidance as to their responsibilities or the limitations of their office. This group soon became notorious for its corruption.

"The present system is . . . worse than anarchy," wrote Robert Semple, the former Bear Flag rebel, in the *California Star*, which he owned. "We have *Alcaldes* all over the country, assuming the power of legislatures, issuing and promulging their *Bandos*, laws and orders, and oppressing the people. . . . The most nefarious scheming, trickery and speculating have been practiced by some that was ever disclosed to the light of heaven." (The term *alcalde*, from the Spanish word meaning "judge" or "magistrate," originated in Andalusian Arabic during Muslim rule of the Iberian Peninsula from the ninth through the fifteenth centuries.)

Even when their intentions were pure, the appointed alcaldes were often powerless to impose law and order on their districts. As a result, disorder prevailed through the countryside. Rural areas were plagued by marauding bandidos, none more renowned than Joaquín Murieta, who was said to conduct his sorties accompanied by a sidekick dubbed Three-Fingered Jack.

Historians debate to this day whether Murieta was a discontented miner wreaking vengeance on the Yankees for dispossessing him of his rightful prospecting fortune or a character of myth. Whatever the truth about Murieta, there is no question that violent assaults were common in the countryside, though Murieta was blamed for many more than he could possibly have committed, assuming he actually existed.

Conditions were not much better in the cities. San Jose, which was inhabited by a large population of Californios who nurtured old resentments against the American settlers, was a particular trouble spot. "Large portions of the population lazy and addicted to gambling have no visible means of livelihood, and of course must support themselves by stealing cattle or horses," a transplanted East Coast businessman named Joseph S. Ruckel complained to Governor Mason in 1847. "Wanted, an *alcalde* who is not afraid to do his duty, and who knows what his duty is."

In San Francisco, merchants took matters into their own hands by creating their own private police force. Known as the Hounds, they were an agglomeration of British convicts who had escaped from transports carrying them to the penal colony of Australia and Americans who had volunteered to fight in the Mexican-American War but arrived after hostilities had ended. The merchants originally hired them to track down and return sailors who had abandoned their ships in order to mine for gold, desertions that had brought trade to a standstill. They soon discovered the downside of endowing ruffians with civil authority. The Hounds took to marching defiantly around San Francisco, waging increasingly violent war on its citizens, extorting protection payments from restaurants and shops, and finally staging a bloody attack on the city's Chilean neighborhood in July 1849. That was the last straw; the day after the attack, more than two hundred citizens were deputized at a public meeting chaired by Samuel Brannan, a Mormon elder who had been sent west by Brigham Young in 1846 as the vanguard of the Mormons' emigration from Nauvoo, Illinois. By nightfall they had rounded up nineteen Hounds and imprisoned them in a navy hulk anchored in the bay. During the next week the prisoners were convicted of riot, robbery, and assault and sentenced to punishments ranging from fines and prison terms to permanent banishment from the city.

The Treaty of Guadalupe Hidalgo, signed on February 2, 1848, ended the Mexican-American War and ceded a vast western territory to the United States, writing a new chapter in California's march toward statehood. But contrary to Polk's desire, annexation had not been achieved without bloodshed.

Statehood now beckoned from beyond the horizon. To reach that goal, the citizens of California would once again be forced to take matters into their own hands. But one more convulsion would interrupt the march to statehood. Its effects would spread not only throughout the annexed territory but across America and worldwide.

4

THE SORDID CRY OF GOLD

ON THE AFTERNOON of January 28, 1848, as John Sutter was working on accounts in his small office in New Helvetia, he was interrupted by his partner James Marshall, who was building a sawmill for the company on the American River forty miles upstream. Sutter, born Johann Augustus Sutter (or Suter) in Switzerland in 1803, felt himself finally to be on the verge of commercial success in his adopted land, having fled a business collapse, crushing debts, and an unhappy marriage to remake himself in California. At thirty-three, James Marshall was not a large man but retained a solid build from his previous trade of backwoods carpentry and wagon building in his native New Jersey. Sutter knew him to be a mercurial sort, generally placid but quick to outbursts of temper. When Marshall, sopping wet from a long ride in a drenching rain, insisted that they repair together to a secluded room and lock the door behind them, Sutter briefly wondered if he should keep his firearm at hand. But Marshall's manner was agitated rather than violent, so Sutter did as he asked.

In the private room, Marshall pulled a soiled pouch from his pocket. At that moment Sutter's clerk came through the door, which Sutter had forgotten to lock. Marshall thrust the sack back in his pocket. Once the clerk excused himself, Marshall groused, "Now lock the doors; didn't I tell you that we might have listeners?" Then he opened the pouch and emptied out its contents: a few pieces of yellow metal, the largest no bigger than a pea and the smallest about the size of a pinhead.

"I believe this is gold," he said, "but the people at the mill laughed at me and called me crazy."

They weighed the metal in water against three silver dollars and determined that its density exceeded that of the silver. Then they applied the classic "acid test," dowsing the metal with aqua fortis, or nitric acid. This curious test is designed to prove a negative; in the presence of impurities, the acid turns color and bubbles, but it is unaffected by pure gold, and it was not affected by Marshall's find. "I declared this to be gold of the finest quality, of at least 23 carats," Sutter wrote later. He encouraged Marshall to stay overnight at New Helvetia so they could return to the sawmill together the next morning, but Marshall would not wait. After Sutter promised to join him at the mill the next day, he rode off in the rain without even staying for supper.

As Marshall later told the tale of finding gold, he and his crew of ten Indians and five Mormons, veterans of a Mormon battalion mustered by Brigham Young to support the US Army in the Mexican-American War, had built a tailrace for the mill and sluiced it clean with river water. Early on the morning of January 24, when Marshall was inspecting the millrace, his attention was caught by the glint of reddish-yellow flakes in the water. Suspecting they were gold, he hammered at one with a stone. It passed the first test of gold, malleability, flattening out without breaking.

Marshall approached his carpenter William Scott, who was building the mill wheel nearby, and said, "I have found it."

"What is it?" Scott asked.

"Gold."

"Oh, no, that can't be."

"I know it to be nothing else," Marshall replied. Four days later, he showed his find to Sutter.

Marshall's discovery and his meeting with Sutter are foundational events of modern California. One can almost divide the state's history into the pre–Gold Rush and post–Gold Rush periods. The Gold Rush that began in the state in 1848 and starting in the following year brought people from across the country—indeed, from around the world—was the fulcrum of California's transformation from a largely agrarian culture into a rapidly industrializing economy; it launched a population surge unprecedented in American history and initiated San Francisco's evolution from a sleepy settlement of squalid tents and combustible wooden shacks into a world-class metropolis.

These changes might well have happened without the discovery of gold but not with the speed that they occurred from 1849 on.

The folklore surrounding the Gold Rush is rich and abundant. One can start with Marshall's discovery at the sawmill, which is often depicted as a bolt from the blue. In fact, he had a fair idea of what he would find when he strolled down to the millrace that January morning. He had studied geology as a schoolboy, and during his search for a mill site he had seen indications of mineral deposits. Rather than being taken by surprise by his discovery, he might have been looking for confirmation of his expectations.

The common notion that great fortunes were made in California's goldfields is on the whole exaggerated. Some prospectors made stupendous finds, but the majority came away with little or nothing. Innumerable fortune-seekers (dubbed "forty-niners" for the year the gold frenzy took hold, or "Argonauts," a reference to the legendary seekers of the Golden Fleece) never reached California at all, abandoning their quest mid-journey due to its hardship or succumbing to Indian attacks or cholera or other diseases along the way.

"Gold mining is Nature's great lottery scheme," Massachusetts emigrant Louise Amelia Clappe wrote from the gold district to her sister Molly in 1852, one of the twenty-three letters she eventually published under the pseudonym Dame Shirley. "A man may work in a claim for many months, and be poorer at the end of the time than when he commenced; or he may 'take out' thousands in a few hours. It is a mere matter of chance."

The period of maximum return to miners in the "diggings" was brief. The average daily take of twenty dollars in 1848 (about $780 at this writing) fell to sixteen dollars in 1849, when competition became intense. It was ten dollars in 1850, declined to eight the following year, and followed the trajectory downward to an average of three dollars a day in 1860. By then the individual miner was reduced to a historical footnote, his role supplanted by wage labor as hand-worked mining gave way to mechanized enterprises. It is true that these figures, especially at the outset of the Gold Rush, handsomely exceeded daily wages back home—in 1849, bricklayers earned an average $1.50 a day, coal miners $1.16, steelworkers $1.40, and railroad engineers, who were considered skilled laborers, $1.98. But work at the diggings was as arduous and the hours as long as the conditions many Argonauts had left behind, and the privations of daily life were greater; as a result, the threshold of frustration when a claim went fallow was low.

Altogether, $670 million worth of gold (at contemporary prices) was drawn out of the California earth and brought back east in the fourteen years following Marshall's discovery—peaking at nearly $67 million in 1852 and falling to $41.6 million in 1861. The truly enduring fortunes, however, were made not by those who attacked the terrain with pick, pan, and shovel but by those who sold those implements to the diggers and kept them fed and clothed. (Hence the quote sometimes attributed to Mark Twain: "When everybody is digging for gold, it's a good time to be in the pick and shovel business.") The victors were retail merchants like Collis P. Huntington and Mark Hopkins, who established their hardware store at 54 K Street, Sacramento, in February 1850 ("Rubber Hose, Belting, Powder, Fuse, Rope, Blocks, Pitch, Tar &c." read the sign out front), and earned enough from the miners to invest in the Central Pacific Railroad, the western reach of the first transcontinental railroad and the project that would engrave their names permanently in California history. Born in upstate New York, they had come west with the Argonauts of 1849, but made their fortunes as capitalists, not prospectors.

SUTTER LATER CLAIMED that he spent a sleepless night after his meeting with Marshall. He told Bancroft that he "saw that night the curse of the thing upon him." Indeed, although he owned the property where gold was discovered, he lacked the nimbleness needed to exploit the find for himself in the face of the widespread frenzy to come. He would die in poverty in 1880 in a hotel room in Washington, DC, where he had journeyed to petition Congress for compensation for the losses he suffered from waves of gold-seeking immigrants. At the end he still owned a ring made from an ounce and a half of the gold extracted from the mill site during his first visit after Marshall's discovery. It was inscribed "The first gold discovered in California, January, 1848," and it was said never to have been taken off his finger even as he was laid in the grave.

Sutter's immediate concern was with the effect that the discovery of gold might have on the lumber and flour mills from which he expected to make his fortune. He was prescient in his fear, for the businesses failed when his crews abandoned him to dig for gold.

The morning after examining Marshall's discovery, he rode to the sawmill, anxious to extract a promise from the workers to say nothing about the find by offering to double their wages in return for about six weeks of silence. He figured that would be long enough to finish the construction of both mills.

But the secret was bound to escape, partially because Sutter himself could not keep his own mouth shut. On February 10 he wrote to his old friend General Vallejo of Sonoma that he had "made a discovery of a gold mine, which, according to experiments we have made, is extraordinarily rich." Sutter also made the mistake of dispatching Charles Bennett, a member of Marshall's crew, to Colonel Richard Barnes Mason, then the military governor of California in Monterey, with a petition for a land grant with mining privileges. Bennett was instructed to say nothing about gold. But he carried a pouch of gold nuggets, and at a roadhouse he fell into conversation with a settler who mentioned that a rich deposit of coal had been found nearby. "Coal!" Bennett exclaimed, producing the pouch. "I have something here which will beat coal, and make this the greatest country in the world."

The news continued to leak out through numerous porous pathways. A teamster bringing supplies to Sutter's Fort was told by a son of Peter Wimmer, another member of Marshall's crew, that gold had been found at the sawmill. When the teamster scoffed, the boy's mother indignantly produced a handful of nuggets as proof. Marshall's crewman Henry Bigler was another conduit of the news through letters to his former Mormon Battalion messmates about his forays with companions into the local ravines, where they pried gold out of the earth with knives. "We have picked up more than a hundred dollars' worth last week," he confided. Bigler's letters soon drew his friends to an island in the south fork of the American River about a mile below the sawmill. This soon became known as the Mormon diggings, one of the richest deposits of all.

The first reports of a gold strike were greeted skeptically in San Francisco; yarns about mineral riches had long been part of settlers' campfire mythmaking. Colonel Mason inquired of a well-traveled friend whether he had heard of a find on the American River. "A few fools have hurried to the place," came the reply, "but you may be sure there is nothing in it."

The *California Star* briefly reported the discovery in early March. Edward C. Kemble, its editor, then decided that "it was in the line of his duty to go and investigate the wonder." He sailed up the Sacramento River to Sutter's Fort, where he was greeted graciously by the guileless proprietor and introduced to Marshall, who was "gruff and evasive" about the gold strike. Despite being told by Marshall's crew that gold could be found "anywhere you're a mind to dig for it," Kemble was so dubious that he scrawled "humbug" across the top of his notebook. The *Star*'s reporting over the subsequent weeks was laced with skepticism. As late as May 20, Kemble was describing "the reputed wealth of that section of country" as "all sham—a supurb take in, as was ever got up to 'guzzle the gullible.' . . . Was there ever anything so superlatively silly?"

Yet Kemble was also prudent enough to hedge his bets. On April 1 he published a freelance correspondent's account that "we saw a few days ago, a beautiful specimen of gold from the mine newly discovered on the American Fork. From all accounts the mine is immensely rich—and already, we learn, the gold from it, collected at random and without any trouble, has become an article of trade at the upper settlements."

With the abruptness of a switch turning, gold fever struck San Francisco—which only the year before had abandoned as too provincial its old name of Yerba Buena. The appearance in town of prospectors laden with bags filled with gold was too hard to ignore. A much-remarked moment was connected with Sam Brannan. After his Mormon party established themselves in San Francisco, Brannan made a reconnaissance trip to the Mormon diggings and came back with a vial of gold dust that he displayed in public. "Brannan took his hat off and swung it. . . . Shouting aloud in the streets that gold was found &c.," Bigler wrote in his diary.

San Francisco, still a hamlet of fewer than a thousand residents, emptied out. "Yesterday and to-day nothing has been talked of but the new gold 'placer,' as people call it," Henry Richard Vizetelly, an English physician, wrote on May 10 in his personal journal. A week later he added, "This place is now in a perfect furor of excitement; all the work-people have struck. . . . Several hundred people of all classes—lawyers, store-keepers, merchants, etc.—are bitten with the fever." Vizetelly was himself preparing to depart for the mines on horseback with a few friends but was delayed because his saddler was overwhelmed with orders. On the day he had been promised delivery he found the saddler's quarters deserted. On the door was pasted a sign reading "Gone to the diggings."

By the end of May, San Francisco was virtually a ghost town, with as many as three-quarters of its adult males off to the mines.

"THE WHOLE COUNTRY, from San Francisco to Los Angeles and from the sea shore to the base of the Sierra Nevada," wrote the weekly *Californian*, "resounds with the sordid cry of 'gold! GOLD!! GOLD!!!' while the field is left half planted, the house half built, and everything neglected but the manufacture of shovels and pickaxes, and the means of transportation to the spot where one man obtained $128 worth of the real stuff in one day's washing, and the average for all concerned is $20 per diem."

Prices for provisions, mining tools, and pack animals soared. "A man would pay $300 for a horse worth $6 a month before," set it loose and buy another when needed, for "he could scrape from the ground the cost of an animal more easily than he could take care of one for a week or two." Flour went for eight hundred dollars a barrel; a pick, shovel, and pan one hundred dollars each. Laborers who stayed behind in San Francisco could demand what had seemed only weeks before to be astronomical wages; a friend told Vizetelly that "his negro waiter has demanded and receives ten dollars a day. He is forced to submit, for 'helps' of all kinds are in great demand, and very difficult to meet with." Reverend Walter Colton, who was serving as mayor of Monterey and shared a house with Mason and Lieutenant J. B. Lanman, commander of the USS *Warren*, reported that "our servants have run, one after another. . . . We had to take to the kitchen, and cook our own breakfast. A general of the United States Army, the commander of a man-of-war, and the *Alcalde* of Monterey, in a smoking kitchen, grinding coffee, toasting a herring, and pealing onions!"

Only two markets saw price declines: San Francisco real estate, which fell in value by half or more as it was left vacant by the exodus, and gold itself. So much metal came into San Francisco that merchants could drive hard bargains with diggers, who sold cheaply and quickly so they could rush back to the goldfields. It was not unheard of for miners to sell their gold for as little as four dollars an ounce when the official government price was $20.67.

The disruption did not spare the military, which battled desertions on all fronts. "For the present, and I fear for years to come, it will be impossible for the United States to maintain any naval or military establishment in California," the commander of the US Pacific fleet, Commodore Thomas ap Catesby Jones (the same officer who had prematurely seized Monterey in 1842), reported to Secretary of the Navy John Y. Mason late in 1848. "To send troops out here would be needless, for they would immediately desert." William Rich, the US military's local paymaster, reported to his Washington superiors that although he had received $130,000 from headquarters for sailors' wages, he needed only about $20,000, "as there are at present but two companies in California," one of which was "reduced to a mere skeleton by desertion," and the other "in a fair way to share the same fate."

Nor were men-of-war the only deserted vessels. "The commerce of this coast may be said to be entirely cut off by desertion," Jones reported to Washington. "No sooner does a merchant ship arrive . . . than all hands leave her; in some instances, captain, cook, and all." The harbor of San Francisco Bay was clogged with abandoned ships, "and such will be the fate of all that subsequently arrive."

Colonel Mason and his young operations adjutant, the future Civil War general William Tecumseh Sherman, took to the road for a personal view of the frenzy. From Monterey they stopped first at San Francisco, where they found that "all, or nearly all its male inhabitants had gone to the mines." As Mason and Sherman subsequently reported to Washington, "The town, which a few months before was so busy and thriving, was then almost deserted."

Twelve days later they reached Sutter's Fort and visited Mormon Island, where they found three hundred men digging for gold. Sherman recounted later that Brannan "was on hand as the high-priest, collecting the tithes," ostensibly for forwarding to Brigham Young in the Great Salt Lake Valley. This appears to have been a conservative estimate; several of the Mormons calculated Brannan's exactions as 30 percent of the miners' gains, describing them as a "toll" or "rent" that Brannan demanded for himself and partners who had laid claim to the island.

Sherman and Mason counted more than four thousand men working in the mines, of whom more than half were Indians. They reported themselves impressed with the diggers' sheer determination. "While the sun blazed down on the heads of the miners with tropical heat, the water was bitter cold, and all hands were either standing in the water or had their clothes wet all the time; yet there were no complaints of rheumatism or cold," Sherman wrote. Their official report estimated that $30,000 to $50,000 worth of gold was being drawn from the earth every day.

The solitary miner of popular imagination, making his fortune armed only with pick, shovel, and pan, was nowhere in evidence. The Mormon mines were worked with a device called a cradle. A box shaped somewhat like a baby's crib, it was six to eight feet long, open at one end and fixed with a coarse grate at the other. The cradle required at least four men—one to dig up the bank, another to empty dirt into the box, the third and fourth to si-phon in water and rock the box back and forth. The goal was to wash the dirt through, leaving a deposit of the heavier gold. The first manifestation of the coordinated activity that would eventually yield to even more sophisticated mechanization, the cradle soon became the standard method of working the mines.

Mason warned Brannan and the diggers that they were working public land and "the gold is the property of the United States; all of you are trespassers." But that was merely a formality, for he added that "as the Government is benefited by your getting out the gold, I do not intend to interfere."

That is where things stood in October and November 1848. The real frenzy was about to begin.

TWO DOCUMENTS EXPANDED the Gold Rush into a national and global phenomenon in 1849. The first was Mason's official report to his army superiors, which was dated August 27, 1848. The report was entrusted to Artillery Lieutenant Lucien Loeser to carry to Washington, along with a "tea caddy" containing 230 ounces of gold that Mason had purchased for ten dollars an ounce in the diggings. For the first time, the rumors of a rich gold strike in the West, which had been published in eastern newspapers in the form of letters from anonymous correspondents, acquired an official imprimatur. Mason's judgment was unequivocal: "I have no hesitation now in saying that there is more gold in the country drained by the Sacramento and San Joaquin Rivers than will pay the cost of the present war with Mexico a hundred times over."* Despite his having witnessed the use of the cradles, Mason reported the remarkable ease with which the gold could be drawn out of the earth: "The laboring man wants nothing but his pick and shovel and tin pan, with which to dig and wash the gravel, and many frequently pick gold out of the crevices of rocks with their butcher knives."

The second document was President Polk's fourth annual message to Congress, delivered in written form on December 5, 1848. Remarking on the natural wealth of California, the president stated: "The accounts of the abundance of gold in that territory are of such an extraordinary character as would scarcely command belief were they not corroborated by the authentic reports of officers in the public service who have visited the mineral district and derived the facts which they detail from personal observation." Polk

---

* The war had officially ended on the previous February 2 with the signing of the Treaty of Guadalupe Hidalgo, but its costs still needed to be covered.

mentioned Mason's visit to the gold district (without identifying the officer) and repeated Mason's estimate that at least four thousand people were working the mines. "The explorations already made warrant the belief that the supply is very large and that gold is found at various places in an extensive district of country," the president concluded.

One final spark came from the Philadelphia Mint, which assayed the gold in Loeser's little chest, determined it to be almost as pure as the metal in US gold coins, and valued it at $3,910.10. As suddenly as the fever had taken hold in California, it now spread nationwide.

SOME THREE HUNDRED thousand Argonauts would strike out for the west by land and sea during a great migration that lasted well into the 1850s. Most of them braved hardships en route that would far outweigh the riches they obtained at their destination. Some ten thousand of them chose what became known as the southern routes—overland byways that converged at Yuma, Arizona, where the Gila River joined the Colorado, and continued along one or another waterless trail, or *jornada*, toward the Pacific Coast. These trails acquired a vicious reputation. One in particular, a desert crossing paralleling the Rio Grande in New Mexico, bore a label that presently became applied to the entire unspeakably harsh road west. It was known variously in Spanish as *la jornada del muerto* or *la jornada de la muerte;* in English as "the journey of death."

Nature in all her forms cast untold perils before the unwary travelers on the *jornada*: disease, brigands, hostile tribes, and the daunting terrain itself. Not even the best-outfitted and well-manned expeditions were immune. John Woodhouse Audubon, the renowned naturalist's younger son, embarked from New York in February as second in command of a party endowed with what was regarded as lavish capital backing of $27,000. On the day of his departure, Audubon was a youthful thirty-six, "tall, strong and alert," as his daughter Maria described him, "keen of vision and hearing, quick in movement and temperament, and with most tender and skillful hands." When he returned home a year later he was broken, "worn out in body and spirit" by his travails on the *jornada* and the loss at sea of all his paintings and sketches and many of his notebooks.

The first blow to strike Audubon's company was cholera, which killed five members and reduced a dozen others to dehydrated wraiths within days of their landing in Texas. The disease seemed to crouch at the very banks of the Rio Grande, poised to spring upon unprepared parties of travelers and claim its horrific tribute. Easily treated today where fresh water is accessible, cholera was then one of the world's most feared diseases. A person could seem perfectly healthy one moment and be racked in the next with indescribably violent vomiting and diarrhea, as though exploding at both ends. Drained of bodily fluids, half the victims died, some within hours of the first symptoms. If their companions knew anything, it was that they were likely to be next, for the disease spread with savage speed.

The survivors pressed on, Audubon collecting botanical specimens and recording in his father's style the wildlife he encountered. In mid-October he and his remaining companions reached the junction of the Gila and the Colorado. "There was not a tree to be seen, nor the least sign of vegetation, and the sun pouring down on us made our journey seem twice the length it really was," he recorded in his journal. "Truly *here* was a scene of desolation."

Broken wagons, dead shriveled up cattle, horses and mules as well, lay baking in the sun, around the dried-up wells that had been opened, in the hopes of getting water. Not a blade of grass or green thing of any kind relieved the monotony of the parched, ash-colored earth, and the most melancholy scene presented itself that I have seen since I left the Rio Grande.

John E. Durivage, a correspondent for the New Orleans *Daily Picayune,* described similar horrors. After crossing the Colorado River, his group ran out of water. All around were remnants of prior expeditions that had reached the limits of their endurance: "Dead mules by scores, saddles, bridles, blankets, broken trunks, bags, pantaloons, packs, *cantinas* (hide panniers), and all sorts of articles. . . . The hot air was laden with the fetid smell of dead mules and horses, and on all sides misery and death seemed to prevail."

Two days later, they staggered up to a well. Durivage reported the water "detestable"—"a tincture of bluelick, iodides of sulphur, Epsom salts, and a strong decoction of decomposed mule flesh." But water was water. The travelers drank freely, gaining from its contents the strength to reach the end of the *jornada* two days later. Durivage's party were among the more fortunate of those who chose the southern routes; others reported having been reduced at their lowest point to drinking their own urine. "One man of the party," recorded the leader of one such cohort, "was found on the hills perfectly insane from his suffering."

Those choosing the sea route—the majority of Argonauts—fared little better. Rather than take the long route around Cape Horn, a voyage that could last as long as seven months, many chose to book passage to Panama, cross the isthmus by foot, mule, or river canoe, and continue by steamship up the West Coast. The isthmus crossing took three days in the best circumstances. It was also the most perilous part of the journey, for in Panama, cholera "broke out in a most malignant form," felling travelers by the score.

Travelers stranded on the Pacific shore jostled for berths on the vessels of the Pacific Mail Steamship Company. The Pacific Mail's first steamship, the *California,* left New York in October 1848 for its maiden voyage around the horn without a single passenger having booked passage all the way to California. In January, when it reached Panama City, it was greeted at the port by a throng of fifteen hundred passengers, of whom the crew could cram only four hundred on board. When the *California* finally steamed into San Francisco Bay on February 28, 1849, it was promptly deserted by its gold-craving officers and crew. Not until June could it assemble a crew for the return journey.

The Argonauts altered the character of San Francisco—indeed, of all California. The city's population more than quintupled to 5,000 by July 1849 and reached 25,000 that December, not counting the seaborne miners who immediately moved on to the gold district after landing in the city. The California population was counted as about 92,600 in 1850, the first time the state was included in the US census (including about 1,000 "free colored" residents but no Native Americans). The vast majority of inhabitants— more than 85,000—were white men, reflecting the heavily male nature of the forty-niner migration. The 1860 census reported a population of about 380,000, roughly four times the population of a decade earlier, including 323,000 whites, 2,500 Blacks, and—counted for the first time—35,000 "Asiatics," or Chinese. Only then did the white population begin to see an influx of women, with just over 96,000 counted versus 227,000 men.

The great migration revived San Francisco's economy, which had been staggered by the flight of workers to the gold mines. Newcomers with an entrepreneurial bent assumed the task of fulfilling the miners' commercial demands. At the start of the Gold Rush, California had no substantial flour mills; by 1860 there were two hundred. A carriage maker named John Studebaker set up shop in Placerville, in the heart of the gold country; he later returned to his native Indiana and deployed the capital he brought home from California to establish one of the earliest American automobile factories. Levi Strauss emigrated from Bavaria to San Francisco in 1853 as a dry-goods merchant; with his partner Jacob Davis, he would patent a process for strengthening men's work clothes with metal rivets at the points of wear. By 1861, observed historian Gerald D. Nash, manufacturers of mining equipment were employing more than one thousand workers in San Francisco, which was now home to thirteen iron foundries, thirty machine shops, and two powder factories.

The financial sector was forced to innovate. California's first constitution, drafted in 1849 prior to statehood, banned banks and paper money. The policy was a holdover of the anti-bank fervor caused by the Panic of 1837, the effects of which were still a drag on the US economy. But the restrictions burdened miners, who had to carry pouches of gold dust on their persons to conduct even the smallest retail transactions and were left at the mercy of private mints, which sprung up to convert their hoards into gold coins at a hard-bargained price. Financial entrepreneurs soon arrived from out of state, notably Henry Wells and William G. Fargo, who had co-founded American Express in Buffalo in 1850 and left the company to serve the California market on their own. The California legislature finally repealed the bans on banks in 1862 and 1864 at the urging of the man who had become the richest landowner in San Francisco, Sam Brannan.

The Gold Rush launched the two narratives of California that compete in the public mind up to the present day. One is the image of California as a place to remake oneself by shedding a disreputable or humdrum past. At first, the popular press filled up with heartbreaking stories of dockside leave-takings between men setting off for the mines and the women and children who were left behind—hopefully for only a year or so. These accounts would eventually be supplanted by stories of "Gold Rush widows" trapped in an endless vigil for the return of their husbands or betrotheds. Many Argonauts set down roots in the West because their experiences opened their eyes to a world they never knew existed. "I never want to work in Ohio for $1 or $1.50 per day," one emigrant wrote to his family, "and I think I shall never do it."

The competing image is of California as a land of bewitching sinfulness. "There never yet has been a nation not irreparably damaged by the sudden opening of the sources of great wealth," Reverend George B. Cheever inveighed from the pulpit of New York's Congregational Church of the

Puritans. "Riches that are gotten . . . by gambling, by hazardous and lucky speculations, by sudden windfalls or by hasty adventures . . . tend to uproot all principles; they throw a man afloat."

Among the clerical leaders sounding the alarm about the Gold Rush was Brigham Young. The Mormon leader seldom missed an opportunity to condemn the quest for gold undertaken by members of his flock in California. "Why don't you dig the gold from the earth?" he asked rhetorically in one discourse. "Because it demoralizes any community or nation on the earth to give them gold and silver to their hearts' content; it will ruin any nation."

Young's words were not rooted in moralistic ground alone; they were partially inspired by his conflict with Sam Brannan over the destiny of the church itself. Brannan, who had been agitating for the Mormons to fulfill their original plan to settle in San Francisco, was frustrated by Young's decision to end their journey in the valley of the Great Salt Lake instead of continuing on to the coast. Their breach was never healed. Brannan went his own way and became rich. Young himself, as it happened, was not above pestering Brannan for a personal tithe in the thousands of dollars—"Bro[ther] Brigham has long been destitute of a home," he wrote Brannan in the third person, "& he wants you to send him a present of twenty thousand dollars in gold dust to help him in his labors."

Whether seen as a blank slate primed for reinvention or an outpost of sin, Northern California during the Gold Rush was anything but a paradise. A cholera outbreak in October 1850 carried off an estimated 15 percent of the population of Sacramento. San Francisco itself was a vermin-infested tent colony and a precinct of wooden shacks which erupted in flames about once a month on average. Street preachers gleefully interpreted the fires as divine retribution for the city's iniquity: "Let the citizens of San Francisco beware!" thundered the self-described Methodist "street preacher" William Taylor after one devastating conflagration. "God is dealing with them. This disaster, dreadful as it appears to be, is but a premonition of 'judgment to come,' in consequence of their sins." In more practical terms, the recurrent blazes prompted city leaders to create a municipal fire brigade in June 1850.

Sacramento, which rose out of the marshy land at the confluence of the American and Sacramento Rivers where Sutter had built his fort, was even less salubrious. In the dry season it was "terribly dusty," reported Frank Marryat, an intrepid English artist who arrived in California in 1850. "The great traffic to and from the mines grinds three or four inches of the top soil into a red powder that distributes itself every where. It is the dirtiest dust I ever saw, and is never visited by a shower until the rainy season sets in, and suddenly converts it into a thick mud." A fleet of "old dismantled hulks" converted into rooming houses occupied the bank next to the levee protecting the town from the rivers. Marryat presumed these derelicts were the source of the rats "distinguished at Sacramento for their size and audacity."

In the countryside, the prospectors wreaked havoc on tribal lifestyles. Native peoples were evicted from their lands, saw the rivers they relied on for water diverted by miners, and faced starvation when the newcomers drove from their natural habitats the wildlife they had hunted for food and clothing.

In the cities, the arrival of thousands of immigrants brought a crime wave. This resulted in the formation in 1851 of a committee of vigilance in San Francisco under the ubiquitous Brannan. This volunteer body took it upon itself to deliver quick extrajudicial sentences. Murder was relatively rare in the city but theft increasingly common and—in accordance with the rough justice of the time—summarily punishable by death. On June 10, for example, a mob caught one John Jenkins allegedly red-handed loading a stolen safe onto a dinghy at the Central Wharf. Jenkins was dragged to Brannan's office, tried by Brannan behind closed doors, found guilty, sentenced to death, and hanged by a mob that held off two police officers who tried to intervene. The arrest happened at ten p.m. and Jenkins, protesting his innocence all the way, was dead by two thirty the next morning.

The Vigilance Committee of 1851 would soon fade away. But the Gold Rush would leave its mark on San Francisco in many ways other than the eruption of crime and the impromptu methods developed to quell it. The Gold Rush wrought changes in labor relations and social and commercial conditions of limitless variety. Perhaps no writer captured the metamorphosis better than Richard Henry Dana, who supplemented his 1840 *Two Years Before the Mast* with an addendum titled "Twenty-Four Years Later." In that chapter, devoted to his visit to the city in 1859, he wrote that the lightly populated trading depot he had visited a quarter of a century earlier had been transformed into a cosmopolitan metropolis "densely crowded with express wagons and hand-carts to take luggage, coaches and cabs for passengers . . . agents of the press, and a greater multitude eager for newspapers and verbal intelligence from the great Atlantic and European world. . . . I can see nothing that recalls the times gone by."

The newly settled population of San Francisco not only clamored for news of the outside world but hoped the outside world would come calling, via the construction of a railroad to provide a permanent link to the rest of the United States. It would be another two decades before that link would be forged, but the transformation of San Francisco, and of the California beyond its borders, was already underway. The first phase had started with gold. The second would be statehood.

5

THE THIRTY-FIRST STAR

THE SOCIAL UPHEAVALS of the Gold Rush required a new approach to politics and civic order in California that proved difficult to impose at first. The state soon acquired a reputation not for the salubriousness of its climate, but for the degeneracy of its inhabitants. Hinton Rowan Helper, a South Carolina–born visitor who would later make a name for himself as an ardent white supremacist, set a standard for censoriousness with a screed entitled *The Land of Gold: Reality Versus Fiction.* "Suffice it to say that we know of no country in which there is so much corruption, villainy, outlawry, intemperance, licentiousness, and every variety of crime, folly and meanness," Helper wrote. "Words fail us to express the shameful depravity and unexampled turpitude of California society."

The biggest obstacle to the establishment of stable government in prestatehood California was a lack of money. There was plenty of it sloshing about the private sector but almost none in public accounts. No legal means of levying taxes existed as long as Congress refused to establish a formal territorial administration or grant California statehood. With every congressional session that passed without action, the issue became more dire. The only money at hand was sequestered in the federal government's "Civil Fund," which held import duties collected from local merchants at the California ports and was ostensibly under the control of the military governors. By 1849, the fund amounted to $600,000, but the authority of Governor Mason to use it was murky—as indeed was the legality of collecting duties at all, since Congress had not yet made the conquered territory subject to federal customs laws.

Congress finally closed that loophole in November 1849 by extending the customs laws to California, but that only inspired cries of taxation without representation. California had been left effectively without a government since May 30, 1848, when the United States and Mexico formally notified each other that they had ratified the Treaty of Guadalupe Hidalgo, ending the Mexican-American War.

Local legislative and administrative bodies sprung up in San Francisco and other cities, while informal laws and regulations were in force in the goldfields. The torrent of new residents brought west by the Gold Rush only underscored the unsatisfactory situation. *"We are in fact without government—a commercial, civilized, and wealthy people, without law, order, or system, to protect and secure them in the peaceful enjoyment of those rights and privileges inestimable,"* complained Peter Burnett, a transplanted Tennessean who would become the state's first elected governor, writing as a member of the San Francisco municipal assembly in June 1849. (Emphasis his.) Congress, Burnett continued, had "assumed the right, not only to tax us without representation, but to *tax us without giving us any government at all.*"

The 1850 census indicated that the settler population had expanded to nearly 100,000, ten times the population in 1846. About 80 percent were young males. The atmosphere verged on anarchy. "Every man carried his code of laws on his hip and administered it according to his own pleasure," wrote Elisha Oscar Crosby, a New York lawyer who arrived in California early in 1849, in his chatty, privately distributed memoirs. "There was no safety of life or property, so far as the intervention of law was concerned there was no police."

It was clear to General Bennet Riley, a stern and much-decorated veteran of command in the Mexican-American War who succeeded Mason as the regional governor in April 1849, that as the settlers' numbers grew they would become increasingly restive under military authority. The necessity of creating something resembling a permanent government was gaining urgency. Riley, who was fully alive to the difficulties of maintaining control over a burgeoning populace with a military garrison shrunk by constant desertions to the diggings, feared that the indignant settlers might simply declare themselves an independent country, Texas-style. He told settler leaders that "he was powerless to enforce any law because all his men had disappeared,"

Crosby recounted. "He could not put a sentinel outside the gate for fifteen minutes, but he would be gone musket and all."

Riley's audacious solution was to call a constitutional convention, with delegates to be elected on August 1 by free male citizens of the region, including any who had been citizens of California under Mexican rule. The convention was to assemble one month later. Riley had no legal authority to take this step, but that scarcely mattered given the national government's neglect of its new acquisition. His action would place California firmly on the road to statehood.

The forty-eight elected delegates represented an accurate cross-section of the fast-growing territory's population in the summer of 1849—or, rather, its white male population, since the vote and the eligibility to serve were denied to women, Blacks, Indians, and Chinese. The delegates' average age was thirty-six. Seven were natives of Mexico and lifelong residents of California; the length of residence of the others ranged from four months to twenty years. Five had been born in Europe, including John Sutter. Of the thirty-six American citizens, twenty-two had come west from northern or free states and fourteen from the South. They were farmers, lawyers, and military officers; one, Benjamin Franklin Moore of Texas, who "carried an enormous Bowie knife & was half drunk most of the time," listed his occupation as "elegant leisure." Despite the hasty electoral process, the delegates' youthfulness, and the absence of legislative experience among them, they took their task seriously. "I don't believe there was ever a deliberative body of men collected with more patriotic sentiments and purposes than prevailed in that convention," judged Crosby, who would later serve in the first state legislature.

The delegates convened on September 3 in a cavernous second-story room of a former Monterey schoolhouse. There was a fireplace at each end and four long meeting tables. The deliberations were recorded in shorthand by J. Ross Browne, an Irish-born traveler and writer who would ultimately produce a 477-page transcript in a nearly superhuman feat of recording and writing. For his five months of labor (including the six weeks of the convention), the members voted Browne an appropriation of $10,000—an immense sum equivalent to almost $400,000 in today's currency. Browne also secured the rights to publish the proceedings for his own profit, which he thought would bring him thousands of dollars more. As he remarked in a letter to his wife, Lucy: "Money amounts to nothing in California, unless in very large piles."

Two related issues were paramount among the convention's concerns: slavery and the boundaries to be proposed to Congress in the application for statehood. The convention disposed of the slavery issue in its very first week, unanimously passing a provision that "neither slavery nor involuntary servitude, unless for the punishment of crimes, shall ever be tolerated in this State."

The speed and decisiveness of the vote surprised even the delegates from northern states, who knew slavery to be a fraught topic of debate nation-wide. It would be an error to view the outcome as an expression of interracial brotherhood or a moral condemnation of slavery as an institution, however. Rather, it reflected the determination of gold miners, who constituted a majority of the voting population, to eliminate what they saw as unfair com-petition from the labor of enslaved people. "All here are diggers and free white diggers wont dig with slaves," Walter Colton, the appointed alcalde of Monterey, wrote in his personal journal. "They have nothing to do with slavery in the abstract, or as it exists in other communities; not one in ten cares a button for its abolition . . . all they look at is their own position; they must themselves swing the pick, and they wont swing it by the side of negro slaves." Some miners believed almost superstitiously that Blacks were preter-naturally skilled at finding gold deposits, others that enslaved people simply augmented their white masters' ability to accumulate wealth in the diggings without those white masters having to make any physical effort themselves.

In fact, the debate over slavery at the convention was shot through with unapologetic racial bigotry. This was unsurprising, as emigrants from slave states, many of whom had brought enslaved people with them, made up a sizable contingent of delegates. Led by William M. Gwin, a former Mis-sissippi slaveholder, they fashioned themselves "Southern Chivalry" Dem-ocrats, or "Chivs." (Their political adversaries among the Democrats were known as the "Shovelry," an allusion to their working-class origins.) "It would appear that the all-wise Creator has created the negro to serve the white race," asserted Chiv delegate Oliver Wozencraft. "If you would wish that all mankind should be free . . . do not bring the lowest in contact with the highest, for be assured that the one will rule and the other must serve." In its earliest version, the antislavery provision was paired with one bar-ring freed enslaved people from entering California; that language was soon struck, out of concerns that interfering with the movement of individuals might be judged unconstitutional and would therefore complicate the campaign for statehood. The convention chose to leave the issue to a future state legislature. The legislators obliged; within two years they also had barred Blacks from serving in the state militia, testifying in court against a white person, and marrying whites.

The boundary issue took up much more of the delegates' time than slavery. The state's proposed western, northern, and southern borders were uncontroversial—the Pacific Ocean on the west, the Oregon Territory on the north, and the border of Mexico on the south. Not so the eastern boundary. Some delegates favored drawing it as far as the 105th meridian west, which runs through the site of present-day Denver. That would encompass virtually all the territory ceded by Mexico to the United States in the Treaty of Guadalupe Hidalgo and even some of the Louisiana Purchase.

The sense of the convention was that such an expansive claim by a non-slave state would generate insurmountable opposition from southerners in Congress. The southerners advocated extending all the way to the Pacific the Missouri Compromise of 1820, which banned slavery in states carved from the Louisiana Purchase north of latitude 36 degrees, 30 minutes. That would cleave California in two, its north admitted as a free state and its south as slave state. In the end, the delegates opted to fix the eastern boundary where it remains today, at longitude 120 degrees from the Oregon Territory to as far south as latitude 39 degrees north, bisecting Lake Tahoe; and following a diagonal path southeast from there to intersect the Colorado River roughly at latitude 35 degrees. From there the state line follows the central channel of the Colorado down to the Mexican border.

In the judgment of delegate William E. Shannon, an Irish-born lawyer, that map would encompass "every prominent and valuable point . . . which is of any real value to the state"—the harbors of San Francisco and San Diego, the inland goldfields, and the rich agricultural land of the Central Valley—while allowing Congress to create as many slave states as it might wish from the remaining treaty spoils.

ON OTHER MATTERS, the constitution reflected the prevailing political currents of the time as well as specific concerns of the miner and settler classes. Dueling was forbidden, but the penalty—barring participants and their seconds from serving in public office or voting—was so weak it would have to be strengthened later by the legislature, which eventually made the practice a crime warranting a prison term. Branch banking and the printing of paper money were forbidden, an artifact of the economic crisis of 1837. The constitution granted suffrage solely to white males. The question of extending the vote to Indians provoked a lengthy battle, since many California-born delegates and former Mexican citizens had Indian blood. A proposal to grant suffrage to Indians was defeated by a single vote; future legislatures were authorized to extend voting rights to Indians, but only by a two-thirds vote of both houses and only in individual "special cases"—that is, on a deliberately laborious case-by-case basis.

On one topic, the property of married women, the convention turned to existing Mexican law, which provided that women retained their right to possessions they acquired before or during their marriage, rather than requiring titles to be transferred to their husbands. To the objection by one delegate that "the God of nature made woman frail, lovely, and dependant; and such the common law pronounces her," delegate Henry W. Halleck, a well-educated physician (and a bachelor) who would later command Union forces in the Civil War, alluded to the dearth of women among the American emigrants: "I do not think we can offer a greater inducement for women of fortune to come to California" than to assure them of their right to their personal property.

In his first address to the convention on September 4, its president, Robert Semple, had voiced the expectation that "we can prove to the world that California has not been settled entirely by unintelligent and unlettered men." His confidence was rewarded. The convention produced a remarkable document that would serve as a foundation of California's civic administration for the next thirty years. The text of the constitution, in English and Spanish, was distributed to voters by messengers on horseback throughout the territory. At a referendum on November 13, it passed by 12,061 to 811. At the same election, the voters chose Burnett as California's first civilian governor and selected legislators to meet in December in San Jose.

That first legislature would acquire the sobriquet of "the legislature of a thousand drinks," which has saddled it with the image of an unruly, dissolute gathering. It was nothing of the kind, but rather one that fully warranted the judgment of historian Judson A. Grenier as "the most creative and probably the most competent" of the early California legislatures. The nickname, Elisha Crosby later recounted, was the product of a daily send-off by Senator Thomas Jefferson Green, an idle lounger who had established a pub down the street from the legislative hall and would close every session with the words "Boys, let's go and take a thousand drinks."

It is true that the legislature lacked the decorum that some might have expected of a lawmaking body. "There was no order of debate . . . but a turbulent dinning colloquy," reported William Kelly, a British judge who stopped by during a grand tour of the American West. The New York–born Argonaut Matthew Van Benschoten Fowler was similarly unimpressed, dismissing the legislature as a "rump parliament, with very little dignity, very little sense, & still less honesty, judging from the imputations of the members against each other." And the acerbic journalist and politician Charles E. Pickett described it as "an infamous, ignorant, drunken, rowdy, perjured and traitorous body of men . . . known to fame for its venality and corruption beyond any legislative body that ever sat in Christendom."

Yet there is no gainsaying the first legislature's accomplishments. It continued the work of the constitutional convention in creating a new state from scratch, without the help or approval of the federal government, while taking care not to complicate the campaign for admission to the union. There was virtually no legislation aimed at putting money in private pockets, legislators' or otherwise. (To be truthful, as Bancroft would observe, at that stage of the government's development "there was nothing to steal.") Burnett marveled at the legislature's successful work, given that "they had to begin at the beginning, and create an entire new code of statute law, with but very few authorities to consult."

The legislature's efforts to place California on a sound fiscal footing included a tax of fifty cents on every hundred dollars of real property and a poll tax of five dollars on every white male between twenty-one and fifty years of age. A tax on foreign miners of twenty dollars per month, designed less to raise revenue than to drive Black, Chinese, and other presumed interlopers out of the goldfields, failed to have any effect, since it was universally ignored. The legislature authorized the issuing of three hundred thousand dollars in bonds at 3 percent a year. The legislators understood that California would still need remittances from the federal government to fund its operations and assumed that, in time, the state would be able to draw from the Civil Fund, which they viewed as California revenues held in trust. (The state would never receive that money.)

On the question of the rights of California's aboriginal inhabitants, the

legislators set the stage for a catastrophe. On April 21, the very last day
of their session, they passed what was misleadingly titled an "Act for the
Government and Protection of Indians." In fact, the measure effectively facilitated the subjection of California Indians to indentured servitude and
legalized the kidnapping and enslavement of Indian children, a practice that,
as we shall see, would continue with unexampled brutality for the next
quarter century.

THE MOST PRESSING duty of the first legislature was to select two senators,
who would be tasked with delivering statehood. They chose Gwin, who had
represented Mississippi in Congress from 1841 to 1843, and Frémont, who
was launching his post-court-martial political career in the region where he
had achieved his greatest fame. The drama now moved to Washington, where
the statehood question would occasion three of the most famous speeches in
Senate history, delivered successively by John C. Calhoun of South Carolina,
Daniel Webster of Massachusetts, and William Seward of New York.

California's admission into the United States was far from a sure thing.
One reason was the irregularity of admitting a new state that had not gone
through the customary first step of territorial status or petitioned for admission as an independent country, like Texas. Another was its remoteness from
the American frontier, which some feared would make it ungovernable from
Washington. This was the view of Zachary Taylor, who succeeded Polk as
president in March 1849. During the inauguration ceremonies, Taylor confided to Polk his view that distant California and Oregon would be better
off as an independent country. Polk, who had maneuvered so assiduously
to annex the western region to the United States, was alarmed to hear his
treasured goal dismissed so casually. He recorded his judgment of Taylor the
next day as "a well meaning old man" who was "uneducated, exceedingly
ignorant of public affairs, and, I should judge, of very ordinary capacity."

Nor was it lost to anyone in Congress that the admission of California as a
free state would aggravate national tensions over slavery. Few expressed this
thought as apocalyptically as Calhoun, who told Gwin from his deathbed
that the equal representation of slave and free-soil states in the Senate was
"the only safeguard the South has against the numerical superiority of the
North." Calhoun warned that "the equilibrium once destroyed, the agitation
of the slave question would become more intense and inevitably result in
civil war and the destruction of the South." He attempted, less convincingly,

to place that prospect in the broader context of equal rights: "With its destruction," he said, "would be obliterated all protection of minorities against the despotic majority; in fact, this government . . . would be the most despotic of any in the civilized world."

Calhoun repeated that viewpoint in his final speech to the Senate, on March 4, 1850, which he was too ill to deliver personally. (It was read into the record by Senator James Murray Mason of Virginia.) Calhoun's target was the proposal of Henry Clay of Kentucky and Stephen A. Douglas of Illinois to admit California as a free state while allowing residents of the territories of New Mexico and Utah, which also were carved out of the Mexican-American War spoils, to decide for themselves whether to allow or forbid slavery. Under what became known as the Compromise of 1850, slavery would be banned in the District of Columbia and the Fugitive Slave Act strengthened to require public officials to capture and return suspected escaped enslaved people to their owners.

"California will become the test question," Calhoun said. "If you admit her . . . you compel us to infer that you intend to exclude us from the whole of the acquired territory [that is, the territory gained by the Treaty of Guadalupe Hidalgo], with the intention of destroying irretrievably the equilibrium between the two sections." The result, he said, would be "disunion," in which the North and South "agree to separate and part in peace."

Webster replied to Calhoun three days later. He placated Calhoun by agreeing that "the North is wrong" to thwart the Fugitive Slave Act by refusing to comply with it—a statement for which he would be pilloried by antislavery Northerners. But he argued that the climates and methods of agricultural production of California and New Mexico made them unsuitable for slavery. He thundered against the very idea of a "peaceable secession" threatened by Calhoun, calling secession an "utter impossibility" that "must produce such a war as I will not describe." In the end he advocated for admitting California to the union "just as she is."

Seward completed the trilogy of notable speeches on March 11, answering Calhoun's complaint that California had breached federal law by writing her own constitution. "She made a constitution for herself under the law, the paramount law, of self preservation," he said, adding that every new state should be welcomed into the union—but that "California, that comes from the clime where the west dies away into the rising east; California, that bounds at once the empire and the continent; California, the youthful queen of the Pacific, in her robes of freedom gorgeously inlaid with gold, is doubly welcome."

The compromise was drafted as five separate measures and submitted for passage in August. By then Calhoun had passed on, as had President Taylor, succumbing to a digestive disorder less than six months into his term. The new president was Millard Fillmore of New York, who favored California statehood. The Senate voted on August 13 to admit California by 34 to 18 and the House by 150 to 56 on September 9. Fillmore applied his signature that very day, which is still observed in California as Admission Day. The news only reached the West Coast on October 18, via banners inscribed "California Is a State" flown from the masts of the steamer *Oregon* as the vessel passed through the Golden Gate. All business in San Francisco came to a halt in celebration. A formal ceremony was held on October 29, when a parade snaked for miles through the city and an American flag with a thirty-first star added to its blue field was hoisted above Portsmouth Square, then the center of civic life (now part of Chinatown).

The moment was recognized as far away as London. "Here was a community of some hundreds of souls collected from all quarters of the known world," wrote the London *Times*. "Polynesians and Peruvians, Englishmen and Mexicans, Germans and New Englanders, Spaniards and Chinese. . . . A third of the time which has been consumed in erecting our house of parliament has here sufficed to create a state with a territory as large as Great Britain, a population difficult to number, and destinies which none can foresee."

The *Times* editorialist artfully glossed over the defining counterfactual of California's birth. For the state remained in thrall to the proslavery Chiv faction of the Democratic Party. The Chivs cherished the dream of eventually converting California to a slave state, notwithstanding its constitutional ban on slavery. Their plan was to convene a second constitutional convention to resurrect the old idea of extending the Missouri Compromise line to the Pacific, with slavery legal in the territory south of that line. ("It will be a glorious day for the South," exulted the *Mississippian*, the daily newspaper of Mississippi's capital, Jackson, "if despite the machinations of her enemies, her institutions should yet be extended over that immense territory [to] the shores of the Pacific.")

The fledgling state legislature was unable to fulfill that goal, but in 1852 it did enact a California version of the federal Fugitive Slave Act. The California measure mostly codified the federal statute as state law but declared further that the antislavery clause in the state constitution was not retro-active, so any people brought into the state in slavery prior to statehood remained in slavery, and therefore any who refused to return with their pu-tative owners to their home states could be tracked down and re-enslaved by force. That applied even if the owners had established residence in California in the meantime; if the owners decided to return to a slave state, their freed slaves had to go with them. California stands apart as the only state to enact its own fugitive slave law.

The California law heartened slavery advocates, who took it as a sign that their cause was not lost. They were not wrong. The status of enslaved people in California had been precarious enough, since the state constitution had left unresolved the question of whether slaves became free merely by their presence in the state or only after due process. The new law decided the issue in favor of slaveholders; abetted by the strongly proslavery leanings of California's freshly minted state judiciary (and by the statutory prohibition of Black testimony against whites in California courts), their rights to force freed people back into bondage were undiminished. California became "a place where the South and the North clashed with profound implications for the country." The evolution of slaveholder rights in the state would cast a long shadow over the slavery debate nationwide, not least through the US Supreme Court's widely reviled 1857 Dred Scott decision, which Chief Jus-tice Roger Taney based in part on case law developed in California.

Yet the state's fugitive slave law also had a more positive impact, if per-versely, for the re-enslavement of freed people would strengthen a sense of community among the state's Black residents. They would agitate for a po-litical voice through a movement marked by the first Colored Convention of California in 1855. "The ability and willingness of blacks to fight for their civil rights was no longer in doubt," one historian observed.

California's white antislavery community was itself energized into di-rect opposition to the Democratic Party's dominance of the state's politics, notably through the formation of the Republican Party of California at a Sacramento meeting in 1856. Its first adherents "could be counted on one's fingers," wrote one of its founding members, the New York–born antislavery lawyer Cornelius Cole. But among them were four men who would exer-cise an outsized influence on the state's history: Collis P. Huntington, Mark Hopkins, Leland Stanford, and Charles Crocker. In time, the Republican Party would supplant the Democrats as the preeminent political power in the state, with Stanford eventually winning election as governor and later as a US senator.

With the new fugitive slave law on the books, proslavery judges began to revoke the freedom that formerly enslaved people had enjoyed as Californians. Their rulings customarily rested on the undocumented claims of former slaveowners. The most widely publicized case involved three former slaves of Charles Perkins, who had left his family's Mississippi plantation in 1849 to seek his fortune in the gold diggings. He had brought with him one enslaved person, Carter Perkins, and eventually was joined by two others, Robert Perkins and Sandy Jones.* Perkins lent all three to a Dr. John Hill on the understanding that once they concluded their duties for Hill (and their earnings were paid over to Perkins), they would be granted their freedom. Hill fulfilled the promise of emancipation in November 1851, after which the three freedmen continued mining on their own, quite profitably. However, at midnight on May 31, 1852, a few weeks after the enactment of the state's fugitive slave act, a gang of armed men raided their cabin and took them into custody at the request of their former owner, who had returned home to Mississippi. The next day, Judge B. D. Fry, a slavery advocate, declared them to be Perkins's property and ordered them transported in bondage back to Mississippi.

Before that could happen, one of Mark Hopkins's Black servants alerted him to the case. Hopkins reached out to Cole, who resolved to use the case to challenge the fugitive slave law before the state supreme court. He failed. Among Cole's arguments, handwritten on ninety pages and read out by him over more than two hours before a packed courtroom on July 29, 1852, was that the state constitution barred the re-enslavement of those who had lived as free residents of the state. A month later, the two judges who heard him— one a former US senator from the slave state Tennessee, the other a native of the slave state Missouri—rejected his position in separate opinions, both ruling that neither the state constitution nor its laws could turn enslaved people into free persons. Perkins's three slaves had come into California prior to statehood as his property, they found, and so they remained when he went home to Mississippi.

Cole later observed that the overt racism of the court's decision proved

* Sandy is often referred to as "Andy" in official documents and in the memoirs of his lawyer, Cornelius Cole.

that "the adoption of a free constitution did not, by any means, abate the aggressiveness of the pro-slavery sentiment in California." Indeed, in his ruling, Chief Justice Hugh Murray (the Missourian) had written that "the increase of free negro population, has for some time past been a matter of serious consideration with the people of this State, in view of the pernicious consequences necessarily resulting from this class of inhabitants. . . . I am satisfied the desire to purge the State of this class of inhabitants, who, in the language of a distinguished jurist, are 'festering sores upon the body politic,' entered largely into the consideration of the Legislature in passing this act." He deemed it the court's "imperative duty" to uphold it.

THE COURT REMANDED the three plaintiffs to Perkins's custody, but whether they ever were returned to Mississippi is unknown. Some sources reported that they escaped from bondage on the way back while traversing Panama, where slavery had been abolished. In any event, they disappeared from history en route.

Five years later, the California court's ruling was cited by lawyers for a family seeking to recover a former slave, Dred Scott, who sued for his freedom on grounds that he had been taken to live in the free states of Minnesota and Illinois before the family returned to Missouri. The US Supreme Court's 1857 decision affirming the status of enslaved people as property and deeming Black people not to be "citizens" under the US Constitution and therefore lacking the right to sue in federal courts stands to this day as the most infamous in the court's history and a major milestone on the road to the Civil War.*

Slavery occasioned several more legal spasms in California following the Perkins ruling and during the run-up to the Civil War. None was more widely noted than the 1858 case of Archy Lee. He had been brought in slavery to California from Mississippi by Charles Stovall, who opened a school in California, a sign that he intended to stay in the state. Stovall later booked passage for Lee on a steamer to return him to Mississippi; Lee escaped and was arrested as a fugitive under the federal law (the state's law had expired in 1855). Eventually his case landed before the state supreme court, where it was heard by two former southerners, Chief Justice David S. Terry and

---

* Soon after the Supreme Court decision in February 1857, Scott and his family were freed by their ultimate owner. Scott died of tuberculosis on September 17, 1858.

Peter Burnett. Terry was a Chiv Democrat. Burnett had condemned slavery as a "great social and political evil" in his 1849 state of the state address as governor, but he also opposed giving those who had been freed from slavery in other states, or "manumitted," the right to work in California, where he believed their presence would provoke "a war . . . between two races."

The judges' efforts to reconcile California law with their racist worldviews produced one of the more bizarre outcomes in the state's judicial history. Burnett, writing the main opinion, found that the state constitution's ban on slavery applied to all but the most transitory visitors to the state. Since Stovall had been in California long enough to be considered a resident, he fell within its strictures. But Burnett ruled that the issue was so novel and poorly understood by most Californians that Stovall deserved a pass. He ordered Archy Lee returned to Stovall's custody, though he warned that "in reference to all future cases, it is our purpose to enforce the rules laid down strictly."

The ruling satisfied nobody, drawing brickbats from editorialists in the proslavery camp, who condemned it for infringing on the rights of traveling slaveholders, and from those in the antislavery camp, who pointed to the absurdity of judging a man to be free yet consigning him again to bondage.

For all that, the proslavery stage of California politics was on the wane, if not entirely extinguished. The Black community had grown more assertive since the Perkins case, funding Lee's numerous courthouse appeals and staging a rescue raid on the ship that was poised to carry him back to Mississippi. Stovall tried one last time to exercise ownership by appealing to the US commissioner in San Francisco, an official empowered to enforce federal law in the states. The commissioner ruled that as Lee had not crossed state lines in asserting his freedom, federal law did not apply and Lee was a free man. A few weeks later, he joined several hundred other freedmen in a mass migration to British Columbia, safely remote from the racial politics of California.

The London *Times* editorialist's celebration of the racial diversity and harmony of the new state of California in 1850 proved to be premature. The hard task of building a state from this raw material still lay ahead.

6

THE AGE OF GENOCIDE

I N FEBRUARY 1860, Bret Harte was eking out a quiet living as an editor
of the *Northern Californian*, the weekly newspaper of the coastal town of
Union (now Arcata), a supply depot for prospectors not far from the Oregon
state line. The tranquility of his existence ended on February 29. That was
when he published a report and editorial about a horrific attack on a peaceful gathering of American Indians three days earlier near Eureka, about ten
miles south of Union and on the far side of Humboldt Bay.

> During the night nearly all the Indians camping on Indian Island, including
> women and children, were killed by parties unknown. Neither age nor sex
> had been spared. Little children and old women were mercilessly stabbed and
> their skulls crushed with axes. . . . When the bodies were landed at Union,
> a more shocking and revolting spectacle never was exhibited to the eyes of
> Christian and civilized people. Old women, wrinkled and decrepit lay wel-
> tering in blood, their brains bashed out and dabbled with their long grey
> hair. Infants scarce a span long, with their faces cloven with hatchets and
> their bodies ghastly with wounds. . . . No resistance was made, it is said, to
> the butchers who did the work, but as they ran or huddled together for pro-
> tection like sheep, they were struck down. . . . Very little shooting was done,
> most of the bodies having wounds to the head.

The Humboldt massacre had begun at four a.m. on February 26, then
spread to nearby Indian settlements—thirty-six Wiyots slain at South Beach

the same day and thirty-five more at Eel River on February 29. Over the following six days, five more attacks took the lives of an estimated two hundred eighty-five Indians.

The killings were unprovoked and so brutish that it seemed they might finally jolt California authorities into taking action against the white perpetrators of Indian massacres. California newspapers editorialized against activities and policies aimed at "exterminating the Indians" and excoriated legislators for their tendency "to come to the assistance of the exterminators," as the *Daily Alta California* put it. But the reckoning was not forthcoming. Indian massacres would continue in California for more than a decade, accompanied by the kidnappings of thousands of women and children and their sale into prostitution and slavery.

From the standpoint of justice, the Humboldt massacres had a familiar result: the perpetrators suffered no punishment. The names of a half dozen attackers were known to authorities but none was ever charged (although four were reportedly killed by Indians in retaliation). After Harte's articles inspired threats on his life—the details of which have never been unearthed—he boarded a steamer for San Francisco and never returned to Union.

THE HARSH TREATMENT of California Indians by whites began with the Spanish expeditions in the sixteenth century. Prior to then, a multiplicity of tribes lived in harmony with the abundance provided by nature. White historians disdained the agricultural prowess of the Indians, but the evidence shows that their practices were well adapted to their environment. Their diets included deer, bear, buffalo, rabbits, geese, quail, and ducks, which were all plentiful on the coast and in the woodlands. Pine nuts, berries, grasshoppers, and acorns were used to make bread and stews. For the most part, the tribes coexisted peacefully with one another, their relationships built primarily around trading. As we have seen, that idyll was disrupted by the arrival of the Spanish.

Three centuries later, the Gold Rush would bring further disruption to tribal existence. "It is now impossible for them to make a living by hunting or fishing, for nearly all the game has been driven from the mining region or killed by the thousands of our people who now occupy the once quiet home of these children of the forest," US Indian agent E. A. Stevenson reported to his superiors in 1853. (The Indian agents were the civilian front men of the Bureau of Indian Affairs, charged with overseeing relations between the tribes on the one hand and settlers and the US Army on the other.) The Sacramento River, which formerly had been "clear as crystal and abounded with the finest salmon," Stevenson wrote, had been turned from its bed and become "so thick with mud that it will scarcely run."

When the tribes acted to relieve their privation by raiding livestock, settlers and the US Army launched ferocious and uncompromising reprisals. "Let a tribe complain that the miners muddied their salmon-streams, or steal a few pack mules," observed ethnographer Stephen Powers in 1877, "and in twenty days there might not be a soul of them living." From 1850 through the mid-1870s, state legislation upgraded the equipment, pay, and funding for the state militia, effectively codifying the punitive treatment of Indians as official state policy.

Throughout this period, the voices of the Indian victims were almost never heard in the white community. For one thing, a historian of the genocide observed, "there were not many survivors" left to tell their stories. Tribal cultures frowned on speaking of the dead, and mass relocations broke the connection between witnesses and the territories where the atrocities occurred. State law barred Indians from giving evidence in court against whites, another factor reducing the contemporary public record to silence. It was mostly the scale of the slaughters, often reported with pride by the perpetrators, that provoked any public backlash at the time. Not until the mid-twentieth century did Native American recollections begin to reach the public to a significant extent.

As many as 130,000 members of Native American tribes are estimated to have lived in the territory that became the state of California prior to 1846. By the 1880 US census, the figure was 16,277. Starvation, disease, dislocation, and homicide had taken their toll, much of it the product of deliberate policy. This treatment is rightly seen today as genocide, although that term did not enter the language until Polish attorney Raphael Lemkin coined it in 1944. Even at the time, however, the goal of attacks on California's Indian tribes was commonly and unblushingly described as their "extermination" or "annihilation."

FROM THE START of the American incursion into California, white colonists perceived the tribes as an ever-present mortal threat. Although the threat was more imagined than real, the settlers repeatedly appealed to the military to take preemptive action. One of the first officers to respond was Frémont. He received a delegation of settlers in the spring of 1846 at the Sacramento Valley ranch of Danish-born settler Peter Lassen, who farmed cotton, wine grapes, and wheat on land that formerly had been occupied by members of the Wintu Tribe. The settlers told Frémont that one thousand Indians had mustered nearby for an attack on the whites. As Kit Carson recalled, they asked Frémont to "drive them back."

Frémont gave permission for a detachment of seventy-six armed men to ride to the encampment of the Wintus, hunter-gatherers who were not known to be particularly hostile to white settlers. The settlers, however, saw them as an obstacle to their ambition to cultivate the land as they wished.

Upon spotting the approaching whites, the Wintus lined up in a defensive formation. The soldiers took this as preparation for an assault. Having been instructed to "ask no quarter and give none" if threatened with attack, the soldiers opened fire. The Wintu bows and arrows were no match for the soldiers' rifles in the first phase of the battle, or for the ferocity of the second phase, in which the attackers sailed into the Indians with sabers and butcher knives, slashing away at women and infants as well as men. "The number killed I cannot say," Carson wrote later. "It was a perfect butchery."

The perpetrators celebrated the outcome of their assault. "This was a rude but necessary measure to prevent injury to the whites," Frémont wrote. "And it had the effect which I intended." Carson agreed that the force "had accomplished what we went for and given the Indians such a chastisement that would be long before they ever again would feel like attacking the settlements"—thereby falsely blaming the Wintu for initiating the violence. This first notable massacre of Indians of the genocide era set a pattern for the coming decades: a surprise preemptive attack provoked by an imagined threat, conducted with unexampled ferocity directed not only at tribal defenders but also at women and children.

Then came the Argonauts.

Many gold-seekers arriving in California in 1849 were predisposed to fear the Indians as a fiendish menace. Stereotypical allusions to Indian savagery was standard fare in popular fiction and eastern newspapers; the *New York Herald*, for example, informed readers in December 1846 of "the daring and predatory habits of the roving bands of Indians . . . who infest the ranchos and villages, and plunder the farmers and peaceable inhabitants." Consequently, the gold diggings bristled with firepower—rifles, pistols, shotguns, and, according to one report, a cannon hauled overland all the way from the East.

Early chronicles of the interactions between American Indians and whites were infused with casual racism. Bancroft, whose opinion of the white settlers in their relations with the tribes was scathing, nevertheless described the Indians as no more advanced socially or intellectually than children. "We do not know why the Digger Indians of California [that is, the Central Valley tribes] . . . were made so much lower in the scale of intelligence than their neighbors," he wrote. The tribes, Bancroft asserted, had been "shabbily treated by nature," rendering them woefully ignorant about agriculture and "religious ideas." Clustered in small communities, "they were kept apart by a confusing multiplicity of tongues." (Ethnographers would come to view this linguistic diversity as the product, not the cause, of the economic and political autonomy of the California tribes.) In any case, Bancroft observed judiciously, "being low, and unsophisticated, in a measure harmless until trodden upon, surely it was not a mark of high merit on the part of the new comers to exterminate them so quickly." Even as late as the 1920s, historian Joseph Ellison leavened his sympathetic analysis of Indian maltreatment in California's first two decades of statehood with the observation that "the California Indians stood low in the scale of civilization."

The bloodiest killing campaign of the Gold Rush period was spurred by the murders of two white landowners who had forced Indians into labor at their ranch at Clear Lake, just north of the Napa Valley. Charles Stone and Andrew Kelsey, who had been among the original Bear Flag rebels, subjugated the Indians by brute force, torture, and the murder of recalcitrant workers. The ranchers kept the workers on the edge of starvation, to the point that the Indians "occasionally took a bullock and killed it themselves," a witness later testified. "If the Kelseys failed to discover the special offenders, they would take any Indian they might suspect, or perhaps one at random, and hang him up by the thumbs, so that his toes just touched the floor. . . . Sometimes they would kill an Indian outright on the spot for some small offence." They routinely subjected the Indian men in camp to beatings, the women and girls to rape.

In December 1849, after a horse in the care of an Indian worker ran away, sixteen Pomo ranch hands met surreptitiously to ponder how to resist the inevitable punitive response by Stone and Kelsey. In light of the cruelty of the ranchers' regime, it was perhaps unsurprising that after an all-night debate, the Indians opted for killing the ranchers. According to the plan, as Pomo storyteller William Ralganal Benson recounted, the Pomo children working as house servants for Stone and Kelsey were to "carrie out all the guns, bows and arrows, knives and everything like weapon" from the ranch house overnight "so the two white men was helpless in defense." The next morning, the ranchers were ambushed when they came outside to light a fire for breakfast. Stone got an arrow in the stomach and fled into the house, where he was killed. Kelsey was shot with an arrow in the back but managed to pull it out and swim across a nearby creek, where he was finished off by a woman whose son he had murdered.

The Stone and Kelsey killings unleashed governmental retaliation on an unprecedented scale. Within days, the US First Dragoons, "a battle-hardened elite mounted infantry unit," was mustered out of its barracks in Sonoma and sent on a murderous rampage. They paused at a village at the northernmost reach of the Napa Valley and opened fire on the Indian residents, indiscriminately killing about thirty-five men, women, and children. They continued on, firing on any Indians they encountered, finally fetching up at the Stone and Kelsey ranch. There the massacre reached its climax. Hearing of the soldiers' advance, the Indians had taken refuge on an island in the lake. The dragoons had been instructed to "waste no time in parley" but to strike the Indians "promptly and heavily." The soldiers landed and turned the island into what Brevet Captain Nathaniel Lyon later described as "a perfect slaughter pen." Lyon estimated the Indian toll at "not less than 75," and probably more than twice that number.

CALIFORNIA LAW ACCOMMODATED whites' perception of the Native tribes as inferior beings. Early in its inaugural session in 1850, the California legislature had taken up a bill proposed by John Bidwell, himself a leading employer of Indian labor, titled "An Act in Relation to the Protection, Punishment, and Government of the Indians." Bidwell's proposal was paternalistic and, in comparison to later measures, almost progressive. It would have established a justice of the peace for Indians to take up abuses of tribal members by non-Indians, though it forbade the conviction of non-Indians on the testimony of Indians alone. The bill required that any labor contracts between non-Indians and Indians have the justice's approval and that the Indians be paid with "two good suits of clothes" when the contracts expired. The justice would also have the authority to approve adoptions of

Indian children by non-Indians, but only if the adoptions were agreed to by the children's parents, who would have to appear personally in court.

The legislature scrapped the Bidwell proposal. Its substitute measure, deceptively titled "An Act for the Government and Protection of Indians," allowed civil judges to place Indian children under the "care, custody, [and] control" of others with the approval of "parents or friends" of the child, giving the vaguely defined "friends" equal authority with parents over their own children. It allowed the children to be worked without pay until they reached the age of eighteen, for boys, and fifteen, for girls. The act legalized convict-leasing of Indians—any Indian jailed for a crime could be bailed out by a stranger and required to work for the bailor until the debt was paid. Indians who were discovered "loitering or strolling about, or frequenting public places where liquors are sold, begging, or leading an immoral or profligate course of life" could be arrested on the complaint of any citizen and hired out to the highest bidder for up to four months without pay. J. Ross Browne—the Irish-born writer who had served as the official reporter at the 1849 constitutional convention—told of Indians being paid in liquor on Saturday, "put in jail next morning for getting drunk, and bailed out on Monday to work out the fine imposed upon them by the local authorities." Thus did the state become the agent and promoter of involuntary servitude. Indians had no legal standing to object to any of these provisions or to their treatment by whites; they had no right of suffrage, and while the act specified that they had the same right as whites to bring complaints to a justice of the peace, they did not have the same right as whites to testify in court, for white defendants could not be convicted of any offense based solely on an Indian's testimony. Nor could Indians serve as jurors or become attorneys.

Amendments enacted in 1860 made it even easier to bind Indians to servitude: Henceforth, Indians could be indentured from their teens up to the age of twenty-five, for women, and thirty, for men. Judges were empowered to place minor Indian children in apprenticeships without the consent of their parents or guardians.

That provision was responsible for a surge in kidnappings of Indian children, often after their parents were slain in punitive expeditions or by freebooting white slavers who engaged in this practice with brazen audacity.

As harsh and unforgiving as the treatment of Indians was nationwide, the conditions in California set such an extreme standard for abuse that they provoked horrified reactions in Congress. "I am informed by officers of the

Army . . . that Indians are hunted down in some portions of the state of California, that the old bucks, as they are called, are killed, and the children taken and disposed of, and in certain cases sold as slaves," Henry Wilson of Massachusetts told his colleagues on the Senate floor in 1860. "The abuses that have been perpetrated upon the Indians in California are shocking to humanity, and this Government owes it to itself to right their wrongs."

Wilson's remarks instantly drew a defensive riposte from Milton Latham, whom the California legislature had just appointed to the US Senate following his mere five-day stint as governor. Latham laid the blame for the kidnappings on the army's failure to keep the tribes in check; this, he believed, had prompted the settlers to take matters into their own hands. The settlers, he said, "have suffered; after their property has been taken; after their children have been slaughtered in the most brutal manner, incensed and indignant, they do get up these expeditions, and oftentimes do that which their calm judgment, reason and humanity . . . would prevent if they did not feel that they were rejected and outraged by the treatment of the Government."

The congressional backlash and rising public disapproval eventually diminished the taste for officially sanctioned punitive expeditions within California. There was more to the kidnappings than the thirst for retribution, however, which kept the practice alive. "Kidnapping Indians has become quite a business of profit," Indian agent George Hanson advised his superiors in 1861, explaining why he had assembled a team of special agents "to counteract this unholy traffic in human blood and souls." After Hanson arrested three kidnappers caught with nine Indian children, aged three to ten years old, in their possession, one of the kidnappers testified that "it was an act of charity . . . to hunt up the children and provide homes for them, because their parents had been killed." When Hanson asked how he knew that the parents had been killed, the kidnapper answered, "Because I killed some of them myself."

Hanson undertook to persuade the state legislature to end the slave trade by repealing the law allowing the indenture of Indians. That would not happen until April 1863.

Federal officials tried repeatedly to end the Californians' attacks on the tribes, largely by removing the Indians from proximity to whites. In 1850 they tried to extend into California the policy they had employed across the midwestern prairie—offering Indians annual financial stipends and guarantees of security if they would consent to move onto reservations. In October, federal Indian Affairs commissioner Ardavan S. Loughery appointed three negotiators to reach treaties with tribal leaders. The negotiators—Redick McKee of Virginia, George Barbour of Kentucky, and Oliver Wozencraft, who had been a delegate at the California constitutional convention (where he had opposed Indian suffrage)—began their work by issuing an open letter addressed to "The People of California." The letter aimed to assuage white sensitivities by describing the Indians as "extremely ignorant, lazy and degraded," albeit "generally harmless and peaceable in their habits." Given that the Indians had been pushed as far west as they could go, there was "but one alternative in relation to these remnants of once numerous and powerful tribes, viz: *extermination or domestication.*" The latter choice meant providing the tribes with land and protection, in exchange for which the whites would receive "a stop to the shedding of blood" (that is, the shedding of white blood by Indians) and a supply of "cheap labor."

The commissioners opened treaty negotiations amid favorable public sentiment. They were prepared to make liberal offers of land and subsistence on the reasoning that it was "*cheaper* to feed the whole flock for a *year* than to *fight* them for a *week*," as they reported to Washington. By January 1852, the three commissioners had signed eighteen treaties with 119 tribes, calling for the establishment of reservations totaling 11,700 square miles, or about 7.5 percent of the area of California.

The white colonists had come to regard the land as their own and the Indians as an inferior race, so the prospect of ceding so much territory to Indians for their exclusive use prompted public opinion to turn against the negotiations. Within weeks of the treaties' signing, the state senate and assembly voted to ask California's US senators to reject ratification and bring the rest of the Senate along if possible. The legislature's resolutions were models of racism and sanctimonious avarice. The state senate version lamented that sequestering the Indians on reserved lands would destroy their value as "indispensable servants to the large rancheros, upon whose estates they were content to live."

The assembly document was even greedier and more condescending. It estimated that the proposed reservations encompassed land worth more than one hundred million dollars and occupied by more than twenty thousand "American citizens" (meaning whites). Allowing Indians to live in "close proximity" to whites even within a reservation, the assembly asserted, would foster rather than quell racial violence: "The Indian is naturally prone to steal, and otherwise depredate upon the white population; and the white man in retaliation takes the life of the Indian." The only suitable option was "removing the Indians beyond the limits of civilization."

These objections bore fruit. On July 8, 1852, five weeks after President Millard Fillmore presented the treaties for ratification, the Senate unanimously rejected all eighteen in a secret session and decreed that their texts were to remain undisclosed. They would not be made public until 1905, more than a half century later.

That the congressional failure to act left the tribes in a desperate situation was not lost on the few federal officials who took the protection of the Indians' welfare as a solemn responsibility. "What justice most demands for these Indians is, that they should have immediate protection from lawless whites," Lieutenant George Falconer Emmons of the Navy Construction Bureau wrote to Henry Schoolcraft, an ethnographer at the Bureau of Indian Affairs. "While we are discussing the propriety of Indian agencies and treaties, they are falling by tens, fifties, and hundreds, before the western rifle."

Edward F. Beale, the federal superintendent of Indian Affairs in California, submitted a more detailed and dismal picture of Indian existence to Indian Affairs commissioner Luke Lea in Washington. Beale had been granted one hundred thousand dollars to sustain the California Indians, an amount he considered woefully inadequate. He pleaded for at least five hundred thousand, lest the government be judged guilty of "intentional and premeditated extinction of our Indian population":

> Driven from their fishing and hunting grounds, hunted themselves like wild beasts, *lassoed*, and torn from homes made miserable by want, and forced into slavery, the wretched remnant which escapes starvation on the one hand, and the relentless whites on the other, only do so to rot and die of a loathsome disease, the penalty of Indian association with frontier civilization. . . . I know that they starve; I know that they perish by hundreds; I know that they are fading away with a startling and shocking rapidity, but I cannot help them.

Early in 1853, Congress took a modest step to fill the void it had created in rejecting the treaties by appropriating $250,000 to establish five "military reservations" of up to twenty-five thousand acres each and to pay for the Indians' relocation. This was about one-sixtieth of the territory provided for in the repudiated treaties. The government's ability to prevent whites from infiltrating and occupying the reservations was uncertain, as was its legal authority to do so. In practice, the reservations exacerbated racial and economic strife between whites and Indians; the Indians resented being forcibly transported to alien territory, and the whites were unnerved at the thought that Indians they imagined to be violence-prone were concentrated in large numbers on lands still disturbingly close to their own settlements.

Some white settlers bristled at what they saw as unwarranted gifts of potentially profitable territory to the tribes. "We are aggrieved," a group of Tehama County whites living on the outskirts of the Nome Lackee Reservation in the Sacramento Valley wrote to Interior Secretary Jacob Thompson in 1859. "The lands occupied by said Reservation are among the best in our State and capable of subsisting a valuable community of settlers." Meanwhile, tribes that resisted relocation to lands the settlers viewed as sufficiently remote and unpromising became targets of further violence. That was the ostensible provocation leading to the Humboldt Bay attack. To paraphrase the treaty negotiators, the Indians who refused to be domesticated were making themselves vulnerable to extermination.

Another focus of discontent among Indians was the behavior of the agents hired to supervise the reservations. J. Ross Browne took the measure of the Indian agent corps after accepting an appointment in 1855 as a federal inspector for Indian Affairs. He found the agents almost universally incompetent and corrupt. "An honest Indian Agent," he wrote, is "the rarest work of God that I know of."

Browne documented for his Treasury Department superiors the agents' practices of allowing their own herds of sheep and cattle to graze on reservation grounds, forcing the Indians in their jurisdiction to labor for the agents' own benefit, and diverting funds meant for reservation inhabitants into their own pockets. The first reservation established in California, the Tejon Rancho due east of Santa Barbara, had been envisioned as a showcase of federal solicitude toward the dislocated tribes; instead, Browne told his superiors, it had become "little more than a private stock ranch," where the reservation's white overseers forced the Indian residents to tend their herd of several thousand sheep.

The Indians fled the reservations by the thousands, disbelieving the government's promises that they would be provided with material sustenance and protection from marauding whites. "Sad experience taught them that these were institutions for the benefit for white men, not Indians," Browne wrote in a scathing and widely republished broadside. "It was wonderful how the employees had prospered on their salaries. They owned fine ranches in the vicinity. . . . [T]he principal work done was to attend to sheep and cattle speculations, and make shepherds out of the few Indians that were left."

Some agents' plundering was so extreme that it could not be overlooked by local settlers. The Tehama County residents who had objected to the interior department about the valuable land sequestered behind the gates of Nome Lackee also complained about the reservation's agent, Vincent E. Geiger, who they said surrounded himself with a "worthless horde" of associates who stole the food and medicines the government provided for the Indians and established a brothel staffed with Indian women forced into prostitution.

THE MASSACRES CONTINUED into the 1860s and 1870s, though at a reduced frequency. In part, this was because "it had become much harder for killers to find California Indians to kill." The remaining Indians also had learned to keep out of the whites' way or had been relocated by the army far from white settlements. In April 1863, in the wake of the Emancipation Proclamation, Governor Leland Stanford signed a law repealing the indenture provisions of the state's earlier Indian laws. (But convict leasing remained legal until 1937.) In 1873 the legislature finally granted Indians the right to testify in state courts, exposing white killers to prosecution.

After that, the Indian genocide was largely forgotten except by the tribes themselves. That changed in the 1940s, when new scholarship revived interest in the period, possibly due to public awareness of the genocidal policies of Nazi Germany. Since then, it has become an important element of California's recognition of its own history; in June 2019, Governor Gavin Newsom apologized on behalf of all California citizens "to all California Native Americans for the many instances of violence, maltreatment and neglect California inflicted on tribes."

The era of Indian genocide would live on in Indian cultural lore. Every year, tribal members stage the Nome Cult Walk, commemorating the 1864 Konkow Maidu Trail of Tears, in which the US Army force-marched 461 Konkow members ninety miles to the Round Valley Reservation in the northern Sacramento Valley for fourteen days without adequate food or water. Only 277 reached the destination; most of the others had been abandoned in mortal distress along the way. In 2021, the board of directors of the

University of California's Hastings College of the Law, which was founded in 1878 by Serranus Hastings, a rancher and the chief justice of the state supreme court, voted to remove his name from the school in light of his complicity in Indian slaughters in the 1850s and 1860s.

There has always been enough blame for the destruction of California's Indian tribes to be liberally spread around, as Browne observed in 1861 while the tragedy was still unfolding. Of the Indians he wrote:

> Wherever they attempted to procure a subsistence, they were hunted down; driven from the reservations by the instinct of self-preservation; shot down by the settlers upon the most frivolous pretexts; and abandoned to their fate by the only power that could have afforded them protection. . . . Their history in California is a melancholy record of neglect and cruelty; and the part taken by public men high in position, in wresting from them the very means of subsistence, is one of which any other than professional politicians would be ashamed. For the Executive Department there is no excuse. There lay the power and the remedy; but a paltry and servile spirit, . . . an utter absence of that high moral tone which is the characteristic trait of statesmen and patriots, have been the distinguishing features of this branch of government for some time past.

This was a reflection and a harbinger of deep-seated ethnic tensions that would surface in paroxysms of prejudice and violence repeatedly throughout California history. The assaults on the tribes might have been the harshest and bloodiest of all, but they would not be the last.

PART II

The RAILROAD ERA

7

"THE CHINESE MUST GO": SAN FRANCISCO
AFTER THE GOLD RUSH

I N A SANDLOT on San Francisco's Nob Hill—the construction site of a new plutocrat's mansion, to join others gazing possessively upon the city below—a stocky man with a fidgety manner and a spellbinding oratorical style launched into a tirade against "thieving millionaires and scoundrelly officials." He threatened them with mob justice at the hands of "the poor and working men." He promised to rid the country of cheap Chinese labor "as soon as possible, and by all the means in our power, because it tends still more to degrade labor and aggrandize capital." He closed his speech with the same phrase with which he had opened it: "The Chinese Must Go!"

It was December 1877 and the speaker was Denis Kearney, an Irish-born drayman—that is, a freight hauler—who was on the verge of upending city and state politics for a short but explosive period. He was a shooting star whose flame would quickly burn out. But the embers of ethnic hatred he left behind would help spread an acrid pall from California to the rest of the country for decades to come.

Kearney had honed his delivery to a fine edge. His rallies, most of them held on Sundays in sandlots around the city, from city hall to Nob Hill, were models of demagoguery. They unfolded in a carnival atmosphere featuring raffles and athletic contests along with soapbox orators attracting well-heeled onlookers slumming in carriages for entertainment as well as working-class crowds. But their more serious character derived from their domination "by rowdies and anti-coolie groups" who were sometimes inspired by Kearney's charismatic exhortations to head from the sandlots to the city's Chinese district, intent on mayhem. (The term *coolie* derived from a South Asian word originally applied by European traders to native laborers in India.)

Kearneyism reflected, and exploited, the tumultuous social and political environment of San Francisco in the decades following the Gold Rush. The Gold Rush had deprived San Francisco of civic stability; the city had never come to grips with its explosive growth after the discovery at Sutter's Mill catapulted it from a frontier outpost into a teeming, jerry-built metropolis of thirty-five thousand souls by 1852. Its population continued to grow, reaching about one hundred fifty thousand by 1870 and nearly a quarter of a million ten years later.

This was a time when "few or none of the respectable classes of the community took sufficient interest in public matters" to go to the polls or accept jury appointments. "An honest man's vote was worthless," observed historian John S. Hittell in 1878, "but if it could under any circumstances be counted as at all effective, care was taken to prevent its being thrown."

The semblance of order established by Sam Brannan's Vigilance Committee of 1851 disappeared after the committee was disbanded late that year. Gangs of bullies and professional ballot-box stuffers rushed to fill the vacuum of authority. Police officers and prosecutors were no more honest and effective than one might have expected in a city where votes were openly for sale; city records showed that of the more than one thousand homicides committed between 1849 and 1856, only one resulted in an execution—that of an immigrant charged with murder who was hanged on Russian Hill on December 10, 1852, in front of an appreciative throng estimated at six to ten thousand people. The common means of settling disputes, whether personal, financial, or political, was by dueling. These contests attained the level of popular entertainment, with spectators eagerly gathering at the publicly announced sites and newspapers reporting the duels like sporting events.

Then an agent of reform appeared in the person of a newspaperman with the peculiar moniker James King of William.* Under King's editorship, the *Daily Evening Bulletin* became the most popular newspaper among San Francisco's twelve dailies and six weeklies, selling 3,500 copies a day.

The critical factor in the *Bulletin*'s astounding success was King's charac-

---

* He had added his father's name to his own to distinguish himself from the numerous other James Kings in his native Washington, DC.

ter. His determination to infuse San Francisco with "public respectability" derived not merely from moral scrupulousness but from his conviction that its gambling and prostitution houses were drivers of public corruption. King looked the part of a crusading journalist—"dark of complexion, with big piercing eyes, aquiline nose, and black beard and whiskers," projecting "a flinty, uncompromising quality of will that would make him a formidable foe." Fearless about calling out graft where he saw it, his prose was correspondingly bold and direct. Having worked at two local banks that had failed due to embezzlement and fraud, he labeled their executives the "Uriah Heeps of San Francisco," evoking the sniveling villain of Dickens's *David Copperfield*. He hammered Democratic Party boss David C. Broderick with allegations of election fraud, referring to him as "David Catiline Broderick," alluding to a politician who had attempted a coup in ancient Rome. King's reporting tied Broderick to not a few municipal scandals, including the so-called Jenny Lind Theater swindle, through which the city paid an inflated two hundred thousand dollars to acquire the building for remodeling into city hall, and named him as the leader of a cabal of politicians who took municipal office "for the sole purpose of filling their pockets with the ill gotten gains of their nefarious schemes, their pilfering and dishonesty."

Broderick's brash personality resembled King's. The son of an Irish stonecutter and his wife, he imported to San Francisco the New York Tammany Hall–style of political roughhousing. He customarily arrived at political meetings in the city behind a wedge of beefy acolytes projecting the air of spoiling for a fight and reigned as the leader of "shoulder-strikers" (that is, violent thugs) and ballot-box stuffers who openly manipulated elections. Many San Franciscans thought this behavior made municipal politics "exciting, dramatic, interesting, and diverting." King opened their eyes to how it drained their municipal treasury and cheated them of a voice in civic affairs.

King editorialized ferociously against the political influence of the city's gambling dens and brothels and their political connections. After a professional gambler and dandy-about-town named Charles Cora murdered William H. Richardson, the federal marshal for California, King predicted that Cora would be freed by the corrupt court system and called in advance for retribution. "If the jury which tries Cora is packed," he wrote, "either *hang the sheriff* or drive him out of town." (Emphasis his.) A complacent Cora appeared in court in high style, wearing a "richly figured velvet vest, and sporting light kids, which, with . . . a neatly trimmed moustache, and his nonchalant air, made up quite a characteristic *tout ensemble*," the *Daily Alta* reported. Fulfilling King's prophecy, the trial ended with a hung jury. "The money of the gambler and the prostitute has succeeded," King wrote in the aftermath. "Rejoice ye gamblers and harlots!"

No one before King "had made a business of preaching concrete righteousness in short and readable paragraphs . . . and with plenty of personal applications scattered all through the editorial columns," observed historian Josiah Royce. Even King's allies could be unnerved by his intemperate zeal and his tendency to collect powerful enemies: William Tell Coleman, who had been an officer of the Vigilance Committee of 1851, described him as "honest, brave, and terribly in earnest, but often rash." That was a charitable description of a crusader known to deploy a bludgeon where a rapier might have better served.

Yet when the retaliatory blow was struck, it came not from the power elite but from James P. Casey, a ballot-box stuffer and political functionary whom King had identified in the *Bulletin* as a former inmate of New York's Sing Sing prison. This was true but, in Casey's view, an unprovoked smear. On the day of its publication, May 14, 1856, Casey accosted King in the street in front of the *Bulletin* and fired a single shot into his chest. King died six days later, leaving a widow and six children.

King's martyrdom provoked a tide of public outrage. At nine o'clock the morning after the shooting, members of the Vigilance Committee of 1851 assembled and asked Coleman to take the helm of a reconstituted committee. The new body soon enrolled eight thousand members, armed them with weapons hijacked in a nighttime raid on a state militia schooner anchored in San Francisco Bay, and drilled them in paramilitary style. Its constitution succinctly set forth the credo that "no thief, burglar, incendiary, assassin, ballot-box stuffer, or other disturber of the peace, shall escape punishment, either by the quibbles of the law . . . or a laxity of those who pretend to administer justice." Coleman rejected Governor J. Neely Johnson's request to stand down in favor of the militia, informing Johnson that it was the inaction of elected officials such as himself that had provoked the people to assume the task of keeping order.

Nothing less than a civic coup d'état was underway.

The 1856 committee was a pivotal event in American vigilantism. The committee was "the best organized, the longest-lived, and the most successful" rebellion against elected government in US history. It was emulated around the world and widely praised as an acceptable, even indispensable, solution to the disorder accompanying any country's transition from an agrarian nation to a modern urbanized state. The committee was not truly deserving of such admiration; in retrospect, its rule marked the peak of the vigilante era and the moment when the movement began to lose its luster. Indeed, less than a month before the founding of the committee, the state legislature had taken the issue of municipal corruption in hand: On April 19 it had passed the Consolidation Act, which merged the city and county of San Francisco into a single civic entity and imposed independent electoral oversight and stringent budgeting rules. Through these provisions and others, proclaimed its author, state senator William W. Hawks of San Francisco, the measure aimed to "throw aside and abjure this disgusting mass of trickery and corruption and fraud" by eliminating the "thousand chances for plunder" afforded under the previously divided government.

The act would help to clean up San Francisco, but it came too late to forestall the committee's formation. Once organized, the committee moved swiftly to deal with the two crimes that had roiled the city. On May 18, while King lay on his deathbed, a squadron of bayonet-flashing members marched to the city jail to take custody of Cora and Casey (whom bystanders had captured at the scene of King's shooting). As the mob gathered, a fretful Sheriff David Scannell approached Casey in his cell. "There are two thousand armed men coming for you," he said, "and I have not thirty men about the jail." Casey waved him off. "Don't peril your life or your officers'," he said. "I'll go with them."

The vigilantes brought Casey and Cora to "Fort Vigilance," the committee's headquarters on Sacramento Street in the center of the city. Their trials took place there on the day of King's death. Swift justice was on the agenda. The defendants were permitted legal representation, but only if they selected their lawyers from among members of the Vigilance Committee's leadership. The outcome was preordained: Both defendants were convicted of murder and sentenced to death. They were hanged from a gibbet erected in front of Fort Vigilance before a crowd estimated at fifteen thousand while King's funeral cortege was making its way to his final resting place, a cemetery at the foot of Lone Mountain, just below the San Francisco Presidio.

Governor Johnson ordered the committee to disband immediately after the executions, arguing that the crisis that led to its creation had been resolved. Yet although the committee's creation had been triggered by two murders, its larger goal was the imposition of a sober new political order upon the raucous city. It was engaged, judged Royce, in a "Business Man's Revolution," the leaders of which were determined to create the moral, economic, and social conditions needed to fulfill the city's ambition to rule as the commercial center of the West. They appreciated, even savored, its reputation as a gaudy, lawless metropolis but felt the time had come to bring down the curtain on old San Francisco.

The business establishment anticipated that the city would become ever more tightly joined to the rest of the country through improved transportation connections, making it the premier entrepôt for the goods trade between the Far East and the continental United States and attracting tourists from around the world. Interest in the construction of a transcontinental railroad was growing apace; by the mid-1850s the project seemed almost inevitable. The business leaders wanted San Francisco to be prepared for its arrival by tidying up its politics and social conditions.

After the hangings of Casey and Cora, the committee turned to cleansing the city of its "notorious ballot-box stuffers and other desperate characters," who exercised their power through threats of violence against independent-minded voters and a device known as a "double improved back-action ballot box," which was built with false sides to conceal faked ballots.

The committee's continued existence alarmed Johnson, who had been elected the year before on the ticket of the Know-Nothings, a party devoted to "nativism," which meant excluding foreign-born individuals and Roman Catholics from eligibility for naturalized citizenship.* On June 3, Johnson declared San Francisco to be in "a state of insurrection" and ordered all volunteer militiamen in the city to report immediately to William Tecumseh Sherman, whom he had commissioned as major general of the state militia only two weeks earlier. Johnson was generally viewed as feckless and given to empty bluster, so his directive was ignored by the committee and the militiamen. Johnson appealed to the US Army for weapons for a planned militia attack on the committee; when the army refused, leaving Sherman without arms or men to reestablish municipal authority, he resigned his commission. It was June 9, and he had served as militia commander for twenty-three days.

---

* The "Know Nothing" sobriquet was not an intimation of members' ignorance but a reference to a code of secrecy in its early period that prompted those queried about their membership to reply that they "knew nothing" of the organization.

The committee did take Johnson's threat of armed counteraction seriously, so it secured its headquarters with a breastworks of sandbags, after which the building became popularly known as "Fort Gunnybags." Meanwhile its members pondered how to deal with election manipulators. They concluded that since hanging was perhaps too stringent a sentence and imprisonment too expensive, the best option was banishment. Over the next few weeks the committee placed sixty-seven names on its "black list," though only twenty-eight individuals would actually be sent into exile, typically at the committee's expense aboard Pacific Mail or Nicaragua steamers headed south. Others targeted by the committee fled the city voluntarily; estimates of their number ranged from eighty to eight hundred, but all figures are necessarily conjectural.

The committee finally disbanded on August 18, having judged the task of purifying "the atmosphere morally and politically" (in Coleman's words) to have been completed. Yet even after formally disbanding, the Vigilance Committee did not entirely vanish. It morphed into the "People's Party," which was formed to pursue the vigilantes' reformist goals. Its leaders and political nominees were drawn chiefly from the middle class, the native-born mercantile caste, as had been the members of the Vigilance Committee. The party would wield political power in San Francisco for more than a decade.

One reason the committee remains controversial after more than 160 years is that a powerful, yet unspoken, ethnic enmity lay at its core. The committee made a formal show of welcoming all applicants to membership (assuming they were of sound moral character and excepting Blacks and Chinese); the motto emblazoned on its official seal read, under the image of an all-seeing eye: "No creed. No party. No sectional issues." In reality, its goals reflected anti-Irish and anti-Catholic prejudice within the city's social and business establishments. Coleman acknowledged that "the largest element" of the committee membership was of "northern and western men, chiefly representing the mercantile, manufacturing, and vested interests." Its blacklist, on the other hand, was replete with Irish names such as Mulligan, Kelley, Cooney, Gallagher and included many members of Broderick's political entourage. For the vigilantes, it was no great stretch to link the political chicanery they were sworn to defeat with the immigrant communities that had swarmed into the city during the Gold Rush, particularly the Irish. In a sense, they were trying to hold back the tide. In 1856, the Irish were the fastest-growing ethnic community in San Francisco. Of the city's thirty-five thousand residents that year, four thousand were Irish-born immigrants and fourteen hundred were US-born children of Irish families; by 1880, Irish Catholics would constitute more than a third of the population. After the Gold Rush and the granting of statehood, San Franciscans had prided themselves on having created a cosmopolitan city, in no small part because the influx of immigrants pointed to future growth in commercial activity and municipal wealth. But the city's increasing diversity was destined to exacerbate its simmering ethnic conflicts and bring them to the surface.

The arrival of women and the formation of families transmuted the overwhelmingly male population of the Gold Rush era. Women accounted for about 7.5 percent of California's population in 1850 but 28 percent ten years later and more than one-third in 1870. This trend, along with the Consolidation Act, would have helped cleanse San Francisco of much of its municipal corruption even if the Vigilance Committee, with its goal of purifying the civic atmosphere, had never existed.

The post-consolidation municipal leadership sharply cut taxes and rescinded corrupt city contracts. A new police commissioner put his officers in uniform, an important step toward professionalizing a force that had previously been known for colluding with criminals. The People's Party built on these reforms by closing prostitution and gambling dens, establishing itself as a party of "home and hearth as well as countinghouse and commercial exchange." After the party triumphed in the 1856 municipal election, the *Bulletin*—now under the editorship of James King of William's brother Thomas—proclaimed a "peaceable, joyous termination of the moral revolution through which we have passed."

This was premature. The streets of San Francisco were crumbling, the gas company still overcharged customers, teachers were unpaid, police and firefighting departments undermanned and ill-equipped. After the Vigilance Committee's dissolution, many of the roughnecks it had banished swarmed back into town. The city's masses, seeking scapegoats for their discontent, soon focused their attention on what historian Alexander Saxton called "the indispensable enemy": the Chinese.

IN THE EARLIEST years of Chinese immigration, San Francisco greeted the newcomers with welcoming arms. "The people of the Flowery Land were received like guests," a committee of Chinese merchants would recall in 1877. Governor John McDougal paid special tribute in 1852 to Chinese laborers who were helping to drain California's swamplands to make them suitable for agriculture, honoring the workers as "one of the most worthy classes of our newly adopted citizens, to whom the climate and the character of these lands are particularly suited." The exotic flavor of San Francisco's China-town became a tourist attraction: "A large business was . . . done in Chinese shawls, and various Chinese curiosities," reported a traveler. "It was greatly the fashion for men, returning home, to take with them a quantity of such articles, as presents for their friends."

The hospitality evaporated after Chinese immigrants began to compete with self-styled "Americans" in business. Originally, the main impetus for immigration had been gold: In 1848, only three Chinese travelers had been recorded landing at the San Francisco Customs House; in 1852, with the Gold Rush in full cry, the number exploded to 20,026. At the gold diggings these new arrivals elicited the same hostility that Mexicans and other "foreigners" had drawn. The calumnies that would become standard against Chinese immigration appeared first in the mining districts—they were dirty, smelly, clannish, and willing to accept lower wages than white laborers. These complaints were mixed with a certain amount of envy, for Chinese miners moved onto placer diggings that whites had abandoned as exhausted and through diligence and toil somehow extracted more gold.

It was not long before politicians recognized the potential of anti-Chinese sentiment for drumming up votes among the white majority and workers feeling fretful about competition for jobs. Among the first to exploit anti-Chinese bigotry was Governor John Bigler. Seeking reelection in 1852, the graceless and unprincipled Bigler called on the state legislature to enact an immigrant tax that would discourage new Chinese arrivals and on Congress to outlaw contracts for "coolie" labor. "In order to enhance the prosperity and to preserve the tranquility of the state," Bigler told legislators, "measures must be adopted to check this tide of Asiatic immigration." His message opened the floodgates in the gold districts for assaults on Chinese miners, who were "subjected to many outrages—driven from their claims, robbed, and murdered."

As the placer mines played out, the Chinese moved into domestic service in the cities, primarily San Francisco, as well as into manual labor such as fruit-picking and road and canal construction. Initially this was welcomed as a remedy for labor shortages. But as more white colonists arrived to fill the same jobs, public antagonism grew and restrictive laws and practices followed. In 1854, the state supreme court extended to Chinese residents the statehood-era ban on trial testimony by Blacks and Indians. (The ruling's author, Chief Justice Hugh C. Murray, expressed horror that if Chinese were allowed to give testimony, Californians would "soon see them at the polls, in the jury box, upon the bench, and in our legislative halls.") In 1859, the Cigar Makers Association, which had reserved cigar-making to whites, expelled a member for "employing China or Cooly apprentices with intent to learn them the cigar trade."

By the early 1860s, public sentiment in California had turned distinctly against the Chinese, thanks to an updraft of Chinese arrivals and a surge in politicians' rhetorical hand-wringing about the mongrelization of the white race through intermarriage. Leland Stanford, elected governor in 1861, launched a prototypical attack on the immigrants in his inaugural address. Delivered on January 10, 1862, it abounded in racist tropes familiar even today.

"Asia, with her numberless millions, sends to our shores the dregs of her population," Stanford said. "There can be no doubt but that the presence among us of numbers of degraded and distinct people must exercise a deleterious influence upon the superior race, and to a certain extent, repel desirable immigration."

Only a few short years later, however, Stanford would play a significant role in increasing Chinese immigration to California, as his Central Pacific Railroad put more than 23,000 Chinese laborers to work speeding the line's progress toward its meeting with the Union Pacific at Promontory Summit in 1869. The railroad was the principal driver of a sharp increase in Chinese immigration into San Francisco, from an average of fewer than 3,100 a year from 1864 to 1867 to an average of 12,500 annually from 1868 to 1870.

"Without them it would be impossible to complete the western portion of this great national enterprise, within the time required by the Acts of Congress," Stanford acknowledged to government officials in an 1865 progress report on federally funded railroad construction. "As a class they are quiet, peaceable, patient, industrious and economical—ready and apt to learn all the different kinds of work required in railroad building, they soon become as efficient as white laborers." Perhaps more to the point, he observed that "they are contented with less wages."

Even after the railroad's completion, California remained the epicenter of Chinese settlement in the United States. This was partially the result of the 1868 Burlingame Treaty between the United States and China, which guaranteed to Chinese nationals the right to immigrate to the United States and travel freely within its borders. In 1870, California's 49,277 Chinese residents outstripped by nearly fourfold their numbers in the rest of the country. In only four other states did the Chinese population even exceed one thousand. This may have facilitated Americans' acceptance of the negative depictions of Chinese character and habits flowing out of California, since the inhabitants of few other states had experiences to contradict the stereotype. That there were any Chinese immigrants at all in the Midwest or East "was accepted as proof that they might be expected to distribute themselves over the entire country in the event of continued immigration." The path was greased for California's anti-Chinese virulence to spread from coast to coast, like a pandemic.

Meanwhile, economic downturns intensified racial resentment in San Francisco. As the yield at placer mines fell to an average of three dollars a day in 1860, the city teemed with disappointed and destitute ex-Argonauts. Drought produced an agricultural recession from 1869 to 1870. The failed attempt by the financial buccaneers Jay Gould and Jim Fisk to corner the gold market in 1869 caused a crash in the price of the metal and provoked a nationwide recession that persisted into 1870. The completion of the railroad failed to bring to San Francisco the prosperity so widely anticipated. Instead, things unfolded much as political economist Henry George, that renowned critic of poverty amid abundance, had forecast.

"The completion of the railroad and the consequent great increase of business and population will not be a benefit to all of us, but only to a portion," George wrote only a few months before the Golden Spike ceremony in May 1869. He foresaw more economic inequality, more exploitation of the working class. "Those who have, it will make wealthier; for those who have not, it will make it more difficult to get. . . . Can we rely upon sufficient intelligence, independence and virtue among the many to resist the political effect of the concentration of great wealth in the hands of a few?" The answer would be no.

During the 1870 slump, a visitor to San Francisco reported, the city's residents, stunned by their reversal of fortunes, "cursed the railroad, they cursed the Bank of California [then the premier banking establishment west of the Mississippi], and they cursed the Chinese, one and all, as parents of their disappointment."

The Chinese bore the brunt of their curses. The railroad and the banks were giant, faceless entities, but Chinese individuals lived among them. Anti-Chinese agitators came together in February 1870 to form an organization called the Industrial Reformers, with the dual goals of forcing the abrogation of the Burlingame Treaty and protecting "white labor" by excluding Chinese workers from all trades and boycotting companies that employed them. An anti-Chinese mass meeting called by the Knights of St. Crispin, a union of boot- and shoemakers, drew representatives from seventeen craft unions.

San Francisco's densely populated Chinatown was blamed for triggering a citywide smallpox outbreak. This inspired a string of anti-Chinese ordinances masquerading as public health measures. A "cubic air" law made it a crime, punishable by a fine of up to five hundred dollars and a jail term of up to three months, to offer lodgings with less than five hundred cubic feet of air per person; Chinese rooming houses were plainly the measure's targets, for it was almost never enforced against the rooming houses serving whites. Further ordinances banned the employment of Chinese workers on public projects and the carrying of baskets on poles slung over shoulders, the practice of Chinese peddlers and laundry workers. The state legislature, for its part, decreed stiff penalties for ship captains landing Chinese passengers without written evidence of their good character; that law was invalidated by the US Supreme Court in 1876.

That same year, the city enacted a so-called queue ordinance, requiring that male Chinese prisoners in the city jail be shorn of their distinctive pig-tails. In an 1879 opinion bristling with indignation over the measure's racism and inhumanity, US Supreme Court Justice Stephen Field, sitting as a circuit judge in San Francisco, declared it unconstitutional largely on grounds that it violated the equal protection clause of the Fourteenth Amendment by singling out Chinese prisoners.

Anti-Chinese discrimination became the sine qua non of political platforms in California. Every party, major or minor, tried to appeal to voters by presenting itself as "*the* anti-Chinese party," Henry George observed. (Emphasis his.)

Hostility toward the Chinese was so widespread that it confounded efforts at ridicule. That was the fate of a poem that Bret Harte—then beginning to win fame as the author of the short stories "The Outcasts of Poker Flat" and "The Luck of Roaring Camp"—published in his *Overland Monthly* in September 1870. Titled "Plain Language from Truthful James," this was a picaresque yarn about a game of euchre between a card sharp named Bill Nye and a Chinese player named Ah Sin, identified by the narrator as "the Heathen Chinee." Nye tries to cheat Ah Sin by hiding cards in his sleeve only to discover that he has been outcheated by his would-be mark, whose sleeves are more capacious.

Nye "rose with a sigh / And said, 'Can this be? / We are ruined by Chinese cheap labor' / and he went for that heathen Chinee." The poem ends with a melee and the narrator's conclusion that "for ways that are dark, / And for tricks that are vain, / The heathen Chinee is peculiar."

Harte wrote the poem as a satire of the anti-Chinese prejudices of day laborers in San Francisco, especially among Irish workers. To his dismay, it was universally misinterpreted as an endorsement of working-class prejudices. It became one of the most popular poems published in America up to that time, reprinted coast to coast under the title "The Heathen Chinee," and it was more responsible for Harte's sudden nationwide fame than his prose stories. Lines from the poem became popular catchphrases, especially those referring to the Chinese expertise in "ways that are dark" and "tricks that are vain." Nye's remark about "Chinese cheap labor," an obvious reference to the customary complaint of white laborers, attracted the sympathy of the reading public. Harte, however, would feel mortified by the poem's popularity to the end of his life.

WHEN IT CAME to broader economic affairs, California remained relatively isolated from the rest of the country even after the railroad's completion. Consequently, the state was inoculated against the immediate consequences of a depression in the East triggered by the Panic of 1873. As 1874 drew to a close, the *Bulletin* declared the year to have been "in some respects one of the most prosperous in the history of California."

It was not to last. The US government's abandonment of silver coinage in 1873 caused a panic in silver-mining stocks. On August 26, 1875, the Bank of California, which had been backed by silver from Nevada's Comstock Lode, suffered a run and closed its doors. The next day, the body of the bank's co-founder, a Gilded Age entrepreneur named William Chapman Ralston, was found floating in San Francisco Bay, his death attributed variously to suicide or a stroke he suffered during a swim. Evidence soon emerged that he had been embezzling bank deposits to finance numerous enterprises in San Francisco and Nevada.

Meanwhile, the national depression sent thousands of workers west to California in search of jobs; in 1875 alone, the state's population swelled by more than sixty-five thousand, an increase of more than 10 percent, bringing the depression to San Francisco. "There is more destitution in our city than has existed in many years," the *Bulletin* reported. More poverty produced more unrest. Then came July 1877, when the unrest boiled over.

The immediate trigger for the crisis of violence that gripped the city was a series of railroad strikes that began in Martinsburg, West Virginia, on July 16. The strike metastasized across the country over the next week, with more than one million railroad workers downing tools in the first labor walkout to unfold on a national scale. In San Francisco, a recently organized local branch of the national Workingmen's Party held a mass meeting on a sandlot in front of city hall on the evening of July 23. An estimated eight thousand spectators assembled for what was described as at first a "quiet, orderly, and good-natured" gathering. Before it ended, however, it was invaded by a gang of hecklers who demanded action against the Chinese with the cry "To Chinatown!" That night and into the next day, Chinese laundries and other businesses were broken into and ransacked, Chinese residents were assaulted, and police trying to quell the violence were overwhelmed by rioters in pitched battles.

Mayor Andrew Jackson Bryant, panicked at signs that the police and militiamen were losing control of the situation, called on William Coleman, the leader of the vigilance committees of 1851 and 1856, to come back into service—not as an adversary of elected authority but as head of a duly-constituted "safety committee." Coleman assembled a volunteer force of fifty-five hundred men and equipped them with hickory pick handles shortened into billy clubs. By Saturday, July 28, following a battle with rioters at the wharves, the city was deemed pacified and the safety committee yielded its authority to the police and the National Guard.

ONE MEMBER OF Coleman's pick-handle brigade was Denis Kearney, who would be described sourly by Henry George as "a man of strict temperance in all except speech." Kearney had acquired his oratorical skills at a local Sunday-afternoon debating club called the Lyceum of Self-Knowledge, where as an independent businessman he was known for "the venom with which he abused the working classes" and for his defense of Chinese immigration as a deserved remedy for white workers' sloth and extravagance. He soon would find his footing on the other side of the immigration issue.

Rejected for membership in the Workingmen's Party of the United States because of his anti-worker rhetoric, Kearney resurfaced as a champion of the workingman, proclaiming at a laborers' meeting in September that "a little judicious hanging would be the best course to pursue with the capitalists." He organized the Workingmen's Party of California and offered fire-breathing addresses all over San Francisco, notably in that sandlot atop Nob Hill, where the city's richest residents built their estates. With every speech Kearney made, his oratory became more extravagantly violent and more directly targeted at the railroad tycoons who had been the principal employers of Chinese workers: "If I give an order to hang Crocker, it will be done. . . . They have got to stop this importation of Chinese, or you will see Jackson Street run knee deep in blood." (His reference was to Charles Crocker, one of the four founding investors of the Central Pacific Railroad.)

At that, city authorities had had enough. They arrested Kearney and several fellow party officials for inciting a riot. (The charges were dismissed on a technicality.) In 1878 Kearney embarked on a lecture tour that brought him to Boston, Chicago, St. Louis, and the White House. There he met with President Rutherford B. Hayes, who (according to an account furnished by Kearney's secretary, Carl Brown) pointed to a box in his office brimming with documents pertaining to what he called "the Chinese question." Hayes acknowledged that the "preponderance of evidence is against the Chinese"; he subsequently presided over a renegotiation of the Burlingame Treaty that would lead to tight restrictions on Chinese immigration.

That same year, Workingmen's Party candidates won mayoral elections in Oakland and Sacramento. Kearneyism was a major factor in the creation of a state constitutional convention in 1878 and the drafting of the notorious article 19 of the new constitution, which voters ratified in 1879. The article barred Chinese persons from working on any public project, forbade any California corporation to employ "any Chinese or Mongolian . . . in any capacity," allowed cities and towns to evict Chinese residents or confine them in ghettos, and called on the legislature to prohibit the immigration of any Chinese person into the state.

Article 19 may have been Kearneyism's bridge too far, for it brought the movement to the apogee of its fame and influence. As critics had predicted, it was overturned by a federal court in 1880. Of the two judges hearing the challenge to the provision, one, Ogden Hoffman, found that the prohibition on employing Chinese workers violated the constitutional rights of employers to employ whomever they chose as well as the Burlingame Treaty's guarantee of Chinese rights to immigrate to and travel within the United States. The second judge, Lorenzo Sawyer, focused more on the violation of Chinese residents' right to equal protection under the law embodied in the US Constitution's Fourteenth Amendment, which had been ratified in 1868.

Negotiations with the Chinese government produced a revised Burlingame Treaty in 1880, allowing the United States to "regulate, limit, or suspend" Chinese immigration short of an absolute prohibition. Congress arguably violated that provision with the Chinese Exclusion Act of 1882, which was drafted as a "temporary" ten-year measure. But the act was renewed for another ten years in 1892 and made permanent in 1902. It would not be repealed until 1943, though a limit of 105 Chinese immigrants per year remained in place until 1968. Chinese arrivals in San Francisco surged to nearly 27,000 in the first seven months of 1882, just ahead of the Chinese Exclusion Act's effective date; after that, the number fell to zero.

Anti-Chinese Kearneyism would pervade race relations in the United States into the twenty-first century. Images of crafty queue-wearing Chinese men became fixed in the American cultural landscape, as did disdain for Asians generally. Casual anti-Asian prejudice was an accepted part of public discourse in California, as was evidenced by the crass reference to the catchphrase that "the only good Chinaman is a dead Chinaman" in a one-sentence notice of the death of a Chinese professor at Harvard, published on the front page of the *Los Angeles Times* on February 15, 1882. It bore the headline "A Good Chinaman."

The fortunes of Kearney's Workingmen's Party tumbled with remarkable swiftness. In 1880 the party elected twenty-six state legislators, in 1881 only fourteen, and by 1883 it no longer existed at all. Its Achilles' heel may well have been its single-minded focus on anti-Chinese politics to the exclusion of any other issues that concerned working people of the time, such as the eight-hour day. When Congress effectively ended Chinese immigration in 1882, the party's raison d'être evaporated.

Kearneyism lived on, however, a virus transmitted from California to the United States at large. Nor did Kearney himself disappear. In 1892 he surfaced at a San Francisco rally attacking the Japanese "menace," which had supplanted that of the Chinese in the popular mind. He harangued the crowd about employers importing "another breed of Asiatic slaves to fill up the gap made vacant by the Chinese who are shut out by our laws," and concluded his tirade with the words "The Japs Must Go!"

Kearney's exhortation did not have the same public appeal of his old words, but anti-Japanese agitation would soon become a movement to be reckoned with.

8

THE OCTOPUS

SACRAMENTO, THURSDAY, JANUARY 8, 1863. Dignitaries huddled on a wooden platform in front of the city levee at the foot of K Street under a chilly drizzle—never mind the report in the next day's *Sacramento Union* that "the skies smiled" upon them.

A brass band was on hand, the stands festooned with the sorts of banners and flags customary for a spectacle of political ballyhoo. Leland Stanford, who had been governor of California for only a year, stepped forward to ladle a shovelful of sand from a cart onto the muddy street. When the burly Charles Crocker, Stanford's partner in the undertaking and master of ceremonies for the day, called for cheers, the crowd of legislators, government officials, and local residents obliged.

Thus was launched the construction of the Central Pacific, the western component of what would become the nation's first transcontinental railroad.

Stanford gave a speech in which he pledged that the work just begun would continue "with no delay, no halting, no uncertainty." The Pacific and the Atlantic would be united "by iron bonds that shall consolidate and strengthen the tries of nationality, and advance with great strides the prosperity of our State and of our country," he said. Crocker closed the event with an assurance that "this is no idle ceremony; that the pile-driver is now while I am talking, driving piles for the foundation of the bridge across the American River." The very next morning, he promised, a subcontractor "will proceed across the river and commence the labor of grading."

Well, not really. It would be months before any of that work began and years, amid great tribulation, before it was finished.

The Pacific railroad had long been viewed in California from two perspectives. One was as the absurd fantasy of "a bunch of local storekeepers trying to build a railroad across the continent." The other, however, matched Stanford's description as the binding together of the nation in iron, unlocking the vast economic potential not only of the United States as a whole but, chiefly, of California itself. The first perspective would be validated by the halting progress of the work in its first years, the second by its lasting impact on California, the West, and the United States.

The concept of a transcontinental railroad with its western terminus in California owed much to an obsessed surveyor named Theodore D. Judah. He had come west from Buffalo after supervising the construction of a portion of the Erie Railroad to take charge of the Sacramento Valley Railroad. This venture aimed to service the placer mines spread along the Sierra foothills. Judah led the efforts to survey the route and promote it among financiers in San Francisco. He produced estimates of the construction and operating costs, weighed them against the revenue potential from carrying freight and passengers, and declared, "It is difficult to conceive of a more profitable undertaking."

Judah was described as a "visionary" at a time when the term signified a person given to hallucinations—as was reflected in the other label by which he was known, "Crazy Judah." Of his initial efforts to raise capital for the Pacific railroad in San Francisco, a contemporary wrote that wealthy investors "heard his story; smiled at his enthusiasm, but they secretly buttoned up their pockets and locked their safes and said wisely to each other that the man was an enthusiastic lunatic." Indeed, by 1859 the rich men of San Francisco had had enough experience with Theodore Judah not to thirst for more. The cost of the Sacramento railroad turned out to be triple Judah's estimates, while its operating fortunes fell far short of his predictions, due in part to a financial panic that swept the gold-rush economy in 1855 and the playing-out of mining profits after six years of exploitation.

Judah had turned his attention to the prospects of a transcontinental railroad even while he was running the Sacramento Valley. "Everything he did from the time he went to California to the day of his death was for the great continental Pacific railway," his wife, Anna, reported later. "It was the burden of his thought, day and night." His enthusiasm was shared by the leading citizens of Northern California, at least in principle; it was the practicality of his program that gave them reason for doubt. He favored a route that had been suggested to him by Daniel Strong, a drugstore owner in Dutch Flat, a hamlet in the gold-mining country of the Sierra foothills. Strong had scoped out pathways through the mountains and invited Judah along on a surveying trip by horseback. They traversed some of the most forbidding country in the region, including the Sierra pass where members of the Donner party had met their maker during the ferocious winter of 1846/1847. "There was no wagon road," Strong recalled, "nothing except the marks left by the Donner party, but there was a regular trail."

Judah and Strong set out to find investors for a new California railroad company under a state law that required a thousand dollars in subscriptions for each mile of the proposed route, which Judah estimated at 115 miles. They found the market slow. "I went to San Francisco," Strong recalled, "and the people there laughed at the idea."

They then turned to Sacramento, the second-largest city in the state. "Less than a dozen of us met in a small room over the store of Huntington & Hopkins on K Street" to hear Judah and Strong one day in 1861, recounted Cornelius Cole, a wealthy lawyer and future US senator. Other than Cole, the attendees included four local merchants, including the two owners of the shop downstairs. Eleven of those present would buy shares in the newly organized railroad company, but seven of them would eventually fall away, leaving a tenacious core: Collis Huntington, Mark Hopkins, Leland Stanford, and Charles Crocker.

And so the "Big Four" enter our story.

Huntington, Hopkins, Stanford, and Crocker had all come west during the Gold Rush and made their fortunes by provisioning the Argonauts with dry goods and hardware. As the founders of the Central Pacific, they would earn a permanent place in the pageant of California history.

The four men's business skills were generally complementary, but their temperaments were distinctly discordant.

Collis Huntington was assigned to watch the money. During his childhood in Harwinton, Connecticut, he had learned from his miserly father how to squeeze a dollar until it screamed for mercy. He was indefatigable in plying customers with wares ranging from foodstuffs to cheap jewelry. He sailed from New York in March 1849 at the age of twenty-seven with an inventory of merchandise that included casks of whiskey and beef jerky, which he was able to sell at a handsome markup in the mining zone.

In contrast to the cold and crafty Huntington, Leland Stanford was superficially an amiable, glad-handing sort, which made him the perfect front man to represent the railroad project in local politics—especially after his election as governor in 1861. But he had an uncompromising streak. A Central Pacific executive described him as displaying "the ambition of an emperor and the spite of a peanut vendor"; at the 1885 dedication of the university he had founded in the name of his recently deceased teenage son, Leland Junior, an audience of eight thousand broiled under a blazing sun for hours while orators praised him for granting "the noblest gift in the history of mankind." Stanford hailed from a suburb of Albany, one of eight children of a farmer and innkeeper. Having acquired a law license in New York, he brought it west to Milwaukee to start a legal career, only to fail after a fire destroyed his office and records. In 1852, at twenty-eight, he abandoned the law and sailed to California to join five brothers who had established a grocery business in Sacramento; presently he became the store's manager.

Of the four partners, Crocker was the least averse to physical exertion, a quality he considered an essential feature of his method of leadership. "I had always been the one to swim a river and carry a rope across," he related to the historian H. H. Bancroft. Born in Troy, New York, not far from Stanford's birthplace, he displayed an entrepreneurial streak from childhood, purchasing the local distributorship for a New York newspaper at the age of twelve. Lured by the gold strike in California, he arrived in March 1850 and opened a dry-goods business in Sacramento, prospering as the city grew.

Mark Hopkins was the senior member of the group, forty-eight at the time of the meeting upstairs from his store. He was tall and "thin as a fence post," ascetic in bearing, as befit a man who had been raised in the snowy, frigid north of New York State on the eastern shore of Lake Ontario, only a few miles from the Canadian border. He ate no meat, enjoyed nothing that could even remotely be considered a luxury, and would serve as the partnership's bulwark against unnecessary risk or complexity. Nor could he be moved once he had taken a stand: "When Hopkins wanted to be, he was the stubbornest man alive," Crocker recalled.

The four men at that K Street meeting had done business with one another for years. They were united not only by commerce but by politics. What had first brought them together was their involvement in organizing a Republican Party committee for Sacramento in 1856, the original purpose of which was to block the further extension of slavery in the United States. Over time, as slavery ebbed as an issue in California, the Sacramento Republicans turned the public funding of a railroad into their principal goal.

At first, Judah faced an uphill challenge in persuading the Sacramento businessmen to part with their money. One obstacle was a California law making stockholders in a corporation "individually and personally liable" for its debts, a risk sure to discourage all but the most stouthearted plungers.

Then there was the magnitude of the financial commitment. The state required railroad companies to have enough capital on hand to complete any proposed line. Judah estimated $8.5 million as the cost of the railroad running from Sacramento to the Nevada border. The law mandated that at least ten investors contribute to the initial required subscription of one thousand dollars for each mile, for a capitalization of $115,000. Although the Big Four would later be depicted as wealthy men going in—thanks in part to inflated estimates provided by Huntington to government investigators in the late 1880s—in truth, Bancroft reported, "none of them were rich." Huntington told the government investigators that he and his partners had access to at least $1.4 million in cash and credit, but other estimates placed their net wealth at less than one-tenth that sum. Huntington acknowledged that, even given his liberal estimate, "we had not enough to build the Pacific Road." On the positive side of the ledger was the law's requirement that only 10 percent of the pledged investments had to be paid in cash. This much they were well able to manage. "We agreed at that first meeting," Cole recalled, "to build the railroad over the mountains, little dreaming of the real difficulties to be encountered in that great work."

The initial capitalization was barely enough to finance a conclusive survey by Judah. For the rest, the partners were counting on federal loans via construction bonds to be floated in accordance with a measure already introduced in Congress, and on contributions from state and local governments whose voters slavered over the prospect of increased land values in the railroad's path and the profits to be made in agriculture from improved transportation from farms to markets. By the time of the railroad's completion, the city of San Francisco had contributed nearly $500,000 to the project, Sacramento another $190,000, and several Northern California counties nearly $400,000. During Stanford's governorship, the state agreed to cover twenty years of interest on $1.5 million in railroad bonds at 7 percent a year.

Cole was right about the unanticipated difficulties in constructing the railroad. Judah once again proved to be a sorry judge of costs. The distance from Sacramento to the state line turned out, upon actual measurement, to be not 115 miles but 140 miles. Judah submitted a new estimate for the cost, not $8.5 million but $13 million, the per-mile cost rising from $74,000 per mile to nearly $93,000. One reason for the increase was that the route would require driving eighteen tunnels through the solid rock of the Sierras, including one nearly a quarter of a mile in length.

Stanford sensed the magnitude of the challenge while accompanying a surveying party to the summit of Donner Pass. "We looked down on Donner Lake, 1,200 feet below us, and then looked at the drifts above us 2,000 feet, and I must confess that it looked very formidable," he told the government investigating commission. Yet he did not doubt that the project promised untold opportunity. "We had an idea, like everybody else on this side"—that is, the California side—"that most of the mountains in Nevada were filled with mineral wealth." To bring it out of the mines and into civilization, only the railroad would do.

THE COMING OF the railroad filled some Californians with visions of a glorious destiny. Mark Twain, penning a valedictory in 1866 to the state where he had lived for some five years (and where he had written "The Celebrated Jumping Frog of Calaveras County," the yarn that first brought him literary fame), declared in the newspaper *Alta California*:

> Over slumbering California is stealing the dawn of a radiant future! The great China Mail Line is established, the Pacific Railroad is creeping across the continent, the commerce of the world is about to be revolutionized. California is Crown Princess of the new dispensation! She stands in the center of the grand highways of the nations; she stands midway between the Old World and the New, and both shall pay her tribute.

Others expressed misgivings. One was Henry George, who had arrived in San Francisco in 1858 at the age of eighteen and spent the formative first two decades of his career in California, a period that coincided with the promotion of the Pacific Railroad and its construction. On New Year's Day 1860, at the end of a performance of Shakespeare's *Richard III* he witnessed from the cheap seats in the gallery, George joined the audience in cheering the image on the drop curtain, "for on that curtain was painted what was then a dream of the far future—the overland train coming into San Francisco." However, George wrote, "After we had shouted ourselves hoarse, I began to think what good is it going to be to men like me—to those who have nothing but their labour? . . . As the country grows, as people come in, wages will go down."

In October 1868, with the Golden Spike ceremony barely six months away, George expanded his original nugget of insight into a full examination of California's coming transformation for an article entitled "What the Railroad Will Bring Us."

Anticipation of limitless growth was spreading across the state, George observed. In San Francisco, "no one who walks our streets can fail to be struck with the stirring atmosphere of rapid growth. . . . San Francisco is fast rising to the ranks of a great metropolis. . . . Her greatest growth will date from the completion of the railroad next year."

So, too, "Oakland is laying out, or at least surveying, docks which will cast those of Jersey City, if not Liverpool, into the shade. . . . San Diego is beginning to look forward to the time when she will have steam communication with St. Louis and New Orleans on the one hand, and China and Japan on the other, and be the second city on the coast." (Not even as farsighted a prophet as George could foresee the growth and domination of Los Angeles, then an inconsiderable pueblo with little to recommend it in terms of natural resources.)

In George's view, the danger was that the railroad would bring progress and wealth to only the well-placed and fortunate few. "The California of the new era will be greater, richer, more powerful than the California of the past," he wrote. "But will she have such general comfort, so little squalor and misery; so little of the grinding, hopeless poverty that chills and cramps the souls of men, and converts them into brutes?" Already, the expectation of riches had driven land values out of reach of ordinary people: "The settler who last year might have had at once a farm of his own, must now either go to work for wages or for some one else." Thus would the railroad become an instrument of subjugation. "The locomotive is a great centralizer," George concluded. "It kills towns and builds up great cities, and in the same way kills little businesses and builds up great ones."

George could not avoid sounding a faintly optimistic note: "A great State is forming; let us see to it that its foundations are laid firm and true." But in his warnings he was more right than he could have known.

IT DID NOT take long for public discontent with the railroad to set in. In the railroad's early stages, the dreams of explosive wealth that had driven the local campaigns for its construction were dashed. In retrospect, this was inevitable. Before the coming of the railroad, San Francisco reigned as the West Coast center of commerce. Almost all goods entering California had to come by water—that is, via San Francisco's wharves—and exports of gold and everything else had to leave the same way.

The railroad, however, allowed traders to bypass the city; the merchants and shippers of Chicago took advantage of the possibilities of transcontinental rail "with customary energy and foresight," while those of San Francisco erroneously assumed that business would simply continue coming their way. When the Central Pacific and Union Pacific met at Promontory Summit, Utah, on May 10, 1869, "Chicago was there represented by her agents, while San Francisco, down by the sea, was reading accounts of the event." Eastern manufacturers responded to the opening of a vast new market by flooding the coast with goods at prices that local manufacturers could not hope to match. Meanwhile, the gold mines were playing out and agricultural production shriveled as a result of a severe drought from 1869 to 1871.

When people caught on to the great fortunes the railroad's owners were poised to make, their respect for the project plummeted. In part this was due to a maneuver that was common in the railroad industry of the era, though brought to near perfection by the owners of the Union Pacific and Central Pacific: diverting subsidies and investments to a wholly owned contracting firm through which they pocketed dividends that should properly have been paid to their investors. In effect, the railroad officers were contracting with themselves.

The company used for the Union Pacific's version of this subterfuge was the Crédit Mobilier of America, the centerpiece of a public scandal that erupted in 1872. The Big Four called their version the Contract and Finance Company. The profits they extracted through it were stupendous. Contract and Finance was eventually estimated to have collected some $47.5 million to build 552 miles of the Central Pacific that probably cost no more than $25 million. The facts could never be precisely determined, because soon after the *New York Sun* exposed the Crédit Mobilier scheme, the Contract and Finance books—all fifteen volumes—vanished. Under questioning by a congressional committee, Huntington explained their disappearance by asserting that after Contract and Finance was formally dissolved, the records were incinerated as wastepaper. He attributed the decision to Mark Hopkins, who at the time of the inquiry was three years in the grave.

The Big Four's more enduring stratagem to secure their profits was an old one: monopoly. In 1870, they rolled several small Northern California regional railroads into the Central Pacific; by 1877 the resulting behemoth, now called the Southern Pacific, controlled more than 85 percent of all the railroad track in California, including almost all the lines in the Bay Area, then the state's economic center. The Southern Pacific's domain stretched from Ogden, Utah, to Sacramento, San Francisco, and Oakland and south as far as Los Angeles, leaving shippers with few other means of moving goods into or out of California.

Stanford in particular never tired of ostentatiously displaying his wealth while simultaneously grousing that the federal government was hounding him and his partners to repay the construction bonds, despite their having performed such valiant service to the public. During one dinner at his Nob Hill mansion, Stanford rattled on bitterly about the government's ingratitude toward the builders. "Yes," whispered Stephen Field, then a state supreme court justice, to a fellow guest, his hand sweeping over the hundreds of thousands of dollars' worth of statuary, paintings, and other objets d'art surrounding them, "one has only to look around him here to see how shamefully these gentlemen have been treated."

One California journalist recalled being escorted around the mansion by Stanford. "It looked as if the old palaces of Europe had been ransacked of their art and other treasures to embellish the home of an American gentleman," he reported. A Sèvres vase for which Stanford had paid one hundred thousand dollars bore an inscription indicating that it had been a gift of Marie Antoinette to a French nobleman. For the journalist, the moment evoked the fate of the French queen and the harvest of abuses of power. "Were I Stanford," he reflected, "I would look upon that beautiful work of art as a 'hoodoo,' and neutralize whatever evil spell it might possess by donating it to some institution where its power for good or evil would expend itself, not on an individual, but on the general public."

He was not the first to notice that the fabulous wealth the railroad brought its owners grew out of a dubious devotion to the public interest. The people of California would feel the discrepancy acutely.

9

THE SHADOW OF MUSSEL SLOUGH

HENRY GEORGE'S PREMONITION that the railroad would concentrate wealth and power in very few hands in California was quickly borne out. Almost from the inception of their enterprise, the Southern Pacific's owners worked to solidify their political influence. Huntington ensconced himself in Washington to keep his eye on Congress, which had the power to support or undermine the railroad's interests almost at whim. From a Washington hotel he maintained a vigorous correspondence with railroad vice president David Colton, a veteran political fixer from Sacramento he had installed as a sort of chief of staff at headquarters. Colton acquired so much authority at the Southern Pacific that local newspapers took to calling the Big Four the "Big Four-and-One-Half."

After Colton's sudden death in October 1878, the correspondence he and Huntington had conducted caused posthumous embarrassment to the railroad. More than three hundred letters preserved by his widow, Ellen, became public in 1883 and 1884, in the course of a lawsuit in which she asserted, probably correctly, that the partners had cheated her in a financial settlement after her husband's passing. The so-called Colton letters gave the shocked public a window into the partners' bribery of congressmen and senators through cash payments, free passes on the railroad, and commissions paid for imaginary legal services.

The correspondence documented Huntington's disdain for the political process and his contempt for its practitioners. He described Congress as "the worst body of men that ever before got together in this country." He called

Representative Gilbert C. Walker of Virginia, whom he had gifted with railroad passes, "a slippery fellow" and advised Colton to "do the best you can
with him," but "don't trust him much." Sending Colton an accounting of
his expenditures to secure passage of an advantageous measure in early 1878,
Huntington remarked, "The boys are very hungry and it will cost us considerable to be saved."

Public discontent over the railroad's political and commercial power had
been rising. "From San Francisco to Ogden, nothing is heard but one contin-
uous murmur of complaint," the *Stockton Independent* observed. "There is not
in a single town on any of their lines of road, either in this state or Nevada,
one individual who . . . will speak well of the company, unless it be one of
their subsidized agents."

Yet the railroad still managed to evade efforts to rein it in. The California
legislature had created a board of transportation commissioners in 1876 to
ride herd on the railroad, but although it had endowed the commissioners
with the right to demand information from the company, they responded
only feebly when the Southern Pacific ignored their demands. The 1878
constitutional convention replaced the board with an elected commission of
three members provided with the power to set freight and passenger rates. To
be sure, there were doubts that the elected regulators would succeed where
their predecessors had failed. An Oakland newspaper warned that the new
commission "would soon become a good thing for the railroad men, for they
would readily capture the Commissioners, and matters would be worse than
at present." Its editorialist was right.

On the surface, the new commission was granted impressive authority
indeed. In addition to setting rates, the commissioners were armed with
the right to audit railroad books. Fines and prison terms were provided for
violations of their orders. The issuance of free passes to public officials was
forbidden. Rate wars, through which the Southern Pacific had been able to
bankrupt its competitors, were effectively outlawed by a rule that any railroad that lowered rates to compete with any other transportation company
could not raise them again without the commission's express permission.

One objection to these regulations heard at the convention was that the
commission would be *too* powerful. Yet the Southern Pacific emerged as the
victor in almost all its battles with the commissioners, who almost invariably
voted 2-to-1 or 3-to-0 in its favor. Although rate cuts were almost always on
the commission's docket, none that the Southern Pacific found objectionable

were ever implemented. Commission reports were "filled with apologies for the existing rates," observed a contemporary critic. In 1883, the commission imposed maximum freight rates of four to six cents per mile—higher than what the railroad was already charging.

The keys to the Southern Pacific's ability to defy regulatory oversight were the commissioners' unfamiliarity with the complexities of railroad operations, and, more important, the siren call of money. C. J. Beerstecher, one of the first commissioners to take office, had been the nominee of Kearney's Workingmen's Party and therefore was expected to maintain a strong anti-railroad stance. In practice, however, "he seemed anxious to take no action not explicitly approved by Towne [A.N. Towne, the Southern Pacific's general manager] or Leland Stanford." Beerstecher was later revealed to have increased his personal wealth by as much as twenty thousand dollars during his four years in office. His "sudden acquisition of wealth while Commissioner . . . admits of no other explanation than that he was bribed," a legislative committee reported. Beerstecher's colleague in the commission's pro-railroad majority, J. S. Cone, a rich Northern California rancher, collected a profit of one hundred thousand dollars through a series of intricate land transactions in which the railroad's treasurer served as the counterparty.

Before the railroad was ten years old, it had infuriated every major commercial interest group in the state. Farmers and manufacturers resented its manipulation of freight rates, exporters its collusion with the overseas steamship line Pacific Mail (and subsequently its creation of a steamship subsidiary of its own), homesteaders its ownership of vast arable acreage.

The last issue would give rise to the prototypical conflict between the railroad and the people. To this day it is known as the Battle of Mussel Slough. Historians continue to ponder its details and meaning, their task somewhat complicated by Frank Norris's overwrought fictionalizing of the episode in his 1901 novel depicting the railroad's despotic influence over California, *The Octopus*.

The Battle of Mussel Slough originated in the Central Valley's unusual topography as a lowland sink. Unlike much of the semi-arid valley, the slough benefited from relatively abundant water, which facilitated irrigation, and from the construction of a Southern Pacific spur to carry produce to market. Hundreds of settlers and their families migrated to the slough starting in the early 1870s; by the end of that decade, its sixty thousand acres constituted the state's most intensively developed agricultural region, with farms and ranches devoted to corn, fruit, and dairy cattle, all dependent on the railroad for access to their markets. But a time bomb was quietly ticking away. Although the railroad owned the land, its interest lay in selling it off quickly to raise capital; the question was, at what price?

The Mussel Slough settlers maintained that the railroad had promised to sell them the land they occupied for $2.50 an acre, as specified by a circular the railroad had distributed. This was a narrow and optimistic reading of the document, which promised sales at "from $2.50 *upward* per acre." (Emphasis added.) That said, the railroad had implied that the farmers would receive a low price; higher rates, the circular stated, were mostly for "land covered by tall timber," which did not exist in Mussel Slough. In practice, however, the Southern Pacific demanded twenty dollars or more per acre, with some settlers charged as much as one hundred.

The image of a profiteering railroad cheating an agricultural yeomanry drew anti-railroad agitators to the settlers' cause. Denis Kearney staged a series of rallies in the slough at which he called on the settlers to "murder the red-eyed monsters." The *San Francisco Chronicle* declared that the settlers were poised to "strike the first blow against land monopoly and corporate greed."

The dismal truth was that the settlers had virtually no legal standing. In a series of decisions starting in December 1879, federal judges ruled that the Southern Pacific's title to the land was unassailable. In other words, settlers who resisted the railroad's offers to sell could be legally ousted as trespassers and squatters. The railroad piled up eviction orders along with judgments for damages. Most of the more than five hundred occupants bowed to the inevitable and reached agreements with the railroad, sometimes at a discount to the railroad's initial demand but nowhere as low as $2.50 an acre. By March 1880, only a few holdouts remained in opposition. They were assembled into a ragged militia by John J. Doyle, an orchestrator of fraudulent land claims, and a luxuriantly bearded former Confederate major and land speculator named Thomas Jefferson McQuiddy. The fuse for the Battle of Mussel Slough was about to be lit.

The detonation came on May 11, 1880. That morning, US Marshal Alonzo Poole rode into Hanford, the main settlement in the slough. Armed and perched on a buggy with a land officer named William H. Clark, Poole intended to evict the last few squatters. Along the way Poole and Clark met up with Mills D. Hartt and Walter Crow, who had purchased properties from the railroad and were to be the beneficiaries of the dispossession and who also carried weapons. The four were approached by a group of armed men on horseback—fifteen by some accounts, more than forty according to others.

Not for the first time in California nor the last, what began as a confused scuffle ended in bloodshed. The most credible version of what ensued is that the horsemen tried to disarm Marshal Poole, who resisted. While he stood his ground, he was kicked by a horse, presumably by accident. At that moment a shot rang out, provoking a general melee. Horses shied out of control; rifle and shotgun blasts filled the air. Seven men were dead or mortally wounded: Hartt, Crow, and five horsemen. Who shot first and who fired at whom will forever be unknown.

Doyle and five squatters were ultimately convicted in federal court of interfering with a federal officer. Each was sentenced to a prison term of one year and a fine of three hundred dollars. McQuiddy eluded arrest for two years, even while campaigning for governor of California on the Greenback Party ticket. Eventually he was taken into custody, but procedural complications delayed his trial so long that his indictment was dismissed.

The episode fixed in the public mind the image of the Southern Pacific as a rapacious, unyielding bully and provided a reliable focal point for anti-railroad agitation for decades to come. This was especially so after Norris published *The Octopus,* twenty years after the event.

The battle also prompted the railroad to take control of its public image, largely by suppressing negative publicity. Settlers trying to transmit news of the confrontation to the outside world in its immediate aftermath discovered that the telegraph operator at Hanford had been instructed to accept only messages addressed to railroad headquarters. The railroad painted the settlers as instigators and thugs, circulating a fabricated report that armed settlers had dragged the telegraph operator from his post and forced him to walk fifteen miles to safety at Goshen.

Having imposed a news blackout about the Battle of Mussel Slough, the railroad proceeded to fill the vacuum with its own version. Charles Crocker led teams of Southern Pacific employees into newspaper offices in San Francisco to reinforce the railroad's portrayal of the settlers as trespassers standing in the way of a lawful transfer of property. San Francisco readers never learned of demonstrations in the Central Valley sympathetic to the squatters, including a line of residents some two miles long accompanying the horse-drawn carts carrying the corpses of the five slain settlers to the cemetery. By the time outside journalists reached Mussel Slough and sent back reports less favorable to the railroad, the public had largely lost interest in the details.

By the 1890s the railroad's ability to protect its franchise and profits from public interference was nearly total. "What chief executive of the state . . . has there been who did not owe his nomination and election to the Southern Pacific Company and in acknowledgment of his debt hasten to obey its slightest command?" asked J. M. Bassett, a former secretary to Leland Stanford, in one of a series of open letters addressed to Huntington published in the 1890s. "How many Superior Courts are there in the State in which a citizen may bring an action against you in full confidence that he will be fairly and impartially dealt with?"

Politicians understood that to thwart the railroad was to risk losing their offices to a railroad nominee. The Southern Pacific's financial patronage was dispensed at the discretion of William F. Herrin, the head of its "political bureau." The three governors who served from 1899 to 1911—Henry T. Gage, George C. Pardee, and James N. Gillett—effectively functioned as railroad stooges. Herrin paid Abraham Ruef, the corrupt political boss of San Francisco, to deliver the city's delegation at the 1906 state Republican convention to Gillett, the railroad's choice for governor. The evening after the vote, Gillett and Ruef were guests of Republican chairman Frank McLaughlin at a dinner party that included five other railroad-anointed politicians. Ruef called for a photographer to commemorate the occasion. The resulting photograph appeared in the *San Francisco Call* over the caption "The Shame of California." Gillett won anyway.

The railroad rendered most of the press docile through generous infusions of cash. When the journalist Fremont Older joined the *San Francisco Bulletin* as managing editor, he learned that the newspaper was receiving $125 per month from the railroad for "friendliness." Since this sum sometimes spelled the difference between red ink and black for the struggling publication, Older was unsuccessful at persuading its owner that there were greater profits to be earned by taking an editorial stance in opposition to the railroad.

"The entire State of California was, at that time, politically controlled by the Southern Pacific Railroad," Older recounted. "Not only did this powerful organization dominate the legislature, the courts, the municipal governments, the county governments . . . but it also had as complete control of the newspapers of the state as was possible, and through them it controlled public opinion."

One exception was William Randolph Hearst's *San Francisco Examiner*, which initially went along, due to monthly thousand-dollar installments of what purported to be a thirty-thousand-dollar contract for advertising. Herrin was not shy, however, about reminding the newspaper's business manager that the sums would be considered grossly excessive if viewed strictly as payments for advertising space alone; rather, he said, "the chief consideration to inure to the Southern Pacific Company . . . was the fair treatment to be accorded by your paper." Hearst ultimately canceled the contract after concluding, as had Older at the *Bulletin*, that more money was to be made by presenting itself to readers as an opponent of the railroad than by accepting its patronage. Another holdout was the *Wasp*, a San Francisco satirical magazine founded in 1876. Under the editorship of the acerbic Ambrose Bierce from 1881 to 1885, the magazine waged an unceasing campaign against the railroad, originally bestowing on it the label of "the Octopus" that Norris later made famous.

In 1886, Hearst lured Bierce to the *Examiner* by inviting him to Washington to cover a congressional fight over a major bill the railroad had concocted. This was known as the Funding Bill. It concerned the timing and cost by which the railroad had to redeem the government bonds that had financed the Central Pacific's construction. The bonds were scheduled to mature between 1895 and 1899, when principal and interest (at 6 percent a year) would come due, totaling as much as $164 million. The railroad proposed to refinance the debt for as long as 125 years at a reduced rate of 2 percent.

The proposal elicited a furious public reaction in California. A mass meeting in San Francisco yielded an open letter addressed to congressional leaders describing the Southern Pacific's owners as "men who have for thirty years been wrecking a railroad, defrauding the Government, corrupting public morals, plundering and oppressing the people, and violating every principle of business probity, or law, right, justice and public policy." Sentiment rose for a government takeover of the company if it failed to meet its obligations.

Bierce launched his coverage for Hearst with a characteristically caustic broadside at Huntington. "Mr. Huntington is not altogether bad," he wrote. "Though severe, he is merciful. . . . He says ugly things of the enemy, but he has the tenderness to be careful that they are mostly lies." Over the subsequent months, he turned out more than sixty articles in this vein. The assignment gave rise to one of the most oft-cited anecdotes from Bierce's life, involving a personal encounter with Huntington on a Washington street. Huntington supposedly asked Bierce to state his price to lay off, to which Bierce replied, "My price is one hundred thirty million dollars. If, when you are ready to pay, I happen to be out of town, you may hand it over to my friend, the Treasurer of the United States."

The railroad's proposal was defeated in Congress in 1897, provoking a citywide celebration in San Francisco reported by the *Examiner* in a front-page article headlined "San Francisco Wild with Joy at Downfall of the Huntington Lobby." Congress finally settled the debt at $58.8 million, to be guaranteed by the entire Southern Pacific, not merely by earnings on the original Central Pacific line, and deferred the maturity date by ten years at a reduced interest rate of 3 percent. That was less than the railroad might have had to pay had the original terms remained in force but still more than it had hoped to pay and on stricter terms than it had proposed.

Huntington's powers of persuasion appeared to be failing. While he was fighting the funding controversy, he was also waging a battle over the construction of a seaport for Los Angeles. The city and its business establishment favored development at San Pedro, about twenty-five miles south of the city center, where a modest harbor dredged out of a salt marsh already existed. Huntington, however, had invested in a coastal tract at Santa Monica, about fifteen miles west of the city, access to which was monopolized by his Southern Pacific. Either location would require a federal subsidy for dredging and for building breakwaters. Huntington waged a vigorous battle to swing the federal judgment toward his choice.

Southern California businesses, which had long felt the sting of the Southern Pacific's monopolistic behavior, mobilized against it. The railroad controlled almost 90 percent of California's rail traffic, charging piratical cargo rates. Business and political leaders foresaw that if Huntington persuaded the government to pump millions of dollars into construction of a port at Santa Monica, the railroad "would seal its grip over them for generations to come." The cry of "anti-monopoly," sounded by such influential local personages as Harrison Gray Otis and by politicians in Sacramento, won the day in Congress. At almost the same moment that the Southern Pacific lost on the funding bill, Huntington lost on the harbor decision, which went to San Pedro.

Huntington still reigned at the railroad, however. The most telling indication of his power came in 1890, when he orchestrated Stanford's resignation as president of the railroad.

Huntington and Stanford were then the last surviving members of the Big Four, Hopkins having died in 1878 and Crocker in 1888. For five years, Huntington had nurtured a seething resentment over Stanford's having cheated one of Huntington's friends out of his candidacy for the US Senate so Stanford could take the job himself. Huntington persuaded Stanford to step aside voluntarily from the railroad's presidency by signing a joint agreement that the partners "shall in good faith refrain from hostile or injurious expressions concerning each other." Stanford, who retained figurehead roles as a member of the railroad's board and chairman of its executive committee, was amenable to the deal. He was in declining health, focused on building his university and serving in the Senate, and satisfied that the agreement would keep the enmity between himself and Huntington a secret.

Huntington promptly blew the agreement to smithereens. With what Stanford's biographer described as "studied malice," Huntington declared in his inaugural speech as the railroad's president: "In no case will I use this great corporation to advance my personal ambition at the expense of its owners, or put my hands into the treasury to defeat the people's choice, and thereby put myself in positions that should be filled by others."

Huntington's transparent attack on his partner's integrity crushed Stanford, who had courted the esteem of the public in his political career; his wife's secretary recalled that when he returned home from the railroad's annual meeting that night, "he appeared to have grown years older than when he left in the morning." Three years later, he was dead.

As the last survivor of the Big Four, Huntington ran the Southern Pacific as a personal fiefdom. He spent his final years rejecting repeated offers from Edward H. Harriman, then the owner of the Union Pacific, who wished to extend his growing empire by acquiring the Southern Pacific. But on August 13, 1900, Huntington suddenly lapsed into a coma and died at his country retreat in upstate New York. His heirs gave in to the blandishments of Harriman, who would prove to be an even more determined monopolist than Huntington and his partners.

The Octopus might have earned its nickname under the original Big Four, but under Harriman, the enterprise became even more powerful, its tentacles extending ever further into the economy of California. The public's reaction would influence state politics through the decades ahead.

10

THE FIRST WATER WAR

THE RAILROAD TYCOONS were the chief beneficiaries of Californians' determination to remake the state's landscape by hand, but they were not alone. Many others were inspired to seek their fortunes by manipulating and exploiting California's natural gifts, the most important of which was water.

Starting in the mid-nineteenth century, California was defined by water—or, to be precise, by its scarcity. The historian Bernard DeVoto, grasping for a precise definition of the West, delivered what is perhaps the best-known rendition. "The West begins," he wrote, "where the average annual rainfall drops below twenty inches." DeVoto placed that demarcation line at the one hundredth meridian, which cleaves through the Dakotas, Nebraska, Kansas, Oklahoma, and Texas. But his definition applied most profoundly to the California of the Gold Rush and the railroad, which deposited passengers beyond the one hundredth meridian to make their fortunes, if they could, in the Golden State.

Before the railroad's completion, the fortune-seekers came by other means. Two German immigrants, Henry Miller and Charles Lux, each reached San Francisco by steamship around the time of the discovery of gold.

Years later, having built a landholding empire based on water rights, Miller boasted of having arrived in San Francisco in 1850 with nothing but a walking stick in his hand and six dollars in his pocket. Born Heinrich Alfred Kreiser in 1827 in Brackenheim, a small town outside Stuttgart, he immigrated to New York in 1847; he later changed his name to Henry Miller in conformance with the steamship ticket to California he bought from an acquaintance, an example of the personal reinvention for which California would become known. The Alsace-born Lux arrived in California in 1849 also by way of New York, where he had immigrated to at the age of sixteen and found work as a butcher's helper for six dollars a month.

LIKE MANY OTHERS who reaped lasting fortunes during the Gold Rush, they made their millions not by toiling in the diggings but by provisioning those who did—in their case, as butchers in San Francisco. In 1851, when Miller and Lux both had accumulated enough capital to open their own retail shops, they jointly purchased a herd of sixteen hundred Texas cattle for slaughter. Four years later they partnered again, this time establishing a lasting enterprise for land acquisition and cattle raising, the Miller and Lux Company.

Lux was the more suave of the two, gliding as smoothly as a swan among San Francisco's emerging high society. He had gained entry into the city's elite by marrying a widow named Miranda Wilmarth Sheldon, a doyenne of the newly developing society district of Nob Hill. Miller tended to shun Lux's social milieu, though he stayed close enough to marry Miranda's sister Nancy and, after her death, to successfully court Nancy's twenty-year-old niece Sarah. In general, Lux stayed in San Francisco to manage the partnership's business affairs and hobnob with the judges and other officials with power over its activities while Miller remained in the field, handling the acquisition of land, livestock, and manpower from his seventeen-hundred-acre farm in rural Gilroy, eighty miles from the city.

Miller acquired much of the company's lands from San Joaquin Valley settlers who had hastened to the goldfields, leaving their properties to go fallow. In this way, according to his first biographer, Edward Treadwell, a sedulous admirer who served as Miller's attorney, he assembled an initial holding of 8,900 acres for a bargain price averaging $1.15 an acre, along with 7,500 head of cattle for five dollars a head.

Miller further exploited a federal program that ceded land to the states for the latter to redistribute as they wished. An 1850 law had granted the states title to "swamp and overflow" federal lands within their borders—some two million acres in California alone. The definition of *swampland* was "a farce and a sham," in the judgment of Horace Greeley, who had been a member of the House of Representatives when the bill was drafted. In fact, Greeley observed, whole expanses of ostensibly waterlogged and worthless acreage "had not muck enough on their surface to accommodate a single fair-sized frog." That did not keep the states from selling these acres to entrepreneurs savvy enough to know the difference between the parcels' legal categorization as wasteland and their true value as pasture. According to an enduring legend, Miller hitched a team of horses to a boat and had it hauled over one tract of dry land so he could claim that the land was waterlogged.

Miller was also adept at exploiting the labor of homeless drifters. He did so by handing out two-bit pieces (twenty-five cents) and letting it be known that a "tramp" could get a meal at a Miller rancho without working but only one meal and only from an already-used plate unless he contributed his labor. "They have established what is called the dirty-plate route in order to keep labor there in the country," economist Edward F. Troy testified to congressional investigators in 1914.

A Miller and Lux employee later estimated the mob of migrants at about one thousand men moving from company farm to company farm, constituting a provisional workforce that resembled today's freelance gig workers. This gave Miller flexibility to meet seasonal needs, such as when thousands of sheep needed to be sheared in the spring.

Others testified to the squalor of the dirty-plate route. "There was not sufficient room, nor were there accommodations for the ordinary decencies of life," wrote H. A. Van Coenen Torchiana, an ex-foreman for Miller and Lux, in an account published in 1930 under the title *California Gringos.* "Often the men slept on manure piles to keep warm . . . The whole system was vicious, and bred industrial oppression on a large scale."

California's farm districts looked nothing like those of other states. One could search in vain for family farmhouses surrounded by fields of tended crops; instead, there were rows of barracks-like shacks and croplands swarming at harvesttime with workers in thrall to slow-moving machines while their masters remained comfortably ensconced in their city mansions. "There is not another State in the Union where everything outside of city limits is so unrural, so contractor-like," one writer observed in 1884. "I did not see ten honest, hard-fisted farmers in my whole journey. . . . For laborers, there are runaway sailors; reformed street thieves; bankrupt German scene-painters"—while "plenty of city-haunting old bachelors and libertines live and die in 'Frisco.'"

As ruthless as Miller and Lux were in acquiring land and managing their workers, they were even stricter when it came to water, the lifeblood of their ranching and agricultural empire. They and their fellow land barons, Troy testified, "have taken every means of driving people off, to get control of the water that is so essential to their land," chiefly "through expensive litigation, and also by means of force." He recounted the experience of a widow in the Central Valley "who wanted to dam up a torrential stream that is dry all the year around except when a little rain comes into it, and Miller & Lux told her if she attempted to dam that up they would take her into court."

The scarcity of water, the cost of husbanding and distributing the supply for irrigation, and the ability of Miller, Lux, and other capitalists to assemble large tracts of arable territory through their connections with the railroad and government officials created a model of the agricultural economy that persists to this day and eventually spread across the country: plantation-scale mechanized farms owned by absentee investors and worked by migrants.

The decades following the Gold Rush saw tracts spanning hundreds of thousands of acres come into the possession of fewer than half a dozen speculators. By 1870, Miller and Lux owned 450,000 acres in parcels so large that enclosing one required 160 miles of fencing. Miller was quoted as boasting that he could drive his livestock from Oregon to Mexico and "sleep every night in one of his own ranches."

Ranchos of this magnitude were not what the state's founding fathers had envisioned. California's third governor, John Bigler, declared after taking office in 1852 that subdividing public lands into small tracts for farming would "induce emigration to the State" and reduce "the power of unscrupulous capitalists and speculators to monopolize the very necessaries of life, and thus to reduce the laboring classes, in many cases, to the verge of starvation."

It was not to be. The government office charged with surveying and entitling land became known for its staggering corruption. Its surveyors were often the owners of huge tracts themselves, and fraudulent transfers to large landowners of properties originally claimed by small farmers were common. In 1872, the largest 122 farms in the state averaged more than 72,000 acres each, encompassing more land than the total occupied by the 33,000 farms that were smaller than 500 acres.

Miller and his compatriots were "the lords of California—lords as truly as ever were ribboned Dukes or belted Barons in any country under the sun," wrote Henry George. "California is not a country of farms, but a country of plantations and estates."

The land barons, George wrote, exacted a merciless toll on settlers who had hoped to sustain themselves and their families by homesteading: There was no state in the union "in which settlers in good faith have been so persecuted, so robbed, as in California." The barons "still make a regular business of blackmailing settlers upon public land, or of appropriating their homes, and this by the power of the law and in the name of justice. Land grabbers have had it pretty much their own way in California—they have moulded the policy of the General Government; have dictated the legislation of the state; have run the land offices and used the courts."

This was no secret—indeed, for the winners, it was the subject of pride. Treadwell wrote admiringly of Miller's ability to exact freight rebates from the Southern Pacific Railroad unavailable to other ranchers and growers: "The railroad was his partner." Like plutocrats throughout history, Miller used his wealth to acquire political influence and used his political influence, in turn, to acquire greater wealth. "Assessors could not over-assess him," Treadwell wrote. "Legislatures could not impose excessive taxes upon him. He belonged to the 'organization,' and the State belonged to the organization too."

Another benefit that monopolization gave Miller and Lux was the ability to exploit riparian water rights. The riparian legal doctrine, which prevailed in the well-watered eastern United States, provided the owners of land adjacent to streams with the right to freely use all the water flowing past their property as long as their usage did not interfere with the rights of landowners downstream. Watering livestock or irrigating crops on a ranch or farm bordering a stream, for instance, was permitted on the reasoning that the water would eventually drain back into the waterway in one form or another.

That could not happen, however, if water was transported out of a stream's watershed, say for the irrigation of distant farms or for the ditches, sluices, and pipelines of mines, which were typically located far from the source.

In those cases, an alternative legal doctrine known as "prior appropriation" came into play. The product of a prospecting tradition that gave the first settler to stake a claim the right to its gold, prior appropriation gave the right to a stream's water to the first person to divert and use it. Under this doctrine, the principle of "first in time, first in right" governed, as long as the priority holder continued to use the water for the original purpose.

Prior appropriation enabled California mining to evolve from the individual and small-group diggings of the first Gold Rush years into a large-scale, industrialized system. The standard technology was hydraulic mining, in which a torrent of water under high pressure blasted away soil and boulders to expose the gold veins underneath. In his autobiographical 1872 work *Roughing It*, Mark Twain described the environmental devastation this unleashed on the Sacramento Valley: "You may still see, in places, its grassy slopes and levels torn and guttered and disfigured by the avaricious spoilers of fifteen and twenty years ago." Hydraulic mining was effectively outlawed by court order in 1884, but its dismaying consequences would inspire naturalists like John Muir to crusade for the preservation of what had not yet been ruined.

The riparian and prior appropriation doctrines were naturally incompatible, since the first forbade the permanent diversion of water while the second established diversion rights as law. Despite their mutual tension, they remained equally entrenched for some three decades after the Gold Rush, each endorsed by state and federal courts alike.

The riparian principle guided Miller and Lux's land purchases through the 1870s. Smallholders had neither the money nor the political capital to stand in their way; ultimately the partners secured ownership of a one-hundred-mile strip of land along the San Joaquin River and another strip of fifty miles along the Kern River, providing them with the water they needed for growing alfalfa for cattle feed. The drought-and-flood weather patterns of central California drove their acquisition of more and more riparian properties, for only through expansive landholdings could nature's extremes be held at bay. Yet sometimes nature would not be denied: During a punishing drought in 1877, Miller informed Lux that "the whole country [is] burned up . . . [a] great deal of stock will be loosed without [we] kill them off, to keep them from starving."

A greater threat to Miller and Lux emerged that same year, when they discovered that water in large quantities was being diverted upstream of their holdings on the Kern River—and not by a small landholder who could be intimidated but by a rival industrialist rich and powerful enough to fight them to a draw. His name was James Ben Ali Haggin. Their battle would span seven years and result in one of the longest opinions ever issued by the California Supreme Court, a landmark two-hundred-page ruling in the case known as *Lux v. Haggin*.

Notwithstanding his exotic middle name—drawn from his maternal grandfather, a Turkish-born physician—Haggin was the scion of a socially prominent family in Louisville, Kentucky. He had established a legal practice in New Orleans before coming west during the Gold Rush for what he expected to be a two-year sojourn. Instead, in partnership with his brother-in-law Lloyd Tevis, he established himself as a successful investor with stakes in San Francisco's gaslighting utility, a mining company in Utah, and the banking and transportation firm Wells, Fargo and Company.

The pair's biggest venture was in the vast semi-arid southern plains of the Central Valley. Perceiving that the territory could become a productive Eden if it was irrigated, they purchased water rights from small farmers who were irrigating their crops by ditch and canal. Much of this acquisition was accomplished by subterfuge in a scheme developed by William B. Carr, a third partner. Carr's unscrupulous character was well known in San Francisco, where the *Argonaut* newspaper identified him as one of "a ring of mercenary bandits who steal to get office and who get office to steal," but he was not as well known in the farming interior. Acting as land agent for Haggin and Tevis, Carr induced smallholders to issue shares in their own farms, ostensibly to attract investment. He then bought up the shares, enabling him to seize the farmers' land and water rights. Haggin and Tevis incorporated the Kern County Land and Water Company as the proprietor of more than four hundred thousand acres. Citing the doctrine of prior appropriation, the company claimed the right to divert three times as much water as the river actually carried.

Haggin posed as the champion of the ordinary farmer. "My object has not been, nor do I wish to monopolize large bodies of land," he asserted publicly, "but I desire to make valuable and available that which I have by extending irrigation ditches over my lands . . . and divide them up and sell them . . . in small tracts with the water rights necessary for irrigation." In other words, Haggin was presenting himself as a defender of prior appropriation against big-money adversaries exploiting their riparian rights to block the upstream farmers' diversions for irrigation—against, that is, Miller and Lux.

Yet Haggin was every bit as ruthless as Miller and Lux when he encountered resistance to his quest for water. He cut off supplies to recalcitrant settlers, forcing them to sell their land to his company, and filed more than one hundred lawsuits against farmers who diverted water from the Kern River for their own use. These court cases were especially menacing because his company had the wealth and influence to obtain favorable rulings from local judges.

That was not likely to faze Miller and Lux, who themselves possessed considerable political influence and whose fortunes depended on preserving their access to the Kern River. For them, the consequences of Haggin's upstream diversions became crystal clear during the 1877 drought, which reduced the river to a nearly dry gulch interspersed with "green and slimy sinks of stagnant water" and "streaks of mud" fouled by the carcasses of dead cattle. They tried to strike a deal with Haggin, bargaining for one-fourth of the river's flow in exchange for relinquishing their riparian rights to the rest. Haggin, encouraged by a mood in the countryside that favored prior appropriation, refused. That provoked Miller and Lux to sue.

The California Supreme Court found for Miller and Lux in 1886. Its monumental ruling, however, failed to clarify the law. The state's high court ruled that riparian doctrine was the prevailing law in California but allowed that it could be outweighed by prior appropriators under certain conditions, such as when diversions were made before a landowner acquired riparian property downstream. This hybrid finding became known as the California doctrine and would soon become the standard in states as far east as Texas. Depending on the conditions of ownership, either doctrine might prevail. In practice, although the court bowed to the riparian doctrine as settled law, the effective principle was still "first in time, first in right." The unstated subtext of the decision was that irrigation, the chief purpose of diverting river water, was important enough to warrant the law's protection in California—even, if necessary, at the expense of riparian rights.

This was not an uncommon or extreme position at the time, when millions of acres of potentially productive land lay fallow for want of water. With the advent of improved rail networks and refrigerated railcars (practical versions of which first appeared in the 1870s), California-grown fruits and other specialty crops could reach nationwide markets hungering for fresh produce all year long, underscoring the hydraulic urgency. The theory, as one historian wrote, was "deliverance through irrigation: irrigation as the people's choice, the benefactor of the common folk, savior of our dreams, defenders of our institutions."

The virtues of irrigation were understood even by the naturalist John Muir. In 1874, the future crusader for preserving the landscape in its natural condition praised the human engineering that distributed the natural bounty of rain from the Sierra Nevadas over the once-parched plains of the Central Valley via a three-foot-deep ditch:

> The thirsty ground is being watered, cheerless shanties, sifted through and through with dry winds, are being displaced by true homes embowered in trees and lovingly broidered with flowers; and contentment, which in California is perhaps the very rarest of the virtues, is now beginning to take root.

Muir did acknowledge that as long as the most important ditches were owned by big companies that refused to sell water to small farmers, "true agricultural independence seems impossible." Still, he asserted, "irriguous revivals are breaking out all over the glad plains."

MILLER AND LUX, who had secured their riparian rights before Haggin began to dam the Kern River, appeared to be the victors in the state supreme court's ruling—legally speaking. In a sense they won too much, for they still needed Haggin's dam to regulate the Kern's flow. In the river "there is more water than we can use, and it does not come at the right time of the year," Miller observed. "It comes in a great flood early in the spring, and in the hot months of summer the river is dry." He made another overture to his adversary, and this time they reached a deal: If Haggin built a reservoir to flatten out the seasonal flows, Miller and Lux would cede to him two-thirds of the streamflow.

With the *Lux v. Haggin* ruling threatening to make "deliverance through irrigation" a remote prospect for small farmers, the state legislature moved to break up the land monopolies that were the real obstacle to saving the common folk. Its solution was the Wright Act, passed in 1887. The act authorized the creation of local irrigation districts with the power to condemn and assume private water rights by eminent domain, making it what the *San Francisco Chronicle* lauded as "all that stands between the rich water monopolist and the poor farmer."

The *Chronicle* was too optimistic about the law. Irrigation expanded in its wake, but at first only to about one and a half million acres, a tiny fraction of the state's twenty-eight million acres of irrigable farmland. Most of the gains occurred on the large estates because only they, not the community water districts, could afford to build waterworks. All but a handful of the dozens of districts formed under the Wright Act failed within a few short years due to legal attacks by rich riparian interests and the dearth of capital. Still, over time and after a series of revisions to the act in the first decades of the twentieth century, irrigation took hold in California, with watered acreage reaching 4.2 million acres by 1920. The "golden age of California agriculture" had begun.

YET THE EXPANSION of irrigation would only sharpen conflicts over water, thanks to the murky principles underlying *Lux v. Haggin*. The ruling has bedeviled California water policy for more than 130 years.

The state supreme court itself struggled to make sense of it, issuing a string of contradictory follow-on rulings from 1886 through 1926, when its dithering over a new lawsuit finally provoked voters to try settling matters through a ballot initiative.

The trigger was a lawsuit pitting a family of landowners on the San Joaquin River against the utility empire of Henry E. Huntington, the nephew and protégé of Collis Huntington. Miller and Lux cast an indirect but heavy shadow over the case, for the landowning family had leased their lands to the firm for cattle raising. The family's complaint was that Huntington's power company was holding seasonal floodwaters in a reservoir for electric generation, reducing the flow downstream. The case involved those two perennially discordant issues in California and across the West: one, private property rights in water, and two, the public's need and desire for economic development.

In *Herminghaus v. Southern California Edison*, the court took a step back from its landmark 1886 ruling by vastly narrowing the ability of appropriators to interfere with riparian landowners' rights. That posed a major threat to the expansion of irrigation and the growth of urban areas, which needed appropriated water to serve their burgeoning populations. The only answer to the threat was to rewrite the law; in 1928, a constitutional amendment limited all water rights to only the water "reasonably required for the beneficial use to be served."

If its goal was to clarify matters, it failed, as it left undefined the terms *reasonably* and *beneficial*. To this day, those terms remain subject to dispute. A resolution of the conflict over water in California seems as distant and unattainable as ever. In this, as in so many other matters, the seeds of a dilemma that affects communities across the country and indeed globally—how to manage ever scarcer water supplies—first sprouted in California. History suggests that the first solutions will appear in California too.

11

"CITY OF THE DAMNED"

FOR DAYS THE weather had been hot and dry, the sun a bleached orb in the sky, a south wind streaming over the parched land and out to sea. It was what San Franciscans called earthquake weather.

James Hopper left the Grand Opera House on Mission Street just after midnight on April 18, 1906. He headed for the *San Francisco Call* newsroom to turn in his report on the performance by the visiting Metropolitan Opera Company of New York, with Enrico Caruso in the role of Don José in *Carmen*. Hopper's ears were still ringing with Don José's wail of grief at realizing that he had slain his beloved Carmen in a fit of jealousy.

"Surely," Hopper thought, "what I have felt tonight is the summit of human emotion."

By the time he reached his rooms and went to bed, it was three a.m. On the way home he had passed a livery stable and been startled by a sudden inhuman cry and the thunder of hoofbeats in the stalls. "Restless tonight," the stableman told him. "Don't know why."

Hopper spent another couple of hours in troubled slumber, dreaming of Caruso and Don José, until a few minutes after five a.m.—"And then," he would write, "I awoke to the city's destruction."

For the first few seconds there was "a feeling of incredulity at the violence of the vibrations . . . Then the feeling of finality." As he dressed to go outside and gauge the extent of the damage, Hopper saw the back wall of his three-story building collapse onto the wooden houses in the alley below. "Then I noted the great silence . . . and it was an awful thing. But now in the alley some one began to groan. It was a woman's groan, soft and low." The streets "were full of people, half-clad, disheveled, but silent, absolutely silent." He wandered about the city, helping to carry residents trapped by debris into the open. Then, having reached the *Call* and been sent out for further reporting, he began to take in the full measure of the catastrophe. He stopped a chauffeured car, offered the driver fifty dollars for the day, and soon found himself enveloped within "a vague kaleidoscopic vision of whirring at whistling speed through a city of the damned." Everywhere they came upon clutches of firemen staging futile defenses against a spreading conflagration. By then Hopper knew that "the earthquake had been but a prologue, and that the tragedy was to be written in fire."

It had begun at about 5:12 a.m.—the exact moment is impossible to pinpoint because of the varying accuracy of local seismographs—when the San Andreas Fault two miles offshore snapped like an overloaded tree branch. After the first shock waves struck the city, the shaking continued for forty-five to sixty seconds, an eternity to those under its assault. The city's residents and those living to its north and south were hard-pressed to put the feeling into words, although a recurrent image in survivors' letters and memoirs was the sensation of being a rat caught in a dog's jaws. The shock wave traveled at a prodigious 8,300 miles per hour, propagating along three hundred miles of the fault, from as far south as Monterey to Cape Mendocino in the north, displacing the terrain by as much as thirty-two feet on a northwestern diagonal.

Within hours, much of what was then the largest metropolis on the West Coast was engulfed in flames and cut off from the outside world. Most of the damage was caused by fires ignited by burst gas lines. The firefighters battled the blazes without water, for the city's mains had been ruptured. The six-hundred-member fire department's chief, Dennis T. Sullivan, was out of action; he was buried by debris in the first moments of the quake and died of his injuries four days later.

The earthquake of 1906 remains the greatest civil disaster in California history. In terms of its impact on San Francisco and the state of California, it ranks with the Gold Rush and the building of Hoover Dam in its transformative effect. Through the quake and subsequent fires, San Francisco delivered a series of lessons to the outside world—how to respond and how not to respond to an immediate crisis; how such an event draws a community together and how it splits it apart; how history can be manipulated when great fortunes are at stake; and how a great city can rise from the ashes against almost insurmountable odds.

Measured in raw numbers, the magnitude of the disaster was stupefying. The property damage was initially estimated at about $350 million, but by the end of the year it was judged to total as much as $1 billion—this at a time when the average annual wage of urban doctors and lawyers was $1,200 and of common laborers $390. Experts termed the three-day conflagration "the most disastrous in the history of the world," noting that it destroyed almost all the property in an area of 514 city blocks, or about three thousand acres, nearly five square miles. (Of the most recent contemporary benchmarks, the Chicago fire of 1871 had spread over 2,112 acres and the Baltimore fire of 1904 only about 140.) About 28,000 buildings were destroyed, along with almost all their contents. City boosters would later observe that the destruction covered only about one-sixth of the city's area, but that was misleading; virtually the entire business district, the civic center, and much of the "better residential section" were consumed. Among the destroyed public buildings were City Hall, the main courthouse, the hall of records, and scores of police stations, firehouses, schools, and libraries.

At the Palace Hotel, where the Metropolitan Opera troupe was housed, Enrico Caruso "tore about in a frantic state." The orchestra conductor, Alfred Hertz (a future conductor of the San Francisco Symphony), encountered Caruso in the lobby. Caruso, "crying like a child, repeatedly insisted that we were doomed and all were about to die." The star tenor decamped with other troupe members for the St. Francis Hotel, which seemed at the time to have survived the shocks. As the performers made their way across Union Square, one passerby heard Caruso muttering, "'Ell of a place. I never come back here."

Jack London, who reigned as California's preeminent literary personage and lived in Sonoma, forty miles from the city, received an assignment from *Collier's* magazine after the first reports of the earthquake reached the East. "Within an hour after the first earthquake shock," he wrote, "the smoke of San Francisco's burning was a lurid tower visible a hundred miles away." He and his wife, Charmian, took a train to Sausalito on the northern side of the bay and then a ferry into the city on the first afternoon following the quake. Out on the water, he wrote, "It was dead calm. Not a flicker of wind stirred. Yet from every side wind was pouring in upon the city." He and Charmian walked across to Union Square, which on that first evening was teeming with thousands of refugees, many with trunks laden with the few heirlooms they had been able to secure in the first panicky hours. They were bedding down on the grass, partaking of free meals cooked by army troops under tents. By half past one that morning "three sides of Union Square were in flames. . . . Union Square, heaped high with mountains of trunks, was deserted. Troops, refugees, and all had retreated."

THE RECOLLECTIONS OF city dwellers told the story from street level. Josephine Baxter, a middle-class housewife, reported to her parents in Omaha that her first thought when "that awful shock came at 5:15" was for her sleeping infant. "I tried my best to get her from the crib, but every shake would pull her from me and throw her against the side of the crib." She reported the destruction of "all my bric-brac" and also that "people were passing our house in all sorts of rigs and every face was terror stricken. . . . No one did a thing but sit around in the street wondering what was going to happen next and what was to be the end of it all."

Dolly Brown, a secretary, described for her absent fiancé, Henry, the hours of terror during the first days and the feeling of destitution that followed. The quake itself left her house standing, but fire reached it at ten o'clock that night. After packing clothes and "a few trifles in two trunks and baskets," she and her siblings pleaded with their mother to come away with them, but she refused. "She was determined to see the house burn down," Dolly recounted. The family hauled their belongings a few blocks to safety, then went back to rescue their mother, who could not be found. "I entered the house in the total darkness with the fire crackling in the rear and looked in all the rooms, fearing that she had fainted or lost her mind, but I had to leave without her." Soon after that they were forced to leave the trunks behind and run for their lives; eventually they found refuge in a firehouse, where they were reunited with their mother.

Golden Gate Park, Brown related, was "one mass of tents and 32 babies were born there night before last and 5 last night . . . the sanitary conditions are very bad and the water peddled is not drinkable. The only thing to be feared now is an epidemic or—another earthquake." Brown's family was "destitute but for $10," though provisions for the city were pouring in by boat and train. "The question is, where are we going to live. Oh well, 300,000 are asking the same question." Brown recounted rumors of civil disorder, that "people have been shot right and left for disobeying the martial law, some for looting, others for refusing to work. Four were shot for assaulting women and three lynched for building fires in the house."

Upon returning to the city after the fires were finally quelled, Margaret Brindley, the daughter of a retired diplomat, found that "everything is gone. Nothing remains of the once beautiful City of the West but skeletons of great buildings gradually crumbling away at the last wind. . . . The roads heaped with bricks, broken glass, half burnt furniture, and a network of broken wires." The disaster was a ruthless social leveler, with every park and vacant lot in the unburned districts "filled with people of all classes—some of whom were millionaires—living under every conceivable kind of shelter, and some with no shelter at all."

Creatures other than human beings suffered in the event too. Cattle that were being driven up Mission Street to the city stockyards when the quake struck were "entangled in the debris, their frenzied bawling echoing through the ruins." A witness identified for the record only as "Captain Kelly of the Corps of Engineers" wrote to his family in Boston of delivery horses that had been lined up in front of the market blocks his detachment had been assigned to guard. The tremor "dropped the fronts of the buildings on the whole bunch," he wrote. "I counted 25 dead horses on one block and 15 on another."

The earthquake was hardly the first to strike San Francisco, but it was the most serious since the city's emergence as the leading commercial and social center of the West Coast. Before then, the regularity of tremors had been an oft-noted feature of San Francisco's Gold Rush–era character, even contributing to its earthy charm. Mark Twain, who lived in California intermittently from 1864 to 1868, wrote of having "enjoyed my first earthquake" in San Francisco in 1865. That quake, which struck on Sunday, October 8, 1865, was known to locals as the "great" earthquake—until 1906. "All was solitude and a Sabbath stillness," Twain wrote. Then "there came a really terrific shock; the ground seemed to roll under me in waves. . . . Every door, of every house, as far as the eye could reach, was vomiting a stream of human beings . . . in all sorts of queer apparel, and some without any at all." Twain could not know that what he saw was merely a harbinger—some four decades in advance—of what nature held in store.

Given the city's image as a hive of immorality—financial and carnal—it was perhaps predictable that the 1906 disaster would be seen in some quarters as a manifestation of divine retribution against what the evangelist preacher R. A. Torrey called "one of the wickedest cities in the country." The *New York Observer*, a Presbyterian newspaper, speculated that the disaster "may have been in some sense a visitation of divine judgment." Some found an almost biblical portentousness in the thought of San Francisco's greedy fortune-seekers being instantaneously wiped off the face of the earth by the flick of nature's tail.

Others saw the event more optimistically as an opportunity for moral rebirth. "It required a convulsion of nature to bring about a change" in the social and political atmosphere of San Francisco, John Young, the official historian of the *San Francisco Chronicle*, observed a few years later. The "disastrous conflagration," he wrote, "was a case of purification by fire."

As it happened, the disaster occurred at a moment when San Francisco was already in turmoil. The cause was politics, and its source was a tactical blunder by James D. Phelan, who had been elected mayor on a reform platform in 1897. Phelan had worked hard to foster a spirit of cooperation between the city's moneyed elite and its growing—and increasingly militant—labor unions. But his failure to quell a general strike in 1901 had lost him the support of unions and employers alike and opened the door to a victory by union supporters in the 1901 municipal election.

Phelan's successor was Eugene E. Schmitz, an orchestra leader and president of the musicians union. Schmitz had been chosen by the city's political boss, Abraham Ruef, largely due to his appealing physical qualities and what Ruef judged to be his willingness to take instruction. He was dapper, tall, and good-looking, with a well-trimmed black beard, and he projected intelligence and culture despite lacking formal higher education. As the mayoral campaign unfolded, Schmitz turned out to have an unexpected talent for speechifying and the other elements of effective electioneering, and he won handily.

Schmitz would serve three two-year terms, presiding over an administration that set a benchmark for civic corruption. The earthquake brought forth both his best and worst qualities. Once the scale of destruction from the earthquake became evident, he mounted an energetic, proactive response. One decision, however, would go down in history as a quintessentially extreme overreaction to a crisis. This was his infamous "Shoot to Kill" proclamation, issued in the first hours after the quake. In the proclamation, printed on handbills circulated throughout the city, Schmitz stated that "the Federal Troops, the members of the Regular Police Force and all Special Police

Officers have been authorized by me to KILL any and all persons found engaged in Looting or in the Commission of Any Other Crime."

The proclamation was the product of the exaggerated panic about looting that had prevailed in the first daylight hours. In fact, there were numerous accounts of unwarranted shootings by law enforcement but few reports of looting—except in Chinatown. There, "wholesale looting . . . by 'respectable' citizens and National Guardsmen took place" without any perpetrators being shot by officers. The *Chronicle* estimated the number of looters, who carried off precious bronzes and china, to be in the thousands. A dozen or so militia members were turned over to military authorities, who found them all to have been innocent of anything other than "sightseeing." Having been destroyed by fire, Chinatown would be rebuilt in the same location near the center of the city.

The toll from trigger-happy officers has never been determined, but the inaccurate perception that San Francisco came under martial law in the days after the quake persisted. In part that was because the story was spread by the city's three leading morning newspapers—the *Chronicle*, the *Call*, and the *Examiner*. With their offices and printing presses all destroyed by fire, the three dailies collaborated to put out what is almost certainly a unique publication in American journalistic history, a free four-page edition dated April 19 and bearing the banners of all three papers (in an order established by the drawing of lots): the *"Call-Chronicle-Examiner."* About forty thousand copies were printed at the facilities of the *Oakland Tribune* across the bay, ten thousand of which were ferried to the stricken city and the rest distributed regionally. The edition's front page bore the banner headline "Earthquake and Fire: San Francisco in Ruins," over a lead article that began: "Death and destruction have been the fate of San Francisco."

Valiant as the tripartite effort was and as valuable as it was as a source of information about the disaster, the front-page account perpetrated the falsehood that "at nine o'clock, under a special message from President Roosevelt, the city was placed under martial law." No such message had been sent. The edition also published a hyperbolic account of public disorder: "Many acts of vandalism were commiteed [*sic*] and during the excitement crooks looted countless damaged stores and office buildings."

Schmitz's shoot-to-kill order was far from the most damaging official initiative during the crisis. That distinction belongs to the decision to use explosives to establish firebreaks by bringing down flammable structures in the path of the fires.

The deployment of explosives was the product of desperation on the part of a fire department struggling without water. When the acting fire chief appealed to army headquarters at the Presidio for military-grade explosives, the army promptly dispatched, no questions asked, forty-eight barrels of "black powder"—that is, gunpowder—to the city center in field caissons and three hundred pounds of dynamite in two wagons. It immediately became apparent that the use of powder was a major blunder, for the powder tended to ignite the very wood structures it was employed to demolish. The incompetent handling of dynamite brought down buildings that might otherwise have been saved and caused untold deaths and injuries. Had the deployment of powder and dynamite been "planned systematically and carried out properly much of the City could have been saved," mining experts observed in a series of postmortem reports. Instead, "the work was done by Dick, Tom, and Harry . . . [who] used a box of dynamite where a pound would have sufficed."

INSIDER ACCOUNTS LATER depicted the city's business leaders as courageous and determined advocates of rapid reconstruction from the very first. Contemporary accounts paint a different picture. On the third day after the quake, with the financial district obliterated by fires that consumed most of the major banks' headquarters along with the most glittering private homes, prominent bankers, attorneys, and business leaders gathered in the parlor of a surviving mansion to take stock. "We appeared to be conscious, but really our brains were in a fog, and our actions were those of automatons," recalled a participant. A banker visiting from Los Angeles said "he had never before met such a dispirited lot of men."

They eventually regained their composure and began to make plans for rebuilding. A common goal was to stamp out the publication of reminiscences of the event and photographs of the destruction. "Are we not damaging the city by every one of these views we send away?" editorialized the *San Francisco Call* on May 20, scarcely one month after the disaster. "If we want to frighten people away from us this is about as good a way as any other." The newspaper condemned "the practice of many persons, mostly women, to go about among their friends armed with doleful predictions . . . of still more terrible catastrophes to come, in which earthquakes, tidal waves, pestilences, conflagrations, tornadoes and all sorts of terrifying cataclysms are presaged with alarming minuteness, even to announcing the exact dates on which they are to occur."

The real concern of the rebuilding party was not the effect on women and children but the effect on investors. "It soon became clear that persons controlling the eastern financial resources needed to rebuild the Bay Area . . . were more afraid of earthquakes than of fire," seismologist Karl V. Steinbrugge observed. "It became fashionable locally to refer to the disaster as 'the fire.' . . . A discussion of earthquakes was as welcome in San Francisco as a discussion of the plague."

Major urban fires were not unfamiliar events. Since these were almost invariably the result of human activity, they theoretically could be addressed by human agency. Earthquakes, however, were mysterious, unpredictable, and largely unknown on the East Coast, at least on the scale of the San Francisco event. To the city's municipal leaders, then, it made sense to pretend that the earthquake barely happened at all. Still, there is no denying that most of the death and damage in San Francisco was due to the three days of fire that succeeded the few seconds of quake—there were 599 killed by asphyxiation, smoke inhalation, or burns, compared to 427 crushed to death on the first day. (Another 472 deaths were due to heart attacks, exposure, or exhaustion, or could not be connected to either earthquake or fires.)

Among the leaders of the reconstruction drive was the intensely energetic Edward H. Harriman, president of the Southern Pacific. For Harriman, reconstruction was an urgent matter. San Francisco was the hub of his western transportation empire, which included the Union Pacific and Wells Fargo Express along with the Southern Pacific. Within hours after receiving the first reports of the earthquake, he boarded a train in New York bound for the stricken Bay Area, where Southern Pacific rolling stock and ferries had been donated—or commandeered—to transfer victims to safety outside the city. He arrived three days later and established his temporary headquarters across the bay in Oakland, from where he could watch black smoke rising over San Francisco.

Among Harriman's contributions to the city's rebirth was an expansive publicity campaign. It began with the distribution of "San Francisco Imperishable," a free seven-page pamphlet exuding confidence in its future as a "city of Opportunity as well as of Destiny." The pamphlet acknowledged that the business district had been "largely reduced to ashes," but "the water front with its miles of wharves and warehouses is intact. The Union Iron Works and other large industries were not disturbed. . . . Five-sixths of San Francisco's area was not touched by fire." This was true but glossed over the fact that the damaged and destroyed sections were the heart of the city's civic and commercial life.

As for the earthquake itself, the pamphlet cited professional opinion that the quake was "the most severe that will ever be felt in California." One of the railroad's seismic experts was "quite willing to risk his reputation on that statement that California will be free from severe quakes for a long time to come and in all probability never again know one as strong as the last. . . . Earthquakes have never been in knowledge of man twice destructive in the same locality." (This cocksure declaration proved to be untrue, as has been shown by several major Bay Area quakes since then, most notably a 6.9 magnitude quake in 1989 that took sixty-three lives and caused an estimated ten billion dollars in damage.)

Harriman drove rescue and recovery efforts through the force of his personality and the application of the Southern Pacific's considerable resources. Special freight trains carrying provisions for residents of the stricken city from Los Angeles, Sacramento, and across the country were given right-of-way on Harriman lines, and more than a thousand carloads of residents were brought out of the city to safety on the nineteenth and twentieth of April. The Harriman system later estimated that in the thirty-five days following the earthquake, its trains brought 1,063 carloads of supplies into the city and nearly 225,000 refugees out for free, giving up an estimated $500,831 in revenue.

This was not the only crisis facing Harriman's Southern Pacific at that moment. Some six hundred miles to the south, the railroad was battling a torrent of Colorado River water threatening to flood and destroy the Imperial Valley, one of California's most productive agricultural regions. Because the railroad had invested in the canal company that inadvertently unleashed the Colorado, President Roosevelt had ordered Harriman to restore the river to its original bed. The battle was on the verge of being lost, Harriman learned upon his arrival in Oakland. He immediately authorized $250,000 in new funding for the effort. It eventually succeeded at a total cost to the railroad of more than three million dollars. (Roosevelt had promised to compensate the railroad for the job, but Congress never approved the payment.) The ultimate solution to the Colorado's flooding threat to the Imperial Valley would be the construction of Hoover Dam three decades later.

THE BOOSTERS' CONVICTION that the destruction of April 1906 would give birth to an even greater San Francisco began to be validated within a few short months. "It was a cruel trick of Fate that made ashes of the heart of the city, and weak hearts were near to despair at the ruin wrought," wrote Charles S. Aiken, who as editor of the Southern Pacific's *Sunset* magazine served as the recovery's proselytizer in chief. "But men and money and will and daring joined hands promptly, and weeks of humming, hustling industry resulted."

There would be much to do in the way of cleaning up and rebuilding in the coming months and years, not only of the city's physical plant but of its political structure. The latter task, which had just gotten underway when the earth trembled, resumed afterward with redoubled energy. The result would produce an even longer-lasting impact on the city and the state.

12

THE PROGRESSIVE REVOLUTION

JUDGING BY HIS family history, Hiram Johnson would appear to be poorly cast as the standard-bearer of California progressives and the archenemy of the Southern Pacific Railroad. His father, Grove, was one of the most conservative members of the state legislature at the turn of the century. Grove's defining legislative position was his sedulous support for the Southern Pacific. Indeed, he would blame his final electoral defeat on his reputation as an ally of the railroad—a relationship he defined defensively as one in which he was "a friend, not a follower or slave."

What Hiram inherited from his father was not his political ideology but a pugnacious approach to lawyering and legislating. According to a local legend, Grove one day decided to call out the corrupt politicians of Sacramento in person. He and his two sons, Hiram and his older brother, Albert, burst in on a meeting held by Frank Rhodes, the city's corrupt boss. "Little more than boys," Hiram and Albert stood by with revolvers drawn as their father fearlessly hectored Rhodes and his backroom cronies with invective and promised that their power would someday be broken. When he finished, he and his sons turned on their heels and walked out.

Biographers tend to doubt this anecdote; its principal source, the San Francisco–born muckraker Lincoln Steffens, acknowledged that the meeting was secret, with "no outsiders present." He never explained how he came by his knowledge. But the story did point to the truculent determination Grove bequeathed to his younger son. In two documented encounters, Hiram came to blows with opponents inside a courthouse. On the first occasion, his adversary was Sacramento district attorney Frank Ryan, whom Johnson called a liar in open court; the second confrontation came during a San Francisco corruption trial, when Johnson lunged across a courtroom table, landed a blow on a defense attorney's cheekbone, and received one in return. Once he began running for political offices, it was a rare campaign photograph that did not depict Hiram Johnson in a pugilistic stance, with his dukes up.

JOHNSON'S POLITICAL CAREER was born in a muckraking campaign in San Francisco launched by the *San Francisco Bulletin's* crusading newspaper editor, Fremont Older. As an individual, Older stood out in a crowd—he was six foot two, rail thin, with a flowing handlebar mustache. As a muckraker, he stood apart from his fellow editors in his adversarial approach to the Southern Pacific. Although he had failed to persuade the newspaper's owner, R. A. Crothers, to wean the paper from the monthly subsidy the railroad paid to guarantee its "friendliness," Crothers did allow him to move its editorial policies closer to the positions of an emerging reform faction in the city.

Under Older, the *Bulletin* waged a fiery campaign to oust the corrupt city-hall cabal of Mayor Eugene Schmitz and Union Labor Party boss Abraham Ruef. The effort, Older wrote, was a "struggle that led into every cross-section of San Francisco life; into the depths of the underworld; to attempted murder; to dynamiting and assassination."

Reform-minded observers marveled at the scale of corruption instigated by Ruef and Schmitz in San Francisco, where they and their allies "took toll everywhere, from everybody, and in almost every imaginable way."

> They went into partnership with dishonest contractors [wrote the political commentator George Kennan]; sold privileges and permits to business men; extorted money from restaurants and saloons . . . shared the profits of houses of prostitution . . . blackmailed gamblers, pool sellers, and promoters of prize-fights; forced beer, whisky, champagne, and cigars on restaurants and saloons on commission. . . . The motto of the administration seemed to be: "Encourage dishonesty, and then let no dishonest dollar escape."

Even Ruef could be shocked by the greed of his own party's members of the board of supervisors, who were swept into office in 1905, when Schmitz won reelection—a gang of grifters so avaricious, Ruef said, they would "eat the paint off a house."

Appalled by the election results, Older offered Francis J. Heney, a federal prosecutor renowned for his success at putting corrupt public officials in jail, one hundred thousand dollars to bring his skills to San Francisco. The money was to be provided by Rudolph Spreckels, the heir to a sugar fortune and brother of the *San Francisco Call*'s owner.

Heney's investigation began in October 1906, when San Francisco was starting to recover from the earthquake and fires. He brought indictments against numerous grifters associated with Ruef and Schmitz, but in the end, the only person to do prison time would be Ruef.

Heney was unable to finish the job he started. On November 13, 1908, during a recess in Ruef's trial, a spectator walked to the front of the courtroom, leveled a pistol at the prosecutor, and shot him in the head. The assailant, Morris Haas, nursed a grievance against Heney for having discharged him from another jury after disclosing his previous conviction for fraud and embezzlement. Heney escaped assassination but was put out of commission for the duration of Ruef's trial. His place at the prosecutor's table was taken by his deputy, Hiram Johnson.

Johnson's theatrical courthouse style and skill at accusatory invective had made him a celebrity in San Francisco. His scathing denunciation of Ruef in his closing argument made him famous statewide. "History contains no instance so base, so wicked, so malign, so avaricious, so corrupt, so horrible as this," he declared in a torrent of vituperation lasting three hours. He contrasted the suffering of ordinary San Franciscans in the earthquake's aftermath with the defendant's uninterrupted campaign of graft: "When all of us were down in the dirt and in disorder, crawling through our streets, begging for aid . . . fighting, indeed, for life—it was at that time that Abe Ruef and the United Railroads sold our town and sold out you." The jury found Ruef guilty the next day. Two weeks later he was sentenced to the maximum term of fourteen years in San Quentin State Prison.

Ruef served four years and seven months. He rebuilt his fortune, which had reached one million dollars before his trial, but later suffered a reversal in the stock market crash. When he died in February 1936, he was bankrupt. Schmitz had been convicted of graft in June 1907, but his conviction was overturned on a technicality by an appeals court and he was acquitted at a second trial when Ruef refused to testify against him.

Of the figures who participated in the great corruption prosecution of San Francisco, one would profit above all: Hiram Johnson, whose performance in the courtroom catapulted him into a career of public service that would have a far more lasting impact on politics in California—and indeed nationally— than the graft trials themselves.

JOHNSON'S UNASSAILABLE PROGRESSIVE politics brought him into contact with reform leaders who judged him to be the ideal candidate for governor in the 1910 election. Among those leaders was the state's outstanding progressive figure, John Randolph Haynes, a Philadelphia surgeon who had moved to Southern California with his family in 1863 for his health. Through timely investments in real estate, oil, and mining, Haynes had accumulated a sizable fortune that he put to work funding progressive causes. His passion, which he pursued with a religious fervor, was "direct legislation." This encompassed ballot-box initiatives and referendums along with a procedure to recall public officials. All were aimed at seizing power back from the corporate interests entrenched in Sacramento and returning it to the voters so they could exercise their will without the interference of self-interested intermediaries such as the Southern Pacific and its wholly owned politicians. The concept was not entirely novel; by 1910, seven states, starting with South Dakota in 1898, had enacted statewide initiative and referendum laws.

Haynes's campaign for direct democracy had borne fruit in Los Angeles in 1902, when voters added the initiative, referendum, and recall to the city charter. The next step was to bring direct democracy statewide. As a candidate, Johnson adopted Haynes's crusade as his own. But the core of his campaign was an attack on the Southern Pacific, his own holy war. The Mussel Slough incident of 1880 was still fresh in Northern California memories, and over the subsequent decades resentment had continued to rise against the railroad statewide.

Across California the railroad's manipulative control of state government through its lobbyist William F. Herrin was a byword. After becoming the head of the Southern Pacific's political bureau in the mid-1890s, Herrin built it into a force that dictated party nominations for governor and derailed unfavorable legislation. Its influence extended to the judiciary; the state supreme court ruled in the railroad's favor in fifty-seven of seventy-nine lawsuits charging it with rate manipulation and other offenses dating as far back as 1895. County bosses in thrall to the railroad were known to provide Herrin with lists of prospective jurors who could be counted on to vote in its favor in railroad cases. "The railroad was the biggest landowner and the biggest employer of labor," observed historian John W. Caughey, "and by arbitrary manipulation of freight rates it could make or break almost any merchant, industrialist, or agriculturalist in the state." For reformers, the Southern Pacific was, in Caughey's words, "public enemy number one." (Indeed, Fremont Older had listed "overturning the Southern Pacific rule of California" among his goals as editor of the *Bulletin*, notwithstanding the subsidy the newspaper was receiving from the railroad.) Johnson's attacks on the railroad, expressed during sixteen-hour days of barnstorming, fell on sympathetic ears in the big cities and in the countryside. He appealed to city folk by promising to curb the Southern Pacific's political influence and to country folk by promising to curb its greediness.

As it happened, by the time Johnson launched his campaign, the Southern Pacific's political power in the state was already waning. During the 1909 legislative session, lawmakers considered two competing measures to curb the railroad's rate-fixing power, replicating the efforts of the 1870s and 1880s. One would give a state commission the authority to set rates and impose fines or even imprison executives for violations; the watered-down version that passed only set maximum rates and limited punishment to corporate fines. That bill was nevertheless the most important anti-railroad measure to pass in California in years. Perhaps more significant, that same year a reform mayoral candidate in Los Angeles defeated a candidate backed by the Southern Pacific machine. The railroad's political power had been "shattered beyond repair," declared the *Los Angeles Express*, somewhat optimistically.

Yet the railroad was still a major landowner, and the new law constrained only modestly its ability to deliver favorable rates to friendly shippers and punish their competitors. As a political target for progressives, the Southern Pacific's value remained unmatched. Johnson made the most of it. Touring the state with his son Jack behind the wheel of a cherry-red Locomobile, Johnson relentlessly bellowed his promise to "kick the Southern Pacific out of politics." In an era when political speechifying was a form of mass entertainment, Johnson's arrival in a town, heralded by the ringing of a cowbell, always drew a crowd. "The first notes of his voice keyed up your nerves to a fighting pitch," wrote an observer. "It grates and snarls and pierces. . . . His hands are nearly always clenched. His jaw, a good strong fighting jaw, is set. . . . He gives you the impression of a man carried away entirely on the flood of his own feelings." Another compared Johnson's effect on his listeners favorably to that of preachers at revival meetings.

Johnson's skill at invective was displayed most vividly in his responses to attacks by the *Los Angeles Times*. The newspaper's owner, Harrison Gray Otis, had no love for the progressive reformists whose banner Johnson carried. That was especially so given the progressives' alliance with Otis's chief bête noire, organized labor. The newspaper's savage broadsides against Johnson often entailed tying him to his father's politics—one editorial cartoon depicted them jointly cleaving a log labeled "State Politics" with a saw labeled "S.P. [Southern Pacific] Tool" under the caption "Like Father Like Son." The accusation that the two family members were collaborating with the railroad was sure to drive Johnson to livid extremes.

The Ohio-born Otis, who had seen action in fifteen Civil War battles and later in the Spanish-American War, had acquired control of the faltering *Times* in 1886 in a timely deal that positioned the new owner to ride a wave of spectacular regional growth. The newspaper's editors marched in lockstep to Otis's command to the end of his life in 1917. Otis established the principle by which the *Times* would be managed for three-quarters of a century: its editorial judgment on any issue was to be dictated by his family's economic interests. Through the 1950s, this principle would render the newspaper politically reactionary and ferociously anti-union.

Johnson struck back at the seventy-four-year-old Otis during a campaign appearance on August 5, 1910, at Simpson's Auditorium in downtown Los Angeles. Prompted by a planted question from the audience, he ostentatiously set his prepared speech aside and strode to the edge of the stage, the ornate decor of which evoked the building's origin as a church. In San Francisco, he declared, "we have been disgraced before the world by crimes unspeakable, but . . . we have never had anything so degraded, so disreputable, so vile as Harrison Gray Otis. . . . Here he sits in senile dementia, with gangrened heart and rotting brain, grimacing at every reform and chattering in impotent rage against decency and morality, while he is going down to his grave in snarling infamy."

Otis's newspaper answered Johnson the very next day, calling his performance "almost a frenzy of vituperation and . . . unspeakably abusive." (The newspaper drove in the blade a little deeper by describing Johnson in its headline as "Old Grove's Son.") The *Times'* anonymous editorialist provided readers with a vivid portrait of the campaigning Johnson in action, albeit one in which a begrudging admiration seemed to leak through: "His voice was cold and precise and metallic. . . . His sarcasm showed that his ideas are stamped out as he talks, by a brain that is like chiseled steel."

In the end, it was Southern California voters who gave Johnson his winning margin of 22,000 votes; he won narrowly in San Francisco but lost in the rest of Northern California and in the Central Valley farm belt. Still, victory was victory. Johnson solidified his progressive credentials by visiting the East Coast to meet with Robert LaFollette, Lincoln Steffens, and former president Theodore Roosevelt. This allowed him to associate himself with those progressive celebrities' renown. But it also gave him the opportunity to educate himself about the progressive principles with which he identified as a candidate but understood only vaguely. Late in the campaign, for instance, when he realized that he might win, he had to ask one of his campaign officials to explain how the initiative, referendum, and recall would actually work in practice.

"FORGOING ANY FORM of pageantry," Johnson strolled from his Sacramento hotel to the state capitol on January 3, 1911, to be sworn in. In the preamble to his inaugural speech, he took the obligatory swipe at the Southern Pacific, declaring that "the first duty that is mine to perform is to eliminate every private interest from the government," especially "the former political master of this State, the Southern Pacific Company." He called for the creation of a railroad commission with genuine power, unlike the mild version of the law enacted in 1909.

He proceeded to embrace several progressive platform planks that had taken a back seat to his attacks on the railroad on the campaign stump, including the initiative, referendum, and recall. He also called for the direct election of US senators rather than their appointment by the state legislature, a system that a majority of states already had abandoned in favor of a rule binding their legislators to the senatorial candidates the voters favored. This was known as the Oregon plan, after the state that pioneered the change in 1908. (The Seventeenth Amendment, which was passed by Congress in 1912 and ratified in 1913, would make direct election of senators the rule nationwide.)

The one progressive plank that Johnson ducked in his speech was women's suffrage, which happened to be one of the few progressive goals that his father supported. Johnson had not mentioned the issue at all during his campaign and was known by friends not "to take serious women seriously, especially in politics." When the legislature placed the issue on the ballot of an October 1911 special election as a constitutional amendment, he quietly acknowledged that he would vote for it. In the event, the referendum passed, making California the sixth state to grant women the right to vote. This was not "universal suffrage" by any means, however: Proposition 4 of 1911 provided that "no native of China, no idiot, no insane person, no person convicted of any infamous crime [that is, felons], no person hereafter convicted of the embezzlement or misappropriation of public money, and no person who shall not be able to read the constitution in the English language and write his or her name" would be granted the franchise. Chinese immigrants were not given the right to vote in state elections until 1943, and the literacy requirement and felon exclusions were not removed until the 1970s. (The Nineteenth Amendment to the US Constitution, granting women the right to vote nationwide, went into effect in August 1920.)

Johnson delivered on the promises of his speech and guided the California legislature to its most creative and accomplished period since the first legislature of 1849–1850. The lawmakers passed the railroad commission bill that had been shunted aside in 1909, endowing the commission with the power to set rates and impose fines or prison sentences for violations. They adopted the Oregon plan and drafted constitutional amendments for women's suffrage and the initiative, referendum, and recall. All twenty-three of the amendments the legislature placed on the special election ballot passed, all but one with more than 60 percent of the vote. The exception was women's suffrage, which received a narrow majority of 51 percent.

The legislature passed an eight-hour workday for women, established an industrial safety commission, and created a workmen's compensation program, which was made voluntary in 1911 and compulsory in 1913. (In his inaugural address, Johnson had approvingly quoted Theodore Roosevelt's maxim that "industry must bear the monetary burden of its human sacrifices.") During Johnson's first term, the legislature passed thirty-nine of the forty-nine pro-labor bills that came to the floor.

These amendments and laws dramatically reshaped government and politics not only in California but nationwide. Although California was not the first state to institute direct democracy through the initiative and referendum, its action significantly advanced the movement, with twelve more states enacting initiative or referendum procedures over the next four years. California has always reigned as the pacesetter in direct democracy; from 1911 through 2022, some 450 initiatives and referenda appeared on the state's ballots, 185 of which were approved.

Still, direct democracy as enacted in California was not universally admired in 1911, even by progressives. Some, like the commentator Herbert Croly, whose liberal credentials were incontestable (he would co-found the *New Republic* in 1914), challenged the "superstitious belief" in the wisdom of voters that lay at the heart of Haynes's faith in citizen democracy. By exercising their unconstrained instincts at the ballot box to combat the dominance of the railroads and other big businesses, Croly warned, "the people . . . may succeed in abolishing one kind of abuse and oppression, but only at the price of its being succeeded by other kinds." He was correct. Over the more than one hundred years since Johnson's innovation, the direct democracy of initiative and referendum has become the servant, not the nemesis, of corporate interests; real estate owners got the property-tax-cutting Proposition 13 enacted in 1978, and in 2020, gig companies persuaded voters to overturn a law mandating that their workers be properly classified as employees rather than independent contractors, a money-saving boon for firms such as Uber and Lyft. As a historian of the process observed, most ballot initiatives ride upon surges of public pressure to address immediate crises "with little concern for long-term effects."

The Johnson administration's pro-labor policies earned it the intensified enmity of General Otis and his *Los Angeles Times*. Yet the *Times'* influence extended only as far as its circulation market. The anti-union sentiment prevalent in Los Angeles was not shared in San Francisco. There, labor support propelled Johnson to an overwhelming victory in his reelection campaign of 1914, when he expanded his margin over his nearest rival from 22,000 votes to nearly 200,000.

The progressives' success in the first years of Johnson's term brought him nationwide fame and a reluctant position as Theodore Roosevelt's vice presidential running mate on the 1912 Progressive ("Bull Moose") Party presidential ticket. As Johnson had feared, the campaign was a disaster; the Progressives split the Republican vote and brought Democrat Woodrow Wilson into the White House.

BACK HOME, JOHNSON could not escape the most noxious feature of California progressivism—its overt anti-Japanese racism, which plunged him into the center of a political maelstrom.

This prejudice in California dated back to 1900, when Japanese immigration caught the attention of the same labor organizations that earlier had spearheaded the anti-Chinese movement in the state. The agitators initially made little distinction between Chinese and Japanese—to them, they were all Asiatic "coolies."

The movement in California gained nationwide notice in 1906, when the San Francisco Board of Education voted to eject all Japanese pupils from the city's primary and grammar schools and segregate them in an "Oriental School." The action, which showed flagrant ingratitude for a generous $246,000 donation to the earthquake relief committee from the citizens and government of Japan in 1906, was widely condemned around the country. To rationalize the policy, the school board asserted that most Japanese pupils were in fact adult men who posed a moral and physical danger to young girls in the crowded confines of the classroom. The claim was easily refuted; the vast majority of Japanese pupils in San Francisco were younger than fifteen and only two had even reached the age of twenty. The Japanese student population was meager, in any case; of the nearly 29,000 schoolchildren in the system, only ninety-three were Japanese. School authorities said they had never received a single complaint against a Japanese student.

The growing anti-Japanese feeling in California created a host of problems for President Roosevelt. He was not averse in principle to excluding Japanese immigrants from the United States. But he personally considered the physical assaults and other attacks suffered by the Japanese on San Francisco streets objectionable and their geopolitical implications even more troubling. With its unexpected yet decisive military victory over Russia in the Russo-Japanese War of 1904–05, Japan had humiliated a world power. Many in America consequently foresaw as inevitable a conflict between the United States and Japan in the Pacific, which each country viewed as lying within its sphere of influence. Roosevelt was not at all eager for Japanese public sentiment to be provoked by demeaning acts against Japanese schoolchildren and adults perpetrated by people he labeled "violent extremists." Hostility toward the Japanese was not merely "most discreditable to us as a people," but "may be fraught with the gravest consequences to the nation," he warned in his annual message to Congress on December 4, 1906. He feared that the combustible politics of San Francisco might lead the United States into armed conflict with a foreign military regime bursting with bellicose self-confidence.*

Meanwhile, the Democratic Party was turning immigration into a campaign issue. Roosevelt, fully alive to the powerful appeal that immigration restrictions had for California voters, tried to evade the controversy by negotiating with the Japanese government for a voluntary crackdown on immigration to the West Coast. The result was the so-called Gentlemen's Agreement of 1907, in which the Japanese government agreed to cease issuing passports to Japanese workers for travel to the coast in return for the San Francisco school board's rescinding its discriminatory policy. Roosevelt summoned the board and its chairman, Mayor Schmitz, to Washington for a browbeating session in the White House. Smarting from the thud of Roosevelt's big stick, the board grudgingly assented.

To Roosevelt's dismay, however, the Gentlemen's Agreement only exacerbated anti-Japanese prejudice in California. The problem was that the deal allowed Japanese residents in the United States to bring over family members. As a result, resident workers' wives were immigrating to the United States by the thousands. The reunited couples were having babies, children who were American citizens by birth. Five anti-Japanese measures were introduced in the 1909 state legislature, including bills to impose Japanese segregation in the schools statewide, allow local officials to create ghettos for Asian residents, and require alien landowners to become citizens of the United States within five years of taking title or lose their land. This provision was openly aimed at the Japanese, who were ineligible for naturalization under federal laws dating back to 1790, when citizenship was restricted to "free White persons." At Roosevelt's behest, Governor James Gillett killed all these measures.

---

* Roosevelt received the Nobel Peace Prize in 1906 for his role in negotiating the Treaty of Portsmouth, which ended the Russo-Japanese war.

The underlying impetus for anti-Japanese antagonism in California was economic, as was the case with the anti-Chinese antagonism of the 1870s and 1880s. The Japanese were seen as threats to the established white order, both as providers of cheap labor and as landholders in the farming regions. Since the progressives had associated themselves politically with labor unions and small farmers, they were cornered into assuming the economically inspired prejudices of their partners.

In the agricultural districts, the Japanese were often viewed as mysteriously successful alpha farmers. "The Japanese does not remain a coolie," was the sour judgment of Chester Rowell, a progressive leader and the owner of the *Fresno Republican,* who was elected mayor of that agricultural city in 1909. "When he can, he buys or rents land. Wherever many Japanese settle, as owners or renters, white men move out, surrendering to the Japanese a voluntary monopoly." Rowell did not explain why white men would give in to the Japanese incursion so meekly, but his concern was wildly overblown: In 1910, only about 19,000 of the 42,500 Japanese living in California (constituting 1.8 percent of a state population of 2.4 million) inhabited the farming regions. Among them were not only farmers but laborers and shopkeepers; Japanese residents owned fewer than thirteen thousand of the state's twenty-seven million acres of farmland.

Rowell explained that what he called "Orientophobia" was a regrettable recognition of political reality, but his view was shot through with overtly racist prejudices. Lurking just beneath the surface of his judgment was a horror of intermarriage that went beyond white middle-class presumptions about the social and cultural incompatibility of the races. The problem was "biological," Rowell wrote, voicing the notion that the races should be seen as distinct species that could not interbreed without producing freaks of nature. The Japanese "are a different race physically, and nature will keep them different through all the generations, unless there is mingling of blood. We owe it to the posterity of both races that this experiment be not tried."

Although Johnson had kept the racial issue out of his first campaign for governor, anti-Japanese discrimination became prominent on the legislative agenda after the 1910 election. During the 1911 legislative session, twenty-seven anti-Japanese measures were introduced in Sacramento. The persistence of anti-Japanese prejudice in California unnerved Roosevelt's Republican successor in the White House, William Howard Taft, who was attempting to conclude a trade treaty with Japan and was as reluctant as his predecessor to unnecessarily antagonize an emerging military power. Johnson assured Taft's secretary of state, Philander C. Knox, that he would quash the entire package of bills in Sacramento. He was as good as his word.

A new concern arose in 1912, however, during the planning for the 1915 Panama-Pacific International Exposition, which was to take place in San Francisco to celebrate the opening of the Panama Canal and mark the city's recovery from the 1906 earthquake, and at which the Japanese government was expected to be a prominent exhibitor.

It was a delicate political moment. Immigration loomed as a major issue in the 1912 presidential campaign, with Democrat Woodrow Wilson eagerly embracing a "national policy of exclusion" and making no secret of his conviction that "we cannot make a homogenous population out of people who do not blend with the Caucasian race."* In the 1912 presidential election, Wilson lost California by only 174 votes out of 700,000 cast, a strong signal that immigration remained a potent issue in the state.

The state legislative hopper for 1913 contained forty anti-immigrant measures, a sizable portion of which pertained to land ownership. The bill attracting the most attention forbade land ownership by aliens and alien-owned corporations. It rapidly became clear, however, that such a comprehensive limitation would hinder the state's commercial and economic development. Legislators eventually amended the Alien Land Bill to allow corporate ownership and limit its restrictions to individuals who were not "eligible for citizenship." This narrowed its application to Japanese residents, then the only alien landowners of any note in the state. The act allowed leases of farmland to Japanese for no more than three consecutive years and barred them from new land purchases. Japanese landowners could transfer their holdings only to citizens or those eligible for naturalization.

When Wilson took office in March 1913, he became the third president in a row to be ensnared in California's racial politics. The day after Wilson's inauguration, the Japanese ambassador to the United States visited him with a plea to block the California land bill. Wilson was boxed into a corner, for he had attacked Roosevelt and Taft during the campaign for interfering with

---

* In 2020, Wilson's racism provoked a reconsideration of his legacy at Princeton University, where he had served as president before coming to the White House. As a result, the university removed his name from what had been known as the Wilson School of Public and International Affairs and the residential Wilson College.

the California legislature and therefore could not be seen applying the same sort of pressure now. He was reduced to sending his secretary of state, William Jennings Bryan, on a mission to pressure Johnson and the legislative leaders into dropping the bill. Bryan, who had no proposals or bargains to offer, was all but laughed out of Sacramento.

On April 17, 1913, a mass protest in Tokyo attracted twenty thousand residents, who cheered as a member of the Diet called for dispatching the imperial fleet to the California coast "to protect Japanese subjects and maintain the nation's dignity." Johnson was unmoved by the international uproar. The issue, he told the legislature, "should be . . . not: Is Japan offended today? But is Japan *justly* offended today?" His answer was a firm no. To Bryan he made the cynical point that the bill did not specifically mention "the Japanese or any other race." After signing the Alien Land Act on May 19, he gloated to Roosevelt, "We have shown the Democratic doctrine of 'States' rights' to be sham and pretense . . . insisted upon when it is their state that is affected but denied when . . . our State is affected."

The Alien Land Act remained on California's books until it was invalidated by the state supreme court in 1952 for infringing on the Fourteenth Amendment's equal protection clause. In any case, the law had been routinely circumvented by Japanese families who transferred title to their American-born children, who after all were citizens. But its discriminatory intent remained deeply offensive to the Japanese, whether resident or nonresident, citizen or noncitizen.

Almost worse than the impact progressive policies of discrimination had on Japanese residents of California in this era was their corrosive impact nationally. What became known as the California position, the predominant feature of which was the prohibition of Japanese land ownership, evolved into the model for anti-Japanese discrimination nationwide. Ultimately it created the foundation for the moral disaster of the incarceration of Japanese residents, including American citizens, during World War II.

13

JOHN MUIR AND THE BATTLE FOR CONSERVATION

ON THE FIRST of April, 1868, John Muir set out on foot for the Yosemite Valley. The Scottish-born naturalist had arrived in California only a few days previously, after having trekked a thousand miles from Indiana to the Gulf of Mexico, boarded a steamer for Cuba, and stayed there for a few months amid the "rich tropical flora" while waiting for a ship to take him to South America, where he intended to seek out the headwaters of the Amazon. Not finding passage, he headed instead for the West Coast, finally disembarking from a Panama steamer in San Francisco, where he recalled inquiring from a passerby "the nearest way out of town."

"But where do you want to go?" he was asked.

"To any place that is wild," he said.

Muir was directed eastward, to the mountains. In his uniquely poetic style he would describe his first impression of the Sierra Nevada range as "miles in height, and so gloriously colored and so radiant, it seemed not clothed with light, but wholly composed of it, like the wall of some celestial city."

His path led him ultimately to the Yosemite. The valley had been unknown to Europeans until the winter of 1850–1851, when an army expedition assigned to corral and relocate Indian tribes accused of harassing Gold Rush prospectors stumbled upon it in pursuit of their quarry.

Over the next four and a half decades, no place on earth would become more closely identified with John Muir, and no man would be more closely identified with the Yosemite. Muir's battle to preserve this magnificent wilderness became the central endeavor of his life. His friends and family would blame his death at the age of seventy-six on the cruel defeat he suffered in his final skirmish on its behalf.

Through Muir's work, California's debate over its lands and waters—so fundamental to the rise of monopolists of its lands and water—expanded into a national debate over the very meaning of the word *conservation*.

Congress had ceded the Yosemite Valley to the State of California for a park in 1864. That action is sometimes portrayed as the national park system's foundational event, though the formal birth of the system is typically attributed to the Yellowstone National Park Act of 1872.

It was in California that the conservation movement reached its full flower, educating the outside world about the virtues of keeping the natural landscape unspoiled and free from commercial development. Thanks to Muir's influence, conservation emerged as a potent political movement, albeit only briefly. The tragedy of his later life was his discovery that even the most valiant and determined efforts to protect natural resources from commercial encroachment could be defeated by money.

That discovery involved a twin of the Yosemite Valley known as Hetch Hetchy. Located about eighteen miles north of Yosemite and still under federal control, Hetch Hetchy was much harder for tourists to reach than its larger sibling and less familiar even to naturalists. To Muir, however, it was a "wonderfully exact counterpart" of Yosemite. In his estimation, Hetch Hetchy's majestic two-thousand-foot granite pyramid, known to the local Miwok Tribe as Korana, rivaled Yosemite's Cathedral Rocks; a massive sheer wall on the north side of the valley evoked Yosemite's El Capitan; and the twin waterfalls cascading over its lip exceeded even Yosemite's distinctive Bridal Veil in their glory. The Hetch Hetchy was in mortal peril, however, because the city of San Francisco wanted to flood it to create a municipal reservoir.

Some of the same physical qualities so admired by Muir made the Hetch Hetchy Valley a natural reservoir. The valley floor was flat. The Tuolumne River entered it through a narrow inlet between perpendicular granite walls hundreds of feet high. For city planners, however, its location inside a national park was a drawback, for that meant that the city could not take it without governmental dispensation. That, in turn, provided Muir and his allies with their main point of defense.

The politics of Hetch Hetchy caused a schism within the conservation movement. During the last half of the nineteenth century, Americans' ideas about the wilderness focused on the opportunity for exploiting the nation's natural resources to advance civilization and prosperity. The historian Frederick Jackson Turner described this impulse in his seminal 1893 paper on the western expansion of the United States, "The Significance of the Frontier in American History."

"American history has been in a large degree the history of the colonization of the Great West," Turner wrote. "The existence of an area of free land . . . and the advance of American settlement westward explain American development."

As the century drew to a close, Turner's frontier had all but disappeared. The wilderness had been colonized; the struggle to tame the wildlands no longer seemed relevant to an increasingly urbanized population. The public turned away from celebrating the nation's natural endowments and toward pondering whether the bounty had been harvested prudently or depleted through wastefulness and profligacy—and whether its management had been done in the public interest or mainly for the benefit of the wealthy. From there it was only a short step to the question of whether the wilderness should serve ends other than exploitation for profit, such as its preservation in pristine form to encourage the meditative contemplation of nature.

Muir was the most effective champion of preservation, which animated his battle to protect the Yosemite as a natural resource of value in and of itself. He wrote eloquently of the invigorating effect of unspoiled nature upon the human psyche: "Climb the mountains and get their good tidings," he wrote. "Nature's peace will flow into you as sunshine flows into trees. The winds will blow their own freshness into you, and the storms their energy, while cares will drop off like autumn leaves." Muir could attest to this effect from personal experience; having taken over the management and subsequently the ownership of his in-laws' vineyard in Martinez, a few miles northeast of San Francisco, he customarily spent the months prior to the autumn grape harvest in solitary exploration of the wilderness, returning home to labor in the vineyards infused with a robust "wilderness health."

Muir's definition of pristine nature did have an important blind spot: his aversion to the Native human inhabitants of the land. After one chance encounter with a group of Miwoks in Yosemite, he described them as "mostly ugly, and some of them altogether hideous. . . . Somehow they seemed to have no right place in the landscape, and I was glad to see them fading out of sight down the pass." As it happened, the creation of several national parks, including Yellowstone, involved the eviction of their Native American occupants; Yosemite escaped the harsher implementations of this policy for many decades, in part because the resident Indians served as a tourist attraction themselves. But the Indians' access to the park shrank over the years under federal administration until the last tribal resident was relocated off the site in 1996.

In all other respects, Muir's celebration of unspoiled wildlands had great popular appeal and attracted wealthy and influential followers. Among them was a Chicago-born outdoorsman named William Kent who had settled near Mount Tamalpais in Marin County, north of the Golden Gate. In 1903 Kent discovered that a canyon on the mountainside bearing a virgin stand of redwoods was being eyed by a local water company for a reservoir. He bought the parcel and offered it to the federal government as a preserve; when Theodore Roosevelt proposed naming the preserve after Kent, he declined, instead arranging to have it called Muir Woods National Monument, a name it still bears. Muir and Kent never met, but Muir wrote the donor in gratitude for "the best tree-lover's monument that could be found in all the forests of the world." Unfortunately, their comradeship would not survive the Hetch Hetchy controversy.

MUIR BROUGHT YOSEMITE'S beauty to nationwide attention through more than 165 articles in regional and national newspapers and magazines. His efforts culminated in the founding of the Sierra Club with twenty-six eminent Northern Californians in 1892. The founders' goal was to end the pillaging of the Yosemite by commercial interests under state ownership. California's Yosemite Valley Commission, which governed the park, was a hive of "ignorance, stupidity and vandalism," wrote William H. Mills, a Sacramento newspaper owner and friend of Muir's, upon resigning from the commission in 1899. Far from preserving the valley in its natural state, the commission encouraged excessive logging and allowed its glorious meadows to be plowed under for the planting of grains behind barbed wire.

Through the 1890s, public support for the return of Yosemite Park from state oversight to federal control increased. The so-called recession movement gained momentum in 1903, when President Roosevelt, whose devotion to "conservation" was an inextricable feature of his public image, visited Yosemite in Muir's company. Following the visit, which yielded a famous photograph of Roosevelt and Muir standing shoulder to shoulder at Yosemite's Glacier Point overlook, the president expressed his support of recession, conditioned on the passage of an enabling act by the state legislature. Recession was opposed by businesses worried that a federal regime would revoke their franchises to build hotels, plant crops, and graze cattle in the valley. But it finally prevailed, in part through the support of Edward H. Harriman, whose ownership of the Southern Pacific Railroad gave him unrivaled influence over California politics. Muir had forged a close friendship with Harriman during an extraordinary two-month, nine-thousand-mile seagoing expedition to Alaska in 1899 on which Harriman hosted thirty scientists, artists, and photographers among the 126 passengers. Not long after they returned from Alaska, Harriman achieved his dream of merging the Southern Pacific Railroad with his Union Pacific, creating one of the dominant railroad companies in the country.

Muir, concerned that the Sierra Club lacked the money and influence in Sacramento to push recession to victory, knew that Harriman had both in abundance. Harriman's personal interest in science, naturalism, and exploration made him receptive to Muir's plea for help. Additionally, the Southern Pacific could easily justify a campaign to save the park as a business venture, for Yosemite was a promising draw for tourists the railroad could transport to the site. Harriman instructed William Herrin, who, as the Southern Pacific's lobbyist in Sacramento, wielded supreme power in the capital, to make the railroad's support for recession known. Opponents of the measure obligingly changed their votes, and recession passed. Roosevelt accepted the park back into the federal government's embrace in June 1906.

With the recession battle won, Muir and the Sierra Club turned their attention to saving the Hetch Hetchy. The ensuing battle might have originated as a regional political conflict, but it turned into what historian Norris Hundley described as "the first confrontation of national significance" between preservationists and conservationists.

ALTHOUGH SURROUNDED BY water on three sides, San Francisco was perennially racked with thirst. The waters of the Pacific Ocean on its west and the estuarial bay on its east were too briny to drink. Its annual rainfall of a mere twenty inches would have made it a poor choice for a colonial settlement if not for its superb harbor.

The shallow wells and inconsequential springs bubbling up from beneath its sandy hills adequately served the city in its first few decades; residents especially admired the purity of a spring located within the Presidio (the Spanish-built fortress overlooking the Golden Gate), the "miraculous qualities" of which were remarked on by General Mariano Guadalupe Vallejo (later the hostage of the Bear Flag rebels). "In proof of my assertions," he wrote, "I appeal to the families of Miramontes, Martinez, Sanchez, Soto, Briones and others, all of whom several times had twins," supposedly due to the "salutary effects" of the spring.

The city's explosive population growth during the Gold Rush turned its chronic water shortage into a crisis. Entrepreneurs swept into the market, delivering water door to door via burros for a dollar a bucket. Adding to the sense of urgency were recurrent fires—six that leveled parts of the largely wooden city between 1850 and 1852 while the fire brigades' pumps ran dry.

Eventually the water entrepreneurs consolidated into the Spring Valley Water Works, which soon owned nearly every source of water within the watershed serving the city. Spring Valley shared the dreary features of monopolies everywhere—namely, indifferent service and extortionate rates. Consequently, city leaders had been fully alive to the necessity of bringing water under municipal control. "An element as vital as the air we breathe," Mayor William Alvord said in 1873, "should not be confined as a merchantable commodity in the hands of a few individuals."

San Francisco struggled to fulfill Alvord's exhortation. Yet as Spring Valley became bigger and richer, it became less inclined to negotiate its own demise. In 1876, when San Francisco offered to buy Spring Valley's holdings outright, the company demanded an extravagant $15.5 million for its assets, more than the city could pay.

The first concrete steps toward commandeering Hetch Hetchy for a municipal reservoir occurred after the election of a reform city administration under Mayor James D. Phelan in 1900. Phelan persuaded the state legislature to award the city a new charter that not merely allowed it to acquire its own water supply but mandated it. The following year Phelan filed a claim to water rights at Hetch Hetchy. A battle commenced that would last for thirteen years.

Preservationists scored the first victory in 1903 when Interior Secretary Ethan Allen Hitchcock—possibly irked by the discovery that the city had entered and surveyed the Hetch Hetchy without federal permission—

rejected its claim. Phelan was unable to appeal Hitchcock's decision because he was no longer in power. In 1902, his reform administration had been swept out of office by Eugene E. Schmitz and by working-class voters under the banner of Ruef's Union Labor Party. Among the bill of particulars later lodged against the Ruef/Schmitz cabal's storied corruption was a scheme to profit illicitly from the water crisis.

From the standpoint of the Hetch Hetchy's defenders, the change in the city administration was tantamount to victory. By 1906, almost all the city officials and staff who had tried under Phelan to make the reservoir a reality were gone. In February of that year the board of supervisors passed a resolution to expend no further "money, energy or time in the futile attempt to acquire the so-called Tuolumne system." A few months later, after the San Francisco earthquake underscored the urgency of securing a municipal water system, five alternative proposals were placed before the board, and one, the purchase of the Bay Cities Water Company for $10.5 million, was selected.

To local muckrakers, the Bay Cities deal smelled to high heaven. Fremont Older's newspaper, the *San Francisco Bulletin,* expressed doubt that "a scheme to sell a water supply system which cost four hundred thousand dollars for ten and a half millions can be put through without bribery." As it ultimately transpired, Bay Cities had promised Ruef a million-dollar "fee" if he could secure approval of the $10.5-milllion purchase. The deal died in 1907 when Ruef and Schmitz were charged with graft and removed from office.

A new phase of the battle, which would involve three presidents and four interior secretaries before reaching its ultimate conclusion, now began.

Opposing Muir were former members of the Phelan administration, among them Marsden Manson, who had been the city's commissioner of public works. Manson had continued promoting the Hetch Hetchy reservoir project while the Phelan administration remained in political exile. In 1905 he managed to obtain a meeting with President Roosevelt and two aides who would ultimately provide crucial support for the reservoir: Chief Forester Gifford Pinchot, who eventually became a leading figure in the conservation movement, and James R. Garfield, who succeeded Hitchcock as interior secretary. Garfield reversed his predecessor's decision, effectively restoring the city's rights to the valley.

Muir did his best to persuade Roosevelt to reject the reservoir, reminding him of their companionable joint visit to the Yosemite in 1903 and pleading

that "to dam and submerge" the Hetch Hetchy "would be hardly less destructive and deplorable in its effects on the Park in general than would be
the damming of Yosemite itself."

Roosevelt's reply, however, suggested that on balance, he favored the reservoir. Regarding "the great natural beauties of this country," he wrote Muir,
"you must remember that . . . if they are to be used so as to interfere with
the permanent material development of the State . . . the result will be
bad." But he grumbled about being obliged to mediate a battle between
conservationists and the forces of economic development: "I have been in
the disagreeable position of seeming to interfere with the development of
the State for the sake of keeping a valley, which apparently hardly anyone
wanted to have kept, under national control."

In California, the battle deteriorated into ad hominem name-calling.
Manson, a member of the Sierra Club, publicly disdained his adversaries as
"mistaken zealots who are witlessly being used as catspaws by these grasping
interests [and] . . . associated water power grabbers." Privately, he disdained
them as "short-haired women and long-haired men" in thrall to "so-called
nature loving societies." Muir was no more polite in describing his opponents: "Everything in the Hetch Hetchy Yosemite Park battle looks fine for
our side, & black for the robbers," Muir told his friend Robert U. Johnson in
1909, when the preservationists were momentarily in ascendance.

Manson's reference to "grasping interests" was meant to evoke the Southern Pacific, which was extremely unpopular throughout the state. Yet for
several reasons the railroad had steered clear of the Hetch Hetchy controversy. The valley offered none of the tourism opportunities of Yosemite,
since it was inaccessible by rail or road. Furthermore, the reservoir battle
was waged largely in Washington, DC, where the railroad could not exercise
the same influence as it did among California state legislators. Years before,
Harriman had split bitterly with Theodore Roosevelt, a former political ally
who in promoting his progressive political platform had taken to identifying
the railroad tycoon as a "malefactor of great wealth." Harriman had almost
no ability to influence Roosevelt in the Hetch Hetchy affair or, indeed, in
any other.

The Hetch Hetchy controversy threatened to rip apart the Sierra Club,
largely because many of its founders and leading members were drawn from
the San Francisco social and political elite that favored the reservoir plan. In

1910, the club staged a vote through which members could opine on whether the Hetch Hetchy "should remain intact and unaltered" or be flooded as a reservoir. Both sides showered members with letters and manifestos. When the ballots were counted, the preservation of the Hetch Hetchy in its natural state won overwhelmingly, 589 to 161. Most of the votes on the losing pro-reservoir camp came from San Francisco.

The Roosevelt administration's approach to conservation leaned more and more in favor of resource development. Gifford Pinchot became a nationally recognized advocate for the view that the purpose of conservation should not be the complete sequestration of natural resources from development but rather their conscientious exploitation to avoid wastefulness. "In every case and in every direction the conservation movement has development for its first principle," he wrote during the Hetch Hetchy battle. "The development of our natural resources and the fullest use of them for the present generation is the first duty of this generation." He was "not much interested in saving the woods for scenic beauty or romantic purposes," acknowledged his biographer M. Nelson McGeary. "Nor was he enthusiastic about turning forest reserves into national parks or game preserves."

By the time of the Sierra Club vote, the main rationale for the Hetch Hetchy reservoir expressed by San Francisco's municipal leaders had evolved from the claim that the valley was its only possible water source to the argument that it was, among several options, the *cheapest* source. This was a winning point for San Francisco voters, who in January 1910 approved a forty-five-million-dollar bond issue to begin work on the reservoir. From then on, the battle to save the Hetch Hetchy was doomed. Congress approved the reservoir at a 1913 special session convened by President Woodrow Wilson, who signed the bill that December.

The conflict over California's natural resources left the preservationist camp in a state of exhaustion. Muir did his best nearly to the end, closing his 1912 book *The Yosemite* with a heartfelt appeal: "Dam Hetch Hetchy! As well dam for water-tanks the people's cathedrals and churches, for no holier temple has ever been consecrated by the heart of man."

From Muir's standpoint, the bitterest betrayal of his cause may have been that of William Kent, who was elected to Congress in 1910 and used his credibility as the donor of Muir Woods National Monument to argue against the preservation of Hetch Hetchy. "The ideal conservation is public social use of resources of our country without waste," he told his colleagues from the House floor, articulating a virtual credo of conservationism. "If Niagara Falls could be totally used up in alleviating the burdens of the overworked in sweatshops of New York City I should be glad to sacrifice that scenic wonder for the welfare of humankind." In private communications to fellow congressmen, he drove the blade in even further by describing Muir as a foolish, starry-eyed idealist: "I hope you will not take my friend, Muir, seriously, for he is a man entirely without social sense," he wrote. "With him, it is me and God and the rock where God put it, and that is the end of the story."

Muir's family was convinced that the battle hastened his death, which came on Christmas Eve, 1914. Following Wilson's approval of the reservoir, Muir had written to a friend, "It's hard to bear. The destruction of the charming groves and gardens, the finest in all California, goes to my heart. But in spite of Satan & Co. some sort of compensation must surely come out of this dark damn-dam-damnation."

No compensation that Muir could have envisioned came out of the dark damnation. The city completed the O'Shaughnessy Dam to impound the waters of the Tuolumne in 1923 and began drawing water from the reservoir in 1934. Today the valley provides San Francisco with 85 percent of its water, so pure from natural filtering through the valley's granite walls that it requires no additional purification before reaching residents' taps. Periodically, however, the proposed restoration of Hetch Hetchy reenters public debate. In 1987, Interior Secretary Donald Hodel, perhaps seeking to counter the anti-environmental reputation of his boss, Ronald Reagan, launched a trial balloon about dismantling the dam and restoring the valley to its natural condition. The idea was promptly quashed by local political leaders, including Democratic Senator Dianne Feinstein, a former mayor of San Francisco, who described the Hetch Hetchy reservoir as the city's "birthright." In 2012, a ballot proposition to appropriate eight million dollars to study draining the reservoir was overwhelmingly defeated by San Francisco voters, 77 percent to 23 percent.

Yet the Sierra Club has never conceded defeat. "Mention Hetch Hetchy Valley to long-time Sierra Club members and their response is immediate: a heartfelt feeling of deep sadness for what has been lost, and a fervent hope that what has been lost can somehow be regained," the club said in 2017. Indeed, in recent decades the rationale for keeping the valley flooded has faded. America has gotten out of the dam-building business—in the present century, nearly one thousand dams have been removed from US rivers, in recognition of environmental costs that include the destruction of natural habitats and the deterioration of water quality. San Francisco now has access to many multiples of the outflow from the O'Shaughnessy Dam from other reservoirs. Yet the Hetch Hetchy remains underwater. A "historic mistake," as the Sierra Club labels it, unredeemed.

PART III

CALIFORNIA ASCENDANT

14

CONJURING LOS ANGELES

THE WRITER MORROW MAYO seldom minced words, especially when his subject was the gaudy, tawdry city where he made his home in the 1920s and 1930s.

"Los Angeles, it should be understood, is not a mere city," he wrote. "On the contrary, it is, and has been since 1888, a *commodity*; something to be advertised and sold to the people of the United States like automobiles, cigarettes and mouth wash. . . . The attitude of the Angelenos towards their city is precisely that of a salesman towards his product, or a football cheering-section towards its team. Here is a spirit of boost which has become a fetish, an obsession, a mania. *Everything* else is secondary to it."

Mayo's acerbic book *Los Angeles* appeared in 1933, when the city was in its second decade as the dominant metropolis of California; in the 1920 census, its population had finally exceeded that of San Francisco, which had been the center of the state's economic and political life since the Gold Rush and the granting of statehood.

That Los Angeles would someday overtake San Francisco in prominence was in some respects preordained. San Francisco is geographically constrained, perched at the tip of a narrow peninsula like a fingernail, with water on three sides. Consequently, its population has never reached even nine hundred thousand. Los Angeles, however, lies nestled within a vast basin stretching from the Pacific Ocean to the San Gabriel and Santa Monica mountain ranges on the north and northwest, some three and a half million acres of mostly undeveloped territory capable, in the fullness of time, of supporting a population of more than thirteen million.

Yet seen from another perspective, nothing could be as surprising as the birth in that particular location of a gigantic, vigorous megalopolis. The Los Angeles Basin is a place seemingly devoid of the resources needed to sustain life and commerce. For most of its history, it has had no reliable supply of water, no port—the best natural harbor in Southern California is San Diego's, one hundred twenty-five miles to the south, and the nearest shore is a thirty-mile trek from the pueblo that the Spaniards of Mexico established as their civic seat early in the nineteenth century. Its rivers are dry gulches for most of the year; Mark Twain is said to have quipped that he once fell into a Southern California river and "come out all dusty."

The Los Angeles that became the queen city of California did not grow naturally but had to be "conjured into existence." Almost everything that made it habitable needed to be imported. Its water came from a river valley two hundred miles away and its electricity from a river canyon three hundred miles to the west, brought to the city via systems that are titanic marvels of human engineering. It is wrong to think of the basin as a void to be filled up; better to view it as a gigantic canvas on which its settlers painted a new, transformative future for their state.

THE CUSTOMARY DATE given for the birth of Los Angeles is September 4, 1781, though whether that reflects some sort of ceremonial formality or the whims of Spanish administrators has been lost in the mist of time. El Pueblo de Nuestra Señora la Reina de Los Angeles ("the Pueblo of our Lady the Queen of the Angels") was one of a string of agricultural settlements the Spanish established to grow provisions for their garrisons, or presidios, in San Jose, San Diego, and Santa Barbara. The regional governor, Felipe de Neve, judged that the Indians whom the Spanish herded into rancherias around the Los Angeles pueblo were incapable of cultivating the land sufficiently to meet the presidios' needs without close supervision, so he dispatched a company of soldiers south into Mexico to recruit able colonists. The soldiers were to return with twenty-four families, each to be headed by a paterfamilias "healthy, robust, and without known vice or defect." Each family group was to include, at a minimum, a mason, a blacksmith, and a carpenter. The recruits were guaranteed rations for three years and the equivalent of ten dollars a month, along with a house lot and land for cultivation. They were required to sell any crops they harvested (beyond their own subsistence needs) exclusively to the presidios for ten years.

The soldiers managed to recruit only twelve families, whom they escorted north starting in April 1781, moving at an easy amble to avoid fatiguing the human travelers or injuring their livestock. They arrived at the Mission of San Gabriel, about nine miles from the site de Neve had mapped out, on August 18. There they stopped for several days to recover from an outbreak of smallpox; they finally reached their destination in the first week of September. The adults were identified in the official record by name and ethnic blood—Spanish, Indians, "mestizos" and "mulattresses," and one Negro. A single male was identified as Chinese, although he bore a Spanish name. There were twelve men ranging in age from twenty-two to sixty-eight, eleven women (whose ages were not recorded), and twenty-three children.

At first, the agricultural output of the Los Angeles pueblo disappointed the Spanish. The year after its founding, de Neve concluded that the pueblo needed an "active and exacting" supervisor "who will bestir the settlers to cultivate their lands [and] care for their crops." Although the soil would be superbly productive if properly watered, the settlers were so negligent that the first wheat harvest was barely half what was expected and the first corn crop entirely lost: "The plants, already sprouted, dried up because of their carelessness in not opening up the irrigation ditch soon enough to water them." Thus did de Neve establish himself as the first observer on record to complain about the supposed lassitude of Southern Californians.

For decades, the economy of the region stretching south of the Tehachapi range stagnated. In 1850, while San Francisco was basking in the stupendous influx of people and wealth produced by the Gold Rush, Los Angeles was still barely a village, with 1,610 inhabitants recorded in the 1850 census and "no newspaper, hospital, public school, college, library, Protestant church, factory, bank, or public utility of any kind." One-third of its residents could neither read nor write.

Residents of the rich northern counties tended to see the inhabitants of the south as almost an alien race, or at least more Mexican than American. Southern Californians also felt themselves to be a breed apart. "So unlike are the California of the North and the California of the South that already two distinct peoples are growing up," wrote J. P. Widney, a pioneering Angeleno, in 1888. "The time is rapidly drawing near when the separation which the working of natural laws is making in the people must become a separation of civil laws as well, and two Californias stand side by side as distinct and separate states." Visitors from all over either disdained the underdevelopment of Los Angeles or condescendingly appreciated it for its quaintness. "The English tongue was as foreign from the speech that one would hear in its streets as it would be in Culiacan or Jalapa," reported a traveler who had come north in 1872 from a sojourn in Mexico.

Angelenos bristled at the hauteur of their neighbors beyond the Tehachapi, an attitude reflected in the south's underrepresentation in the state legislature and its consequent over-taxation; the six thousand voting residents of the six southern "cow counties," as they were dismissively described, paid a total of $42,000 in property taxes into the state treasury, while the 120,000 residents of the north paid half that sum. A movement sprang up to sunder the state in two and establish the southern counties as the "Territory of Colorado" or even as a Pacific Republic. The advocates got as far as calling a convention to implement the division amid strong indications that a majority of southern voters would grant approval, but before the issue could be presented to Congress, the Civil War broke out and the movement withered away.

With one exception, the Gold Rush left almost no trace of itself in the portion of California from Monterey south to the Mexican border. The exception was the Southern California cattle industry, which briefly prospered thanks to the gold miners' demand for beef. Yet in time, the cattle ranchers fell victim to the emergent boom-and-bust pattern of the Southern California economy. Beef prices were driven so high by the surge in demand that Mexican ranchers flooded the market with livestock, eroding what had been a Southern California monopoly; by 1855, the competition had sent prices plummeting by 75 percent. Then came a series of natural catastrophes, starting with punishing droughts in 1856 and 1860. They were followed perversely by torrential rains in 1861, which drowned hundreds of head. Yet another drought arrived in 1863, killing cattle by the tens of thousands; for years to come travelers in the south would be "often startled by coming suddenly on a veritable Golgotha, a place of skulls, the long horns standing out in defiant attitude, as if protecting the fleshless bones."

Despite the productive potential of irrigated land in the south, commercial truck farming was slow to develop. One problem was the settlers' get-rich-quick approach to agriculture. An early boom centered on the cultivation of silkworms. This was triggered by the proselytizing of a French-born settler named Louis Prevost, who in the 1860s established an orchard of mulberry trees in present-day Riverside to nurture the voracious cocoon-spinning worms and persuaded the state legislature to support it with subsidies. Yet instead of building factories to produce silk, which might have given birth to a sustainable industry, the farmers opted for short-term profits by selling eggs and trees to collect the government grants. By 1869 the market for silkworm eggs was saturated, the state repealed the subsidy, and the industry imploded.

The next craze was for wool production, with output more than doubling between 1868 and 1871, only to fall victim to the competition from Australia, France, and Mexico attracted by a spurt in demand for wool. Their entry into the market produced a glut and ended the boom.

Meanwhile, the city of Los Angeles gained an image as a crime-ridden "haven for thugs" and "staging place for drifters"—most of them disaffected and unemployed ex-prospectors, soldiers, and ranchers. The homicide rate of 158 per 100,000 in the 1850s and 1860s was nearly twenty times that of New York City. The town was "policed in theory alone." An exasperated editorialist at the *Los Angeles Star* pronounced its six-member police force "rotten from head to foot" and deeply in thrall to criminal gangs. San Francisco had experienced a similar period of civic disorder in the 1850s, but Los Angeles lacked the critical mass of wealthy civic leaders who had organized the committees of vigilance of 1851 and 1856 in San Francisco and enabled that city to fill its vacuum of law enforcement with specially appointed lawmen.

The two cities shared a tendency toward political corruption, however. Fraud was so pervasive in Los Angeles that "a man could sell his vote at election times as easily as he could buy a drink at all other times." The *Los Angeles Express* estimated that about $20,000 had changed hands within a largely inebriated electorate during the primary election day of September 6, 1871.

No event testified to the lawlessness of Los Angeles more than the horrific outbreak of anti-Chinese violence on October 24, 1871, which took the lives of eighteen Chinese residents. The massacre could be traced to two sources. The immediate cause was a quarrel that erupted between two Chinese gangs over a prostitute who had been the victim of serial abductions by those two gangs, each of which claimed to own her. As an accused kidnapper was being escorted from his arraignment on the morning of October 24, a gunfight broke out between the gangs. A white policeman was wounded, as was a white saloon owner who had come out from behind his bar upon hearing a police whistle. Within hours, the district was overrun by an armed mob spoiling for battle.

The broader context was the 1863 state law barring Chinese from testifying against whites in California courts. The law merely extended to Chinese people the ban on testimony by Indians against whites enacted by the first state legislature in 1850, but it obviously exposed Chinese residents to robbery, injury, and murder by white hoodlums, who could evade arrest and punishment as long as their crimes were committed only before Chinese witnesses. In San Francisco, civic leaders organized a force of special police to patrol the city and arrest anyone found abusing Chinese residents. No such effort emerged in Los Angeles, where unprovoked assaults on Chinese men and women became widespread.

Anti-Chinese antagonism in Los Angeles was less rooted in economic rivalry between Chinese and whites than it was in San Francisco. Unlike Chinese residents in Northern California, who competed directly with whites for work in factories and on farms, in Southern California they typically worked as launderers, cooks, domestic servants, and vegetable peddlers, occupations shunned by whites. But the white residents were nevertheless receptive to the generalized contempt for Asians communicated by political leaders and the press, which depicted the Chinese as resistant to assimilation, eager to work for absurdly low wages, and morally depraved. Among the most virulent sources of vitriolic anti-Chinese hatred was the *Los Angeles News*, which was affiliated with labor unions and the Democratic Party and "relentlessly castigated the Chinese people as 'an inferior and idolatrous race . . . and a foul blot on our civilization.'" To the whites of Los Angeles no less than to those of San Francisco, the Chinese were aliens who could be treated with scorn.

This surely contributed to the savagery of the violence of October 24. The white marauders, who were estimated to exceed five hundred, dragged Chinese residents from their beds and lynched them in the street. No distinction was made between Chinese gunmen and innocents; among the victims was a popular doctor named Chien Lee "Gene" Tong, who was robbed and shot in the head. The crowd strung him up and entertained itself by tugging on the rope so hard his head struck the crossbeam again and again. When the killing was over, four hours after it began, the bodies of the eighteen murdered Chinese residents—one out of every ten Chinese inhabitants of

Los Angeles—were deposited under tarpaulins in front of the police station, some still with ropes around their necks, and their homes were ransacked.

The carnage elicited horror and condemnation from coast to coast. Any expectation that the worst mass lynching in US history would produce a soul-searching about the treatment of Asians in California or nationwide was quickly dashed, however. A grand jury returned thirty-seven indictments in November, but only ten suspects were ever brought to trial. Eight were convicted of manslaughter in the killing of Gene Tong and sentenced to terms ranging from two to six years. The state supreme court overturned the convictions on the technicality that the indictments had not explicitly specified that Tong had been murdered.

Rather than producing pangs of conscience, the 1871 massacre led to a redoubling of official discrimination against the Chinese in America. The lesson that California communicated to the nation at large was that the solution to anti-Asian antagonism was to bar Asians from coming to America at all. The product of this approach was the Chinese Exclusion Act of 1882, that artifact of Kearneyist racial discrimination.

The local press, which had done so much to foment anti-Chinese hostility, engaged in no self-reflection and showed no remorse after the massacre, but continued to disparage Chinese culture and behavior. Only a week after the massacre, the *Star* was predicting that the event would result in "no evil of consequence" for Los Angeles and would "be forgotten in a brief time."

The *Star* was correct. The Chinese who had fled Los Angeles after the massacre soon returned, moved into apartments in the Chinese district left vacant by their countrymen's murders, and took up their former livelihoods. When the Chinese New Year arrived the following February, they celebrated the holiday with the customary noisemakers and fireworks.

The impulse to bury the memory of this unprecedented outbreak of violence arose from the local boosters' desire to exploit for tourism and economic development Southern California's one manifestly marketable feature: its weather.

The promotion of Southern California's Mediterranean climate took hold in the first decade after the Gold Rush and continued into the new century. Travel writers praised the region's moderate temperatures and lack of humidity—dry, but not *too* dry—and described its healthful effects as almost miraculous. "The diseases of children prevalent elsewhere are unknown here," reported Charles Dudley Warner, the coauthor with Mark Twain of the 1873 novel *The Gilded Age.* "They cut their teeth without risk, and *cholera infantum* never visits them. Diseases of the bowels are practically unknown. . . . Renal diseases are also wanting; disorders of the liver and kidneys, gout, and rheumatism, are not native. . . . These facts are derived from medical practice."

Major Ben C. Truman, an East Coast transplant, compiled the death rates from all causes in American cities for his 1885 book *Homes and Happiness in the Golden State of California* and found thirty-seven deaths per thousand inhabitants in New Orleans; twenty-four in St. Louis, Boston, and Chicago; and a mere thirteen in Los Angeles. "Fevers and diseases of the malarial character carry off about half of mankind, and diseases of the respiratory organs one-fourth," he wrote. "From such diseases many of the towns of California are remarkably free. . . . *Cholera, yellow fever, sunstroke, and ravages by wind storms are unknown!*" (His emphasis.)

The German-born journalist Charles Nordhoff* wrote glowingly of the regional climate's health-giving qualities for tuberculosis patients, describing it as the French Riviera's equal, lacking only the deluxe hospitality infrastructure of that renowned gathering place of the rich: "You will not find . . . tasteful pleasure-grounds or large, finely-laid-out places. Nature has done much; man has not, so far, helped her." If he was trying to alert resort developers to the existence of a blank slate to be written on for great profit, he could hardly have done better.

The ballyhoo had its limits, however. The completion of the first transcontinental railroad in 1869 opened the West Coast to a flood of immigrants, but the flood initially reached no farther than San Francisco. The striking of the Golden Spike "meant no more to Southern Californians than if they had been citizens of the Hawaiian Islands." The route from the railhead at Sacramento to Los Angeles traversed 450 miles of rutted roads, leaving travelers sore from days spent "bouncing over the mountains" in a "creaking, swaying coach."

Following its creation in 1870, the Southern Pacific took steps to drive its rails from Northern California south toward San Diego. This was the Angelenos' dream, for a rail connection was the one element needed to transform the pueblo into a big city. The railroad could choose from any number of routes south, however, and could select as its southern terminus one of any number

---

* Not to be confused with his grandson, the Charles Nordhoff who coauthored the 1932 novel *Mutiny on the Bounty.*

of largely undeveloped communities. Los Angeles (population 5,700), San Diego (2,300), and Santa Ana (1,445) were the largest settlements in the region south of the Tehachapi range. From the railroad's standpoint, they were all "little country towns," none more suitable than any other.

Facing the risk that their community would be circumvented by the Southern Pacific and thus be forever condemned to inconsequence, Los Angeles leaders embarked on a campaign of civic persuasion. Recognizing that a link between the Southern Pacific and the San Pedro harbor by way of Los Angeles would be essential, the boosters' first step was to build a line inland from the port. The goal was to convert the twenty-one miles of dusty cow paths over which stagecoaches carried goods and passengers into a paved connector. Taking charge of this project was Phineas Banning, a barrel-chested glad-hander whose herd of five hundred cargo-carrying mules and fleet of harbor tugs had made him the king of the Southern California freight business. To secure the voters' approval of the $225,000 bond needed to build the port line, Banning advertised the bond as the key to securing a glowing future of limitless growth and prosperity, thereby creating a model for Los Angeles civic financing campaigns for decades to come.

Once the San Pedro line was completed, Banning and his fellow boosters ran into another obstacle: the Southern Pacific's buccaneering temperament. "Railway companies are soulless corporations," a local newspaper warned. "They are invariably selfish and love money." The city promised the railroad a healthy subsidy, leaving only its size to be negotiated. The Southern Pacific's demand was the maximum permitted by law, 5 percent of the county's assessed valuation, which was calculated at $10,554,592. In other words, its price was $527,730, to which the city added another $75,000 worth of stock in the harbor line, for a total of nearly $603,000, not including sixty acres of land the city donated for a depot. In return, the railroad agreed to build fifty miles of trunk line within the county and designate Los Angeles as its terminus. The deal was approved by voters in November 1872. After the line's completion, the city staged an inaugural ceremony on September 5, 1876, with the Southern Pacific's David D. Colton hammering down a golden spike as the final link in the steel chain connecting Los Angeles and San Francisco.

What appeared at first to be an extortionate subsidy proved in the long run to be a great bargain for Los Angeles. Just as city leaders had hoped, the extension of the Southern Pacific south from San Francisco launched the transformation of Los Angeles into a "full-fledged metropolis." But it did not end the need for civic boosterism—if anything, the demand for hoopla increased. The reason was that the Southern Pacific was little known by eastern bankers, whose capital was crucial for the railroad's continued expansion; investors who were aware of the railroad at all concluded that its southern branch traversed territory that was as yet so unproductive and lightly populated that it would be many years before the freight and passenger traffic could cover the cost of construction.

Consequently, the Southern Pacific turned itself into one of the chief boosters of Southern California, the same service it would perform for San Francisco after the 1906 earthquake. It did so through *Sunset* magazine, its house organ, which depicted the southland's virtues in photographs, drawings, and unblushing promotional testimony. "I have caught every fish on the Atlantic coast and know every fishing ground, but the finest fishing, to my mind, in the world is to be found at Santa Catalina island," the magazine quoted one Franklin S. Schenck of Brooklyn.

Soon Southern California was reveling in its first major land boom. The condescending reference to the "cow counties" south of the Tehachapi had to be retired, especially after 1885, when the Atchison, Topeka, and Santa Fe Railroad completed the nation's second transcontinental line by driving its tracks into Los Angeles and provoking a rate war with the Southern Pacific. The fare from New York and Chicago to Southern California dropped to $100 from $125; by March 1887, the rate from Kansas City had fallen as low as one dollar per passenger. Visitors who had been intrigued by the books of Nordhoff and Truman now could satisfy their curiosity at a bargain price. That year, some 120,000 passengers were brought into Los Angeles by the Southern Pacific, while the Santa Fe served the region with as many as four passenger trains a day. Tourists jammed hotels and boardinghouses, but they were not the only newcomers. The steady rise of land values attracted fortune-seekers eyeing the prospect of making a killing in real estate as well as families with the simpler ambition of making new lives in the West. Between 1880 and 1890 the city's population nearly quintupled, from 11,000 to 50,000. Los Angeles "suddenly changed from a very old city to a very young one." In 1890, more than three-fourths of its residents had lived in the city for fewer than four years.

Recounted travel writer H. Ellington Brook, "Everybody that could find an office went into the real-estate business . . . a crowd of speculators settled down upon Los Angeles like flies upon a bowl of sugar." The railroads brought swarms of sharp operators who had already drained the Midwest of its potential for land fraud and detected on the West Coast a "golden opportunity of the fakir and humbug and the man with the past that he wanted forgotten," a municipal historian wrote. Thus was born Southern California's image as a place to start anew, especially among those with reason to shed memories of a previous life.

To a great extent, the boom in real estate values was based on fiction. Los Angeles still had almost no industry to sustain its growing population—indeed, virtually no economic activity at all other than real estate speculation. Promoters established new townsites on every patch of vacant land, building hotels and laying down concrete sidewalks and community halls: "A miniature city appeared, like a scene conjured up by Aladdin's lamp, where a few months ago the jack-rabbit sported and the coyote howled," wrote Brook. "Old settlers, who had declared that land was dear at $5 an acre, looked aghast to see people tumbling over each other to secure lots at $500 each"—one-third cash down, the rest to be paid over six or twelve months. "Every clerk, and waiter, and car-driver, and servant girl scrimped and saved to make a first payment" on a lot in one of the scores of "paper cities" that sprang up during the summer of 1887. Promoters lured crowds to land auctions with brass bands and free lunches as well as "advertisements rich in descriptions and profuse in promises that were never intended to be fulfilled . . . lithographs of colleges about to materialize . . . railroads that began and ended in the imagination of the projectors." They promised that values would continue rising without limit: "Buy land in Los Angeles and wear diamonds," read a boom-time advertisement.

The boom penetrated all the way to San Diego, where "gambling was open and flagrant . . . painted women paraded the town in carriages," and "theft, murder . . . highway robbery and licentiousness gave to the passing show in boomtime San Diego many of the characteristics of the frontier camp." So wrote the war correspondent Walter Gifford Smith, scanning the city as if it were a new beachhead in California's eternal battle between virtue and vice.

But this boom ended as all must—with a resounding crash. From October 1886 to August 1887, monthly real estate sales had grown from $2.2 million to $11.5 million. Then the buyers hastened to realize their gains by selling. Townsites that had been mapped out to accommodate homesteaders by the thousands were abandoned without having attracted any inhabitants at all, save perhaps for a watchman to keep guard over abandoned housing plots. The brass bands fell silent. The banks called in their loans and refused new applications. The boom evaporated almost overnight.

Still, all was not blight. The 1880s frenzy created a foundation for growth spurts to come. Not every promised college was fictitious. The University of Southern California was founded in 1880 and Occidental College in 1887. In 1891 a Pasadena philanthropist named Amos Throop founded Throop University, a technical institute that would evolve into the California Institute of Technology, or Caltech. The first streetcar lines were mapped out and water systems built. An estimated 137,000 boom-time tourists set down roots in the region, populating new communities that would develop into Long Beach, Glendale, and other cities that remain part of Southern California's geography.

The boosters stayed on the job. In October 1888, the Los Angeles Chamber of Commerce was founded at the initiative of Harrison Gray Otis, who brought together the city's leading business owners to create a program for nationwide municipal marketing. The chamber sent a railcar dubbed "California on Wheels" to visit every important town in the Midwest, displaying agricultural produce amid scenic photographs and charts projecting remarkable growth for the city. It was a rare civic exposition that did not boast a Los Angeles pavilion. Trade delegations visiting the city were feted in high style. By the turn of the century Los Angeles had acquired the reputation of "the best advertised city in America."

Entrepreneurs spent lavishly to refashion the physical landscape. The most spectacular undertaking was the handiwork of Abbot Kinney, a New Jersey transplant with blood connections to luminaries such as Ralph Waldo Emerson and Oliver Wendell Holmes and a fat bankroll provided by his family's cigarette company. A "white-bearded, black moustached, starry-eyed combination of booster and dreamer" who had been asthmatic from childhood, Kinney discovered the health-giving qualities of the Southern California climate during a stay at a resort in the Sierra Madre mountains in 1880 and decided to make the region his new home. He bought a 160-acre parcel of salt marsh south of Santa Monica and hired engineers and architects to drain it, dredge out a system of four-foot-deep canals, and erect replicas of the Venetian doges' Renaissance palaces and the Rialto Bridge spanning the Grand Canal. He imported gondolas along with gondoliers and opened "The

Venice of America" in 1905. The place became a tourist attraction, though by 1925 the elegant canal network had deteriorated into a hodgepodge of freak shows, honkytonks, and stagnant pools. At that point the community's inhabitants pleaded for annexation by the city of Los Angeles, which paved over most of the canals and converted Venice, California, from a glittering tourist trap into an urban beach neighborhood.

Southern California continued to attract tourists by the thousands, many of them lured by a romantic mythology centered on the Mission era. In its original manifestation, this was the product of the 1884 publication of Helen Hunt Jackson's novel *Ramona*.

Jackson had come west from Amherst, Massachusetts, as a tourist in the 1880s, during which she absorbed what the writer Carey McWilliams called "odds and ends of gossip, folk tales, and Mission-inspired allegories" concerning the California Indians. She fell under the spell of the region's temperate climate, which she ascribed to its being walled off from the rest of the continent by the mountains. That rendered it "climatically insulated," she wrote—"a sort of island on land."*

Jackson intended *Ramona* to be a social justice tract akin to Harriet Beecher Stowe's *Uncle Tom's Cabin*; her goal was to unmask the persecution and abuse visited upon the Indians by the Mission fathers and the Spanish military. The public would utterly miss the point.

Ramona tells the story of the orphaned daughter of a white father and Indian mother who elopes with an Indian named Alessandro. The young lovers are evicted by a white landlord and lose their daughter to illness because of neglect by a white doctor. Ramona is widowed when Alessandro is murdered after being wrongly accused as a horse thief. Finally, she remarries and moves to Mexico to find lifelong peace.

Contrary to Jackson's intentions, *Ramona* seized the public's imagination as a romantic narrative of star-crossed lovers. A *Ramona* craze took hold. Tourists swarmed Southern California to discover the scenery that gave Jackson her inspiration. Promoters fed the frenzy with picture postcards depicting the purported locales of the book, and the Southern Pacific staged excursions to the most popular locations. The book received numerous dramatizations,

---

* McWilliams used Jackson's line as the subtitle of his book *Southern California Country*. He misquoted it, however, as "an island on the land," thus giving her phrase a universality it does not possess in the original.

including at least three film features. A live version is staged annually in the desert community of Hemet, sometimes with amateur local actors, sometimes with professionals (in 1959 Raquel Welch appeared as Ramona, one of her first professional acting assignments). That the book's plot and characters bore little resemblance to real life—among other distinctions, the book treated the Franciscan padres as kind and protective, and depicted the gringos exclusively as villainous monsters—mattered little.

The sugarcoating of the historically distant Mission era as an example of civilized Spanish colonization of a backward land was augmented by the work of Charles Fletcher Lummis, who as an editor of the *Los Angeles Times* had acquired a taste for Mission architecture along with vexation at the old Spanish chapels' drift into disrepair. In 1895, Lummis launched a campaign for their renovation, which required bathing the missionaries' less than creditable activities in an inspirational glow that would shine for the better part of a century, until the advent of a more discerning historiography.

CLIMATE, ROMANTIC MYTHOLOGY, the lure of real estate wealth—all these factors set the stage for one of the greatest booms of all. Nearly 1.5 million new residents moved into Southern California between 1920 and 1930, an influx that was labeled "the largest internal migration in the history of the American people," and one that would not be exceeded until the postwar 1940s and 1950s.

The explosive growth brought with it gimlet-eyed reassessments of what it had taken to bring Los Angeles to its newfound stature as reigning metropolis of the West. More acerbic even than Morrow Mayo was a Slovenian transplant named Louis Adamic, who had immigrated to the United States in 1913 and settled among fellow Croatians in the port community of San Pedro, where he held down a job with the harbor pilot's office. As an outsider, Adamic scrutinized his Southern California with pitiless objectivity in essays and books. "Healing is a tremendous industry in Los Angeles," he wrote in 1930. "There are thousands of regular physicians and surgeons and dentists, and hundreds of chiropractors, osteopaths, 'drugless doctors,' electro-therapeutists, Christian Science practitioners, other faith-healers like Aimee McPherson . . . magicians, spellbinders, mesmerists, mystics, miracle men and women, wonder workers, yogis, and quacks and charlatans of all descriptions."

But Adamic could not overlook the city's growth. During the 1920s, he observed, its population had passed one million, and "now the go-getters . . . look confidently ahead to 1935, when the third million will be on the way. Big things are immediately ahead."

While the city's population did not reach three million until the 1980s, its civic character was already written. It was a place controlled by a handful of fabulously wealthy men whose greed and political power would play a momentous role in the city's history.

Chief among those men was Otis, whose obdurate hostility to organized labor became a credo of the city's business establishment. When unionized typographers went on strike in 1890 after Otis and other publishers cut wages by one-fifth and locked out scores of protesting employees, the *Times* continued to operate with scab workers for five years, at which point the union ended its strike in defeat. Otis would boast of never again employing a union man at the *Times*.

Although the city's newspapers all filled their columns with unrelenting anti-union rhetoric, the *Times'* "bitterness of attack has never been matched by any other newspaper in the United States or elsewhere," a prominent labor historian observed. Its attacks on organized labor intensified after the Pullman strike of 1894 halted rail service into and out of Chicago, threatening to isolate California from the rest of the country and stranding its perishable fruits and vegetables at depots in Los Angeles. (The strike was broken by a court injunction and President Grover Cleveland's deployment of federal troops.)

In the strike's wake Otis led the city's employers to form the Merchants and Manufacturers Association. The M&M became the nation's most powerful lobby for the open shop—that is, the rule that employment cannot be tied to union membership. The M&M's founders perceived that the greatest advantage their city could have over San Francisco, the state's heavily unionized industrial and trade center, was a lower wage scale. Wages in Los Angeles undercut those in San Francisco by as much as 40 percent. The stream of homesteaders into Southern California provided a steady supply of laborers competing fiercely with one another for work, and many newcomers were vulnerable to exploitation—they were invalids seeking light jobs, farmers aiming to escape the short growing seasons and punishing weather back east, and nearly penniless migrants willing to work for little.

Otis and his fellows spread open-shop propaganda to the point where few major employers tolerated union members or organizing activities on their premises. They pressured the city council to pass in July 1910 one of the first anti-picketing ordinances in the country and certainly the most stringent. Within weeks, 470 workers had been arrested.*

Rather than quell labor unrest, the employers' campaign provoked an uproar in the working class. The unions and the Socialist Party, feeling their position strengthened, mustered workers by the tens of thousands for street parades.

Then came October 1, 1910.

Shortly after one o'clock that morning, two powerful blasts detonated at the *Times* building at Broadway and First Street, igniting barrels of flammable ink. One hundred workers were trapped in the inferno. Twenty-one died.

The *Times* labeled the explosion "the crime of the century" and "one of the worst atrocities in the history of the world" and blamed union agitators. The Los Angeles labor community held the belief that a gas leak inside the building had caused the explosions. But the following April, two union members, brothers James B. and John J. McNamara, were arrested for the dynamiting. They pleaded not guilty, and the American Federation of Labor hired Clarence Darrow for the defense. On Labor Day, a crowd of twenty-five thousand assembled by the Socialist Party and union leaders massed at the county jail where the brothers were held to serenade them raucously with "La Marseillaise," the socialist anthem.

As the brothers' trial approached, so did the city's mayoral election, threatening the M&M with its worst nightmare—a Socialist mayor of Los Angeles. That candidate was Job Harriman, a lawyer who was a member of the McNamaras' legal team. Harriman saw the open shop as an instrument of the same capitalist power that endowed railroad tycoons with their mastery over the law and politics: "They seek an open shop to keep the worker disorganized and weak, so that they may reap the greatest harvest to themselves constantly," he would tell a government investigating commission in 1916. After he won the Democratic primary with a plurality at the end

---

* A yarn beloved of Los Angeles historians holds that Otis rode around in a limousine with a cannon mounted on the hood, at the ready to fend off hordes of violent unionists. The cannon is mythical, however; the object was a horn that vaguely resembled a miniature artillery piece but blew only air.

of October, the threat he represented to the city's entrenched plutocrats became tangible.

Otis's newspaper warned that the election of Harriman would be a disaster touching the lives of all Los Angelenos, portending "an orgie of evil, in a season of stagnation in business . . . in the withdrawal of capital, in hunger in the homes and rioting on the highways."

The employers were saved, as it happened, by the inconvenient fact that the McNamaras were guilty—or at least, in Darrow's view, that the evidence against them was so strong they were sure to be convicted. He turned his efforts to saving their lives. In return for guilty pleas, James, who had the more direct role in the dynamiting, would be spared the death penalty, which Darrow had long campaigned against as "a cruel, brutal, useless barbarism." John would be sentenced to ten years in prison. Despite the agreement, the judge sentenced John to fifteen years. Both men died in 1941, James at San Quentin and John in Butte, Montana.

The city's labor and socialist voters reacted with revulsion to the McNamaras' guilty pleas, which were filed only days before the election. They took their anger out on Harriman, who lost to George Alexander, the incumbent mayor he had trounced in the primary, by 34,000 votes.

The pleas also knocked the wind out of a nascent union campaign to mandate closed shops—in which union membership is a condition for employment—in Los Angeles, and bolstered Otis's campaign against organized labor. Coverage of the pleas at the *Times* had a triumphalist tone: "Industrial freedom reigns supreme," the newspaper crowed. (The main entrance to the 1930s-era headquarters building the *Times* erected in downtown Los Angeles would be etched with a creed similarly dedicating the structure to "the cause of true industrial freedom," and a bronze statuette of an eagle, which somehow the 1910 explosion had failed to dislodge from its perch atop the old building, was installed in the lobby, where it stared down visitors waiting for the elevators for the next eighty-five years.)

Otis's successor as owner of the *Times,* his son-in-law Harry Chandler, carried on Otis's fiercely anti-union stance. Chandler inherited the newspaper upon Otis's death in 1917, expanded his family's wealth through canny investments in real estate, and soon exercised nearly absolute authority over Southern California's political and business establishments. By the mid-1920s there were few ventures or investments in the region into which his fingers did not reach. Estimates of his wealth approached half a billion dollars, and in the corridors of the *Los Angeles Times* he was said to be the eleventh richest person in the world.

Chandler's *Times* agitated for even harsher anti-union legislation than had been enacted during Otis's life. In 1919 a campaign by the newspaper to stoke hysteria over the Industrial Workers of the World, the union known familiarly as the "Wobblies," resulted in the state's Criminal Syndicalism Act, under which hundreds of labor organizers were sent to prison as "radicals." Arrests under the law were invariably granted front-page coverage in the *Times*. Los Angeles district attorney Thomas L. Woolwine officially declared even membership in the Wobblies to be a felony under the act, a decree praised by the *Times* as a "war of extermination on I.W.W." Ultimately, nearly twenty states would pass anti-syndicalism laws based on California's model. The California law was upheld by the US Supreme Court in 1927, declared unconstitutional as an infringement on free speech in 1969, but not officially repealed in California until 1991.

Otis and Chandler had made Los Angeles vehemently hostile to organized labor. Yet they could not keep it from becoming a seedbed for grassroots utopian movements, such as the one that would almost sweep the socialist writer Upton Sinclair into the governorship.

The 1920s would make Los Angeles and Southern California modern. The missing factors were water and a new technology for mythmaking—the movies.

15

GHOSTS OF THE OWENS VALLEY

CALIFORNIA HAD NEVER experienced an event like it. The celebrations accompanying the announcement of statehood in 1850 and the driving of the Golden Spike in 1869 had been enthusiastic enough, but they had not attracted anything like the crowd of more than thirty thousand assembled at the north end of the San Fernando Valley to witness the coming of the water.

It was November 5, 1913. On that day the last valve on the Los Angeles Aqueduct was to be opened. The water would flow to Los Angeles from the bucolic Owens River Valley more than two hundred miles to the north. Crews from navy ships at harbor were granted leave to attend, Shriners paused their Los Angeles convention to join the throng, and families came aboard special trains put on by the Southern Pacific. Awaiting the big moment, the crowd was entertained by the world-famous coloratura soprano Ellen Beach Yaw, who made her home in Southern California and who visibly struggled to keep her windblown feather boa out of her mouth, lest it muffle the words of the anthem—"California, Hail the Waters"—she had composed for this moment.

There were speeches by Congressman William Stephens, a former mayor and future governor, and General Harrison Gray Otis, a prime beneficiary of the fabulous profits the water would bring to the city's more fortunate and farsighted landowners. (Otis had been commissioned as a brigadier general during the Spanish-American War.) Then came Mayor Henry Rose's introduction of William Mulholland as "the man who built the aqueduct." Mulholland stood up to unfurl an American flag as the signal to let the water flow. A thin stream trickled from under heavy iron gates. As the gates rose ponderously, the trickle grew into a torrent, cascading down the concrete spillway that moments before had been as dry as a desert arroyo. A gun salute resounded over the crowd's cheers. Mulholland stepped back to the podium and uttered what remain to this day the most famous five words in Los Angeles history. "There it is," he croaked. "Take it."

WHETHER THE TALE is seen as a victory over nature or an act of ruthless thievery, the story of Los Angeles and the Owens Valley has something for everyone, from academic historians to freewheeling mythmakers. The narrative handed down for longer than a century bubbles like a rich stew with incident and personality—explosive violence, embezzlements, allegations of fraud, and a suicide—posing fundamental questions of morality and the injustice of plutocratic power wielded against the defenseless. Nonfiction writers, novelists, and moviemakers have found the story irresistible, right up to the classic film *Chinatown* (1974), which transposes the story to the 1930s, treats every claim of official and private skullduggery as gospel truth, and sets it all against a blood-soaked backdrop of murder and incest.

In its most extreme versions, the Owens Valley case has been presented as a saga of merciless cruelty. Morrow Mayo set the standard for this approach in his 1933 book *Los Angeles*, in which he asserted that the city got its water by "one of the costliest, crookedest, most unscrupulous deals ever perpetrated." Mayo accused the city of having "deliberately ruined Owens Valley" in an "obscene enterprise from beginning to end." The phraseology of his crowning judgment is broad in its implications and purposefully salacious: "The Federal Government of the United States held Owens Valley," he wrote, "while Los Angeles raped it."

Yet the story is not so simple. The romanticization of the Owens Valley saga as a David-and-Goliath battle in which a valiant David was vanquished has long poisoned efforts to balance valuations of water as an agricultural resource, a crucial commodity for urban dwellers, and a life-giving necessity for nature's flora and fauna. Water is the most contentious resource in the world, and part of the blame belongs to the story of Owens Valley. Since the first trickles appeared under the gates in the San Fernando Valley, policymakers in California have tried to lay the ghost of Owens Valley to rest. The effort continues, because the contests waged for water among rural, agricultural, and urban Americans extend beyond California's borders to the rest of the country.

It is true that the aqueduct made some of the richest tycoons in Los Angeles unimaginably richer but not true that their greed was all that motivated its construction. It is also true that the individuals most often pictured as the villains of the case, Mulholland and former Los Angeles mayor Fred Eaton, were not among those who reaped the greatest profits. Nor is it true that the goal of Los Angeles was to ruin the valley, as Mayo had it. Most owners of water rights in the valley knew that what they were selling was valuable. They held out for the best price, gaining far more financially by selling their water to Los Angeles than they would have as farmers.

Still, there can be no denying that subterfuge played a role in how Los Angeles initially acquired its water rights in the valley. Mulholland admitted that the city kept the valley in the dark about its interest in the purchases, otherwise "we never could have obtained the water for anything like the price we are to pay." It is also true that some key figures played multiple roles as public officials and private businessmen that would be condemned today as disqualifying conflicts of interest. Unprincipled as they may have been, however, they were not acting outside contemporary law. The lesson, then as now, may be that what shocks the conscience most is not what is illegal but what is legal.

THE IDEA OF bringing water to Los Angeles from a far-off river originated in the early 1890s in the mind of Fred Eaton. The city was suffering from a prolonged drought, causing farmers to siphon so much water out of underground aquifers that even those seemingly inexhaustible supplies began to go dry and the city's most important surface source, the limpid Los Angeles River, shriveled into a patchwork of shallow ponds.

Eaton was that rare figure of the time—an actual native of Los Angeles, the son of a forty-niner from Missouri who had set out his shingle as a lawyer after his dream of striking it rich in the goldfields failed. In 1871, at age fifteen, Fred landed an apprenticeship with the Los Angeles City Water Company, the private concern that held an exclusive thirty-year franchise to provide the city with water. His affinity for engineering enabled him to rise to the exalted position of general superintendent before he turned twenty. Over the years, he also insinuated himself into municipal politics, first by winning election as city engineer in 1886 and subsequently as mayor, serving a single term from 1898 to 1900. What he brought to those jobs was the conviction that Los Angeles was destined to grow but to do so it would have to import water to supplement what could be drawn from the river. He would impart that conviction to another self-taught engineer, his protégé William Mulholland.

Mulholland became superintendent of the water company's works in 1888 through a combination of luck, a superhuman capacity for physical labor, a restless intellect, and the patronage of Eaton, who gave him his first job in the system as a deputy *zanjero* on the river, the title derived from the Spanish word for "ditch." The Dublin-born Mulholland had come across the Atlantic as a merchant seaman, jumped ship in New York in 1874 at age eighteen, and made his way west via a series of jobs in midwestern lumber camps and aboard Great Lakes freighters. He landed in Los Angeles in 1877 and started at the very bottom of the water-company pyramid. For the task of "clearing brush and debris, removing dead animals from the stream, and keeping the flow in proper channels," Mulholland received $1.50 a day and a tumbledown shack to live in. He labored by day and studied engineering and geometry from library books by candlelight. By 1880 he had become foreman of a pipe-laying crew, which paid two dollars a day and provided another shack, this one equipped with a woodstove that, he complained, emitted more smoke than heat.

The self-educated Mulholland was a man of sharp contrasts. He evinced a taste for literature and music yet wielded a profanity-laced vocabulary that would put a stevedore to shame. As he rose through the ranks of the city's water bureaucracy, he gained a reputation as both an autocratic boss and a figure of unquestioned expertise and integrity, ultimately becoming venerated by municipal employees as simply "the Chief."

The city's public water department was the product of a civic takeover staged in 1899, reflecting the same impulse to bring a municipal water supply under public control that would prompt San Francisco to dam the Hetch Hetchy. Los Angeles had been in thrall to the City Water Company since 1868, when municipal officials unwisely granted the company its thirty-year franchise. That contract required the company to develop a water supply at Crystal Springs, a swampy area north of the city. But the company got most of its water from a secret tunnel it built to tap the river—a "liquid embezzlement" that foreshadowed all the acts of subterfuge that would color the city's water affairs for decades. As the expiration of the franchise approached in 1898, a city takeover seemed inevitable. The water company was widely cursed for excessive charges and atrocious service. One expert estimated that its bills were so inflated that of the average household water charge of fifteen dollars a year, five dollars covered the cost of water and the rest flowed directly to the company's profits. Water pressure was so feeble that the fire department sometimes had to let buildings burn because their hoses ran dry. The city purchased the company's network of pipes and pumps for two million dollars in 1899, funded by a bond issue eagerly endorsed by the voters.

Mulholland moved smoothly from superintendent of the private company's waterworks to the same job as a public employee. In 1888, when he was superintendent of the water company, the river was providing forty million gallons a day to a city of only fifty thousand souls. Eaton continually warned him that this limited supply would be a constraint on growth, but as Mulholland later recounted, "I laughed at him." He told Eaton, "We have enough water in the river to supply the city for the next fifty years." Eaton shot back, "You are wrong. . . . I was born here and have seen dry years, years that you know nothing about. Wait and see." In 1902, the crisis that Eaton foretold erupted in the form of an implacable drought, and Mulholland recognized that Eaton was right.

Eaton had spent years hunting for alternative water sources, partially to serve the city and partially with an eye to turning a personal profit. He identified the most suitable source as the Owens River, which flowed through a 120-mile-long valley east of the Sierra Nevada range. The river terminated at Owens Lake, a fetid alkaline pond that by one estimate contained "enough bicarbonate of soda to supply the entire world." Eaton perceived that, given the valley's average elevation of more than 3,600 feet above sea level, building an intake upstream of the lake would allow the river's bounty to flow to Los Angeles by gravity, without the need for expensive pumping.

Eaton quietly bought up land and water rights along the river starting in the fall of 1904. His plan was to sell enough water to the city at his cost to serve its needs via an aqueduct while retaining rights to the excess, which he could sell to local farmers and ranchers for irrigation. His actions fed the later impression that the city acquired the Owens Valley water through bad faith. With some sellers he posed as a farmer and rancher just like them; a contemporary photograph shows him leaning on the wooden handle of a scythe, wearing a slouch hat and an unbuttoned denim vest. At the General Land Office in the Inyo County seat of Independence, which he visited regularly to record his options and purchases, the registrars assumed that he was an agent of the federal government, assembling the landholdings to build a reservoir for local irrigation—a misimpression he did not bother to correct. In less than a year, he acquired 22,670 acres in the valley. He then presented his idea of a public-private arrangement to the city, only to be promptly turned down.

There were two major obstacles to Eaton's scheme. One was the federal government's Reclamation Service, which had been formed in 1902 to implement President Theodore Roosevelt's conception of conservation as the efficient husbanding of natural resources for use. The service had placed the Owens Valley on its roster of possible irrigation projects. Aware of the city's interest in taking the water rights for its own purposes, it assigned its regional engineer, Joseph B. Lippincott, to establish whether the best use of the river would be for irrigation locally or to satisfy the thirst of distant Los Angeles. Lippincott reported that either purpose was plausible, but he pointed out that since the service's financial resources were limited and many other candidates for irrigation funding were on the drawing board, the better course was to let the city have the water. Reclamation was willing to step aside in the city's favor, but only for a project that was entirely publicly owned. That ruled out Eaton's proposal for a public-private partnership.

The second obstacle was Mulholland's conviction that any system providing a resource as precious as water should be under the public's control. Mulholland was so respected a voice on water issues that his viewpoint prompted voters to amend the city charter in 1903 to guarantee that water service would remain a municipal responsibility in perpetuity.

One more factor would color the city's quest for water. Lippincott was not only Reclamation's regional supervising engineer; he also maintained a private consulting practice in which his most important client was the City of Los Angeles. His divided loyalties annoyed his superiors at Reclamation, who repeatedly demanded that he choose one role or the other. But his dual loyalties were unknown, for the moment, to the people of the Owens Valley.

The city's board of water commissioners concluded in April 1905 that the valley was the only new water source that could be acquired at a reasonable price and authorized Mulholland to buy Eaton out before continuing land purchases in its name. The ultimate price of nearly $234,000 produced a decent profit for Eaton, if not one that approached his original ambitions.

The city did take pains to keep its land acquisitions confidential. Its officials prevailed on local newspapers to keep silent in order to serve the public's interest in obtaining water rights at the best price. But the agreement broke down one day after Mulholland reported to the commissioners that he had completed all the necessary land acquisitions in the Owens Valley. "The last spike has been driven," he told them; "the deal by which Los Angeles city becomes the owner of thirty thousand inches of the purest snow water has been nailed." The next morning, July 29, 1905, the *Times* scooped its competitors with a front-page headline announcing a "Titanic Project to Give City a River."

The *Times* generously apportioned credit among Mulholland, Eaton, and Lippincott—discomfiting the latter two, who were less than pleased to have their machinations exposed, even amid unstinting praise. Eaton found himself suddenly surrounded that very day by valley ranchers incensed by the revelations, which made plain that they would not be getting the irrigation reservoir they hoped for. (He related that they warned him that "I shall never take the water out of the valley; that when I go back for my cattle, they will drown me in the river.") Lippincott, whose "interest and cooperation" were described admiringly by the *Times* as crucial factors in the project's development, vehemently maintained that Los Angeles had always been Reclamation's preferred destination for the Owens River water. But he resigned from Reclamation a year later to take a job with the city at a salary of $6,000 a year, a substantial raise from the $4,200 he had earned on the federal payroll.

The *Times* scoop introduced Los Angeles residents to a part of California of which most were almost entirely unaware. Owens Lake had been named by John Charles Frémont in 1859 after Richard Owens, one of his guides. In Frémont's time, the valley was inhabited by Paiute-Shoshone Indians who lived off its rabbits, antelopes, berries, and pine nuts. Within three years of Frémont's arrival it had become the site of some of the most savage massacres that white settlers and their military protectors waged upon California tribes. Like tribes elsewhere, the Owens Valley Indians suffered from settlers' diversions of streams and clearing of wildlife habitats for farming and ranching. Like other dispossessed tribes, they resorted to stealing cattle and horses. Once the valley gained the reputation of a retreat for "horse thief Indians," the Army marked the inhabitants for annihilation, staging two campaigns known as the Owens Valley Wars in 1862–63 and 1864–65. By the time of Eaton's land acquisitions, the tribes were long gone and the valley was inhabited by small farmers eking out a meager existence on marginally productive land.

To present-day Angelenos, who can motor north on a highway paved smooth as glass and refresh themselves at tourist restaurants and curio shops along the way, the Owens Valley beckons as a summer vacation destination and a winter gateway to skiing resorts. During the city's incursion, however, the region seemed impossibly remote and virtually inaccessible. In March 1906, Mulholland led Mayor Owen McAleer and members of the board of water commissioners on an inspection tour of the valley that proved to be nothing like a relaxing junket. It took the party six days to reach Bishop, the largest town in the valley. Along the way, their automobiles got trapped in quicksand and mired in flooded roads from which they had to be extricated by block and tackle with ropes anchored to trees. At Haiwee, 180 miles from home and still 90 miles from Bishop, they stopped for the night but had to sleep in a barn.

The valley dwellers had fantasized about its agricultural potential, envisioning irrigation ditches brimming with carp and sprawling fields of alfalfa serving vast dairy ranches, a semi-arid bowl turned into an Eden by irrigation. For Lippincott and others, however, determining the highest and best use of the water was subject to the remorseless laws of economics. "The total population of all Inyo County is but 4,500 people, the assessed valuation of the entire county is $2,505,000, and a cubic foot per second of water in that locality is not over $1,250," Lippincott wrote in 1905. By contrast, "the population of Los Angeles County is about 375,000; the assessed valuation of the county is $235,000,000, and the value of a cubic foot per second of water is approximately $100,000."

Such a calculation appealed to President Roosevelt, who at the same time was trying to find a compromise between the views of John Muir and the conservationists in his own inner circle over the damming of the Hetch Hetchy. Gifford Pinchot's opinion that the goal of conservation should be the conscientious exploitation of natural resources to avoid wastefulness, not their preservation in pristine condition, found fitting application in the Owens Valley and swayed Roosevelt toward Lippincott's stance.

The Hetch Hetchy and Owens Valley projects both involved balancing competing claims on water. In both cases Roosevelt invoked the utilitarian goal of the greatest use for the greatest number of people. In September 1906, he decisively closed the Owens River issue by accepting Mulholland's assertion that the water would fill the needs of Los Angeles for the next half century. "It is a hundred or a thousand fold more important to state that this is more valuable to the people as a whole if used by the city than if used

This map of the western hemisphere, attributed to the Spanish cartographer Diego Gutiérrez and dated 1562, is thought to be among the first on which the name California appears, attached to a cape at the very southern tip of Baja California. LIBRARY OF CONGRESS

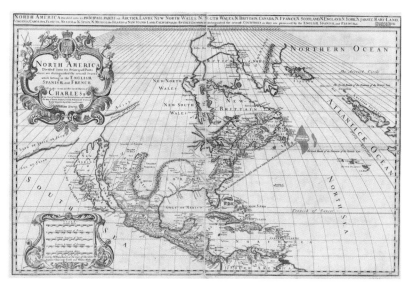

One of many contemporary maps, based on an original by French cartographer Nicolas Sanson in 1650, that depicts California as an island, an error that persisted for more than a century after Spanish explorations proved it wrong.
LIBRARY OF CONGRESS

The Bear Flag raised by American rebels in Sonoma in 1846, designed by William L. Todd and executed with red paint or berry juice, bore crude versions of all the elements that remain part of today's official state flag—a grizzly bear, a red star, and the legend "California Republic." CALIFORNIA STATE LIBRARY

Explorer, soldier, and adventurer John Charles Frémont injected himself into the conflicts between settlers and Mexican Californians prior to the Mexican War. After statehood, he briefly served as one of California's first two US senators.

CALIFORNIA STATE LIBRARY

James Marshall in front of the mill where he discovered gold in 1848.
LIBRARY OF CONGRESS

The port of San Francisco teemed with vessels during the Gold Rush in 1850, when 805 ships arrived, bearing 62,000 passengers. CALIFORNIA HISTORICAL SOCIETY

Public executions were a source of popular entertainment in post–Gold Rush San Francisco. Here, a crowd of 15,000 gathered for the hangings of murderers James Casey and Charles Cora on May 22, 1856. Their bodies dangle from the rooftop of the building at the left of the square.
FRANK LESLIE'S ILLUSTRATED NEWSPAPER, JULY 19, 1856

"Protecting the Settlers," an illustration for
J. Ross Browne's book *Crusoe's Island*, in which
Browne denounced the whites' punitive
butchery of California Indian tribes.

J. ROSS BROWNE, *CRUSOE'S ISLAND* (1864)

Harper's Weekly, lamenting in 1877 that American Indians were almost invariably
depicted "scalping, stealing, or hunting," offered this sketch by illustrator Paul
Frenzeny of a family of Mission Indians in the San Diego area as "an interesting
exception to the rule." HARPER'S WEEKLY, OCT. 20, 1877

Ambrose Bierce's publication
The Wasp lampooned Denis
Kearney as a false protector of
the workingman; Kearney is
depicted in this 1878 illustration
by George Frederick Keller as
a jackass in a military uniform
(*center*), labeled "This Ass Soon
Will Take a Walk."

THE WASP, MAY 4, 1878

Thomas Nast
compared anti-Chinese
discrimination to Black
discrimination in 1879.

Collis Huntington and Mark Hopkins provisioned the forty-niners from this
general store in Sacramento, generating the seed money for their investment in
the Central Pacific Railroad.

THE BIG FOUR

Leland Stanford

Mark Hopkins

Collis P. Huntington

Charles Crocker

THE CURSE OF CALIFORNIA.

Keller endowed the Southern Pacific with its enduring nickname, "The Octopus," with this cover illustration for *The Wasp*; the figures in its eyes are Stanford and Crocker.

THE WASP, AUG. 18, 1882

Edward H. Harriman, lord of the Union Pacific and Southern Pacific Railroads.

A panorama of San Francisco after the quake and fires in April 1906.

Abraham Ruef, who oversaw the most corrupt administration in San Francisco history from behind the scenes but was the only figure to spend time in jail as a result . . .

. . . and his principal henchman, Mayor Eugene Schmitz.

Theodore Roosevelt and John Muir at Yosemite's Glacier Point, May 1903. Their companionable three-day tour of the park did not keep Roosevelt from disappointing Muir by allowing the neighboring Hetch Hetchy Valley to be flooded for a reservoir.

Hiram Johnson—California governor, "Bull Moose" Party vice presidential nominee, and US senator—in his signature pugilistic stance.

Harrison Gray Otis, owner of the *Los Angeles Times*, in Philippine-American War regalia.

The *Times* building after the 1910 bombing, showing its trademark bronze eagle still on its parapet.   C. C. PIERCE COLLECTION OF PHOTOGRAPHS, THE HUNTINGTON LIBRARY, SAN MARINO, CALIFORNIA

395:—Across the Lagoon, Venice, Calif.

Cigar heir Abbot Kinney dredged canals and imported gondolas to create his "Venice of America" on the Southern California coast in 1905, but by 1925 most of the canals had been filled in.   WALTER VON BOLTENSTERN POSTCARD COLLECTION, LOYOLA MARYMOUNT UNIVERSITY

The Los Angeles Air Meet of 1910 brought 200,000 spectators to Southern California to see aviators from all over the world display their aircraft, seen here in a composite photo by C. C. Pierce. The meet helped turn the state into a leader of the nascent aeronautics industry.

The first water arrives to Los Angeles from the Owens Valley, Nov. 5, 1913.

Hop pickers in the Central Valley, led by the "Wobblies," went on strike in 1913, launching an era of labor unrest in the burgeoning agricultural region.

The charismatic Aimee Semple McPherson, seen here preaching at Christmastime 1923, brought audiences of thousands to her temple in Los Angeles and reached millions as a pioneering radio evangelist. COPYRIGHT PROTECTED. USED BY EXPRESS CONSENT OF INTERNATIONAL CHURCH OF THE FOURSQUARE GOSPEL.

Dr. Francis Everett Townsend of Long Beach (*right*) conceived a national old-age pension program during the Depression that inspired Congress to move ahead with what became Social Security. LIBRARY OF CONGRESS

The Cuckoo!

Upton Sinclair's campaign on the EPIC (End Poverty in California) platform nearly won him the governorship but was countered by relentless derision from the press, such as this cartoon published by the *Times*.   LOS ANGELES TIMES

Wartime hysteria led to the relocation and incarceration of some 110,000 Californians of Japanese descent. The US Army sent them to concentration camps such as Manzanar in the Sierra foothills, the subject of this photograph by Ansel Adams.
LIBRARY OF CONGRESS

Congressman Richard Nixon of California, seen here examining a "Pumpkin Papers" filmstrip with Robert Stripling, chief investigator of the House Un-American Affairs Committee, parlayed his role in the Alger Hiss case into national renown and ultimately to the presidency.
BETTMAN/GETTY

Ronald Reagan exploited unrest on the UC Berkeley campus to win the California governorship from Democrat Edmund G. "Pat" Brown in 1966.

An oil-covered duck on a Santa Barbara beach following the disastrous offshore oil spill of 1969. Images like this, transmitted around the world, triggered an unprecedented surge in environmental activism and federal oversight of the fossil fuel industry.

California vintner John Giumarra Sr. raises his arms in mock surrender to Cesar Chavez (*left*) and his United Farm Workers Union after signing a landmark contract with the UFW in 1970.   BETTMAN/GETTY

The *Los Angeles Times*'s Paul Conrad interprets defeat of a water project that would bring water from Northern to Southern California.
LOS ANGELES TIMES

In 2009, during his second term as governor, Arnold Schwarzenegger reached a deal with the legislature to close a massive budget deficit through sharp cuts to the state's safety net and other services.   MAX WHITTAKER/GETTY

Governor Jerry Brown campaigns in 2012 for Proposition 30, which would raise taxes to close a multibillion-dollar state budget deficit. The measure passed, reversing more than three decades of tax resistance.   KEVORK DJANSEZIAN/GETTY

by the people of Owens Valley," he told his interior secretary, the Missourian Ethan Allen Hitchcock. He acknowledged that the interest of "a few settlers in Owens Valley . . . is genuine" but decided that it "must unfortunately be disregarded in view of the infinitely greater interest to be served by putting the water in Los Angeles."

Roosevelt's decision ceded federal claims on the valley's water to the city and settled the congressional dispute. But it did not resolve the broader politics of water, then or for the future.

THE TIMES DID not exaggerate by calling the aqueduct "titanic." As a public works project, it was reckoned to be second in scale and ambition only to the Panama Canal. Indeed, Mulholland was lauded as "the Goethals of the West"—a reference to George Washington Goethals, who oversaw the canal's completion in 1914. The aqueduct overmatched the construction techniques of the time and required new methods to be invented on the spot. Experts doubted it could be done—Arthur Powell Davis, the nephew of explorer John Wesley Powell and Lippincott's engineering superior at the Reclamation Service, ridiculed the project, calling it "as unlikely as the city of Washington tapping the Ohio River." Upon the aqueduct's completion, however, an awestruck Davis pronounced it "the best piece of work of a big project I have ever seen."

The 233-mile aqueduct included sixty miles of open canals and ninety-eight miles of covered conduits, as well as five reservoirs and one hundred fifty tunnels ranging in length from a hundred and fifty feet to one that was more than five miles. That was the magnificent Elizabeth Lake tunnel, driven from both ends through solid granite with such precision that at their meeting, the two excavations were misaligned by only two and a quarter inches. The total cost was $24.5 million (about $800 million in modern terms), funded by bond issues approved by Los Angeles voters in 1905 and 1907. Mulholland left nothing to chance in the run-up to the first vote, to authorize $1.5 million for the acquisition of water rights in the Owens Valley. He kept up a drumbeat of hyperbolic warnings about a drought emergency and an incipient "water famine." Nature cooperated just before election day by smothering the city in a heat wave that drove temperatures above a hundred degrees. Mulholland also linked the aqueduct to the city's ambitions for growth, alarming voters with the prediction that "if Los Angeles runs out of water for one week, the city within a year will not have a population of 100,000." At the time, the city's population was already twice that number.

Mulholland would make it a practice throughout his career—notably in campaigning for the construction of Hoover Dam in the 1920s—to depict water projects designed to serve the region's future growth as "emergency" projects needed to forestall immediate shortages. In this case, his overselling was probably unnecessary, for the voters were foursquare behind the project, approving the first expenditure by a fourteen-to-one margin and the second, for a construction bond of $23 million, by ten to one.

With the impending completion of the aqueduct came a pressing question: What to do with the water? The answer would open the next great chapter in Los Angeles' expansion. A far larger volume of water would be carried by the aqueduct than the city would need for years, even decades. Some city officials advocated selling the surplus to farmers for irrigation, an option Mulholland vehemently opposed. The city eventually would need all the water, he warned. Selling it to outsiders only to reclaim it later "would be practicing a base deception on . . . innocent purchasers" who would have spent millions on land improvements dependent on the water, only to have it all snatched away. Instead, he successfully advocated providing the surplus only to communities that had agreed to become part of the city by annexation. The result transformed Los Angeles into what its boosters anticipated would be "the greater Los Angeles that is to be" and the "metropolis of the Pacific Coast." In the two years following the aqueduct's completion, annexations nearly tripled the city's area, to 285 square miles from 108.

The largest single addition was the vast San Fernando Valley. This also was the annexation that generated the greatest public suspicion. Real estate developers coveted the valley as early as 1903, when a syndicate formed by Otis, his son-in-law Harry Chandler, Southern Pacific president Edward H. Harriman, and a handful of fellow millionaires acquired an option on 16,000 acres for about $35 an acre. In 1909 the partners acquired another 47,500 acres for about $53 each. The San Fernando Valley was not then a part of Los Angeles and was therefore ineligible to receive the water. But once the valley could be incorporated into the city and endowed with its water, the land was expected to fetch as much as a thousand dollars an acre. The fortune Otis and Chandler garnered from the San Fernando Valley would far outstrip what they earned as proprietors of the *Los Angeles Times*.

The *Times* scoop of July 1905 gave the tycoons' game away. "The cable that has held the San Fernando Valley vassal to the arid demon is about to be severed by the magic scimitar of modern engineering skill," the newspaper crowed. This premature celebration by Otis's house organ has "ever since tantalized historians and conspiracy-theory devotees alike," a prominent historian observed. Yet there is no evidence that the syndicate members prompted the aqueduct project or influenced the mapping of its right-of-way; Mulholland had long planned to terminate the aqueduct at the northern end of the San Fernando Valley so he could use that valley's vast underground aquifer for storage. What is more likely is that the tycoons capitalized on advance information about the aqueduct's trajectory, enabling them to make exquisitely timely land purchases. Their presumed source was Moses H. Sherman, a local railroad entrepreneur who was privy to the aqueduct planning as a member of the city's board of water commissioners. Sherman became a member of the Otis/Chandler syndicate as it was acquiring its landholdings, a presumptive indication that he had exploited his public position for private profit.

SO WHAT ARE we to make of the enduring claim that Los Angeles stole the Owens Valley's water?

The city did pay for the property and water rights of Owens Valley landowners. At the center of the theft narrative is the question of whether the price was fair. The valley's farmers set their expectations according to the water's value to Los Angeles; the city's offer was based on its much lower estimation of the water's value to the farmers. The gap between these two values was not easily bridged, but the prices of land purchases by the city from 1924 through 1934 suggest that the farmers generally collected more than they would have earned from agriculture because the Owens Valley was not likely to be as productive as its farmers expected, though it is true that they collected less than the city was (secretly) willing to pay.

In terms of the relative gains from the water sales, there is no question that Los Angeles was the winner. The major losers arguably were the nonlandowning residents of the Owens Valley—shopkeepers, laborers, schoolteachers, blacksmiths, physicians, and others deprived of their livelihoods as the valley's farming economy shriveled away. Their plight forms the bedrock of the narrative of ruthless subjugation of a vulnerable countryside by a greedy city and drives the moral condemnation of the city to this day. Their resentment turned the valley into "a hotbed of suspicions, prejudices and hatred . . . full of whisperings, mutterings, recrimination and suggestion of threat of one kind or another," an investigative committee of the city water board reported.

Rather than stand silently by as their customers disappeared, the residents reacted in two ways. One was to agitate for the payment of reparations by the city. The other was by violence. In taking the latter step, they wrote the final chapter of the Owens Valley saga.

The reparations movement began in the 1920s, when the city bought up additional land and water rights in the northern valley to counteract yet another drought. Its impetus came from the valley's two leading bankers, brothers Mark and Wilfred Watterson, and was further fueled in April and May 1924 by a series of articles titled "The Valley of Broken Hearts" in the *San Francisco Call* by Court E. Kunze, the editor of the *Owens Valley Herald* and the brother-in-law of Wilfred Watterson. On May 21 a dynamite blast ripped away a concrete section of the aqueduct and part of the hillside. The Owens Valley water war had begun.

Over the next three years, sections of the aqueduct were torn apart by dynamiting twelve more times. None of the blasts did lasting damage, but they did force the city to spend hundreds of thousands of dollars on repairs. The most significant attack began early on the morning of November 16, 1924, when one hundred men in a caravan of vehicles led by Mark Watterson made their way to the Alabama Gates, a key flood-control structure on the aqueduct. The makeshift army quickly overpowered the surprised watchman and opened the gates, diverting the aqueduct's entire flow onto the parched land and into the dust-choked hollow that had once been Owens Lake.

The Alabama Gates occupation evolved into a festive community event attended by a crowd that swelled to more than seven hundred. Housewives arrived from Bishop with pies, and local butchers and grocers contributed food for a giant barbecue. Cowboy star Tom Mix, filming a movie in the Sierra foothills, made an appearance, drawing newspaper and magazine coverage from the national press. ("California's Little Civil War" was the headline in the *Literary Digest*, which observed, not inaccurately: "The history of the settlement of our West is largely a history of fights for the control of water.") For the attack's organizers, the nationwide attention was the point. "The only weapon we have is publicity," Mark Watterson said, "and that is about the only thing the City of Los Angeles seems to fear."

He was right. The Alabama standoff ended after only five days, but in its wake even the *Los Angeles Times* urged a more conciliatory approach to the "honest, earnest, hard-working American citizens" of the Owens Valley "who look upon Los Angeles as an octopus about to strangle out their lives." In 1925, the campaign for reparations brought about a state law requiring the buyers of water rights to pay for the business losses resulting from the transfers. Owens Valley residents presented the city with 528 itemized claims totaling more than $2.8 million, ranging from a few hundred dollars for personal effects to $113,000 from a garage and hardware store owned by the Wattersons. But the law's mandate applied only to future water purchases; in the case of preexisting deals, it empowered but did not require the buyers to pay reparations. The city rejected every claim.

Still, Los Angeles did step up its land purchases from farmers and landowners. By 1933, when the final land deals were completed, the city had spent more than twenty-five million dollars to acquire more than 95 percent of the agricultural properties in the Owens Valley and 98 percent of the landholdings in the towns. Residents could aptly complain that these transfers fundamentally changed the character of the valley—the city had little interest in operating its properties as farms but leased them instead to ranchers. A more dire effect on the valley, however, came from an event with which the city had no direct connection.

This was the sudden bankruptcy of the Wattersons' banks. The brothers blamed the city's "years of destructive work," but government examiners established that they had systematically embezzled millions of dollars from their institutions. Hundreds of depositors lost their life savings, including money they had received from land and water sales to Los Angeles. Farmers and businesses were crushed by their losses. The betrayal rippled across the valley, prompting one of the brothers' closest allies, newspaper editor Harry Glasscock, to take his own life. The Wattersons were convicted of embezzlement in November 1927 and sentenced to ten-year terms in San Quentin.

Without the Owens Valley water, Los Angeles could not have continued to grow through the first decades of the twentieth century. But it was still not enough. Even before the city finalized the last of its land deals, it was angling for yet another source of water, one much greater than the Owens Valley—indeed, great enough to fuel growth all across the arid west. That source was the Colorado River.

16

THE UTOPIANS

THEY CAME BY automobile and streetcar and on aching feet, massing in front of the colonnaded front doors in the hope of gaining admission. Inside, the vast hall resounded with the clamor of expectation of the spectacle ahead—every seat filled, and people spilling into the aisles, many on crutches or in wheelchairs. Then came a sudden fanfare of trumpets, and an eerie hush fell over the crowd of more than five thousand. A baton was raised, and the whole orchestra—a full brass band, plus a grand piano at one side of the stage and an organ at the other—broke into "The Star Spangled Banner" as colored lights swirled over the stage.

A female figure sheathed in white satin and garlanded with flowers descended a tall staircase, and the entire crowd rose as one to deliver a thunderous standing ovation. She lifted her arms and cried out, "Glory! Glory! Glory!" The crowd shouted back, *"Glory!"* She smiled a beatific smile and said, "Brothers and sisters, is there anyone here who wants to be cured tonight? Let him come up and if he has faith he will be cured. Those who were blind will be able to see; those who are deaf will be able to hear; those who are crippled will be able to walk. . . . Come up, come up."

They came up, long lines shuffling the aisles up to the stage. The blind staggered off, crying, "I can see!" The hobbled threw their crutches aside. The audience gasped with wonder.

Thus the entrance, repeated every Sunday evening at seven, of Aimee Semple McPherson, "Sister Aimee" to her faithful, onto the stage at her vast wedge-shaped, cream-colored Angelus Temple, just at the edge of downtown Los Angeles.

Sister Aimee was not the most intellectual of evangelical preachers or the most theologically consistent. But she was certainly the most theatrical, and that was what counted in the Roaring Twenties. No one was better at investing spiritualism with Hollywood-style stagecraft. The Angelus Temple, built for three hundred thousand dollars in 1922 (more than five million in today's money), boasted "a brass band bigger and louder than the late Sousa's, an organ worthy of any movie cathedral, a female choir bigger and more beautiful than the Metropolitan chorus, a costume wardrobe comparable to the late Ziegfeld's," wrote Morrow Mayo. McPherson was also innovative, broadcasting her sermons to listeners nationwide from a radio station she installed at the temple for seventy-five thousand dollars (call letters KFSG, for "Church of the Four Square Gospel," her evangelical congregation). She had been bathed from childhood in the punitive, premonitory images of hellfire and brimstone at the heart of evangelism's northeastern traditions, but she put them through a Southern California filter from which they emerged soaked in light and love and fellow feeling. Her approach was uniquely suited to her new milieu. "In bleakest Vermont a theological sadist might prosper for years by threatening old ladies with hellfire and damnation," Mayo observed, but that would hardly serve in "a sun-kissed, flower-garden land of eternal June."

Born in Ontario, Canada, Aimee Kennedy would be married twice—widowed once and divorced once—by the age of twenty-eight. She had found her religious calling in Pentecostalism, which incorporated speaking in tongues and faith healing as manifestations of the Holy Spirit. She joined her mother, Minnie, later known as "Ma Kennedy," who worked the highways and byways as an itinerant preacher. On these journeys she picked up the methods of theatrically demonstrative sects such as the Holy Rollers before surfacing in San Diego in 1918, where she attracted notice by "scattering religious tracts from an airplane and holding revival meetings in a boxing arena." She moved to Los Angeles in 1922 with Minnie, two children, a battered jalopy, and one hundred dollars in cash. There she underwent an astonishing apotheosis, to the extent that at any McPherson event, the Almighty Himself was granted only a secondary role. Her stage business had her driving the devil out of the theater with a pitchfork or posing in uniform as George Washington crossing the Delaware.

Aimee's appeal was broad. She fascinated middle-class middle-Americans and Jazz Age Southern California flappers, theologians and Hollywood stars. Her fan base consisted of true believers and mere curiosity-seekers, journalists of all leanings, and literary figures as distinguished as John Updike (although he did not come under her spell until long after her death). Carey McWilliams, though generally a skeptical observer of California culture, challenged the impression that Aimee was merely a money-grubbing charlatan, concluding instead that "her followers always felt that they had received full value in exchange for their liberal donations" and praising her for her philanthropic outreach to all comers, whatever their ethnic origin or economic standing. "She made migrants feel at home in Los Angeles," he wrote, adding that in his experience, she had never been heard to "attack any individual or any group."

H. L. Mencken was enthralled by the McPherson phenomenon but immune to her personal magnetism. He described a service he had witnessed at the Angelus Temple as "the time-honored evangelical hokum, made a bit more raucous than usual by the loud-speakers strewn all over the hall" and saw Aimee herself as a "commonplace and transparent mountebank." He explained her success by "the plain reason that there were more morons collected in Los Angeles than in any other place on Earth," as evidenced by the region's having become "swarmed with swamis, spiritualists, Christian Scientists, crystal-gazers and the allied necromancers."

There was no doubting her charisma. Often described as plump, even dowdy—"An ample lady of early middle years," wrote Sarah Comstock of *Harper's Monthly* in 1927, when Aimee was thirty-seven years old. With marcelled hair that varied in color from bright red to auburn to blond and a kindly smile fixed on her face, she somehow exerted a spellbinding effect on awestruck crowds. The actor Anthony Quinn, who first met her at the age of fourteen and as a youth played saxophone in her orchestra and interpreted for her during her outreaching forays into the Mexican neighborhoods of Los Angeles, called her "the most magnetic personality I was ever to encounter . . . As magnificent as I could find Anna Magnani, Ingrid Bergman, Laurette Taylor, Katharine Hepburn, Greta Garbo and Ethel Barrymore, they all fell short of the first electric shock Aimee Semple McPherson produced in me."

On May 18, 1926, she staged a climactic drama. Bathing at the beach in Santa Monica, she disappeared, presumed drowned. The outpouring of grief included a vast memorial service at the Angelus Temple (at which $35,000 was collected). But a few days after the service, on June 23, she reappeared in Douglas, Arizona, with a yarn about having been abducted at the beach, spirited to a shack in the Sonoran desert, and confined there for five weeks until she was able to saw through her bindings with the sharp edge of a tin can and spend seventeen hours walking twenty miles to freedom in the blazing heat.

Although her return to Los Angeles inspired an outburst of jubilation among her followers, it was not long before the local newspapers picked apart her story. It emerged that she had spent her "abduction" in a love nest in Carmel, on the Northern California coast. Prosecutors charged her with moral turpitude and giving false information to the police, but she never wavered from her story, so they dropped the charges. The stillborn prosecution was widely condemned, regionally and nationally, as the handiwork of Southern California local pastors who had been rattled by her popularity. Aimee won even Mencken's sympathy, if only because he judged the local clergy and the "town Babbitts" who attacked her to be even more contemptible than she was. She continued to preach, often to crowds far from Los Angeles, while at home the finances of the Angelus Temple deteriorated.

Aimee's popularity drained away slowly but steadily. She died of an overdose of sleeping pills, presumed to be accidental, in 1944. The legacy she left behind was quintessentially Californian in its giving the old-time Bible-thumping religiosity a modern theatrical gloss and a relevance to the modern world that has never disappeared.

AIMEE SEMPLE MCPHERSON was not the first person to find California a nurturing ground for a utopian mission of rebirth and reformation, though she provided a model for the utopians who came in her wake. The phenomenon had gathered force after the appearance in 1888 of Edward Bellamy's visionary novel *Looking Backward 2000–1887*. Bellamy told the story of a Rip van Winkle character named Julian West who falls asleep in 1887 and awakens 113 years later in a socialist paradise where industry has been nationalized and labor and production regimented to foster equality. Bellamy's novel found an especially receptive audience in California; nearly one-third of the nation's more than 160 Nationalist Clubs, formed to promote the political and social movement Bellamy described, were founded in the state.

One utopian community that profited from the *Looking Backward* excitement was the Kaweah Co-Operative Commonwealth, which was founded by

Burnette G. Haskell, a labor lawyer with piercing gray eyes and a political outlook fired by Marxism and anarchism. Haskell laid claim to a large tract of land in the forested central California foothills near Visalia and tried to create a community spirit among the laborers, farmers, engineers, and artists lured by what appeared to be a Bellamy-like community in the making. It was a kaleidoscopic "United States in microcosm," Haskell would reflect. "There were temperance men and their opposites," he wrote, "churchmen and agnostics, free-thinkers, Darwinists, and spiritualists, bad poets and good. . . . There were dress-reform cranks and phonetic spelling fanatics, word purists and vegetarians. It was a mad, mad world, and being so small its madness was the more visible."

Haskell discovered that anarchism functions poorly as an organizing principle in the real world. "Instead of the fraternal, friendly feeling hoped for, one found Kaweah divided into factions, and fractions of factions," he wrote. "Otherwise good people seem to take a delight in finding flaws in their neighbors." A more serious threat to Kaweah's survival came from the federal government, which invalidated Burnett's land claims because the properties intruded on the new Sequoia National Forest. Haskell's idealism battled with his heartbreak at Kaweah's failure to the bitter end. The final entry of his journal, on April 18, 1892, recorded the fate of his poor homestead garden: "The pigs ate up all the potatoes on the flat today; also the squash. Oh, Hell!"

As more settlers arrived in the late nineteenth century and into the twentieth, the state's center of utopian gravity shifted south. The factors that made Southern California a rich incubator for utopian movements are not hard to identify. One is certainly its balmy climate, which is free of the extremes of cold and heat that might interfere with the serene contemplation of nature and humanity in a paradisiacal setting. The climate also attracted those suffering from ailments that doctors could not cure but believed could be eased by a temperate and dry milieu; these desperate souls were susceptible to faith healers and quacks awaiting their arrival in the West. There was also the region's remoteness from the rest of America; the writer Edmund Wilson called it "the jumping-off place," where invalids rubbed shoulders with those who had done something shameful or disgraceful in their past lives, all engaged in a final search for health or redemption before permanently shedding their worldly cares by suicide. For those not quite certain that they had reached the end of the road, there was the dream of the fresh start "out in the golden land," Joan Didion would write, "where every day the world is born anew."

The most important factor was economics, which played out in the eternal conflicts between employers and labor. In this case, those conflicts exposed the working class to the seductions of a promised utopian future.

When Los Angeles was experiencing its first major boom, in the 1880s and 1890s, the anti-union obduracy of the city's ruling class sabotaged whatever social stability could have been created by broad-based prosperity. The conflict over unionization climaxed with the 1910 bombing of the *Los Angeles Times* building. The aftermath of the bombers' guilty pleas was the defeat of socialist Job Harriman in his race for mayor, but that steered him toward a new career path. Pondering his loss, Harriman dreamed of taking refuge in a cooperative colony governed by socialist principles. In 1914, having exploited his still considerable personal popularity among socialists to raise the necessary funds, he acquired ten thousand acres of wildland on the edge of the Mojave Desert about sixty-five miles north of Los Angeles, an area he christened Llano del Rio, or "Plain of the River." By August 1917, Llano del Rio boasted a population of nine hundred people raising hogs, cattle, and chickens for market. They grew alfalfa and potatoes on soil reclaimed by brute labor from its native vegetation of creosote, brush, and Joshua trees and watered by a nearby creek. The community built schools and sponsored dances and music recitals. Rent and medical care were free, and food and clothing were provided through deductions from the four dollars a day paid to every colonist. Over time, however, Llano fell victim to the same ills that had afflicted Kaweah: organizational strife and human frailty. There were conflicts over how to deal with slackers and shirkers who failed to put in their eight hours of solid work. Llano's governing general assembly deteriorated into "an inquisition, a mental pillory, a madhouse of meddlesomeness . . . democracy with the lid off," in the words of a member. What delivered the death knell was lack of water. Harriman ultimately led a migration of more than two hundred members to Louisiana, where they established New Llano, which functioned in socialist style until disbanding in 1937.

AS AIMEE SEMPLE MCPHERSON'S star was dimming, the Great Depression was taking hold, creating another seedbed of discontent in Southern California to be farmed by dispensers of utopian relief. "Swarms of self-appointed 'saviors' poured out of every pecan grove, each with a large pink pill for the cure of every social and economic ill," reported George Creel, a keen observer of California politics and culture.

The "saviors" tended to project a messianic sincerity, none so much as the socialist Upton Sinclair.

The Baltimore-born Sinclair had already established a precocious career as an author of military potboilers when he published his masterwork *The Jungle* in 1906 at the age of twenty-eight. Based on seven weeks' research inside the Chicago meatpacking industry, the exposé became a bestseller, crystallizing Sinclair's renown. He proceeded to turn out a string of politically charged novels on such topics as the coal and oil industries and the Sacco and Vanzetti case, as well as militantly critical tracts on religion, the newspaper industry, finance, and education. In the 1920s he moved to Pasadena, where he embarked on a quintessentially Californian transformation from expository writer to politician, conducting two failed campaigns for the state legislature on the Socialist Party ticket. In August 1933, an elderly Democratic committeeman from Santa Monica urged him to run for governor as a Democrat. "This old gentleman would not be put off," Sinclair recollected.

The political landscape looked encouraging. After sending Republicans to the governor's mansion for thirty-seven years straight, California had joined the Franklin Delano Roosevelt landslide in 1932. The incumbent Republican governor, the colorless Frank Merriam, was widely abominated for continuing a sales tax that overburdened the middle class while vetoing an income tax, thus sparing the state's affluent residents from shouldering their fair share of public expenses. But the Democratic Party had withered during its decades out of power. Sinclair stepped into the vacuum with a radical economic platform. The plan, which he called EPIC, for "End Poverty in California," was published in 1933 as a pamphlet styled after Bellamy's *Looking Backward* and titled *I, Governor of California and How I Ended Poverty—a True Story of the Future*.

Convinced that California's economic stagnation sprang from its failure to bring together industrial assets and human capital, both of which were abundant but inefficiently utilized, Sinclair proposed to establish a public agency called the California Authority for Land (CAL) to acquire idle land, a California Authority for Production (CAP) to acquire idle factories, and a California Authority for Money (CAM) to issue scrip to pay workers employed on the "state land colonies" established as centers for production. The sales tax would be replaced by a progressive income tax and a steep property tax to redistribute entrenched and dynastic wealth. Elderly, disabled, and needy residents would be guaranteed a state pension of fifty dollars a month.

"I say, positively and without qualification, we can end poverty in California," Sinclair wrote. "I will put the job through—and I won't take more than one or two of my four years." The Depression, he asserted, was a crisis "of abundance, not of scarcity. . . . The cause of the trouble is that a small class has the wealth, while the rest have the debts."

Sinclair's program disregarded basic economic realities. Among other flaws, his new taxes could not come close to replacing the revenues lost by the sales tax repeal. The pension plan would cost three hundred million dollars a year in a state already struggling with a thirty-million-dollar deficit. Yet EPIC's promise was seductive for Californians devastated by the economic downturn. *I, Governor* sold two hundred thousand copies, and eight hundred Sinclair Clubs sprouted across the state, luring voters with rodeos, picnics, and barbecues. EPIC brought into being a political base that shared common features with Sister Aimee's following and Kaweah's membership: "socially-minded clergymen, quack astronomers, single taxers, mind readers, members of the powerful Utopian Society, leaders of the unemployed co-operatives, a few Santa Barbara dowagers. . . . [and] miscellaneous political has-beens," McWilliams reported. Yet there was more to it. Sinclair was unique among California politicians in speaking directly to the disaffected and dispossessed working class. These voters, like those other more marginal groups, fell under Sinclair's spell, McWilliams wrote, "as if by default."

Underscoring the Democrats' disarray, in the 1934 primary Sinclair faced seven challengers. He outpolled the entire field by fifty thousand votes. As he had also outpolled Governor Merriam, he looked to be the presumptive victor in the November election. The Roosevelt White House, which had avoided taking sides in the California election, now recognized that Sinclair's campaign warranted its attention. FDR granted Sinclair's request for a meeting, with the condition that no politics would be discussed—a proviso Sinclair accepted, recognizing that the nomination of a onetime Socialist would put the president "very much 'on the spot'" in his own reelection campaign in 1936.

Their meeting took place on September 5 at Roosevelt's estate in Hyde Park, New York. Present were New Deal aides Harry Hopkins and Rexford Tugwell, who were relieved to find Sinclair nothing like the fanatic depicted by California newspapers. "He wanted the Presidential blessing," Tugwell reflected, "and was happy to be regarded as respectable after a lifetime of being more or less an outcast."

Sinclair was thoroughly charmed by FDR. "I found that he had read my book and knew the EPIC plan," he wrote later, perhaps naively. If anything, the Hyde Park meeting marked the high-water mark of Sinclair's campaign. Establishment Democrats, who began repudiating Sinclair almost as soon as the primary results were in, joined with Republicans in excavating damagingly radical statements from the abundant material in his books and pamphlets. These included a 1918 tract entitled "The Profits of Religion" in which Sinclair lumped together the Episcopal, Roman Catholic, Mormon, and Christian Science Churches as havens for quacks and liars.

California's movie studios, which were headed by some of its most reactionary businessmen, distributed newsreels and still photographs showing tramps and hobos surging over the state line to partake of EPIC's generous pensions, much of the "documentation" drawn from feature films already in production or nestled in their vaults. Newspapers lampooned Sinclair mercilessly, depicting him as, among other things, an eyelash-batting southern belle, a starry-eyed goblin, and Don Quixote tilting at a windmill.

Democrats tried in vain to persuade Sinclair to drop out of the race in favor of a compromise candidate lest his campaign hand victory to Merriam. On Election Day Merriam won by 1,138,620 votes to Sinclair's 879,537. Sinclair returned home to write his campaign memoir, which was issued in 1934 under the pungent title *I, Candidate for Governor—and How I Got Licked.* There he recapitulated all the offenses mustered against him by the Democratic Party and the press: "They had a staff of political chemists at work, preparing poisons to be let loose in the California atmosphere."

Sinclair's campaign memoir is almost forgotten today, but one line from it may be his most oft-quoted utterance: "It is difficult to get a man to understand something, when his salary depends on his not understanding it!"

Sinclair retired from politics, taking comfort from Merriam's adoption of much of EPIC's program, including a state income tax and an old-age program. Merriam also made the sales tax marginally less regressive by exempting groceries and proposed a severance tax on oil (that is, a tax on oil as it is taken out of the ground).* These initiatives cost Merriam his supporters on

---

* At this writing, California remains the only major oil-producing state without a severance tax.

the right, including the *Los Angeles Times*, which condemned him for trying to "palliate lunacy by adopting some of the folly of the lunatics." He lost his bid for reelection in 1938 to Culbert Olson, who became California's first Democratic governor in forty years.

BY THE TIME of Sinclair's defeat, California-bred utopianism had already produced a new avatar. He was Francis Everett Townsend, a physician who, like Sinclair, proposed a radical redistribution of wealth in the name of economic recovery. But Townsend would acquire an even greater, and more unlikely, eminence than Sinclair on the national political scene.

The origin legend of the Townsend movement was that in 1933, the doctor, unemployed at the age of sixty-six, glanced out his bathroom window in Long Beach while shaving one morning and spotted three "haggard, very old women" in an alley, rooting in garbage cans for food. The doctor let loose a profane tirade, bringing his wife scurrying to his side. "Doctor, you mustn't shout like that! All the neighbors will hear you!" she cried.

"I want all the neighbors to hear me!" he bellowed back. "I want God Almighty to hear me! I'm going to shout till the whole country hears!"

The story was most likely concocted by Townsend's business partner, a slick real estate man named Robert E. Clemens, years after the Townsend movement spread across the United States. The movement's birth can be more reliably traced back to a letter Townsend wrote to his local newspaper, the *Long Beach Press-Telegram*, in September 1933, in which he proposed coaxing workers sixty and older into retirement by granting them a monthly government pension of two hundred dollars financed from a broad-based sales tax, thereby increasing the circulation of money and creating job openings for younger people.

The idea caught fire. In short order there were Townsend newsletters, Townsend flyers, Townsend Clubs all over the country claiming membership of more than five million and followers numbering twenty million more. The Townsend movement became the first true mass lobby for old-age security in the nation's history and the largest grassroots movement in the country. In 1934 several new members of Congress won election on the Townsend platform, alarming incumbents, who would soon be asked to approve a national old-age pension program.

In person, Townsend was soft-spoken and diffident, professing a desire merely to get the country moving again. He disavowed any ambition for public office, playing the role instead of a "gentle general of a growing army." He had been born in 1867 in an Illinois farmhouse, a genuine log cabin located in an agricultural community, and began his medical studies in Omaha at age thirty-one, the oldest student in the first class of the University of Nebraska's medical school. He practiced medicine in the Black Hills of South Dakota for nearly twenty years until 1919, when an attack of peritonitis prompted him to seek out the mild climate of Long Beach, where oil had recently been struck beneath a mound-shaped outcropping known as Signal Hill. The bounty financed parks and promenades and the public health clinic that employed Townsend, but the 1929 crash left thousands of residents on the outside looking in. As the Depression deepened, Townsend came face-to-face with the "soul-wracking" image of "men and women suddenly reduced to absolute begging penury from comparative affluence."

The worst were the homes where unemployed men and women had taken in their fathers and mothers. "The aged were in the way of the young," Townsend observed. In one home, he discovered that an aged gentleman he earlier had seen on his rounds had taken his own life. "He knew himself a burden upon those he loved. He killed himself so his grandchildren might have more to eat."

When the public health service was dissolved, another victim of the Depression, Townsend felt himself too old, at sixty-six, to start over. His answer to his predicament and that of millions of other aged Americans like him—indeed, for the nation as a whole—was the Townsend plan.

As was true of Sinclair's EPIC, the pension program Townsend laid out in that letter on September 30 bore an alluring but misleading simplicity. Recipients of the monthly two-hundred-dollar stipends would have to give up all employment. A mandate that they spend the money within thirty days guaranteed a potent economic impact from the high "velocity" of currency. Financing the program was also simplicity itself: a 2 percent sales tax. "The easiest tax in the world to collect," Townsend maintained, "for all would realize that the tax was a provision for their own future, as well as the assurance of good business now."

The Townsend plan attracted critics among conservative commentators as well as middle-of-the-road economists. At the rate of $2,400 a year per recipient, it meant funneling some $24 billion a year to about 9 percent of the country (based on a conservative estimate of ten million recipients) at a time when total personal income in the United States came to only $40 billion.

The tax would amount to more than twice the total of federal, state, and local taxes already levied from the Atlantic to the Pacific.

New Deal officials struggled to explain the plan's folly to members of Congress unnerved by its popularity yet captivated by its apparent simplicity. Frances Perkins, FDR's labor secretary, who was trying to usher her own national old-age program through Congress, placed it "in the realm of fancy rather than in the realm of practical statesmanship." Political commentator Walter Lippmann learned from correspondence with the physician that Townsend had "read somewhere that in 1929 'the United States did $1,208,000,000,000 of business.'" In other words, he had mistaken the sum of all transactions in the United States for the actual volume of business. A mere 2 percent of that $1.2 trillion, Townsend reasoned, would pay the pension bill.

Spending $2,400 annually per person—$4,800 for a couple—was another challenge at a time when a new Ford sedan could be had for about $600. Townsend's acolytes issued sample budgets for the expenditure of the windfall—$75 a month for the wages of a chauffeur and $20 to $30 a month for fuel; when gasoline cost less than 20 cents a gallon and the average car delivered up to 20 miles per gallon, this implied travel of as much as 3,000 miles a month, or about the distance between California and the East Coast.

In truth, the millions of Townsend Club members had no more interest in the mathematical details of the program than many churchgoers do in the practical plausibility of Biblical miracles. As 1934 drew to a close with the Townsend movement scarcely one year old, it seemed to many in Washington, in the words of the *New Republic*, that "whatever the exaggerations of its publicity . . . it will score to the extent of giving an immense impetus to some form of national legislation on old-age pensions."

That was correct. When Franklin Roosevelt expressed doubts in late 1934 about the national pension program Perkins was crafting, she defended it by warning him that the expectations stirred up by movements like Townsend's warranted drastic action. Roosevelt promptly came around, acknowledging that "Congress can't stand the pressure of the Townsend plan unless we have a real old-age insurance system." That system is Social Security.

17

EXECUTIVE ORDER 9066

CALIFORNIA'S POPULAR REPUBLICAN attorney general Earl Warren—a future governor and later the most liberal chief justice in American history—strode into a meeting room in the old Post Office Building on San Francisco's Embarcadero at ten o'clock one Saturday morning in 1942.

Warren took a seat facing three members of a select congressional committee. Although all were Democrats, Warren was confident of a solicitous reception. The chairman, John H. Tolan, was a friend and neighbor in Oakland. More important, Warren and the congressmen were very much on the same page when it came to the subject at hand, national security. Comfortably settled in, Warren spent the next two hours delivering an unremittingly racist tirade, his targets the more than 110,000 residents of his state with Japanese ancestry, including 66,000 who were native-born American citizens.

"It seems quite plain," Warren said, "that the necessities of the present situation require the removal of the Japanese from a considerable portion if not from all of California."

It was February 21. The Japanese attack on Pearl Harbor had occurred two and a half months earlier; the Battle of Midway, in which the US Navy would reestablish its primacy in Pacific waters after seeming to have lost it in the wreckage of Pearl, was as yet more than three months in the future. On February 19, only two days before Warren's appearance, President Franklin Roosevelt had issued Executive Order 9066, authorizing Secretary of War Henry Stimson to designate any portions of the western United States as "military areas . . . from which any or all persons may be excluded." Nowhere in the order's five terse paragraphs did the words *Japanese* or *Japanese-Americans* appear, but as historian Roger Daniels observed, "they, and they alone, felt its sting."

Thus was launched one of the most shameful episodes in American history, in which dehumanizing prejudice and discrimination was visited upon Japanese immigrants and American citizens of Japanese descent in California, then exported from California to the rest of the country. More than 120,000 people were relocated and incarcerated by the US government starting in 1942 and continuing well into 1946. The vast majority were California residents. Most would be confined in remote camps in the western deserts, giant installations thrown together on a shoestring to house tens of thousands of evictees. The details of the incarcerations remained largely unknown to most Americans until the late 1960s, when a flood of oral histories and memoirs began to reach print.

Roosevelt and his inner circle are often blamed for the relocation and incarceration of Japanese residents, but its genesis was wholly Californian. That was recognized in 2020, when the state assembly passed a resolution acknowledging the state's role. "During the years leading up to World War II," said Assemblyman Al Muratsuchi, a Japanese native who introduced the resolution, "California led the nation in fanning the flames of racism."

But the resolution did not mention Warren's all-important role in fanning those flames.

Warren's defenders argue that since Roosevelt had issued the exclusion order before he testified to the congressional committee, he should not be held responsible for the calamity Japanese families faced during the war. But that overlooks Warren's role in condoning, even encouraging, anti-Japanese passions in the weeks following Pearl Harbor. He met regularly with California governor Culbert Olson, Los Angeles mayor Fletcher Bowron, and other California politicians who advocated the removal of Japanese residents. The participants in these sessions spent hours stoking one another's hysteria about clandestine contacts between Japanese residents on land and the Japanese military at sea, the potential for Japanese sabotage, and the prospects for a Japanese invasion of the coast, and spreading it to the population at large. "It is known that there are Japanese residents of California who have sought to aid the Japanese enemy by way of communicating information, or have shown indications of preparation for fifth column activities," Olson stated in a radio speech on February 4, 1942. The very next day, Bowron warned his own radio audience: "If there is intrigue going on—and it is reasonably certain that there is—right here is the hotbed the nerve center of the spy system, of planning for sabotage. Right here in our own city are those who may spring to action at an appointed time in accordance with a prearranged plan."

As military and intelligence sources would establish, these fears were entirely unwarranted.

By early February, Warren was fully in agreement with his political colleagues that all Japanese residents—immigrants, citizens, children, those suspected of collaboration with Japan, and those against whom no suspicions had been lodged—had to be removed from their homes and sent away. He became an adviser and confidant to John L. DeWitt, the aging lieutenant general who would oversee the eviction and relocation of Japanese residents, passing on to DeWitt every unfounded rumor and fantasy about Japanese sabotage and invasion plans that reached his own desk. DeWitt was openly racist, contemptuous of Japanese and Blacks alike, and "at once insecure and arrogant, panicky, prone to outburst and susceptible to paranoia"—the worst combination of character flaws for a military officer entrusted with a major military enterprise.

There were some inconsistencies in Warren's actions. Even after he began agitating privately for the relocation of the Japanese, he reproached the California State Personnel Board for deciding to fire all public workers who were "descendants" of foreign enemies, a decision plainly aimed at the Japanese. To question the loyalty of native-born Japanese and place them "in a category different from other citizens is not only cruel in its effect upon them but is also disruptive of the national unity which is so essential in these times," he advised the board on February 7. He took a similar position in a formal opinion on February 17 overruling Governor Olson's order to state agriculture officials to revoke the produce-handling licenses of all "enemy aliens."

By then, however, Warren had become a source for visiting political and media figures seeking insights into the parlous security situation on the coast. One visitor was Walter Lippmann, the syndicated columnist regarded as the preeminent political commentator in the land. On February 2, Warren hosted a meeting at which he and DeWitt filled Lippmann's ears with panicky judgments about the Japanese threat in California. Warren had asked local district attorneys to prepare maps of their counties showing "all lands owned, occupied, or controlled by Japanese," both immigrants and American-born. He displayed these to Lippmann, who was duly impressed.

The harvest was an alarming column titled "The Fifth Column on the Coast," distributed for publication on February 12 to Lippmann's more than two hundred newspaper clients. "The Pacific Coast is in imminent danger of a combined attack from within and from without," he wrote. "It is a fact that the Japanese navy has been reconnoitering the Pacific Coast more or less continually and for a considerable period of time, testing and feeling out the American defenses." Washington policymakers, he admonished, were operating with "one hand tied down" by the assumption that the problem was one of "enemy aliens." Instead, it was "a problem of native-born American citizens." He described the Pacific Coast as "officially a combat zone; some part of it may at any moment be a battlefield. Nobody's constitutional rights include the right to reside and do business on a battlefield."

More sober minds in Washington privately repudiated Lippmann's words. In a memo to Roosevelt on February 17, Attorney General Francis Biddle denounced Lippmann, arch-conservative Westbrook Pegler, and other saber-rattling columnists as "armchair Strategists and Junior G-Men." Biddle acknowledged the "increasing demands for evacuation of all Japanese, aliens and citizens alike, from the West Coast states," but dismissed the oft-cited justification of "military necessity." Lippmann and his fellow columnists, he advised, came "close to shouting FIRE! in the theater; and if race riots occur, these writers will bear a heavy responsibility . . . Either Lippman [sic] has information which the War Department and the F.B.I. apparently do not have, or is acting with dangerous irresponsibility."

The real reasons for the alarming rhetoric were economic and racial, Biddle told Roosevelt. He identified as the salient element of the relocation mania the animosity that many white Californians harbored against the Japanese dating back to the turn of the century, originating partially from resentment at the success that Japanese farmers had achieved: "A great many of the West Coast people distrust the Japanese, [and] various special interests would welcome their removal from good farmland and the elimination of their competition." Federal agricultural officials agreed, chalking up anti-Japanese sentiment in California to a "propaganda campaign" by white farmers aiming to "eliminate Japanese competition."

At the time of the Pearl Harbor attack, nearly half the gainfully employed Japanese on the West Coast were working in agriculture. They produced nearly half of all the vegetables raised in California. Nearly five thousand people were employed in the more than one thousand Japanese fruit and vegetable stands in Los Angeles alone. The Issei farmers—that is, first-generation Japanese immigrants—had helped to establish California as the nation's premier farming state through their efforts to "reclaim and improve thousands of acres of worthless lands . . . which the white man abhorred," according to agricultural historian Masakazu Iwata.

The public hysteria triggered by the Pearl Harbor attack only layered a contemporary theme on top of these long-existing resentments.

Warren and his political colleagues, along with Lippmann and his fellow public intellectuals, did much to normalize a policy that many authorities regarded as flagrantly illegal, even unconstitutional. James H. Rowe Jr., an ardent New Dealer who was Biddle's assistant at the Department of Justice, warned FDR on February 2 that the mass eviction of Japanese citizens and aliens from their homes "would probably require suspension of the writ of habeas corpus," leaving the administration with "another Supreme Court fight on our hands." The day before, Rowe had attended a meeting in Biddle's office with War Department and army officials, among them DeWitt's partner in relocation planning, Colonel Karl Bendetsen. Biddle presented them with a proposed press release stating that the War and Justice Departments "are in agreement that the present military situation does not at this time require the removal of American citizens of the Japanese race," but the Pentagon declined to join in the public disavowal. DeWitt had told Bendetsen that pressure for relocation of the entire Japanese population was "not being instigated or developed by people who are not thinking but by the best people of California"—the governor, attorney general, and mayors of the biggest cities. "They don't trust the Japanese, none of them."

Under increasing pressure from West Coast politicians and the military, Roosevelt ignored his advisers' legal opinions and issued his executive order. Rowe would later defend FDR by observing that the president might have been preoccupied by the immediate crises of warfare in the Far East, to the point that Japanese relocation "must have been a fringe matter for him in those weeks." Roosevelt could have transcended the clamor for relocation spreading outward from California in the first weeks of 1942 but failed to do so; the fault is his alone. In the end, the Justice Department refused to have anything to do with the relocation and incarceration policy, thus leaving its implementation to the army.

In his testimony to the Tolan committee, Warren placed the most sinister interpretation on every nugget of information he presented. Referring to the maps of Japanese landholdings supplied by the district attorneys, he said that they showed "a disturbing situation. . . . Along the coast from Marin County to the Mexican border virtually every important strategic location and installation has one or more Japanese in its immediate vicinity."

Warren acknowledged the possibility that "the presence of many of these persons in their present location is mere coincidence, but it would seem equally beyond doubt that the presence of others is not coincidence." In fact, the location of many of these landholdings resulted from a historical injustice: Forbidden by California law to own land or to lease it for more than three years at a time, immigrant Japanese had gravitated toward parcels disdained by whites who were burdened by no such restrictions, acquiring "scraps of property along railroads and electrical lines because it was cheap and available." In many cases their farms predated construction of the "strategic" installations they were accused of surveilling.

California's law enforcement community, Warren told the committee, generally considered that "there is more potential danger among the group of Japanese who are born in this country than from the alien Japanese who were born in Japan." He explained this counterintuitive assertion by noting that, "in the first place, there are twice as many of them"—citing census records showing that 66,000 US-born versus 33,000 foreign-born Japanese lived in California—and assuring the committee that the immigrant generation was too aged to be a threat. Since Japanese immigration to the United States had been curtailed after 1924, the Issei were mostly aged fifty-five or older. On the other hand, Warren said, some of their children "have been sent to Japan for their education . . . and while they are over there they are indoctrinated with the idea of Japanese imperialism. . . . They come back here imbued with the ideas and the policies of Imperial Japan."

Asked by a committee member how one could distinguish loyal US-born Japanese residents from those whose allegiance was to Japan, Warren opined that "there is no way. . . . We believe that when we are dealing with the Caucasian race we have methods that will test the loyalty of them and we believe that we can, in dealing with the Germans and the Italians, arrive at some fairly sound conclusions because of our knowledge of the way they live in the community and have lived for many years."

This was no time for complacency, Warren said: "Many of our people and

some of our authorities . . . are of the opinion that because we have had no
sabotage and no fifth column activities in this State since the beginning of
the war, that means that none have been planned for us." By his reckoning,
Japanese residents' apparently blameless behavior and the absence of known
cases of sabotage were themselves the best evidence of sinister intent. "That
is the most ominous sign in our whole situation," he testified. "I believe that
we are just being lulled into a false sense of security and that the only reason
we haven't had a disaster in California is because it has been timed for a
different date. . . . We are approaching an invisible deadline."

Tolan: "They would be fools to tip their hands now, wouldn't they?"

"Exactly," Warren replied.

Warren devoted some of his testimony to the "one-half of the problem"
that had not received sufficient attention thus far: where to house the relocated residents after their evictions. "There are many, many Japanese who
are now roaming around the Western States in a condition that will un-
questionably bring about race riots and prejudice and hysteria and excesses
of all kinds," he said. "People do not want these Japanese just loaded from
one community to another." Western governors, chambers of commerce,
and other civic authorities were already informing federal officials that they
expected the relocated Japanese to be sequestered behind government fences.
"They don't want them either," Richard Neustadt, an official overseeing federal programs on the West Coast, told the Tolan panel.

WORD OF THE attack on Pearl Harbor on December 7, 1941, filled Japanese
families in California with dread—even those who had been part of their
communities for decades. Twenty-seven-year-old Mary Tsukamoto, who had
grown up on her father's strawberry farm and attended a segregated high
school in the Sacramento suburb of Florin, was playing piano for her church's
adult Issei service when her husband ran in with the news.

"Suddenly the whole world turned dark," she recalled. "We started to
speak in whispers, and we immediately sensed something terrible was going
to happen. . . . We knew that we needed to be prepared for the worst."

After the attack, the FBI began rounding up male heads of households,
evidently working from a secret list. Yoshiko Uchida arrived home in Oakland from a Sunday spent studying for her finals at the University of California
at Berkeley to discover a stranger being served tea by her nervous mother in
the living room. He was an FBI agent, one of the team assigned to take her

father away and left in place to intercept incoming phone calls. The family would not learn the whereabouts of Uchida's father or even if he was alive until six days later, when they received a postcard from him asking for his shaving kit and clean clothes to be sent to an address in San Francisco. The Uchidas were finally reunited in mid-May, after the family had been relocated to a windswept camp in a Utah wasteland known as Topaz.

Donald Nakahata, who was twelve at the time of Pearl Harbor, recalled that his father disappeared on December 7 or 8—the exact date was unknown because the senior Nakahata was arrested while working for a Japanese community group in San Jose, far from the family home in San Francisco. The family never saw him again. They learned much later that he had died after suffering a series of strokes while being transferred from camp to camp in Oklahoma, Louisiana, North Dakota, and New Mexico.

The Japanese incarceration process has been compared to the forced displacement of Jewish communities by the Nazis during World War II. Unlike Nazi policy, the Japanese relocation was not aimed at extermination, but the two procedures shared certain features, notably the dehumanization of the affected population. To be fair, this was a goal of Nazi policy and merely a byproduct of the US process. Still, the US Army displayed a wanton indifference to the physical and emotional well-being of the more than 120,000 individuals placed in its charge. The indifference flowed from the top; DeWitt assumed that the Japanese and Japanese Americans were "a dangerous element, whether loyal or not" and regardless of whether they were citizens. "It makes no difference whether he is an American; theoretically, he is still a Japanese. . . . You can't change him by giving him a piece of paper."

Casual cruelty was baked into the process. Among the first people to feel the pain were the Japanese residents of Terminal Island. This narrow spit of land within Los Angeles Harbor was occupied entirely by Japanese fishermen, cannery workers, and their families—about five hundred households and thirty-five hundred residents in all. The island was reachable only via a drawbridge and ferry, its residents so isolated that they had developed their own dialect, a mélange of English and a regional dialect from Japan. On the reasoning that the island was perilously close to a harborside naval station, the army notified the residents on February 14 that they would have to vacate by March 14. On February 25, however, they were abruptly informed that they would have to leave within forty-eight hours.

Panic swept the community. Permitted to take away only what they could carry, the residents fell into the clutches of a mob of secondhand goods traders. "Unscrupulous vultures in the form of human beings taking advantage of bewildered housewives . . . offered pittances for practically new furniture and appliances: refrigerators, radio consoles, etc.," recalled an evictee. Residents who had invested their life savings in boats and fishing nets had to leave them behind to be pillaged by white fishermen; the navy commandeered the fishing boats and razed the settlement with bulldozers.*

Jeanne Wakatsuki's family had hurriedly moved from their home in the Ocean Park section of Santa Monica to Terminal Island in the first weeks of the roundup to be close to relatives, bringing with them only their silver, family heirlooms, and a fine set of porcelain china. "The secondhand dealers had been prowling around for weeks, like wolves, offering humiliating prices for goods and furniture they knew many of us would have to sell sooner or later," Wakatsuki recalled. A dealer offered her mother fifteen dollars for the china, a full setting for twelve she believed was worth more than ten times the price. When he refused to go above $17.50, "she reached into the red velvet case, took out a dinner plate and hurled at the floor right in front of his feet. . . . Mama took out another dinner plate and hurled it at the floor, then another and another, never moving, never opening her mouth, just quivering and glaring at the retreating dealer, with tears streaming down her cheeks."

Yuri Tateishi was living in a rented home in West Los Angeles with four children when the order came for her to vacate the exclusion zone, forcing her to sell a brand-new living-room set and a refrigerator on which she and her husband had just made the final payment. The morning they were to start their journey to the concentration camp Manzanar, in the Mojave Desert of California, Tateishi's two-year-old son came down with measles. She assembled for the bus with her sleeping child swaddled in a blanket. "Then a nurse came up to me and said, 'May I see your baby?'" Tateishi recounted. "She said, 'I'm sorry but I'm going to have to take him away.'" Tateishi pictured her child waking up in a strange place among strangers: "He probably would just cry all day or all night . . . but there was nothing we could do but leave him." Fortunately, some neighbors promised to keep an eye on him, and he was reunited with his mother in Manzanar three weeks later.

---

* In the 1970s, a memorial featuring a statue of Japanese fishermen and historical placards was erected at the village site, which is now nestled within the ports of Los Angeles and Long Beach.

The evicted residents were brought to camps hurriedly erected in secluded and desolate locations. Since the army had decreed that the camps be far from any installation that could be considered "strategic," they were built on undeveloped government-owned lands—parched, stifling, and devoid of vegetation, "places where nobody lived before and no one has lived since."

Recollections of arrival at the camps all bear a dismal sameness. Upon reporting to the debarkation points, the evictees were shocked to find themselves herded onto buses by armed soldiers and sent on their way. Bay Area residents were first housed at the Tanforan Race Track south of San Francisco, where families were crowded into vacated horse stalls and instructed to stand in line to receive their meals—a couple of canned sausages each that a cook retrieved from a dishpan with his fingers, a hunk of boiled potato, and a slice of unbuttered bread. This was merely the beginning of their degradation.

The desert camps were bleak habitations, reached after hours on crowded trains. Topaz rose behind barbed wire in the Sevier Desert of Utah, an arid bowl surrounded by settlements with sinister names such as Robbers Roost and Skull Rock. Its elevation was 4,600 feet, its temperature reached 106 degrees in the summer and fell below freezing in the winter, and its defining characteristics were a wind that kept up "a seldom interrupted whirl of dust" and rock-hard soil that rain turned into a "gummy muck" swarming with mosquitoes.

The earlier arrivals greeting the newcomers were covered in white dust, as if they had been dipped in a flour barrel or reduced to ghosts. The dust penetrated through spaces between the wallboards and floorboards and the unfilled knotholes of barracks that had been erected hurriedly and indifferently by government contractors. Overnight it accumulated inches thick on their bedding and covered laundry that had been hung out to dry. There had been no time for camp builders to provide the living quarters with heat for the frigid desert nights or serviceable latrines or running water, much less schoolrooms for the children and social gathering places for adolescents and adults. Hospitals would not be completed in many camps until late in 1942; the dearth of medical personnel persisted throughout the incarceration. Sanitation was rudimentary; dysentery outbreaks occurred at Topaz as well as the camps at Minidoka, Idaho (where a typhoid epidemic was also reported), and Jerome, Arkansas. Polio struck Granada, Colorado. At Poston, Arizona, 140 cases of tuberculosis were reported in a span of only eight months.

The evacuees suffered incalculable economic losses. Many had been forced to vacate their homes before they could arrange for security or upkeep during their absence. "Businesses lost their good will, their reputation, their customers," the Commission on Wartime Relocation reported in 1982. Farmland was left fallow, professional careers disrupted. Meanwhile, mortgage and tax obligations continued to mount on families deprived of the resources to pay them. The commission estimated the evacuees' total losses at $810 million to $2 billion in 1982 dollars. The federal government eventually paid about $37 million on property claims filed under a 1948 congressional act by relocated Japanese individuals and families, obviously a minuscule fraction of its obligation.

In February 1943, the government's War Relocation Authority, which supervised the evacuations and ran the camps, stumbled on a way to add insult to injury. This was a loyalty questionnaire developed to help the army recruit volunteers for a segregated all-Japanese combat unit.

The WRA administered the questionnaire to all camp residents over the age of seventeen, male and female. The document's question 28 became infamous. It asked whether the respondent would "swear unqualified allegiance to the United States . . . and forswear any form of allegiance or obedience to the Japanese emperor" or "any other foreign government."

For Issei, who were ineligible by law to become American citizens, a *no* would imply that they were disloyal to the United States, but a *yes* would effectively reduce them to stateless persons vulnerable to a nearly infinite variety of mistreatments. The question was eventually rewritten to ask whether the respondents would "swear to abide by the laws of the United States and to take no action" to interfere with its war effort. It still provoked resentment among evacuees subjected to the manifold indignities of camp life, but in the end more than 65,000 of the 75,000 evacuees administered the test answered *yes* to question 28. About 6,700 answered *no*, and another 2,000 qualified their answers with statements such as "Yes, if my rights as [a] citizen are restored."

The Japanese residents' hopes that the US Supreme Court would defend their rights were destined to be dashed. In a series of decisions beginning with *Hirabayashi v. United States* in 1943 and culminating with *Korematsu v. United States* and *Ex Parte Endo*, both handed down on December 18, 1944, the court betrayed them by upholding the constitutionality of the relocations and incarcerations. All three plaintiffs were American-born US citizens. Legal scholar Eugene V. Rostow later described the rulings as "timid and evasive" and even "sinister." Several justices who came to be regarded as lions of liberal judicial temperament made themselves complicit in a historic miscarriage of justice.

In *Hirabayashi*, liberal chief justice Harlan Fiske Stone, writing for a unanimous court, upheld the relocation and incarcerations, thereby allowing wartime hysteria to trump the constitutional rights of residents and citizens and even for racial judgments to be accepted as government policy. William O. Douglas, one of the most liberal justices ever to serve on the court, concurred in Stone's opinion on the narrow grounds that the plaintiff, Seattle-born Gordon Hirabayashi, had properly been convicted of the crime of defying a government curfew. Liberal justice Frank Murphy filed a concurrence that read more like a dissent—as it may have been originally intended, according to evidence suggesting that Murphy recast it as a concurrence under pressure from his intransigent colleague Felix Frankfurter.

In the *Korematsu* opinion, written by Hugo Black for a 6 to 3 majority, the court accepted DeWitt's position that the relocation was "a matter of military necessity." As Black wrote: "True, exclusion from the area in which one's home is located" was a great deprivation that could be justified by "nothing short of apprehension by the proper military authorities of the gravest imminent danger to the public safety." But he found that in this case "exclusion from a threatened area . . . has a definite and close relationship to the prevention of espionage and sabotage."

Dissenting from Black's opinion, Justice Murphy stated that the evacuation "goes over 'the very brink of constitutional power,'" and falls into the ugly abyss of racism," but his objection was unavailing. In *Endo*, a unanimous decision written by Douglas, the court ruled that the habeas corpus rights of plaintiff Mitsuye Endo had been violated when she was denied release from Topaz. The court ordered her freed but again declined to come to grips with the broader issue of the policy's constitutionality.

Not until 2018, in a decision upholding President Donald Trump's anti-Muslim travel ban, did the court invalidate *Korematsu*, if only in passing. "*Korematsu* was gravely wrong the day it was decided, has been overruled in the court of history, and—to be clear—'has no place in law under the Constitution,'" Chief Justice John Roberts wrote.

Earl Warren sometimes expressed regret at his role in the incarceration in private conversations with friends and his Supreme Court clerks. But although he was often asked to justify himself, to the end of his life he refused to comment publicly on the matter. One notable incident took place in April 1969 following his speech at a human rights conference at Berkeley's law school, his alma mater. Warren was approached by a delegation of twenty-five Sansei-generation—that is, children and grandchildren of those who had been incarcerated—Japanese American students.

"We are here to ask you to publicly apologize," they said.

"I never apologize for a past act," Warren responded uneasily. "That is just a matter of history now."

A public apology, such as it was, appeared only in Warren's memoirs, published posthumously in 1977, three years after his death. "I have since deeply regretted the removal order and my own testimony regarding it," he commented, "because it was not in keeping with our American concept of freedom and the rights of citizens."

The relocation and incarceration originated in California's historical antipathy to Japanese immigrants, but they profoundly disgraced the moral values of the nation. The stain did not disappear with the end of the policy, for America's efforts to redress the injustice were halting at best. A Commission on Wartime Relocation recommended in 1983 that the government make a onetime tax-free payment of twenty thousand dollars to every survivor of the camps then living, a group of about sixty-five thousand individuals, on top of the payments on property claims authorized in the 1940s. Not until 1990 did the payments, inadequate as they were, begin.

Fred Korematsu's conviction for violating the government's exclusion order was overturned in 1983. He died in 2005 at the age of eighty-six, seven years after receiving from President Bill Clinton the Presidential Medal of Freedom, the nation's highest civilian honor, for his court battle against one of the most discreditable policies in American history.

18

THE SELLING OF RICHARD NIXON

ON NOVEMBER 2, 1945, a regional Republican Party committee met in a hotel room in Whittier, a suburban city near Los Angeles, to screen potential candidates for the coming year's congressional election. The race would be challenging. Although the Democratic incumbent, Jerry Voorhis, was rather more liberal than the district's voters, his reputation for integrity and diligence had kept him in his seat for nearly a decade; a few years earlier, the Washington press corps had voted him the most honest congressman and one of the most intelligent.

Still, the committee members had an inkling that the 1946 election might be a turning point for the GOP. World War II was over. Returning servicemen ready to settle down and start families were unhappy with the housing shortages, exorbitant rents, and persistent scarcities in consumer goods they encountered. These were conditions for which the Democrats, who had held the White House and both chambers of Congress since 1933, were likely to be blamed. What the committee needed was a credible candidate; during the long Democratic reign, Republican nominees in California had been a sorry collection of nobodies and right-wing demagogues. The local leaders' efforts to anoint a better class of candidate had been stymied by fate. Their first choice, a retired president of Whittier College, had succumbed to a heart attack in mid-October. Their second choice was General George S. Patton, a Southern California native, but Patton showed no interest.

One of the men interviewed during that meeting in November was a local boy, a navy lawyer and Whittier College alumnus named Richard Nixon.

A committee member and friend of the Nixon family had thrown his name into the ring. The committee flew Nixon in from Baltimore, where he held down a job managing navy contracts, for a look-see. He proved to be personable, intelligent, and intrigued by the possibilities of a political career. The committee chairman, an advertising executive named Roy Day, was immediately taken with the thirty-two-year-old political neophyte.

"You know," he said prophetically upon leaving the committee room, "that is saleable merchandise."

Nixon was unknown in the district but appealingly youthful and distinctly conservative. When the committee met again on November 28 to pick a candidate, he was its unanimous choice.

Nixon had advantages in the campaign that the Voorhis camp failed to comprehend at first. During the initial months Voorhis was stuck in Washington, where the House was debating the complex issues of price controls and public authority over nuclear technology amid the emerging Cold War. Meanwhile, Nixon was free to give speeches all over the district about "the mess in Washington" and to inveigh against government bureaucrats. Not only was Voorhis unavailable to meet with his own constituents, he had no opportunity to size up his opponent.

Consequently, Nixon's considerable speaking and debating skills left Voorhis flatfooted at the first of their five face-to-face debates, which took place on September 13. Voorhis had not undergone the pre-debate prep so routine in politics today. "All of us simply assumed that, in any debate on legislative issues, the experienced congressman would slaughter his opponent," Voorhis aide Paul Bullock would recall. Voorhis was also disadvantaged by the debating rules, which limited him to three-minute sound bites to explicate the nuances of Washington policymaking for his audience. Consequently, Bullock later wrote, "his answers seemed fuzzy or incomplete . . . whereas Nixon was always ready with a quick and acceptable response."

During that debate, Nixon unveiled what would become his principal tactic: questioning Voorhis's character by insinuating that he associated with Communists via the political action committee of the Congress of Industrial Organizations, or CIO-PAC. It was true that Communist Party members were active in the CIO, but CIO-PAC was by no means a Communist front; founded in 1943, it was chiefly a conduit through which CIO-affiliated unions steered their political contributions to progressive candidates. In any case, a cautious Voorhis had let it be known that he would not accept an endorsement from CIO-PAC (nor was one ever offered).

Nevertheless, labeling Voorhis as "the CIO-PAC candidate" became shorthand for Nixon's insinuations that his opponent was a disloyal American. "Voorhis would never know what hit him," Bullock recalled.

The truth was that Voorhis had solid anti-Communist credentials. He was a member of the House Un-American Activities Committee (which was known as the Dies Committee after its chairman, the Texas Democrat Martin Dies). As a committee member, he explained, he had tried to "do my part in exposing . . . the facts about such actually disloyal organizations as the Communist Party" while also moderating the committee's bullying tactics and blocking its "unfair accusations against perfectly loyal Americans." He had introduced what became known as the Voorhis Act, which required all organizations subject to foreign control and devoted to overthrowing federal, state, or local government to disclose to the Department of Justice their members, meeting places and times, and other information.*

None of that mattered. Nixon hammered Voorhis with accusations of Communist sympathies to the very end: "A vote for Nixon is a vote against the Communist-dominated PAC with its gigantic slush fund," read an ad placed in district newspapers late in the campaign. Nixon's campaign supplemented this line of attack with the manifestly untrue claim that Voorhis had been an ineffective legislator during his decade in Congress. Voorhis tried to counter Nixon's onslaught with a newspaper ad listing his legislative accomplishments in numbing detail on a full page of gray print, but by appearing to protest too much, Voorhis in effect granted Nixon's accusation a hint of legitimacy.

Nixon won the election by the unexpectedly large margin of more than fifteen thousand votes. How much his smearing of Voorhis as a Communist sympathizer affected the election is uncertain; in his memoirs, Nixon cited "the quality of life in postwar America" as the decisive issue. Voters "had 'had enough' . . . and they decided to do something about it." Voorhis himself attributed his loss to the bare-knuckle tactics developed by Nixon's campaign manager, Murray Chotiner, whose formula involved discrediting one's opponent as early in the contest as possible, using misrepresentations of the opponent's record wherever necessary. Voorhis identified himself as

---

* The Voorhis Act remains in effect as of this writing.

"the first victim of the Nixon-Chotiner formula for political success." He would not be the last.

AS A POLITICAL figure, Nixon was the beneficiary of California's home-grown variety of anti-Communism and the carrier of its DNA to the nation at large, where it would erupt convulsively as McCarthyism in the early 1950s. California's Red Scare period was more intense and lasted longer than that of any other state. For many of the same reasons that California had been a fertile seedbed for utopians in the 1920s and 1930s, its voters proved uncannily receptive to Red-baiting politicians in the 1940s.

One factor was the impotence of its party organizations. This was an outgrowth of the direct legislation reforms of Hiram Johnson, which undermined party control by moving legislative authority to the ballot box through the initiative and referendum. Johnson built upon Californians' resistance to partisanship dating back to the pre-statehood era by enacting a "cross-filing" law that allowed candidates to run in multiple party primaries, further eroding party authority. By the mid-twentieth century, noted a veteran political journalist, a California party organization typically consisted of "a letterhead, offices in San Francisco and Los Angeles with skeletal staffs, and a dispersion of unpaid, spare-time officers who have no way of mobilizing efforts on behalf of the party except through unpredictable tides of sentiment."

New residents diverse in ethnicity, occupation, and political leanings poured into the state in the 1930s and 1940s, nearly doubling its population from 5.7 million to 10.6 million—further undermining party authority. This produced a pluralistic electorate in which "a motley of interest groups and powerful individuals competed with one another" while the parties could only watch from the sidelines.

Southern California was an especially rich nursery for right-wing movements. Generations of demographers and political scientists have tried to pinpoint the peculiar factors that made it so. Often their judgments have shaded into caricature: "Flagrant self-seeking and corruption have coexisted with intense assertions of moral purity since the early migrations," read a retrospective look in 1970. "With its high mobility, rootless population, and church-saturated atmosphere, southern California has long been seen as the home of the 'isms.'"

An important factor may have been an alliance between the region's conservative business leaders and its law enforcement bodies, through which the latter suppressed outbreaks of leftist and union activity, often violently. The relationship blossomed in the 1920s, a period of notable labor activism, after the founding of the Better America Federation, a business coalition devoted to suppressing union activity. Under its leader Harry E. Haldeman, the federation opposed almost any governmental intervention in the economy, even measures to outlaw child labor.*

With the support of the *Los Angeles Times*, the federation lobbied the city of Los Angeles to create its notorious "red squad" (formally the police department's intelligence bureau), which for fifteen years would employ "a host of spies, stool pigeons, and informers to disrupt trade unions, to provoke violence, and to ferret out the 'reds.'" Carey McWilliams witnessed the squad "break up meetings in halls and public parks with a generous use of tear-gas bombs and clubs." From the employers' standpoint, the squad was particularly effective during the 1934 longshoremen's strike that shut down ports all along the Pacific Coast; in Los Angeles, the squad deployed three hundred police officers and one hundred twenty-five sheriff's deputies to sequester 3,600 strikebreakers—"pasty-faced clerks, house-to-house salesmen, college students and a motley array of unemployed," as one strikebreaker described his fellows—in what was called "a concentration camp at the harbor," ostensibly to protect them from union toughs but really to exclude union organizers. The squad's expenses were not covered by the city budget but paid by the employers.

The 1934 strike was a watershed event in American labor history. Launched on May 9 by the International Longshoremen's Association, it provoked a violent response from employers in Los Angeles, Portland, Seattle, and San Francisco, where strikers who gathered along the Embarcadero were confronted by police "armed with riot clubs, revolvers, tear-gas guns, and riot guns," short-barreled shotguns loaded with buckshot. The eighty-three-day walkout ended with an agreement through which the union's hiring hall supplanted the exploitative employers' system that had previously controlled hiring. The contract, negotiated with the assistance of Labor Secretary Frances Perkins, formalized the workers' right to collective

---

* Haldeman's grandson Harry Robbins (H.R.) Haldeman became chief of staff to President Richard M. Nixon and served eighteen months in prison after being convicted of conspiracy, obstruction of justice, and perjury in connection with the Watergate scandal.

bargaining and brought national renown to strike leader Harry Bridges, an Australia-born longshoreman.

The notion that extreme measures were necessary to root out "subversives" from all walks of life persisted in Southern California and statewide long after the longshoremen returned to work. Civil liberties hung in the balance. A leading exponent of this notion was a state legislator named Jack B. Tenney.

An inveterate publicity hound whose quest for attention had led him on a journey across the political spectrum from left to right, Tenney had started his legislative career in 1936 as a protégé of Art Samish, a hulking, three-hundred-pound Democratic lobbyist in Sacramento who fashioned himself, not inaccurately, as "the secret boss of California." Seeking a candidate who could fill a vacant state assembly seat in Los Angeles and be trusted to follow the party line, Samish recruited Tenney after learning that he had just passed the bar and was interested in moving beyond his middling career as a bandleader and an officer of the musicians union. Asked what he had done before studying for the law, Tenney told Samish, "I played piano in a whorehouse in Mexicali." A delighted Samish replied, "You'll make a good legislator."

Tenney served three two-year terms in the assembly as a supporter of the New Deal even as he affiliated himself with the increasingly febrile anti-Communist movement in California. Two years after the Los Angeles red squad was abolished by the incoming liberal Democratic mayor, Fletcher Bowron, in 1938, Tenney pushed through the creation of a state committee on un-American activities, which soon became known as the "little Dies committee," and served as its chairman.

Tenney's rightward trajectory helped him win a state senate seat as a Republican in 1942. He launched his committee on a series of hearings into alleged Communist subversion targeting "labor, welfare, educational, Progressive Party and 'communist front' groups."

Among Tenney's chief targets was the University of California at Berkeley. In 1947 he turned his sights on the Radiation Laboratory of Ernest O. Lawrence, whose invention of the cyclotron, a pioneering atom smasher, had brought him the Nobel Prize in Physics in 1939. In 1947, Lawrence was the most eminent scientist on the Berkeley faculty. He was one of the top scientific brains behind the wartime Manhattan Project, which developed the atomic bombs dropped on Japan in 1945, and his credentials as a defender of national security were unassailable. That did not protect him from Tenney's search for subversives. At a committee hearing in San Francisco, Tenney homed in on purportedly lax security at the Lawrence lab. His star witness was his chief investigator, R. E. Combs, who told of having ambled up to the lab perimeter one night, flashlight in hand, and crawled under an unguarded fence. Combs was able to wander around without ever being challenged, thereby—so he asserted—exposing an enormous hole in the security fabric of the nation.

This became ammunition for Tenney's broader war with the university. In early 1949 he introduced a package of thirteen bills targeting suspected Communists in state government, including a measure requiring all teachers in the state, including Berkeley faculty, to sign a loyalty oath. This would be a major step, for the state constitution explicitly immunized the university from political pressures. Hoping to head off wholesale interference in university affairs by a conservative legislature, the university's president, Robert Gordon Sproul, rewrote the university's 1942-vintage oath of office so every signer would have to swear explicitly that "I am not a member of, nor do I support, any party or organization that believes in, advocates, or teaches the overthrow of the United States Government."

A craze for anti-Communist loyalty oaths had already swept across the state. Before it faded out, one out of ten Californians would be required to swear an oath, many of them more than once. At the university, most faculty members signed, for the Board of Regents threatened to fire anyone who refused.

Sproul's endorsement of the loyalty oath alienated the faculty and did immeasurable damage to Berkeley's reputation as a haven of academic freedom. Many faculty members were repulsed at the thought of having to affirm their political loyalty. That was especially so among Berkeley's European-born scientists. Even the most ardent anti-Communists among them found the oath reminiscent of the government censorship they had suffered in their homelands. So many émigré physicists quit that the department of physics did not fully regain its academic reputation for years. The controversy also permanently damaged Lawrence's stature at Berkeley, for he had been seen as one of the very few professors who could stand up to Sproul and the regents without fear of retribution; instead, he had tried to enforce the regents' order inside his lab.

Nixon assiduously exploited the anti-Communist fervor that Tenney and others nurtured to advance his own political career. In his freshman congressional term, he succeeded Voorhis on the House Un-American Activities Committee, ultimately using his seat to maneuver himself into the central role of what became arguably the highest-profile espionage case in American history.

The Alger Hiss affair galvanized American public opinion about Communist subversion. "Until the Hiss case," Nixon wrote in his memoirs, "domestic communism . . . was generally not seen as a clear and present danger to our way of life." The affair showed Americans that Communist infiltration posed "a serious threat to our liberties." That might have been a dubious proposition, but the case certainly catapulted Nixon into national prominence, into a place on the 1952 Republican presidential ticket as Dwight Eisenhower's vice presidential running mate, and eventually into the White House.

The Hiss case began with an appearance at a public HUAC hearing by Whittaker Chambers, an editor at *Time* and a self-confessed defector from the Communist Party. Chambers named a half a dozen low-level New Deal functionaries as people he had met at party meetings. Among them, Alger Hiss's name stood out. Hiss was a former State Department aide who had helped organize the international conferences at Dumbarton Oaks in Washington, DC, and San Francisco at which the founding principles of the United Nations were worked out. He also had traveled with the American delegation to the February 1945 Yalta Conference at which Franklin Roosevelt, Winston Churchill, and Joseph Stalin drew the post–World War II geopolitical map. In 1946 he had been named president of the prestigious Carnegie Endowment for International Peace.

Chambers's allegation against Hiss led newspaper accounts the next day.

Hiss denied knowing Chambers and demanded the opportunity to confront his accuser face-to-face. It would be hard to conceive of two more dissimilar people than Alger Hiss and his accuser. Nixon himself described Hiss, a well-bred graduate of Harvard Law School (where he had been a protégé of future Supreme Court justice Felix Frankfurter) and a former clerk for Supreme Court justice Oliver Wendell Holmes Jr., as "tall, elegant, handsome, and perfectly poised." Nixon remembered Chambers as "one of the most disheveled-looking persons I had ever seen." His most distinctive physical feature was "a mouth full of rotting teeth." Hiss testified forthrightly in his defense; Chambers seemed perpetually to be holding something back.

The committee was inclined to drop the investigation until Nixon proposed to interrogate Chambers privately to draw out any evidence that could be used to impeach Hiss.

What drove Nixon's determined pursuit of Hiss? Certainly he got under Nixon's skin. "His manner was coldly courteous and, at times, almost condescending," Nixon wrote of Hiss's first appearance before HUAC. It is easy to imagine that Hiss's socially lubricated journey to high diplomatic and political echelons grated on Nixon, whose own life journey was burdened by his penurious working-class upbringing and had brought him, at that time, only as far as a congressional seat in a suburban district.

The Hiss case gave Nixon an irresistible opportunity to raise his political profile. Sure enough, his efforts soon placed him many steps closer to the most prominent names in the GOP. His role on the committee enabled him to orchestrate what became a landmark news moment, a nationally televised confrontation between Chambers and Hiss in a congressional hearing room, the first such telecast from the Capitol.

There would be one more major turn in the case to solidify Nixon's stature as a spy hunter. Late in 1948, Chambers revealed that he possessed a cache of papers that would prove that Hiss was guilty of espionage—sixty-five pages of government documents purportedly retyped by Hiss on a personal typewriter. Chambers escorted HUAC investigators to a garden patch behind a farmhouse he owned outside of Baltimore, where he extracted five film canisters from a hollowed-out pumpkin. Nixon turned the discoveries into a personal coup de théâtre. The press labeled the sixty-five pages on the filmstrips as the "Pumpkin Papers." Photographs of Nixon holding the strips up to the light and scrutinizing them with a magnifying glass duly appeared on front pages nationwide.

Hiss was ultimately convicted of perjury, for lying to a federal grand jury by testifying that he had never given any documents to Chambers and that he had never met with Chambers after 1936, and served forty-four months in federal prison. He insisted on his innocence to the end of his life. The case obliterated his promise as a young professional in the diplomatic sphere. Nixon, however, would ride it to his next political step higher, the US Senate.

THE REPUBLICAN PARTY suffered a catastrophic defeat in the 1948 elections, losing the control of both houses of Congress that they had wrested from Democrats only two years earlier while watching their standard-bearer,

Thomas E. Dewey, suffer an utterly unexpected loss to Harry Truman in the race for president. For Nixon, the results were a particular blow. As he wrote later, they turned him overnight into "a junior member of the minority party, a 'comer' with no place to go." He had been content to patiently move up the ranks into a position of power in the House of Representatives, but now his prospects appeared to be reduced to spinning his wheels as part of "a vocal but ineffective minority."

Of a host of uninviting career options, the only remotely promising choice seemed to be a run for the Senate in 1950. Nixon's political inner circle tried to dissuade him. The Democratic incumbent was the affable Sheridan Downey, running for his third term. A former New Deal liberal who had run for lieutenant governor on Upton Sinclair's EPIC ticket in 1934 and had actively supported Francis Townsend's old-age-pension movement, Downey had moved distinctly to the right after reaching the Senate in 1939, which narrowed Nixon's opportunities for attack. Downey was popular with the voters and backed by the oil industry and Hollywood, the interests of which he represented ably in Washington.

Nixon's ambition won out, strengthened by his recognition, as he would recall, of "the worth of the nationwide publicity that the Hiss case had given me—publicity on a scale that most congressmen only dream of achieving." He also held a trump card: Kyle Palmer, the kingmaking political editor of the Los Angeles Times, had guaranteed him the newspaper's endorsement in a Senate run. Early in the campaign, Downey dropped out of the race, citing health problems, a stroke of luck that improved Nixon's prospects, for Democratic voters replaced Downey on the ballot with Helen Gahagan Douglas, who Nixon thought would be a weaker adversary. She became the second victim of the Nixon-Chotiner political formula.

Idealistic and liberal, Douglas was in her third congressional term. She was also a member of Hollywood aristocracy. A stage actress and opera singer, she had moved west with her husband, Melvyn Douglas, who became one of movieland's best known leading men. The Douglases reigned as the most glamorous couple in Los Angeles liberal circles. Helen's movie career had never taken off, so it was not hard for her to abandon it for a new career in Democratic politics starting in 1938.

Through the early 1940s, Helen Douglas built up a reservoir of appreciative sentiment among Southern California Democrats by mobilizing women's groups for Democratic candidates. She received credit for the party's successful showing in the 1942 congressional races in Southern California, where Democrats won three of six crucial districts while losing seventy House seats nationwide. In 1944, the party persuaded her to run for a House seat in downtown and central Los Angeles, a district that brought together some of the poorest and richest neighborhoods in the city. The district was about 25 percent Black and included Chinese, Japanese, and Mexican communities as well as a slice of Hollywood itself. Douglas showed remarkable energy as a campaigner, speaking at dozens of meetings in voters' homes at which she made the case for herself as a devoted supporter of the New Deal and Franklin Roosevelt.

Having eked out a narrow victory of four thousand votes out of the 137,500 cast, Douglas came to Washington as a member of a Democratic Party majority. She was part of an ideological minority, however, for southern Democrats had made common cause with Republicans to resist such progressive legislative goals as civil rights. Her positions reflected the concerns of her mostly liberal constituents, which enabled her to increase her margin of victory in the 1946 election even as Republicans won control of both chambers of Congress for the first time since the 1930s. While the GOP majority pursued an ever more reactionary course, rejecting President Truman's Fair Deal program, which aimed to extend the New Deal into the postwar period, Douglas solidified her liberal credentials. In 1948 she won again, this time garnering more than two-thirds of the vote.

By then, however, Douglas was showing signs of having become captivated by her own public standing. She collected civic awards and citations by the bucketful and received an unceasing flow of speaking invitations from local, state, and national Democratic organizations. The attention undoubtedly contributed to her decision to mount what many political observers considered a quixotic primary challenge against Downey for the Senate in 1950. After Downey's withdrawal, she won the nomination by a plurality, besting a Los Angeles newspaper publisher and Nixon, who had filed in the Democratic primary under the state's progressive-era cross-filing rule. The Douglas-Nixon race was on.

As Nixon anticipated, political ferment in 1950 played into his anti-Communist persona. In October 1949, Mao Zedong had established the People's Republic of China, triggering a "who lost China" debate that painted Truman and the Democrats as feckless adversaries of the Reds. In January 1950, Manhattan Project physicist Klaus Fuchs confessed to having passed atomic bomb secrets to the Soviets. On February 9, Republican senator Joseph McCarthy of Wisconsin delivered a keynote speech at the Republican Party's annual Lincoln Day dinner in Wheeling, West Virginia, in which he claimed to have in his hand a list of 205 State Department officials who were members of the Communist Party. The Korean civil war erupted in June, and the United States was fully drawn into the conflict before summer's end.

In launching his Senate campaign, Nixon promised "no name-calling, no smears, no misrepresentations." Virtually in the next breath, he accused Douglas of being soft on Communism. Among other things, he cited her opposition to loyalty oaths for federal employees and to budget appropriations for the House Un-American Affairs Committee. In truth, Douglas's anti-Communist credentials were as solid as those of Jerry Voorhis, but in the hands of Nixon and Chotiner, they were twisted to appear just the opposite.

Early in the campaign, Nixon released what has become notorious as the "Pink Sheet." This was a leaflet, printed in red ink on suggestive pink paper, falsely associating Douglas with the far-left wing of the Democratic Party. Privately, Nixon's surrogates described Douglas as "pink down to her underwear," a salacious image Nixon himself was careful not to evoke in public. "Dirty tricks" of the sort that would become essential features of Nixon's campaign arsenal originated in this race; at the University of Southern California, members of a campus fraternity disrupted a Douglas appearance by spraying her with seltzer water and flinging bales of hay at her. Among the frat brothers were several men who would later turn up as White House aides and political operatives during the Watergate era, including Donald Segretti, Gordon Strachan, and Dwight Chapin. Another sub rosa Nixon surrogate, the anti-Semite and white supremacist Gerald L. K. Smith, was heard on the radio exhorting listeners to reject Douglas because she "sleeps with a Jew" (that is, her husband, Melvyn).

The *Los Angeles Times*, true to Kyle Palmer's word, amplified Nixon's attacks on Douglas. Late in the campaign, the newspaper's editorial writers called Nixon "the most conspicuous opponent of Communists and Communism in the present Congress," and labeled Douglas "the darling of the Hollywood parlor pinks and Reds."

Nixon's attacks kept Douglas off-balance from the start. Her camp labeled Nixon "Tricky Dick," a nickname that would stick to him for the rest of his career in public life. But the political winds were against her. Adding to her burden was the ineptitude of the California Democratic Party, whose gubernatorial candidate, James Roosevelt (son of the late president), had been unable to land a punch on the hugely popular Republican incumbent, Earl Warren. With this weakness at the top of the ticket, Douglas had to wage a lonely, poorly funded battle. On Election Day Nixon beat her 2,200,000 votes to 1,500,000. She never ran for elected office again.

There can be little doubt that sexism also played a role in Douglas's defeat. A woman running for such an exalted office was still regarded as a curiosity in 1950. At the time, only seven women had ever served in the US Senate, none from California. Douglas was only the third woman to serve California in the House of Representatives, following Mae Nolan and Florence Prag Kahn, who had won their seats in 1923 and 1925, respectively, to fill out the unexpired terms of their late husbands. No women served California in the US Senate until Dianne Feinstein and Barbara Boxer were elected in 1992.

Nixon was forever defensive about the character of his sole Senate campaign. "Mrs. Douglas and many of her friends and supporters claimed that I had impugned her loyalty and smeared her character," he wrote. Rather, he asserted, California voters "were not prepared to elect . . . anyone with a left-wing voting record or anyone they perceived as being soft on or naïve about communism." But the smear campaign reflected a cruder philosophy: "The purpose of an election," Chotiner held, "is not to defeat your opponent, but to destroy him."

19

TOMORROWLAND

HERE IS THE world's prize collection of cranks, semi-cranks, placid creatures whose bovine expression shows that each of them is studying, without much hope of success, to be a high-grade moron, angry or ecstatic exponents of food fads, sun-bathing . . . diaphragm breathing and the imminent second coming of Christ."

Thus a sample of the pejorative clichés East Coast pundits often used to describe Los Angeles in the 1930s—this one written by Bruce Bliven, editor of the *New Republic*. Yet even in 1935, when Bliven set down those words, they were hopelessly outdated. Southern California was already displaying the industrial dynamism that would transform it into an economic behemoth.

By 1950, Los Angeles "handled more seaport tonnage than San Francisco, landed more fish than Boston and Gloucester . . . made more planes than any other metropolis on earth," historian Richard G. Lillard wrote. "Los Angeles also assembled more cars than any city but Detroit, baked more tires than any city but Akron, made more furniture than Grand Rapids."

Southern California's consumer economy set the standard for the wave of postwar prosperity washing over the entire country. In the fifties, retail sales in Los Angeles County outstripped those in Oregon, Washington, Colorado, and Arizona put together. The county had more passenger cars than any other metropolis in the land—"40 percent more than in all the New York City boroughs, 47 percent more than in Chicago's Cook County," Lillard calculated. Flush times provided the wherewithal to build infrastructure to accommodate what was seen as California's "car culture"; the twenty-two miles of state-funded freeways in LA County in 1952 expanded to eighty-three at the end of the decade. By the turn of the century, when the freeway-construction boom finally ended, there would be 515 miles of freeway among nearly five thousand miles of publicly maintained major arterials.

The hankering of Angelenos for recognition as model mainstream Americans rather than parochial crackpots never lay far beneath the surface for much of the city's history. But it intensified as the city's economic self-confidence grew. Mayor Norris Poulson's enticing of the Brooklyn Dodgers to LA before the 1958 baseball season, an act that turned Dodgers owner Walter O'Malley into a venerated hero in his adopted new home and an enduring villain in Brooklyn lore, was only one example, if an especially high-profile one, of the city's quest to be seen as a world-class metropolis.

In 1948, Walt Disney began conceiving a unique amusement park that would open in 1955 as Disneyland, segmented into five "lands" including Tomorrowland, the theme of which was space travel and the future. That fit well with Californians' efforts to occupy the technological vanguard, which dated back almost to the turn of the century. Disney accepted his consultants' advice to locate the park on a 160-acre tract of orange groves and walnut orchards in the semi-rural Orange County community of Anaheim, on the expectation that residential growth would eventually turn it into the hub of a vast metroplex. The consultants were, plainly, correct.

Southern California's spectacular development in the postwar era grew out of its response to wartime industrial demand and its embrace of entirely new industries advancing new technologies. That characteristic could be traced back to an eleven-day open-air exhibition that placed the region at the center of what was then the new world of aviation.

THE LOS ANGELES International Air Meet opened on January 10, 1910, bringing two hundred thousand onlookers to a hilltop a few windswept miles from the Pacific shore. The show featured hot-air balloons and cigar-shaped dirigibles, but those were old hat. The crowds were drawn more by the barnstorming pilots who had been making their names in Europe with gossamer-winged biplanes and monoplanes whose roaring engines were powerful enough to send them careening around aerial racecourses at previously unimaginable speeds of up to sixty miles per hour.

Southern California's business boosters had found the idea of an international air meet irresistible from the moment that Dick Ferris, a theatrical

promoter representing a group of aviation pioneers, strode into the newsroom of William Randolph Hearst's *Los Angeles Examiner* and laid out the
proposal. His timing was perfect; the city was still struggling to recover
from an economic slump that had struck so hard in 1908 that local banks
were reduced to paying their depositors in scrip. The city's Merchants and
Manufacturers Association, the brainchild of the *Los Angeles Times'* Harrison
Gray Otis, and the Southern Pacific Railroad, which would ferry spectators
to the site for a round-trip fare of thirty-five cents on trains every forty-five
minutes, joined in the ballyhoo.

The site was Dominguez Hill, an undeveloped parcel south of the city
center and overlooking the harbor. The aviators hoped to capitalize on the
excitement generated by the very first international air meet, held in Rheims,
France, in August 1909. Los Angeles offered the opportunity to organize an
American sequel without worrying about the winter weather that ruled out
eastern and midwestern locations.

The two biggest stars were Glenn H. Curtiss, who hailed from upstate
New York, and Louis Paulhan of France, who had battled each other for
prizes in the skies over Rheims. The two aeronauts could not have been
more different. Curtiss was an austere soul with a permanent scowl fixed on
his face. Everything he did was in service to the business of selling flying
machines made in his factory outside of Buffalo, New York, his aerial performance having "about as much sensational atmosphere as that of a busy man
leaving home in his auto for his office." The slightly built Paulhan—five foot
four inches and 140 pounds—was a born showman, a former circus tightrope
walker who had only begun flying in 1909 but loved to thrill spectators
with daredevil stunts. At Dominguez Hill, "he soared like a restless chicken
hawk; swooped down to scare people in the infield like a facetious falcon;
skimmed over the heads in the grand stand; mocked slow dirigibles in their
majestic flight."

Paulhan gave a ride to the *Examiner*'s owner, William Randolph Hearst,
who wedged his two hundred pounds into the aviator's Bleriot monoplane
and emerged from the flight sufficiently enthralled to offer a fifty-thousand-
dollar prize to the first aviator to fly coast to coast in under thirty days. (The
prize expired, unclaimed, in November 1911.)

The air show with its huge, enthusiastic crowds bathed Southern California in a lasting promotional glow. The *Times*, with pardonable pride,
declared the meet "one of the greatest public events in the history of the

West. . . . It has been demonstrated that Los Angeles is a metropolis great and influential enough to handle the biggest of world's events." Los Angeles business and political leaders pondered how to turn the public spectacle at Dominguez Hill into a solid industrial base.

It would take somewhat longer than they expected. In 1925, fifteen years after the air show, there were still only four companies employing only 203 workers building aircraft, less than 10 percent of the workforce of an industry still based mostly in New York and Ohio. Yet within another dozen years, Southern California had become the nation's leading aircraft-manufacturing region, with twenty-four established companies employing more than 11,500 workers, nearly half of the national aviation workforce.

Among the earliest entrepreneurs was Glenn L. Martin, a transplanted Kansan who began building airplanes in a rented former Methodist church in Santa Ana. At midnight on July 31, 1909, he and his three engineers wheeled a craft four miles overland to a lima bean field owned by James Irvine, whose sprawling agricultural estate would eventually become one of Orange County's most important residential and commercial communities. At first light, Martin gunned the throttle and achieved a twelve-second, one-hundred-foot flight, the first of a heavier-than-air craft in California.

Historians have often attributed the growth spurt of aircraft manufacturing in California to the state's salubrious climate and the availability of acres of cheap undeveloped land, but a more important factor was technological. That factor originated with the arrival of Donald Douglas, a recent MIT graduate whom Martin lured away from the school's offer of an assistant professorship in 1915 to become his chief engineer at age twenty-three. Five years later, Douglas founded his own company. Douglas's initial backer was David R. Davis, a self-made millionaire and aircraft designer who advanced him $40,000 to build a plane capable of completing the first nonstop trans-continental flight. The long-range Cloudster biplane was the first plane with the power to lift a payload equal to its own weight. But it crashed in El Paso on its trial flight in 1921, and two army fliers beat it to Davis's goal of a non-stop transcontinental flight two years later. The experience cured Davis of his fascination with aircraft manufacturing. He sold his interest to Douglas, who had won a contract to build a torpedo plane for the Navy. Davis's with-drawal had left him without the capital to carry the contract through, but he was rescued by a syndicate of ten local businessmen assembled by Harry Chandler. They fronted Douglas fifteen thousand dollars, allowing him to move his factory to a vacant former movie studio in Santa Monica that would become the long-term home of the Douglas Aircraft Company.

One breakthrough was the development in 1933 of the L-10 Electra by Lockheed, a company founded in San Francisco in 1916 by the brothers Allan and Malcolm Loughead, who subsequently moved to Santa Barbara. (The Lougheads simplified the spelling of their name in 1926.) The L-10 was a twin-engine all-metal craft with the company's distinctive double vertical tails and retractable landing gear with eight passenger seats.*

The more important innovation, however, belonged to Douglas—specifically, his creation of the DC line of aircraft that would dominate commercial aviation well into the postwar period. Douglas's DC line was conceived as a response to the introduction of the Boeing 247 in 1930, a revolutionary aircraft that could carry ten passengers without giving up space for the US Mail, then the cash cow of America's domestic airlines. Priced at a market-topping $68,000, the 247 was "faster and plushier" than any other airliner on the market, with a top speed of 160 miles per hour that cut the coast-to-coast flying time from twenty-seven hours to nineteen and a half. Douglas Aircraft had been largely a supplier of military aircraft to the government until a letter arrived from Jack Frye, a top executive of Transcontinental and Western Airlines—TWA, later renamed Trans World Airlines—asking him to produce a plane with room for a dozen passengers, a top speed of 185 miles per hour, and a range of 1,080 miles. The result was the DC-1, which rolled out of its Santa Monica hangar on June 22, 1933. That September, Frye and his friend Eddie Rickenbacker, the World War I flying ace who was an executive of Eastern Air Lines, flew it on a test run with a full load of mail from Burbank to Newark, New Jersey, setting a record for a coast-to-coast flight of thirteen hours and four minutes.

The first commercial version of Douglas's plane, the DC-2, rolled out in 1934. It was followed by the DC-3, which could carry twenty-one passengers in comfort. Douglas calculated that he would break even with the sale of seventy-five DC-3s. By the time production ended in 1950, more than sixteen thousand had been built. The DC-3's global popularity derived from both its robust design and the ease of control that became an aviation byword—"an amiable cow . . . marvelously forgiving of the most clumsy

---

* The L-10 acquired a baleful role in aviation history as the plane piloted by Amelia Earhart when she disappeared over the Pacific in 1937.

pilot," as it was described by the novelist and pilot Ernest K. Gann. Most important, perhaps, it made money—the first aircraft that could turn a profit for its owner by carrying passengers rather than cargo. Hundreds of DC-3s can still be found flying air routes all around the world.

Lockheed's L-10 and the DC-3 turned Southern California into the aircraft-manufacturing center of the world. In 1933, Lockheed produced about 11 percent of all the new aircraft bought by US civilian air carriers and Douglas just over 1 percent; by 1935 their shares were 33 percent and 59 percent, respectively. Two years later, Douglas had decisively won the contest, accounting for 87 percent of all new orders, with Lockheed trailing at a distance with 11 percent. The DC-3 then accounted for 95 percent of all civil air traffic in the nation.

THE AIRCRAFT INDUSTRY'S technological sophistication fueled the growth of the electronics and computer industries, which would carry the state's economic arc into the twenty-first century. It also harked back to the state's past. Californians had become experts in using innovative technologies—such as the dams, aqueducts, and canals that collected water and moved it hundreds of miles to farmers and city dwellers—to tame their varied and recalcitrant environment.

The California industry that would be most successful in exploiting technological innovation to generate profits was moviemaking.

The film industry began to appreciate the virtues of Southern California as early as 1917, when William Selig shot a feature in Santa Monica; two years later, he established a studio in downtown Los Angeles. By the time the most important moguls began to immigrate west, led by Louis B. Mayer in 1918, Southern California was already hosting seventy companies producing 80 percent of the world's movies.

The region appealed to the major producers for several reasons. There was its temperate climate, facilitating outdoor shooting year-round, and its varied topography, allowing producers to film "Westerns in the desert, sea stories at the beach, and a weird concoction of Indian-Spanish dramas in front of the missions."

Another factor was the rudimentary social hierarchy in Los Angeles. This was especially appealing to the Jewish immigrants who ruled the movie industry—Carl Laemmle, the founder of Universal, came from Southern Germany; Adolph Zukor and William Fox, founders of Paramount and Fox respectively, from Hungary; Mayer (MGM) from Russia; and the Warner brothers from Poland—yet faced a withering condescension from high society in the East. Hollywood, the Los Angeles enclave where several of them first settled, seemed as distant from the hurly-burly of the metropolitan East Coast as one could imagine: "Apples, avocados, pineapples, orange and lemon trees, calla lilies and geraniums all grew wild . . . and coyotes howled at night." More to the point, it was a blank slate on which to write their new personal histories, a place in which they would craft the idealized vision of America they conjured from their own hopes and dreams to send forth to the world.

For all its cultural adornments, filmmaking was, and is, a fundamentally technological undertaking, continually advanced by innovation. Perhaps the most notable example is sound. In popular imagination, the "talkies" revolution struck like a thunderbolt on October 6, 1927, with the release by Warner Brothers of *The Jazz Singer*, provoking full-blown industry-wide chaos. The truth is rather different.

Efforts to add sound to moving pictures dated to the 1890s, when Thomas Edison tried to market what he called a Kinetophone. This device played an unsynchronized musical accompaniment for what was then known as a "peep show," a strip of film viewed by one person at a time through a small lens. The result was too crude to be successful, but at a New York theater in 1913 Edison demonstrated a more sophisticated version with synchronized clips of a performer smashing a plate, playing a violin, and prompting a dog to bark. The program, which concluded with a chorus singing "The Star Spangled Banner," was well received by the premiere audience, but the equipment was still so tetchy and the synchronization so uneven that this version flopped too.

Even during the "silent era," Hollywood movies were not truly silent; they were always accompanied by either a separately recorded soundtrack or a musician or band in the theater. The challenge was to find a way to match soundtrack and the image closely enough to create the illusion of a performer speaking the words. The film studios had always welcomed advances in film developing, camera and lens design, lighting, and projection technology. In the twenties, they became especially eager to try any innovation in sound. For one thing, there were signs that audiences were becoming bored with the movies, the quality of which had settled into a lethargy-inducing mediocrity. Meanwhile, radio had emerged as a competitive threat by bringing entertainment programming directly into the home. The industry was primed to welcome yet another technological step forward.

As it happened, the main impetus for perfecting a technology for recording and reproducing sound came not from the movie industry but from AT&T, which was trying to improve the intelligibility of telephone conversations; RCA, which was trying to improve the quality of radio sound; and other technological enterprises. AT&T formed Vitaphone with Warner Brothers in 1925 to produce sound movies. Four months later, the first Vitaphone program premiered in New York, featuring a brief comic sketch and the New York Philharmonic in a selection of opera and concert pieces. Growing demand prompted Warner Brothers to erect specially built soundstages in Hollywood to turn out five Vitaphone shorts a week.

The rest of the industry was not idle.

Three other sound systems had entered the market in the 1920s using varied technologies: RCA's Photophone, inventor Lee De Forest's Phonofilm, and Movietone, which had been developed by the inventor Theodore Case and acquired by Fox Film Corporation's William Fox in 1926. In February 1927, five major studios—Paramount, MGM, Fox, Universal, and United Artists—reached an agreement to select one sound system out of the several options as a standard.

Then came *The Jazz Singer*. The film itself, a shameless tearjerker about a Jewish cantor's son torn between his career as a popular entertainer and his promise to his dying father to sing the Kol Nidre hymn at a Yom Kippur service, elicited mixed reviews. But Al Jolson's star quality exploded from the screen in five musical numbers interpolated into a scenario told mostly through the silent-film technique of title cards.

Jolson's presence was probably the most important factor in making *The Jazz Singer* the biggest hit of the 1927–1928 season. But its success did validate the studio moguls' instinct that sound would be a crucial attraction for audiences. Accordingly, sound systems spread rapidly. By September 1929, all the studios had completed transitions to all-talkie production. By January 1930, AT&T was installing nine sound systems a day and by 1932 scarcely a single theater in America was unequipped to show talkies. The public's love affair with Hollywood movies was rekindled; Warner Brothers' profits increased to fourteen million dollars in 1929 from two million the year before. The other studios also saw profits cascade in.

There was a significant downside to the post-talkies boom, however. The big studios had been tightening their grip on the distribution of their own films by restricting them to their own theater chains and excluding features from competing studios. With the surge in post-talkie profits, this behavior caught the attention of government trust-busters. A federal antitrust lawsuit reached the Supreme Court in 1946, resulting in a 1948 court order forcing the studios to sell off their theater subsidiaries. With the divestment order, the wheel turned again, for it helped to trigger the rise of a new threat to Hollywood that far exceeded the threat from radio in the 1920s: television. Seeking new revenue to replace the loss of theater admissions, the studios licensed their film libraries to TV networks. Former film stars launched revitalized careers on TV. As the audiences for television grew through the 1950s, the audiences for films declined. New technologies such as widescreen projection and Cinerama would eventually appear, continuing the historical cycle in which every innovation eventually played out, driving the eternal quest for something new.

ALTHOUGH SPIN-OFFS FROM aviation manufacturing provided a firm economic bedrock for the entire state's eventual domination of technology-oriented industries, the wealth created by the aeronautics industry and Hollywood was concentrated in Southern California. Part of the influence, oddly enough, resulted from the boom-and-bust cycles of aeronautics. Waves of layoffs in the peacetime interludes between World War II and the Korean and Vietnam Wars put thousands of trained manufacturing workers on the street, where they could be snapped up for "improvised factories that began in old loft buildings, in Quonset huts, and in backyard garages," making everything from chinaware to automobile parts and units for prefabricated houses; putting this military surplus manpower to work from 1947 through 1957 drove manufacturing employment growth in the city of Los Angeles that outstripped that of the rest of the country tenfold.

Another factor in the expansion of the innovation economy statewide was government money.

Before he faced Nixon's anti-Communist zeal, Ernest O. Lawrence ushered in an unprecedented era of government-funded technology research in California. He arrived at Berkeley as a young physics PhD in 1928, lured by the promise of a rapid ascent up the academic ladder, impossible at seniority-bound Yale. Within a year, he had stumbled upon the principle of the cyclotron, a peerlessly efficient and effective atom smasher that would launch particle physics on a new phase of discovery. The invention would garner Lawrence the Nobel Prize in Physics in 1939, the first to be awarded for a scientific instrument rather than a theory or experimental result.

Cyclotron technology was constantly evolving; Lawrence was conceiving ever more powerful machines. The series of technological advances he oversaw combined with his talent for raising funds from private foundations and government sources brought a torrent of capital funding to the University of California.

With the advent of World War II, the government spigot opened wider. In 1936, the federal government had spent thirty-three million dollars on research and development nationwide, a mere 15 percent of the total spent by industry, academia, and philanthropic foundations. Starting in 1941 and through the war, the government's share of R and D averaged five hundred million dollars a year, or 83 percent of the total. More important, the trend continued after war's end; in 1947, the federal research budget reached $625 million, still more than half of a rapidly expanding national investment in scientific research. Due initially to Lawrence's wartime rapport with the Manhattan Project's military boss, General Leslie Groves, whom he had served as a key scientific adviser, the University of California remained securely at or near the top of the list of institutions receiving government research funding in physics for decades to come.

Another factor was at play in the Bay Area. There, a fortuitous confluence of the academic, investment, legal, and advertising communities gave birth to what became known as Silicon Valley, which to this day dominates high-technology research and development worldwide.

That story began in 1937 with the founding of Hewlett-Packard Corporation by William Hewlett and David Packard in the backyard garage of a home in Palo Alto, a few miles from the campus of Stanford University. The guiding spirit behind their partnership was Frederick Terman, a Stanford electrical engineering professor, who, by lending them a few hundred dollars as seed money, persuaded his two graduate students to commercialize the audio-oscillator Hewlett had invented. Their initial order, for eight units, came from Walt Disney.

After serving through the war in a government research laboratory in Boston, Terman had returned to California sensitive to Stanford's position as an "underprivileged institution" that, unlike Berkeley, had been uninvolved with developing the technology deployed during the war. Launching a campaign to improve the school's intellectual resources, he succeeded to a degree that no one could have anticipated.

Terman's approach was to engage local electronics companies in a collaborative relationship with the university. The first step was the establishment of Stanford Research Institute in 1946 to pursue research that "might not be fully compatible internally with the traditional roles of the university"— that is, commercially focused industrial research. (It was SRI experts who advised Walt Disney on the location of his amusement park.) The university also encouraged professional employees at local companies to enroll in graduate classes they could attend via closed-circuit television in their offices. The masterstroke may have been the creation of Stanford Industrial Park on 4,500 undeveloped acres bequeathed to the university by its founder, Leland Stanford. Only companies whose businesses met Terman's standards for innovativeness were eligible to lease space. The tenants often hired Stanford faculty or graduate students as employees or consultants, augmenting university/industry collaborations. In 1955, the industrial park covered 220 acres; five years later it had tripled in size and housed twenty-five companies with eleven thousand employees. The university's surroundings were now a hotbed of advanced inventive engineering.

That was especially so after the arrival of William Shockley, whose role as what a professional colleague called "the Moses of Silicon Valley" was unique—and not entirely for the most praiseworthy reasons.

Raised in Palo Alto and Los Angeles and educated at Caltech and MIT, Shockley had been the managing member of a three-man team (with John Bardeen and Walter Brattain) that invented the transistor at AT&T's Bell Laboratories in 1947. Sidelined at Bell Labs because of his abrasive managerial style, Shockley struck a deal in which the Los Angeles industrialist Arnold O. Beckman financed his independent state-of-the-art semiconductor research-and-development facility. Hearing the siren call of Terman's ambitions for Stanford, Shockley established his company in Palo Alto in early 1956. That November, he and his former teammates at Bell Labs were awarded the Nobel Prize in Physics for inventing the transistor.

Shockley was a peerless judge of technological brainpower and a seductive recruiter, though Northern California's salubrious climate played its part in tempting candidates away from the cold, snowy East and Midwest. The Quonset hut rented by his company, Shockley Semiconductor Laboratory, was filled with the cream of the crop of research talent. But then it began to empty out. The problem was that Shockley was an abusive, condescending, and paranoid boss.

The exodus started with Robert Noyce, a masterful research manager; Gordon Moore, a gifted engineer; and six colleagues. Shockley would refer to them as the "traitorous eight" to the end of his life. Backed by the New York industrialist Sherman Fairchild, they set up shop as Fairchild Semiconductor in 1957. Others abandoned Shockley over the next five or six years to start their own companies or join companies already established in the area. (Moore would become famous as the originator of "Moore's Law," which observed that the number of transistors on an integrated circuit doubles roughly every two years—a pointer to the rapid improvement of computing power over the last seven decades.)

In January 1971, Don C. Hoefler, a writer for the weekly trade newspaper *Electronic News*, outlined the family tree of companies that traced their lineage to Shockley's firm. By then there were nearly twenty-five, as Hoefler calculated in a series of three articles he headlined "Silicon Valley U.S.A.," thus contributing to the American business lexicon a term that denotes not only the industrial corridor extending south from San Francisco to San Jose but an entire industry and even a state of mind. (The name derived from silicon dioxide, a material used in semiconductor manufacture.)

Perhaps out of a sense of charity, Hoefler did not delve too deeply into what drove the "traitorous eight" out of Shockley's company. He attributed their departure to dissension over Shockley's insistence on their working on a four-layer diode, a brilliant and farsighted idea that was utterly impractical at the time.

Shockley resigned from his own company in 1963 to accept an engineering professorship at Stanford. At that point he entered the most corrosive phase of his career, a descent into the darkest catacombs of racist eugenics. "If you look at the median Negro I.Q., it almost always turns out not to be as good as the median white I.Q.," he declared in an interview in the November 22, 1965, issue of *US News and World Report*. "How much of this is genetic in origin? How much is environmental?"

Yet his professional legacy was inescapable—Silicon Valley's defining phenomenon of new enterprises begotten from the old. Moore and Noyce continued the trend, leaving Fairchild to found Intel Corporation in 1968, advancing the microprocessor's evolution in conformity with Moore's Law. They were again in the vanguard, as Fairchild Semiconductor succeeded Shockley

Transistor as the quintessential forebear of Silicon Valley start-ups—among
the four hundred men attending a 1969 semiconductor industry conference
in the valley, all but a couple of dozen had worked for Fairchild at one time
or another.

Silicon Valley's cultural ecosystem included the academic linchpins of
Stanford and Berkeley along with venture investors—many of whom, such as
Eugene Kleiner, one of the "traitorous eight," had made their fortunes in the
industry itself—and networks of law, public relations, and marketing firms,
which acquired expertise in financing start-ups, patenting their inventions
and discoveries, and commercializing their products.

The spirit of what a local historian labeled "competitive individualism"
was produced by not only the corporate family ties of its entrepreneurs but
also the valley's geographic insularity, with all this activity shoehorned onto
a narrow peninsula extending south from San Francisco between San Francisco Bay and the Pacific Ocean for about thirty miles. Computer scientists
and engineers could seek out new opportunities by shifting from firm to firm
without upending their families with cross-country relocations.

East Coast companies and government agencies, such as IBM, Westing-
house, Raytheon, and the National Advisory Committee for Aeronautics
(later rechristened NASA), situated their technology laboratories in Silicon
Valley to exploit its innovative spirit. The most significant such move occurred when Xerox Corporation established its Palo Alto Research Center, or
PARC, on a hillside just beyond the confines of the Stanford campus.

Xerox was then flush with capital from its 914 copier, the most commercially successful piece of office equipment in history. Fearful that technological advances might render its cash cow obsolete, however, the company
decided to establish a lab to draw a road map for the "office of the future."
The company's chief scientist, Jacob E. Goldman, opted to locate the lab on
the West Coast to insulate it from the hidebound copier engineers at the corporate headquarters in Rochester, New York. The first recruits moved into a
space recently vacated by the *Encyclopedia Britannica* in 1970. They were led
by Robert W. Taylor, who was lured from his job as a computer technology
official at the Pentagon's Advanced Research Projects Agency. At ARPA,
Taylor had overseen grants to universities working with time-sharing computers all based on proprietary hardware and software and therefore incompatible with one another. Consequently, his office filled up with terminals
that could not talk to one another. He was soon funding grants to design a

single network that could make them mutually intelligible. The result was a network initially called the Arpanet. It would become the foundation of the internet.

An inspired manager of research talent, Taylor assembled a cadre of young computer scientists and engineers who in the span of a few short years invented, among other innovations, the first personal computer (at PARC it was dubbed the Alto), a networking protocol known as Ethernet, the laser printer, and a graphical computer display that liberated computing from the limitations of typed verbal commands and replies.

The scruffy PARC staff failed to mesh with the buttoned-down culture of Xerox headquarters. But they seeded a new cycle of Silicon Valley start-ups. The process had begun in December 1979, when the co-founder of a small private company building personal computers for the hobbyist market demanded and received a look at the research lab's closely guarded secrets, including the Alto and the graphical display. He was granted the access in return for allowing Xerox to invest in his company—a rare occasion in which a start-up was beguiling enough to pick and choose among financial suitors. He was Steve Jobs, and his company was Apple Computer.

Jobs brought his technology brain trust to PARC for two demonstrations that have since gained the halo of Silicon Valley legend. The engineers emerged from the lab with the determination to implement many of its innovations in their own products. Many were ultimately incorporated into the Macintosh computer, which set a standard for "user-friendly" personal computing when it was introduced in 1984.

Even before the fateful demonstrations for Jobs and the Apple engineers, talent was beginning to leak out of PARC, staffing or begetting yet another wave of start-ups. One of the first to go was Robert M. Metcalfe, the co-inventor of Ethernet at PARC (with David Boggs), who mapped out a new company to market communications technologies on the proverbial restaurant napkin and founded it as 3Com in 1979. Metcalfe established himself as a sort of spiritual counselor to his former colleagues discontented with Xerox's inability, even uninterest, in commercializing the technologies they had invented.

The outflow continued, proliferating throughout Silicon Valley. PARC begat a family tree as distinguished and influential as Shockley Transistor and Fairchild Semiconductor before it.

Larry Tesler, who had helped develop the operating software for the Alto and had participated in the demonstrations for Jobs, joined Apple, where he contributed to the design of the Macintosh. Alan Kay, whose ideas about personal computing and creativity had inspired the Alto, left in 1981 to become chief scientist at Atari, which was marketing a consumer PC, later moving to Apple and ultimately to the Walt Disney Company. Charles Geschke and John Warnock, who developed programs at PARC to enable desktop publishing, left to found Adobe Systems, which created the portable document format (PDF) and Photoshop, a pioneering digital image editor. Taylor was fired in 1983 after a shake-up at Xerox headquarters in Stamford, Connecticut, resulted in a decree that PARC work on products with more relevance to the parent company businesses, rather than on speculative technologies. He moved to Digital Equipment Corporation, which built him a new lab in Palo Alto. Fifteen of his former PARC team members followed him there, developing advanced programming languages and the pioneering web search engine AltaVista.

The industrial ecosystem established in the 1970s gave California a dominance over investments in the technologies of the future that it has never relinquished, despite more than half a century of efforts by competing states and regions to dislodge it, through economic booms and slumps and the occasional crash, such as the dot-com bubble and crash of 1995–2000, and through repeated technological transitions. In 2021, California companies attracted $157.5 billion in venture investments, more than triple the nearly $50 billion flowing into the second-place state, New York, and more than four times the $35.5 billion invested in the third-place state, Massachusetts. Funds based in California accounted for half of all the venture capital invested in the United States. Statistics also attested to the degree to which California's technology wealth generated its own unique momentum—of the money invested in California companies, more than 81 percent came from California investors.

The seeds planted by Frederick Terman had not ceased to sprout. California's leadership in technology, entertainment, commerce, and international trade was secure. The question was whether it had reached a peak.

PART IV

The ERA *of* LIMITS

20

RONALD REAGAN AND THE LEGACY OF PAT BROWN

O N MAY 12, 1966, Ronald Reagan—former Hollywood actor, onetime New Deal Democrat, experienced corporate pitchman, and now a rising star in the conservative GOP firmament—strode to the podium at a rally of California Republicans in San Francisco's cavernous Cow Palace convention center. Introduced to the crowd by television's Rifleman, Chuck Connors, Reagan stood with a floor-to-rafters American flag at his right. Bathed in the incandescent gaze of his wife, Nancy, he launched into what he would turn into the central theme of his gubernatorial campaign: the imperative to clean up "the mess in Berkeley."

Reagan had announced his candidacy for governor of California four months earlier, on January 4. In a pretaped speech broadcast statewide on fifteen television stations, he touched on many of the themes beloved of the Republican Party's right wing: cutting taxes, having "faith in our free economy," pushing back the rising tide of crime. But he introduced an element of culture war by alluding to the student protests that had erupted at Berkeley in support of civil rights and in opposition to the Vietnam War. The university administration's efforts to drive the protests off campus had spawned the free speech movement, which intensified the atmosphere of outcry. "Will we allow a great university to be brought to its knees by a noisy dissident minority?" Reagan asked on the tape. "Will we meet their neurotic vulgarities with vacillation and weakness?"

Reagan expanded on that theme at the Cow Palace. Across the bay, he said, "a small minority of beatniks, radicals, and filthy speech advocates have

brought shame on a great university, so much so that applications for enrollment have dropped 21 percent and there's evidence that they'll continue to
drop even more." He cited a report published only days before by the state
senate committee on un-American activities that labeled the anti-war protests a "rebellion" and called the campus "a rallying point for communists
and a center for sexual misconduct." He admitted that he had not read the
report—"I only know what I've read in the paper about it"—but quoted
almost verbatim its description of a dance sponsored by the campus anti-war
Vietnam Day Committee on March 25. During the dance held in a campus
gymnasium, Reagan told his audience,

> three rock and roll bands were in the center of the gymnasium, playing si-
> multaneously . . . and all during the dance movies were shown on two screens
> at the opposite ends of the gymnasium. . . . They consisted of color sequences
> that gave the appearance of different colored liquids spreading across the
> screen, followed by shots of men and women, on occasion, shots [of] the
> men and women's nude torsos, on occasion, and persons twisted and gyrated
> in provocative and sensual fashion. The young people were seen standing
> against the walls or lying on the floors and steps in a dazed condition with
> glazed eyes consistent with a condition of being under the influence of nar-
> cotics. Sexual misconduct was blatant. The smell of marijuana was prevalent
> all over the entire building.

Reagan ascribed this behavior to "a leadership gap and a morality and
decency gap" at Berkeley. "The ringleaders should have been taken by the
scruff of the neck and thrown out of the university, once and for all."

Reagan's listeners interrupted him with repeated ovations. Many of
them surely recognized his speech as a direct attack on his prospective opponent, Democratic governor Edmund G. "Pat" Brown, and on Brown's most
significant gubernatorial achievement, the 1960 Master Plan for Higher
Education, which reinforced the stature of the University of California—
consisting in 1966 of Berkeley and seven other undergraduate campuses—as
the preeminent tuition-free public system in the nation.

THE MASTER PLAN underscored California's position as a national pacesetter in social and economic policy. Thanks to numerous lucrative industries
now firmly in place across the state, California's ascendance had seemed al-

most irresistible. The state was unimaginably rich, not only in dollars and cents but in ideas for using its material affluence to achieve social progress. It was nothing less than "a state rushing to redefine the American Dream." In early 1963 it became the most populous state in the nation.

The major question Californians faced was how to manage the postwar influx of wealth so it would serve more than a narrow segment of its burgeoning population—the very question that Henry George had raised nearly one hundred years earlier, when he contemplated the coming of the transcontinental railroad to San Francisco. "The California of the new era will be greater, richer, more powerful than the California of the past," George had written. "She will have more wealth . . . but will she have such general comfort, so little squalor and misery; so little of the grinding, hopeless poverty that chills and cramps the souls of men, and converts them into brutes?"

Public education was the tool Brown hoped would spread the wealth equitably. This was a quintessentially Californian concept; David Starr Jordan, though the founding president of the private Stanford University, had declared public higher education to be the "coming glory of democracy" in a 1903 address to students.

In the 1920s, California boasted the largest public education enrollment despite ranking only eleventh in population among the states. Observed historian John Aubrey Douglass, "To a degree unmatched by any other state in the twentieth century, California embraced public higher education as a tool of socioeconomic engineering."

Most other states had founded public universities, especially after the federal Morrill Act of 1862 provided funding for so-called land-grant colleges. But California was unique in creating a coherent state structure for its public institutions, aimed at providing all high-school graduates with access to higher education. The dream, wrote Douglass, was "a higher education system to match the ambitions of Californians." The University of California became not only the nation's largest university in enrollment but the first multicampus university and the first public university to receive direct state funding.

The university was also granted constitutionally protected independence from legislative meddling, although this status was not invariably honored during periods of partisan tumult (such as during the Red Scare of the 1950s). Its role as a premier research institution was safeguarded by the creation of two complementary higher education systems dating back to the turn of the century: a network of two-year junior colleges later known as community colleges, and a system of "normal schools" that expanded from institutions for teacher training into the California State University. By the twenty-first century it comprised twenty-three campuses with combined enrollment of nearly half a million students.

This interrelated system guaranteeing universal access to higher education at several levels became known in educational circles as the California Idea. Its principal achievement, in the view of educational theorists early in the twentieth century, was overcoming the competing goals and missions that had torn apart public universities in other states. The California system, observed the education advocate Edwin Emery Slosson in 1910, was one that "cultivates both mechanics and metaphysics with . . . equal success," that "looks so far into space, and, at the same time, comes so close to the lives of the people," and that "excavates the tombs of the Pharaohs and Incas while it is inventing new plants for the agriculture of the future."

CALIFORNIA'S POSTWAR GROWTH spurt added new urgency to the state's educational policymaking. "We faced this enormous tidal wave, 600,000 students added to higher education in California in a single decade," recalled Clark Kerr, president of the University of California and the master plan's principal architect. "It looked like an absolutely enormous, perhaps even impossible, challenge." But Californians showed a predisposition to support their university system: In 1960, about 45 percent of graduating high-school students went on to college when the national average was 25 percent. The master plan's goal was to improve on that record by creating "a place in higher education for every single young person who had a high school degree."

The master plan aimed to manage the further expansion of higher education by codifying the system's three rungs of the "educational ladder." The University of California was to select from among the top 12.5 percent of the state's graduating seniors and received the exclusive authority to issue doctorates and professional degrees, such as those in law and medicine. One rung down, California State University campuses focused on undergraduate instruction and teaching degrees. Finally, the network of two-year community colleges provided academic and vocational education, remedial instruction, adult courses, and workplace training. The plan also confirmed the principle that the system should be tuition-free to state residents.

Notwithstanding its historical roots, the master plan was very much a product of its time. The 1950s were an era of unexampled national prosperity, the start of a period in which "the United States came closer to becoming a meritocratic nation than at any time before or since." After the Soviet Union's launch of Sputnik in 1957 provoked a nationwide panic over America's apparent inferiority in technical know-how, government investment in education was seen as "not just legitimate, but . . . expected."

The master plan's authors foresaw annual public expenditures on education rising from four hundred million dollars in 1960 to seven hundred million in 1975. (Both figures work out to about four billion dollars a year in today's buying power.) To the question raised in a chapter titled "Will California Pay the Bill?," the drafters answered with a hopeful yes, despite the necessity of funding the expansion through new taxes and bond issues.

Perhaps inevitably, the master plan produced a partisan backlash, and not only because of its cost. The plan also coincided with a period of extraordinary social and political unrest in the United States. During the sixties, the civil rights movement came to maturity. Mass protests and demonstrations during congressional debates over the Civil Rights Acts of 1960 and 1964 and the Voting Rights Act of 1965 were often met with violent official responses in the South. Protests against the Vietnam War took root beginning in 1965. It was entirely natural for these movements to manifest on university campuses and also natural that Berkeley, where the student body was diverse, inquisitive, and politically engaged, would be the epicenter from which the intellectual energy of the protests radiated nationwide.

Berkeley activists held the nation's second teach-in against the Vietnam War in May 1965 (following a similar event in March at the University of Michigan), drawing to the campus prominent war critics from university faculties around the country.

The campus was already simmering with discontent. Since the 1930s, the university had been a major recipient of government contracts. By the 1960s, Berkeley's undergraduates felt thoroughly neglected amid the university's focus on government research. "Students were alienated and ripe for revolt," observed a historian of the period.

GOVERNOR BROWN HAD won his party's nomination for reelection virtually unopposed in 1962 and had seen off a challenge from former vice president Richard Nixon in the general election. Nixon took the loss hard.

Meeting with reporters in a famous encounter the next day, he told them, "You won't have Nixon to kick around anymore, because, gentlemen, this is my last press conference."

Still, there were disquieting signals for Democrats in the 1962 results. The party had won all but one statewide office in the 1958 election that brought Brown to the governorship. This time, however, Brown's vote majority ran behind the Democrats' commanding lead in voter registration. Polls had shown Brown and Nixon running roughly neck and neck all during the campaign—until the Cuban missile crisis. President Kennedy's October 22 televised announcement of the discovery of Soviet missiles in Cuba and of his decision to "quarantine" the island to block further deliveries upended election campaigns nationwide. Analysts eventually found it to have favored incumbents in close races, as voters showed a reluctance to change political leadership in that fraught atmosphere.

Brown's popularity continued to fade after the election; a race riot in the Watts neighborhood of Los Angeles in August 1965 and the protests at Berkeley beginning in 1964 gave voters the impression that civil society was breaking down. Brown was almost defenseless against Reagan's promise to bring tranquility back to the streets of California.

Reagan's attack on Berkeley at the Cow Palace presaged the tactics he would employ throughout his governorship and presidency. He uttered assertions of dubious veracity with earnest self-confidence, pledging to relieve voters of their kitchen-table economic concerns and re-create an era of gold-hued serenity that was largely mythical. His demeaning implication at the Cow Palace that the Berkeley protesters were a fringe of "beatniks, radicals, and filthy speech advocates" minimized the breadth of anti-war sentiment on the campus. As for his claim that campus disorder was the reason for the 21 percent decline in applications to the flagship school, university officials attributed the drop to both a new requirement that applicants submit scores from the Scholastic Aptitude Test and to their own efforts to steer students away from overcrowded Berkeley in favor of one of the system's seven other undergraduate campuses. In any case, instead of continuing to fall the following year as Reagan had predicted, applications to Berkeley rose by 36 percent.

When Reagan launched his political career in the 1960s, the conservative movement was searching for a way to become relevant again. The members of the old guard of the 1950s Republican right were either dead (Ohio senator Robert A. Taft), retired (General Douglas MacArthur), or discredited (Wisconsin senator Joseph McCarthy).

Barry Goldwater, who donned the mantle of conservatism, calculatedly clothed himself in cowboy iconography, conjuring up "the classic western hero of popular culture"—the very image of rugged individualism—and associating himself with "the cult of 'true westernness.'"

One of the best descriptions of the power of this image came from Henry Kissinger, who scrutinized this all-American character with the eyes of an immigrant, an outsider—albeit one who would spend his career embedded in the highest echelons of American politics: "Americans like the cowboy who leads the wagon train by riding ahead alone on his horse, the cowboy who rides alone into the town, the village, with his horse and nothing else," Kissinger said. "He acts . . . by being in the right place at the right time. In short, a Western." Goldwater's stock campaign photo played that image for all it was worth, showing him with a shotgun perched on one knee, "in jeans, rawhide jacket, and a cowboy hat, a saguaro by his side."

Goldwater's presidential ambitions, however, ended with his landslide loss to Lyndon Johnson in 1964. Conservatism again had a vacuum to fill.

It was a stemwinding, nationally televised speech late in the 1964 campaign in which Reagan extolled Goldwater's candidacy that led Republicans to perceive the former actor's potential as a national political figure. Reagan embodied the man in the right place at the right time. Among his finer qualities, he gave the conservative movement a California polish. (Reagan was not the only entertainment figure to move smoothly into the California political arena; Helen Douglas had preceded him in the 1940s, song-and-dance man George Murphy was elected to the US Senate in 1964, and Arnold Schwarzenegger was elected governor in 2003.)

In his Hollywood career, Reagan had not been cast in many westerns; the public probably knew him best from his portrayal of the doomed Notre Dame football player George Gipp in *Knute Rockne All American* (1940) and as second banana to a chimpanzee in *Bedtime for Bonzo* (1951). But having honed his skills as a pitchman and public speaker first as the host of the omnibus drama program *General Electric Theater*, then as a roving ambassador for GE, he knew how to project the valor and steadfastness of iconic cowboy heroes. "Reagan was a competent actor with limited range," his biographer Lou Cannon wrote. "As a politician, however, he was so enormously gifted that he seemed a president-in-waiting almost as soon as he began campaigning."

Reagan's personality appealed to a circle of wealthy California entrepreneurs looking for a successor to Goldwater as the flag carrier of Republican conservatism. Chief among them was Holmes Tuttle, the owner of a string of Ford dealerships who had supported Goldwater and had known Reagan since the 1940s. During the 1960 campaign, Tuttle had invited Reagan to speak at a thousand-dollar-a-plate dinner for Goldwater in Los Angeles. There he gave the speech for Goldwater in which he inveighed against government involvement in Americans' lives that he later delivered on national television. It was titled "A Time for Choosing."

THE REBELLIOUS BERKELEY students were ideal foils for Reagan. His stance required, first, redefining as a threat to democratic principles what actually had begun as a student demand for "the right to participate as citizens in a democratic society," in the words of Mario Savio, the wiry, twenty-one-year-old philosophy student who led the free speech movement. Although Savio's goal theoretically dovetailed with Reagan's campaign theme of giving citizens a greater voice in their own government, Reagan painted the student protesters as youthful renegades who needed to be taught a lesson. He posed as the polar opposite of the university administrators and political leaders who chose to spare the rod and let spoiled youngsters run roughshod over the university.

The Berkeley protests had originated in a bureaucratic snafu. The university had long tolerated students distributing political literature, including leaflets supporting the civil rights movement, to passersby from tables on a plaza at the edge of campus. This was based on the mistaken assumption that the space was city property and therefore the students were not violating the university rule banning political activities from campus. Before the 1964 academic year began, however, it was discovered that the plaza actually belonged to the university, which then ordered the tables to be removed. The students predictably did not see this as a neutral act. The tinderbox was lit and the free speech movement, which became the organizing body of the protests, was born.

"The University was apparently under considerable pressure to 'crackdown' on the student activists from the right-wing in California business in politics," Savio wrote later. He blamed former US senator William Knowland, the arch-conservative publisher of the *Oakland Tribune* who had been trounced by Brown in the 1958 gubernatorial election, for having created the myth of Berkeley as the "little red school house"—in other words, a haven for Communists.

The conflict escalated through the fall into a series of rallies and sit-ins amid threats of expulsions and negotiated concessions by the administration. This phase of the Berkeley unrest culminated in a student takeover of Sproul Hall, the administration building, on December 2, after Savio addressed a rally with the words that would always be associated with him: "There is a time when the operation of the machine becomes so odious, makes you so sick at heart, that you can't take part . . . and you've got to put your bodies upon the gears and upon the wheels, upon the levers, upon all the apparatus and you've got to make it stop."

After a one-day occupation, Brown ordered the police to clear the building and arrest the occupiers. This resulted in 773 arrests, "the largest mass arrest in California's history."

Brown remained on the defensive. One reason was the feeble performance of Kerr, who was weak-kneed and indecisive in dealing with a student-led crisis. That had forced Brown to take the tough stand that led to the arrival of police on campus and the mass arrests, which cost him the support of moderate Democrats. The name *Berkeley* became a "buzz word," recalled another Brown adviser. "In our polls, it was the most negative word you could mention." To the right wing, *Berkeley* evoked Communism; to the left, it symbolized official overreaction to peaceful protest; and to the center it exemplified social disorder.

Reagan beat Brown in 1966 by a landslide margin of nearly one million votes, carrying traditionally Democratic strongholds such as working-class districts in Los Angeles as well as suburban and rural districts with Democratic majority registrations. The Reagan tide swept out Democratic officeholders statewide.

As governor, Reagan turned up the heat on the university. Soon after taking office, he goaded the university's twenty-four-member Board of Regents, on which he had a single ex officio vote, into firing Kerr. Unlike previous governors, Reagan often attended regents meetings in person, turning the board into his "personal political arena," as one regent complained anonymously to the *Los Angeles Times*. The board rejected Reagan's demand to institute a tuition fee at the university, which would have negated the principle of free education enshrined in the master plan. The regents did, however, agree to impose a "student charge" of unspecified size. In time, this evolved into tuition by another name.

Reagan continued to use the university and its unruly students and faculty for partisan fodder. He recognized that taking a hard line against them would reinforce his "tough guy" image and exploit the backlash against liberals in academia that his aides had detected during the governor's race. Long-haired students were the butt of his constant jokes. He ridiculed protesters for carrying signs reading "Make Love Not War," remarking, "The only trouble was they didn't look like they were capable of doing either"—a "surefire applause line," Cannon reported. In another oft-repeated jape, he described a hippie as "someone who dresses like Tarzan, has hair like Jane, and smells like Cheetah."

More grimly, he gave his view of the law in one of his last speeches as governor-elect: "No one is compelled to attend the university," he said. "Those who do attend should accept and obey the prescribed rules or pack up and get out."

Liberal professors received their share of rhetorical abuse. Reagan asserted, groundlessly, that "there are political tests in certain departments [where] if a man is not far enough left, he doesn't get hired." He mused out loud about developing "a concerted plan to get rid of those professors who have made it apparent that they are far more interested in closing the school than they are in fulfilling their contract to teach." Although faculty members saw Reagan's attacks largely as political theater, they were demoralized by his constant assault on educational principles. "Reagan chose to exploit his role as an outsider in politics—voicing opinions that the public wanted to hear rather than softening public opinion to protect the state's educational institutions during a time of crisis," reflected William J. McGill, then the chancellor of UC San Diego.

Yet Reagan was not playing to the broad public as much as to a minority bloc of education critics inspired by extremist right-wing organizations such as the John Birch Society. Their movement had begun with a successful recall campaign in 1961 in the suburban Orange County community of Anaheim waged against a progressive school board member named Joel Dvorman, ostensibly because he had held a meeting of the American Civil Liberties Union in his backyard. In short order, seventeen recall campaigns were launched against school board and city council members in the county, which became the epicenter of conservative extremism in California. Small groups disrupted school board meetings, protesting sex-education classes and schoolbooks containing "pro–United Nations" content and the incorporation of evolution in science texts.

The protests intensified in 1965, when state authorities mandated the use of *Land of the Free,* an eighth-grade history textbook produced by a team led by the eminent UCLA historian John W. Caughey. The book's inclusive sweep and critical approach infuriated conservatives, who preferred "a romanticized, top-down, and memorization-based version of U.S. history," observed scholar Elaine Lewinnek. The controversy foreshadowed partisan attacks on "woke" policies in the 2020s, which similarly favored a simplified hero-oriented depiction of American history. *Land of the Free* remained part of the California school curriculum, but the ferment continued through the 1960s, providing grist for Reagan's campaigns.

The low point of Reagan's conflict with Berkeley came during the People's Park controversy of 1969, which concerned a weed-choked vacant lot that the university, its owner, decided to turn into a playing field despite local residents' preference for a community park. At a meeting with Berkeley professors after student protesters blocked the construction work, Reagan engaged in a finger-pointing shouting match with physicist Owen Chamberlain, a Nobel laureate, who told him the lot's fate was still being negotiated by the university and the student protesters. "What is there to negotiate?" Reagan asked incredulously. "All of it began the first time that some of you who know better and are old enough to know better let young people think that they have the right to choose what laws they would obey as long as they were doing it in the name of social protest." Then he stormed out of the meeting.

Matters escalated until May 15, since known as Bloody Thursday, when state and local police summoned by Reagan arrived. In the resulting melee, 128 residents were injured and an uninvolved spectator, watching from a distance, was shot and killed by police.

During his two terms as governor, Reagan honed his political skills and polished his political image, establishing himself as the most important Republican conservative on the national scene and leading to his victory in the 1980 presidential election. His appeal was uniquely Californian, marrying the state's sunny glow to a Hollywood-crafted image as a tough adversary with a self-deprecating twinkle in his eye, evoking a bygone era of simple values while fronting for the nation's privileged class.

Political insiders in California came to understand that on many issues, he was more bark than bite. For one thing, he learned to choose his targets carefully. As Kerr observed in 1973, Reagan never acted on his threats to get rid of politically active professors.

"He wasn't restrained with the students," Kerr reflected, "but he was with the faculty. A couple of serious academic freedom cases could have blown the place apart." Reagan did not want that, for he viewed UC as "the foundation upon which California's high-tech industry was based," historian Gerard J. De Groot noted in 1996. During Reagan's governorship, UC received 25 percent of all Defense Department research contracts. Pressing to fire "leftist" faculty members, Reagan understood, might have led to the withdrawal of government patronage. When he did advocate faculty dismissals, he maneuvered the regents into taking the lead; that was the case with the 1969 firing of Angela Davis from the UCLA philosophy department on the grounds that she was a member of the Communist Party. A state judge overturned the regents' policy forbidding the employment of Communist Party members and ordered Davis reinstated.

Reagan also learned the virtue of compromise. The best example of that was a long battle over California's welfare budget, culminating in the passage of the California Welfare Reform Act of 1971, in which Reagan played the role of "the patient, almost Madisonian seeker of compromise to achieve good policy."

The state's share of spending on the federal Aid to Families with Dependent Children program, or AFDC, had been soaring, from $283 million in 1965 to more than $1 billion in 1971. Much of the increase was due to the 1970–1971 recession, but if the trend continued, the state would face a budgetary catastrophe. Reagan came to the table armed with nothing but anti-welfare mythology. "Reagan had his head up his ass," recalled the acid-tongued liberal Democrat John L. Burton, then an assemblyman representing San Francisco. "He kept talking about some woman with eight kids from eight different fathers driving a Cadillac and having a color TV—I mean just stupid stuff." This was another case of Reagan's playing to the gallery, but if he stuck to it, the prospects for welfare reform were nil.

Instead, Reagan crafted an alliance with Democratic assembly speaker

Bob Moretti of Los Angeles around a welfare-reform package, a deal that would catapult Reagan to new political heights. Moretti recalled that at their first meeting over the issue, he told Reagan, "Look, governor, I don't like you particularly and I know you don't like me but we don't have to be in love to work together." The two politicians' representatives produced a package that preserved, even increased, benefits for "honest" welfare recipients and granted them cost-of-living increases, which were Democratic demands. The Republicans got a tightening of eligibility standards, including a one-year-residency requirement. Welfare rolls promptly began to shrink, although that was almost certainly the result of a powerful nationwide economic recovery. Both sides were able to declare victory, but it was Reagan who harvested the political gains. He had the "abundant good luck" to institute a moderate policy just at the moment when demographics and economics would bring the "welfare explosion" to an end. But the reform act had to be assessed as a major achievement of the Reagan governorship. It was one of many factors that would propel him to the White House, where he would remake the national Republican Party in his own image.

21

La Causa

JOHN GIUMARRA JR. reached across the table at the UFW headquarters in Delano, California, and shook the hand of Cesar Chavez. Giumarra was the scion of a leading agricultural family, Chavez the farm union leader who had led a five-year strike of California grape pickers and a two-year boycott of California grapes.

It had been a long journey, but on July 29, 1970, it ended in triumph for the farmworkers. As the most prominent and influential grape growers in the San Joaquin Valley, the Giumarras had been the standard-bearers for the industry's ferocious battle against Chavez's union, the United Farm Workers. The family had accused the UFW of threatening and intimidating its workers and at one point obtained a contempt citation against Chavez himself, which might have landed him in jail. They had held fast against the union's demand for higher wages, protection from the growers' heavy use of pesticides, and even the basic right to organize into unions. Conditions for farmworkers had not changed much since the 1920s. They were grossly underpaid and worked under the sun with insufficient access to water and sanitary facilities. Child labor was rampant. There were no health or retirement benefits.

On this day in a meeting room at UFW headquarters in Delano, the heart of the California grape-growing region, Giumarra's father, a smiling John Senior, had thrown up his arms in mock surrender. The contract he had just signed—in front of the head of the church committee that had helped broker the deal and an audience of about four hundred farmworkers—committed his company and twenty-five others to an immediate raise in hourly wages, from \$1.65 to \$1.80, with twenty-five cents an hour more in raises to be paid over the subsequent two years. There would be an hourly bonus to fund health and welfare benefits, safety standards for pesticide usage, and the establishment of hiring halls by the UFW to replace the old corps of labor contractors who extracted a percentage of the workers' wages to provide them with jobs.

The path to the contract had started in September 1965 with a strike by Filipino grape workers. The Filipinos were members of a union affiliated with the AFL-CIO, but their numbers were small in relation to the largely Mexican agricultural workforce, and the AFL-CIO was not especially attentive to their concerns. Chavez chose to have his fledgling union, then known as the National Farm Workers Association, throw in its lot with the Filipino workers, launching the five-year struggle. Before it was over, he would lead protest marches hundreds of miles to bring the unionization drive to the doors of the state legislature in Sacramento and stage a month-long fast (replicating a pressure tactic of his idol, Mahatma Gandhi).

The key to the union's success was a nationwide boycott of California table grapes, which was opposed by political leaders in Washington, DC, and Sacramento, who openly favored the growers. President Richard Nixon ostentatiously munched grapes in public and more than quadrupled grape shipments to troops in Vietnam to compensate for a steep decline in domestic sales; Governor Ronald Reagan condemned the boycott as "immoral" and "blackmail." But it worked.

Reagan had been president of the Screen Actors Guild, a Hollywood union, from 1947 to 1952, but he displayed no sympathy for the UFW's membership. "It is tragic that the workers . . . have no choice in determining whether or not they want to join the union," he grumbled after the contract deal was reached.

The two sides ended the signing ceremony with words of amity, hope . . . and caution. "This experiment in social justice, as they call it, or this revolution in agriculture," said Giumarra Junior, "if it works here it can work elsewhere. But if it doesn't work here, it won't work anywhere." Chavez responded, "This event justifies the belief that through the theory of nonviolent action social justice can be gotten." At a follow-up news conference, however, he pledged to carry the fight to the Teamsters union, which had won agreements with lettuce, carrots, celery, and strawberry growers on

terms the growers found more accommodating than those sought by the
UFW. A multifront war lay ahead. For the moment, though, a revolution in
the fields had been won. An industry rooted in the nineteenth century had
entered the twentieth.

THE EVOLUTION OF California agriculture into a corporatized source of
fruits and vegetables could be traced to the completion of the first transcontinental railroad in 1869 and the introduction in the 1870s of refrigerated railcars, which made the shipment of crops to markets in the East
and Midwest feasible. The vast majority of arable acreage was then in the
hands of a small number of land barons who traced their ownership rights
to pre-statehood Mexican land grants and to the acquisition of tracts the
government had given the railroad as construction incentives. The monopolization of land forced small farmers off their properties and reduced them to
itinerant workers. The land-hoarding railroad's outrageous freight rates for
individual farmers ruined those who tried to eke out a living independently;
big shippers enjoyed far more reasonable rates. By the mid-1930s, the army
of farm laborers numbered two hundred thousand "homeless, starving, destitute" individuals. (At this writing, nearly one hundred years later, migrant
farmworkers in California number about eight hundred thousand.)

Interest in agriculture as a durable source of wealth had grown as gold production waned. Seducing the semi-arid valleys of California into full bloom
with hundreds of varieties of salable crops depended on the new technology
of irrigation. Through the relocation of water via networks of pumps, canals, and aqueducts of unprecedented scale and sophistication, "deserts have
been changed into orchards; wastelands and sloughs have been converted
into gardens," wrote Carey McWilliams. Like gold prospecting, California
farming became mechanized and industrialized. Through the introduction
of "huge plows drawn by dozens of horses" and steam-powered machines that
combined harvesting and threshing into a single operation, California farms
grew into vast plantations of sixty or seventy thousand acres as if in a single
leap. By 1869, the state's exports of its robust variety of hard white wheat
made it "the granary of the world," boasted *California Farmer*, an agriculture
journal of the era. Hugh Glenn, a former dentist, became the largest wheat
grower in the world, producing more than one million bushels a year on a
66,000-acre spread fronting on sixteen miles of the Sacramento River. When

the wheat trade ebbed in the 1880s, the state's resourceful growers planted apricots, peaches, plums, pears, oranges, lemons, and wine grapes, their fortunes enhanced by the labor of legions of Chinese workers left jobless after the completion of the Central Pacific Railroad.

Demand for seasonal workers followed the natural cycles of California agriculture, tracking the vagaries of climate, weather, and the social environment. Anti-Chinese sentiment soared in the 1880s. Race riots and boycotts of Chinese-employing businesses spread from the cities into the farm valleys. "White men and women who desire to earn a living" staged "protests against vineyardists and packers employing Chinese in preference to whites," the *Los Angeles Times* reported in 1893. Riots in Fresno and its environs drove Chinese workers from the fields. In the citrus belt of Southern California, Chinese workers were robbed in broad daylight and their camps violently raided at night. The growers resisted the anti-Chinese movement as long as they could but finally succumbed after a boycott of their crops: "Indispensable as the Chinese are," one farmer was reported to lament, "they must go." The growers suffered from their own faintheartedness: After the Chinese were ejected and before Japanese newcomers replaced them, more than a half a million acres of California farmland had to be taken out of cultivation. A drought in 1898 and the consequences of overexpansion compounded these challenges; the orchard business collapsed, and fruit trees were cut down for firewood. Then the big growers were saved by a new crop—sugar beets.

The expansion of beet farming was triggered by a punishing federal tariff imposed on imported sugar in 1897. The cultivation and harvesting of sugar beets were especially labor-intensive—one estimate had it that for every man who had worked in the wheat fields, more than forty-one were needed in the beet fields. The growing season was only three months long and the harvest had to be accomplished quickly for the beets were prone to spoilage, thus creating an immense demand for short-term migrant labor.

Growers soon branched into crops with dissimilar growing seasons, such as strawberries and citrus fruits, and workers began to move around the state en masse, following the seasonal harvests. By the 1920s, California agriculture comprised some 180 different crops, keeping farmworking families on the road year-round. "We reach from the Imperial Valley to the perpetual snows," S. Parker Frisselle, the chairman of the agricultural committee of the Fresno Chamber of Commerce, said at a congressional hearing in 1926.

"We have a cycle and these people travel. . . . They start at the border with the cantaloupes and the lettuce, and they go on up to the grape and citrus harvests."

When cotton growing entered the equation in the 1930s—surging from 1,500 acres in 1921 to 600,000 in 1937—it filled gaps in the harvest calendar from October through January. The demand for child labor in the fields also rose. "There are thousands of boys and girls in California's public schools who are [outside] the range of the child labor laws," the *California Cotton Journal* editorialized, arguing that the laws should be interpreted freely enough to allow this army of unemployed children to be put to work to alleviate the farm-labor shortage.

From the end of the nineteenth century through the first decades of the twentieth, farmwork was identified with a succession of ethnic communities. After the Chinese Exclusion Act of 1882 shut off the flow of Chinese labor into the fields, growers began to import Japanese workers via incentives offered in their native land—"quietly," to avoid reenergizing anti-Asian prejudices. In 1890, there were an estimated 2,000 Japanese in California; by 1910, they numbered more than 72,000 and provided more than 70 percent of the labor on celery, berries, asparagus, tree fruit, and lettuce, and virtually 100 percent of labor on sugar beets. From the growers' standpoint, the Japanese workforce was a mixed blessing, because as energetic as the workers were, their ambition was not merely to work the land but ultimately to own it. As they acquired property, they became competitors, a transition that contributed to the ferocity of the anti-Japanese fervor that eventually emerged in California and to laws prohibiting their long-term ownership of land.

Starting around 1907, Hindustanis from the Indian subcontinent supplanted the Japanese in the cotton fields of the Imperial Valley, where they were admired for their supposed imperviousness to the heat. But they too moved into land ownership; in any case, the influx was cut off by the Immigration Act of 1917, which prohibited immigration from India and the other countries in a "barred zone" stretching from the Middle East to Southeast Asia. The bans would not be rescinded until 1952.

Certain ethnic groups became identified with certain crops—Armenians dominated in the raisin industry, Italians the vineyards, Portuguese the dairies, traditional relationships that in some respects continue to the present day.

The migrant workforce in California eventually became largely Mexican. Growers brought an average of 58,000 Mexicans a year into California during the 1920s, often in convoys of a hundred trucks at a time. This first wave of Mexican immigration into California coincided with an outbreak of economic and political unrest south of the border, starting with government policies that encouraged the formation of large farms, or haciendas, and thus dispossessed small landholders. The disorder continued with the forced abdication of the detested Mexican president Porfirio Díaz in 1911, which led to nearly a decade of political violence and civil war. Higher demand for labor north of the border and better wages than the workers could earn at home kept the wave alive.

In the farm districts, the Mexicans elicited a sort of resentful appreciation mixed with ethnic disdain; the growers preferred that Mexican laborers be brought to the United States under conditions that prevented them from socializing with other workers or unionizing; the Mexicans often were sequestered in camps closed to outsiders. "With the Mexican comes a social problem," Frisselle told the congressional committee. "We, gentlemen, are just as anxious as you are not to build the civilization of California or any other western district upon a Mexican foundation. . . . We would prefer white agricultural labor and we recognize the social problem incident to the importation of Mexicans . . . but after a complete survey of all possibilities, it seems that we have no choice in the matter. The Mexican seems to be our only source of supply." Farmers thought of their Mexican workers much as the railroad barons had thought of their Chinese workers in the 1860s—as "cheap, plentiful, and docile." They paid whole families—men, women, and children—four to six dollars a day to harvest grapes; since the workers technically had entered the country illegally, the threat of deportation kept them submissive.

Starting in 1930, the Dust Bowl—the deterioration of arable land by drought and unsustainable farming practices—drew waves of white laborers into California from the parched Midwest, as was chronicled by John Steinbeck in his classic 1939 novel *The Grapes of Wrath*. By 1940, one in five of California's seven million residents was an immigrant from the Midwest. The difference between the lifeless plains these so-called "Okies" and "Arkies" had abandoned and the fruitful California valleys where they fetched up left them almost stupefied. None described the feeling as well as the

balladeer Woody Guthrie, who fled a dust-blown Oklahoma farm to join the
swarm heading west.

> Indio to Edom, rich farm lands. Edom to Banning, with the trees popping
> up everywhere. Banning to Beaumont, with the fruit hanging all over the
> trees, and groceries all over the ground. . . . Beaumont to Redlands, the world
> turned into such a thick green garden of fruits and vegetables that I didn't
> know if I was dreaming or not. Coming out of the dustbowl, the colors so
> bright and smells so thick all around, that it seemed almost too good to be
> true.

Such romantic impressions were not to last. The newcomers quickly discovered that they were to be condemned to a life of backbreaking work, their
new homesteads reduced to places of "filth, squalor, and entire absence of
sanitation, and a crowding of human beings into totally inadequate tents or
crude structures built of boards, weeds, and anything that was found at hand
to give a pitiful semblance of a home at its worst," according to a National
Labor Board report in 1934. The experience left an indelible imprint on the
lives of those who suffered through it, not least on Guthrie, whose songs
would be marked by fierce advocacy for working people.

The vast emigration from the Dust Bowl rendered the Mexican labor
force superfluous. The white establishment came to see the dispossessed
Mexican laborers as a burden on taxpayers in the cities, where families bereft
of employment in the fields gathered. Mexicans were also beginning to put
down roots, since many of them had children who were born in the United
States and therefore were American citizens. Most of the Mexicans who had
settled in California lived in Los Angeles, which was still the center of an
agricultural region. In 1930, the city's 190,000 Mexican residents accounted
for 15 percent of the population.

The establishment's solution was to ship the migrant workers back to
Mexico. The "repatriation" process had the veneer of voluntary acquiescence
by Mexican families, but in many respects it amounted to forced deportation. The Southern Pacific agreed to carry deported families to Mexico City
for $14.70 per person, charged to taxpayers; local officials saw the fare as a
bargain, as it was much lower than the cost of keeping the families in room
and board for a week. In the first ten months of 1931, more than 120,000
Mexicans were sent back across the border, against only about a thousand

visas issued to Mexicans for entry into the United States. (Most visa applications were denied.) The US State Department declared that "the problem of new immigration from Mexico . . . appears to be solved." From 1929 through 1944, some 400,000 California residents of Mexican descent, including some American citizens, were forcibly relocated to Mexico. But the farmers' thirst for cheap and complaisant workers never really ebbed, and their clamor for a migrant workforce soon reappeared.

LABOR UNREST IN California's fields dated back to August 1913. The so-called Wheatland Riot involved 2,800 men, women, and children who were employed for pennies a day to pick hops and had to camp under a pitiless sun and without access to water in Wheatland, about forty miles north of Sacramento. The filthy conditions attracted organizers from the Industrial Workers of the World, or Wobblies. A mass meeting called by the Wobblies was interrupted by gunfire from a sheriff's posse, provoking a panicky melee. That prompted Governor Hiram Johnson to call out four companies of the National Guard. The pickers dispersed and a statewide dragnet for Wobblies ensued, resulting in hundreds of arrests and summary convictions under the state's 1919 Criminal Syndicalism Act, an anti-union statute by another name. The riot and subsequent investigations opened the public's eyes to the conditions of migrant workers in California agriculture for the first time but also launched a period of repression that hampered efforts to organize farmworkers for more than a decade.

The year 1928 brought the first new attempt at farmhand organizing, a strike by cantaloupe pickers in the Imperial Valley. The strike collapsed after the Imperial County sheriff threatened a "general deportation" of all Mexican laborers in the county. About one hundred strikers were arrested for vagrancy and other trumped-up charges, and hundreds more were deported.

Conflict in the fields continued to mount as the depression in agriculture intensified throughout the 1920s, predating the general depression that followed the 1929 stock market crash. California farm wages had been declining and living conditions deteriorating throughout the decade even as the gross value of crops continued to rise—a formula that could not help but stoke discontent. The average daily wage fell by almost half, from $3.56 in 1929 to $1.91 in 1933. Pickers who were paid by piecework fared even worse. Seven-year-old Roy Dominguez told a California state commission in 1933 that he worked from seven a.m. to nightfall picking cotton for sixty cents per hundredweight, which, at his average production of sixty-five pounds per day, yielded about three cents an hour. The treatment of farmworkers produced an unprecedented wave of agricultural strikes in California from 1929 through 1939. During that decade, more than 180 separate strikes involving about one hundred thousand farmworkers broke out.

Many farmworker strikes were led by the Communist-influenced Agricultural Workers Industrial Union, which morphed into the Cannery and Agricultural Workers Industrial Union in early 1932. The CAWIU organized strikes by cannery workers in the Santa Clara Valley in 1931, fruit pickers in Vacaville in the Central Valley in 1932, pea pickers in 1933, and peach, pear, cotton, and grape workers subsequently. The union organizers followed the worker migrations south to the Imperial Valley in the winter (lettuce and peas) and back north in the spring, exploiting discontent over repeated wage cuts. The striking workers were able to extract modest wage increases from growers frustrated by seeing their crops rotting on the trees and in the fields. But the strikes also unleashed a savage response from the farmers' "strike-breakers, vigilantes [and] private shock-troop squads." An accounting of the thousands of California workers and innocent noncombatants who had been gassed, shot, and beaten to within an inch of their lives took up five full columns in small agate type of an August 1934 issue of *The Nation*.

With the coming of war, migrant farmworking reappeared under new management—the US and Mexican governments. This was the bracero program, created at the behest of growers who complained to Congress that wartime mobilization had produced a critical labor scarcity in the fields. Under the bracero program (the term is colloquial for "manual worker") the Department of Agriculture was empowered to recruit, transport, and provide room and board for Mexican "stoop workers"—that is, those required to wield a short-handled hoe known as *el cortito* that forced them into almost doubling over. This punishing implement would remain in use in California until 1975, when it was banned by a court order resulting from a lawsuit brought by the UFW.

The bracero program was supposed to operate under strict government oversight to guarantee the workers had decent wages, food, and housing, which persuaded the Mexican government to sign on. The guarantees were indifferently enforced and often honored in the breach, as the growers kept wages low and invested only skimpily on housing. The program also suppressed unionization by regimenting the activities and movement of the migrant laborers and holding the threat of deportation over their heads. This was a potent means of intimidation—although bracero wages were lower than those paid to other agricultural workers, they were still higher than rates in Mexico. Unwilling to forgo this abundant and submissive workforce, the growers lobbied to keep the program in place even after the war's end, when returning soldiers should have become available to fill the slots occupied by braceros. In one form or another, the program continued until 1964, by which time a cumulative total of nearly five million workers had been employed.

The bracero program had something of a mixed outcome in immigration terms. Rather than relegating Mexican migrants to the permanent status of guest workers, the program ended up encouraging both legal and unauthorized immigration, as braceros acquired useful knowledge of employment opportunities and migration routes into the United States. On occasion, the inflow of unauthorized workers provoked the US government to harsh countermeasures: In 1954, the Border Patrol launched a program of forced repatriations known by the demeaning title Operation Wetback. But despite those efforts, a demographic transformation of California was underway.

This was the world Cesar Chavez was born into on March 31, 1927. His family grew cotton, alfalfa, and watermelons on a small compound in Arizona about one mile east of the California border. In 1939 the family lost their home in a foreclosure and headed west, picking avocados and peas. They fetched up in the Mexican barrio of San Jose, where they spent two years living in garages, barns, shacks, and tents before moving to the Imperial County community of Brawley. There Cesar attended school through the eighth grade. He then went to work in the fields, traveling the migrant circuit with his family to plant and harvest the crops—beets, cauliflower, melons, plums, grapes, and cotton—that produced a bounty of billions of dollars a year for growers.

The family ultimately settled in the Central Valley community of Delano, which was surrounded by vineyards and cotton fields that provided fairly stable employment for its Mexican and Filipino residents. After a stint in the postwar Navy, Cesar returned home and began working with a church-affiliated Mexican American group called the Community Service Organization. In 1962, having absorbed the organizing principles laid down by one of the CSO's patrons, the political activist Saul Alinsky, he embarked on the quixotic crusade that would make his name a household word: the creation of a farmworkers union. He turned the quest into a movement. Its slogan was *Viva la causa* ("Long live the cause"), its symbol a black Aztec eagle in a white circle against a red background.

THE HANDSHAKE BETWEEN John Giumarra Jr. and Cesar Chavez on that July day in 1970 was close to the high-water mark of the United Farm Workers. Within a year, the union represented forty thousand workers via 180 contracts and seemed poised to achieve the unprecedented stature of a major national union. But by 1973 it was down to forty contracts and forty thousand members. As the expiration date of the 1970 pacts approached, its old nemesis the Teamsters union renewed its efforts to organize farmworkers by reaching tentative deals with twenty-eight growers, which cut the UFW's membership to 6,500. The Teamsters had made an offer that resonated with the growers: an end to the UFW hiring halls, which in the growers' view were hopelessly inefficient at getting workers to the fields when they were needed. The Teamsters' effort provoked a war with the UFW that was finally settled with the Teamsters' withdrawal of their contracts and ultimately by its abandonment of farm-labor organizing entirely. But the conflict pointed to deeper problems within the UFW. Chavez had been inspiring as a leader during the organizing drives of the 1960s, but the union was inept at managing the nuts and bolts of representing members' interests. Farmworkers voted the union out in a series of elections in 1977; in 1987, the UFW lost thirty-nine decertification votes. A significant blow came in 2005, when the UFW lost a crucial election at the Giumarra winery. The victories of 1970 were but a dim memory if they were remembered at all by a workforce increasingly composed of unauthorized immigrants. Chavez had died in 1993, at the age of sixty-six. Dolores Huerta, his indispensable partner in the organizing drives—she had coined the UFW's motto *Sí se puede* ("Yes, it can be done")—had retired.

By 2022, the UFW was at a low ebb, with only seven thousand members and contracts with only twenty-two growers. Labor experts wondered if it had long to survive. After the 1980s, reflected William B. Gould, a Stanford law professor who had served as chair of the National Labor Relations Board and of California's Agricultural Labor Relations Board, "the UFW stopped organizing. . . . That is the brutal reality. The UFW is moribund." The union had not staged an organizing drive in five years when it won a vote at Premiere Raspberries in Watsonville, but that company, ordered by a state court to comply with a contract calling for a 15 percent raise, benefits, paid holidays, and back overtime pay, chose instead to shut down, throwing three hundred employees out of work.

There were intermittent signs of life, reminiscent of an era when the UFW wielded significant political influence. In 2022, it applied pressure to Governor Gavin Newsom to approve a bill making it easier for agricultural unions to organize and conduct certification elections. Newsom had vetoed a similar bill the year before; this time, he heard from President Joseph Biden and House Speaker Nancy Pelosi, a San Francisco Democrat, and signed the measure.

Yet farmworkers across California still suffered the same mistreatment and abuse as had those whom Chavez had organized decades before. A survey established that nearly half were not provided with protection from the heat, a violation of state law. One in five had been cheated of wages. Two-thirds lived and worked in fear of deportation. Among female workers, miscarriages were common. The COVID pandemic swept through the migrant worker population, infecting 70 percent. For all that Chavez had accomplished to meld them into a coherent workforce with real political status, his crusade was a work in progress. At this writing, it still is.

22

DISASTER AT PLATFORM A

THE STRING OF violent winter storms that had swept across Southern California finally passed. The residents of the charming coastal city of Santa Barbara emerged from ten days of enforced solitude to shake off the effects of cabin fever and inspect the havoc wrought by nature.

Santa Barbara had escaped the worst of the damage, which had been so bad that President Richard Nixon declared the entire state a disaster area. Nearly one hundred people had lost their lives. Flooding around the Santa Ynez River, which traversed Santa Barbara County from the inland mountains to the sea, was so devastating that the farmland on its banks was expected to be unusable for at least five years.

On January 28, 1969, Santa Barbara awoke to one of those crisp, sunny days so typical of a Southern California winter. The storms had deposited mounds of driftwood, seaweed, and garbage on its treasured beachfront, but that could all be quickly cleared away, leaving the gleaming white strand that lured tourists by the thousands. The view south to the low mountain ridge of Santa Cruz Island, just over five miles offshore, was so crystalline that the Santa Barbara Channel seemed more like a wide, calm pond than an arm of the Pacific. Those who gathered on the beach to be enchanted by the vista tried not to focus on the structures marring this idyllic scene: oil platforms, bristling with derricks and cranes, situated on stilts in the water a few miles out. What they could not foresee that morning was that one of these structures, Union Oil Company's Platform A, was about to deliver the worst environmental catastrophe in the history of Santa Barbara—indeed, in the history of all California.

At 10:45 that morning, crews on Platform A had finished drilling well A-21 to its maximum depth of 3,479 feet, sufficient to punch through the thin layer of rock sitting atop a primordial reservoir of oil. This was the fifth well drilled from the platform, which was designed to accommodate a total of fifty-six wells costing about a quarter of a million dollars each. The crew pulled up seven of the eight ninety-foot sections of drill pipe one by one and laid them aside on racks so the drilled hole could be lined with steel casing and the siphoning of oil begun. They were working on the last one when they heard a loud, alarming hiss from the open hole. Drill hand Bill Robinson looked up to see a geyser of drilling mud shoot ninety feet into the air and shower down on the men and equipment clustered around the hole.

Slipping and sliding on the muddy platform and enveloped by a miasma of gas that could detonate at any second, the crew managed to pull the eighth section of pipe up and tried to plug the hole with a blowout preventer valve, only to have it blasted free by the torrent gushing upward. Their last option for plugging the hole was to activate a pair of "blind rams," blocks with rubber linings designed to come together with the push of a button like the jaws of a steel trap. The rams slammed shut and the well was plugged. Thirteen minutes had elapsed since the initial blowout. All the personnel on the platform except for Robinson and his crew had already been evacuated by boat. Now it was their turn. From the deck of the launch carrying him to Union's Platform B a half a mile away, Robinson looked back to see the surface of the water just beyond Platform A surging and bubbling. Then he spotted a second boil on the surface. The thin layers of sand, shale, and rock that had kept a pool of oil contained for millennia had shattered, and now it was surging into the channel from every seam, fissure, and fault.

As the day progressed, Coast Guard officials, oil executives, and the few residents aware of the blowout breathed easier. An unfathomable quantity of oil had spilled out, but the wind and ocean currents seemed to be carrying it out to sea, away from the Santa Barbara beach and the pristine shores of Santa Cruz and the other islands in the channel. When the sun rose the next morning, an oil slick of one hundred fifty square miles bobbed on the water's surface from Santa Barbara south toward Ventura.

Then the wind shifted, and the slick headed for shore.

Describing the event demanded the skills of a novelist—in this case, Kenneth Millar, a Santa Barbara resident whose novels under the pen name Ross Macdonald featuring detective Lew Archer were set in Southern California's cultural underbelly. As Macdonald's narrator describes the aftermath in one book, the oil "lay on the blue water off Pacific Point in a free-form slick . . . An offshore oil platform stood up out of its windward end like the metal handle of a dagger that had stabbed the world and made it spill black blood."

By the first week of February, twelve miles of Santa Barbara beaches had been blackened with oil. Thousands of seabirds and uncounted fish and marine mammals perished. But there were positive outcomes from the disaster. These included a new social awareness of the threat posed by human activities to the ecology of the planet, the creation of Earth Day, and the establishment of entirely new environmental laws and agencies, including the National Environmental Policy Act and the Environmental Protection Agency. California's disaster brought home to the rest of the country the urgent necessity of protecting its air and water from the consequences of human activity.

Before 1969, environmentalist Russell Train observed, environmentalism was an "amorphous concern" searching for a circumstance or event that would enable it to crystallize into an international movement. That event happened five miles off the Santa Barbara shore.

CALIFORNIA'S LOVE-HATE AFFAIR with one of its most lucrative industries originated in the 1850s, shortly after statehood, when geologists started to assess the value of its natural resources. Among the resources they identified was bitumen, or asphalt, a heavy, coal-like mineral that seeped from the ground all along the coast. The expectation was that bitumen would find a ready market in roofing and road paving and would be in even more demand if it could be distilled into gas, which was increasingly sought for lighting; in 1853, San Francisco started laying a pipe network and became the first city in the American West to be entirely illuminated by gas.

The geologists' discoveries were by no means a surprise. Native American tribes had long used the tarry deposits washed ashore or seeping from the ground to waterproof their canoes. The utility of this material did not escape the notice of European explorers in the eighteenth century; Juan Crespi, the diarist of the Portolá expedition of 1769, wrote of finding "large marshes of a certain substance like pitch" that were "boiling and bubbling" with such abundance "that it would serve to caulk many ships." Traversing the Santa Barbara Channel in November 1793, the English navigator George Vancouver reported that the water's surface was "covered with a thick slimy substance . . . whilst the light breeze that came principally from the shore brought with it a strong smell of tar. . . . The next morning the sea had the appearance of dissolved tar floating upon its surface, which covered the ocean in all directions."

In 1867, a well drilled near Ojai produced the state's first gusher, yet no one could be sure the oil was commercially marketable. Refined into kerosene, it yielded a gunky, smoky product that clogged lamps. As a lubricant it was even less serviceable, flowing almost as thin as water. In 1880 a San Francisco business newspaper reported that California oil was regarded as so low in quality compared to what was drawn from the ground in Pennsylvania that "many dealers . . . believe that the production in this state will never be a success."

But new markets soon emerged. Western railroads discovered that California oil was a cheaper and more efficient locomotive fuel than coal, especially since in the far West there was "practically no commercial supply" of coal, which consequently had to be imported from the East Coast or British Columbia at great expense. The usefulness of California oil as a marine fuel triggered more drilling. California production surged from 307,000 barrels in 1890 to more than 4.3 million by the turn of the century, and surpassed 23 million in 1903. Every year between 1894 and 1918, California ranked either first or second in oil production, trading the lead back and forth with Oklahoma. The state's output reached nearly 262.9 million barrels in 1923, when California accounted for nearly a third of the nation's output amid an explosion in nationwide demand for gasoline to power the rapidly expanding fleet of private automobiles. It finally topped out at nearly 405 million barrels in 1986. "As gold was the California mineral of the nineteenth century," an industrial historian wrote in 1970, "so oil has been the mineral of our time." That year, four of the six most productive oil fields in the nation were in California.

Oil-industry tycoons would write their names into California history. Edward L. Doheny, who had found modest success mining for silver in Nevada, was lured to Los Angeles in 1892 by the prospect of a real estate killing. He and a partner paid four hundred dollars for a lease on a downtown parcel not far from the La Brea Tar Pits, which were a known source of pitch for caulking. They sank a shaft manually with picks, shovels, and a sharpened eucalyptus trunk. On November 4, 1892, they struck oil, which they bailed out with a bucket. Their strike set off the Southern California oil boom. Derricks sprang up like fruit trees in residential backyards across the west side of Los Angeles; Doheny himself soon had sixty-nine wells pumping. (Doheny would be indicted in 1930 for having bribed Interior Secretary Albert B. Fall in 1921 to obtain an oil lease on federal land in the scandal that became known as Teapot Dome; he was acquitted, even though Fall had earlier been convicted of accepting the bribe.)

The craze drew charlatans too. The most audacious fraud was launched in 1920 by Chauncey "CC" Julian, a former oil-field roustabout who eventually ensnared forty thousand investors with a line of chatter "as breezy as a circus barker." Julian promised investors "the squarest and surest opportunity for big returns it is humanly possible to make." But his unproductive wells served chiefly as a front for his issuance of watered stock on a spectacular scale. The crash came on May 7, 1927, when trading in his company was halted. Julian fled from criminal charges to Shanghai, where he committed suicide by taking poison in 1934.

OIL DRILLERS TURNED their attention to the coastline early in the boom. The world's first offshore well was sunk in the waters off Summerland, six miles east of Santa Barbara, in 1895. Jetties ran a third of a mile into the shallow waters, sprouting derricks and pumps at their far end. The works were such marvels of contemporary technology that the Southern Pacific, ever on the lookout for passenger-enticing scenery, advertised its Los Angeles–Santa Barbara route by inviting tourists to "See the Oil Wells in the Sea."

Early in the twentieth century, offshore drilling provoked an extended tug-of-war between the states and the federal government. The issue was jurisdiction over the seabed out to the three-mile limit and over the outer continental shelf beyond. The federal Mineral Leasing Act of 1920 authorized the granting of oil leases on public property onshore and offshore, though in practice the government refused to grant leases on the tidelands (the land between the water levels at low and high tide)—a tacit admission that those lands stood under state jurisdiction. California enacted its own lease law in 1921 and began to grant copious drilling permits in the tidelands.

The temptation, naturally enough, was money. California's law charged oil producers a 5 percent royalty on tidelands oil. In Santa Barbara, the conflict between money and aesthetics was especially acute, for Santa Barbara County collected millions of dollars in revenue from the industry even as residents blamed it for despoiling the environment—ninety-eight million dollars would flow to the county treasury in 1965 alone. The tide turned, so to speak, in 1921, when the state began rejecting drilling bids based on a finding by California attorney general Ulysses S. Webb that state law allowed only fishing, not oil production, in the tidelands. The state supreme court overturned Webb's interpretation in 1928, and the legislature promptly responded by explicitly banning new drilling in the channel. By then, as it happened, oil companies had lost interest in offshore drilling, for offshore wells were extremely expensive and the industry feared that new sources of supply would only drive crude prices lower.

After World War II, the calculus changed. The Truman administration sought jurisdiction over all waters beyond low tide by bringing a lawsuit against California. When the case reached the US Supreme Court in 1947, the justices ruled that by law, the federal government held rights to all the seabed within three miles of shore. This placed the issue squarely in the political sphere. The Republican-controlled Congress voted to return the tidelands to the states in 1952, but Truman vetoed the measure. Dwight Eisenhower owed at least some of his electoral victory that year to his support of "states' rights" as represented by the tidelands controversy. In his first year as president, he signed a bill almost identical to the one Truman had vetoed.

California resumed granting offshore leases to oil drillers despite complaints by residents of Santa Barbara and other coastal communities about increased beach pollution. The drillers blamed merchant and navy ships for discharging oily wastes into the water as they cruised along the coast and reminded residents that natural seepage of crude had been documented for more than two centuries. The real problem was that state clean-water laws punishing vessels for discharging oil into harbors and three miles out to sea were risibly toothless and resources for enforcement almost nonexistent. When the Mobil Oil Company spilled 12,600 gallons of oil into Los Angeles Harbor in 1967, its entire fine came to one hundred dollars.

The state legislature had fallen firmly under the thumb of the oil industry, an echo of the political power of the Southern Pacific Railroad earlier in the century. In 1955, lawmakers opened more than one hundred fifty miles of tidelands to drilling; during the subsequent decade, drillers punched more than five hundred exploratory holes in the Santa Barbara Channel. In

1958, the first offshore platform in the channel, Platform Hazel—a virtual city, with living quarters and offices along with the equipment to drill scores of wells—was towed from San Diego to an anchorage two miles from Summerland by its owners, Humble Oil and Standard Oil of California (later rebranded Chevron). Meanwhile the Lyndon Johnson administration, voracious for oil revenues to fund the Vietnam War, pursued an aggressive campaign to expand federal jurisdiction over California's coastal waters. Supreme Court decisions in 1965 and 1966 awarded ownership of the waters out to the three-mile limit from the coastline and three miles around the Santa Barbara Channel islands to the state. But those rulings left jurisdiction over most of the offshore tracts sought by oil companies in the hands of the federal government.

The stage was set for an immense lease sale in 1968 even as the world was reeling from the worst oil spill in history: the wreck of the supertanker *Torrey Canyon* off the British coast the previous year.

Plans for the channel sale placed Johnson's interior secretary, Stewart Udall, in the hot seat. A former three-term Democratic congressman from Arizona, Udall was a member of one of the most politically progressive families in the West. As a college student he had helped desegregate the campus of the University of Arizona, and his bestselling 1963 book *The Quiet Crisis* shared with Rachel Carson's *Silent Spring* credit for the 1960s' awakening of environmental consciousness.

"America today stands poised on a pinnacle of wealth and power," Udall wrote in his book, "yet we live in a land of vanishing beauty, of increasing ugliness, of shrinking open space, and of an overall environment that is diminished daily by pollution and noise and blight." Johnson kept him in his post after the Kennedy assassination, reportedly at the personal request of Jacqueline Kennedy. Under the new president, Udall expanded the national parks system and advanced a raft of environmental laws, including the Endangered Species Act of 1966.

Now Udall had to decide whether to permit an oil-lease auction that was expected to be the largest in American history. Trapped between Johnson's determination to hold the sale and Santa Barbara's wealthy and politically influential citizens' opposition to reopening the channel to any drilling, he "agonized" over the decision: "My science adviser was one of the best California oceanographers and I kept asking questions, 'Well, what risk are we running; this is an earthquake prone area and this is a magnificent stretch of coastline; are there going to be spills?' and so on." Finally, persuaded that rigorous regulatory oversight could prevent the drilling from damaging the environment, he approved the auction of leases on 845 square miles of tidelands in the Santa Barbara Channel. The auction, which took place on February 8, validated the government's anticipation of a hugely remunerative sale: The successful bids totaled $603 million, almost twice what had been forecast, drawing gasps from oil executives watching from a ballroom at the Biltmore Hotel in Los Angeles. One tract bought by Union Oil and three partners drew the highest bid, nearly $62 million, a record price of $11,373 per acre. That would be the site of Platform A, which was anchored in place in September and began drilling in January 1969.

Udall, who never ceased to regret his role in the ensuing disaster, would call the auction "the conservation Bay of Pigs." He publicly took responsibility for the decisions that led to the spill. That was a big favor to his successor as interior secretary, former Alaska governor Walter Hickel, but it was only fair, since when the spill happened, it was only Hickel's fifth day in office.

THE OIL CONTINUED to flow from around Platform A for ten and a half days; the well was finally plugged with cement on February 7. By then an estimated 2,300,000 gallons had streamed into the channel. Photographs of befouled beaches and oil-covered seabirds and sea lions captivated the world in a historic illustration of the consequences of humankind's complacent exploitation of its natural environment.

The responses by Governor Ronald Reagan and President Richard Nixon, who had been inaugurated eight days before the blowout, were confused and chaotic. On the day of the blowout, Hickel announced at a press conference in Santa Barbara that he saw no reason to halt offshore drilling. The very next day, January 29, at a hearing before the county board of supervisors, he acknowledged that a temporary halt in the channel would be "reasonable." He then took a flight over the channel to survey the spreading oil slick. Upon landing, he called on the oil industry to voluntarily suspend drilling until the dangers could be more carefully assessed. Philips, Gulf, Mobil, and Texaco immediately shut down, though all resumed operating before dawn the next day. But less than one week later, on February 6, with a political clamor growing from coast to coast, President Nixon suspended all drilling in the channel.

It became obvious that the oil industry had no idea how to cap an offshore blowout. Nor had it developed methods to corral an offshore oil slick to keep it from fouling beaches and marine habitats. The drilling companies flailed about with largely ineffective tools. These included booms constructed from telephone poles and buoyant inflatable bladders, both of which were defeated by the ocean's choppy waters. Chemical dispersants sprayed on the surface proved to be even more injurious to marine life than the oil. Tent-shaped plastic hoods were placed over the well to contain the underwater leaks, but initially these collected only about 10 percent of the leakage. Bales of straw were spread on the beaches to absorb the oil and then trucked off to landfills. A presidential panel that convened in May to ponder solutions heard proposals so implausible, they were not immediately released to the public; one called for paving twenty square miles of the ocean floor with a giant slab of concrete, another for setting off a twenty-kiloton nuclear bomb in the channel to excavate an undersea reservoir for the oil.

The industry placed its faith in the weather and offshore currents and more so in the power of propaganda. In the first days after the blowout, the *Oil and Gas Journal*, an industry publication, disdained coverage of the spill as "hysterical." The July/August 1969 issue of Union Oil's house organ featured an article titled "Santa Barbara Is Alive and Well in California," illustrated with twenty-three color photographs of "children romping in the surf, bikini-clad beauties strolling along the beach, small boats under sail in the harbor"—but not a single shot of the platforms lurking on the horizon.

A counternarrative was gaining steam, however. The environmental movement that would flower into prominence in the wake of the spill had been gestating for years, although it seldom penetrated into the higher echelons of Congress and the White House. Carson's *Silent Spring* had burst onto the scene as a bestseller in 1962, bringing to public awareness the long-term adverse effects of excessive use of pesticides such as DDT and exposing the corporate financial self-interest that kept regulation at bay. Udall's book *The Quiet Crisis*, published the following year, placed the imperative of environmental stewardship in the historical context of America's heedless exploitation of its natural resources and arrived endowed with the prestige of an author serving as a member of Congress. But legislation had languished in Washington without any apparent chance of passage.

Following the disaster at Platform A, these measures were moved to the front burner. On the morning of February 5, Senator Edmund Muskie, Democrat of Maine, convened a previously scheduled hearing of his air and water pollution subcommittee. It was standing room only, with fifty reporters and cameras from all three television networks present. Santa Barbara had become the number one topic in the capital.

Among the witnesses was Fred Hartley, the chief executive (and subsequently chairman) of Union Oil, who in his public statements had consistently minimized the scale and consequences of the oil leak. Hartley spent nearly three hours on the witness stand trying to defend his company but succeeded only in displaying for a national audience the complicity of Big Government and Big Business in an unprecedented natural catastrophe. He told the lawmakers that he had personally called Governor Reagan to advise him that shutting down all offshore drilling in California would be tantamount to "shutting down the whole university system because of a riot at San Francisco"; indeed, Reagan steadfastly defended the drilling industry throughout the crisis. Hartley dismissed the spill's aftermath by suggesting that news coverage was overwrought compared to the coverage of an airliner accident in Los Angeles that had taken the lives of fifteen passengers three weeks earlier: "I am always tremendously impressed at the publicity that death of birds receives versus the loss of people in our country in this day and age." (In fact, the crash had been front-page news nationwide.)

Politicians who had pressed fruitlessly for environmental regulations moved quickly to take advantage of the publicity surrounding the spill. On February 18, Republican senator Henry "Scoop" Jackson of Washington successfully revived a measure he had originally introduced in 1967, now fashioned as the National Environmental Policy Act. The act established a Council on Environmental Quality inside the White House (Russell Train would be its first chairman) and presaged the creation of the Environmental Protection Agency as the nation's independent environmental regulator in 1970. Democratic senator Gaylord Nelson of Wisconsin, who had been known as the "conservation governor" during his term in the statehouse, drew his idea for a national conference on environment policy from the teach-ins opposing the Vietnam War held on the University of California campuses in Santa Barbara and Berkeley. He allied with California Republican congressman Paul N. "Pete" McCloskey to persuade Congress to endorse the idea, which culminated in the first Earth Day, April 22, 1970.

Those were national analogs of movements that also took root in Santa Barbara and California. When the oil slick, thickened by evaporation and wind and waves into a mass of tarry gunk, began to coat the beaches,

Bud Bottoms, a graphic artist at a General Electric think tank in Santa Barbara, exclaimed to an office colleague, "We've got to get oil out!" They founded a local grassroots organization dubbed Get Oil Out, or GOO.

NO ONE COULD say that Richard Nixon was not an astute politician. He was also a Californian, whose "Western White House" stood on the beach at San Clemente, about one hundred fifty miles south of Santa Barbara. Watching the threads of public outrage and legislative action braiding together, he recognized the imperative of associating himself with the nascent environmental movement to keep environmental policy from becoming his political albatross. On a pilgrimage to Santa Barbara on March 21, he surveyed the beach from a helicopter, then landed and strolled along the strand flanked by Fred Hartley and Gordon MacDonald, an environmental scientist who was vice chancellor of UC Santa Barbara. They were trailed by a mob of journalists. On a boat anchored in the channel, a group from GOO unfurled a sign calling for a drilling halt. Nixon strode gingerly along the beach in his oxford brogues while Hartley, still desperately trying to downplay the disaster, remarked, "See, Mr. President, the beaches are absolutely clean and no damage has been done." MacDonald, who knew that the stretch of beach where they stood had been painstakingly groomed for the presidential visit, responded, "Mr. President, the tides come in, the tides go out, and right under this clean sand I bet you there is a layer of oil or oily sand." He kicked hard at the surface, revealing a dark black splotch of oil.

Nixon would attempt to portray himself as an environmentally minded president, not least by creating the Environmental Protection Agency. But his administration never developed a firm policy for regulating offshore oil development. On April 2, Hickel lifted the February 6 moratorium on drilling in the Santa Barbara Channel. His action reflected the impossible position in which he had been placed by the tension between public pressure for environmental protection and the power of the oil lobby.

Hickel had ruled in favor of environmental protection and imposed the drilling moratorium despite opposition from the oil industry. Nixon's creation of the EPA, as it happened, was the first subtle indication of the president's discontent with how Hickel had navigated between the Scylla and Charybdis of oil policy, for most of the functions and authority brought under the new agency's jurisdiction were commandeered from the Interior Department.

Then, on November 25, 1970, Hickel was summoned to the White House and fired. He had come into office amid profound doubts in the environmental community about his willingness to stand up to industry but left mourned as a martyr. None other than Gaylord Nelson, who had voted against his confirmation in 1969, praised him for having turned out to have "a great instinct for what was right and the guts to act on his convictions. . . . Conservationists have lost a great fighter and a great friend." He was right: During his brief tenure at Interior, Hickel had courageously issued rulings that industrialists deeply resented, such as blocking the construction of a jetport because it threatened Florida's Everglades and bringing a lawsuit charging Chevron with nine hundred violations of the federal Outer Continental Shelf Act for its failure to install mandated safety equipment on ninety wells.

THE SANTA BARBARA oil spill dramatically changed public opinion in the United States about offshore drilling. Henceforth, plans to punch holes in the bedrock below the ocean surface in search of fossil fuels would have to be weighed against their potential for environmental damage. But that would not end all oil exploration off the coast of California or elsewhere in America. After the spill, California halted new leases in state waters and codified the moratorium in 1994 with legislation placing the coast off-limits to new drilling. The federal government maintained an informal moratorium on new drilling off California until the energy crisis of 1973, when panic over the Arab oil embargo prompted the government to resume leasing. The first bids in six years were opened in 1975, followed by a second lease sale in 1979. New offshore rigs sprouted off the coast of Southern California in 1981, located so close to the shipping lanes serving the ports of Los Angeles and Long Beach that the Coast Guard warned of the hazards. But in the end, it was the shipping lanes that were moved, not the platforms.

The federal and state governments resumed their pre-1969 disputes over drilling activities on the continental shelf. In 2018, California governor Jerry Brown signed a measure outlawing pipelines and other onshore infrastructure that served rigs in federal waters. The trigger for the new legislation was a plan by the Trump administration to reopen drilling off the California coast. California and other states managed to hold off Trump until he left office in 2021.

In the interim, the perils of offshore drilling continued to mount. The tanker *Exxon Valdez* ran aground in Alaska's Prince William Sound in March 1989, spilling eleven million gallons and creating one of the worst ecological disasters in US history, killing an estimated 250,000 seabirds, 2,800 otters, 250 bald eagles, and untold salmon and herring eggs and leaving some species endangered to this day. In April 2010 a blowout destroyed the Deepwater Horizon, a rig operating in the Gulf of Mexico, causing the largest marine oil spill in history.

Despite their magnitude, neither event could match the Santa Barbara spill for lasting social and political impact. Following Trump's departure from the White House, opponents of California offshore drilling began to sense victory. In 2021, federal officials established plans for decommissioning and dismantling the twenty-three outdated platforms still lurking off the California coast, including the accursed Platform A. Still, at this writing, oil continues to be pumped from four platforms. Production also continues from four artificial islands adorned with palm trees and colored panels to obscure their true purpose from spectators on the Long Beach shore. The pressure for expanding oil exploration in the seabed remains, to this day, unrelenting, an inescapable reminder of the deep-seated tension between commercial interests and environmentalism in California.

23

SIX DAYS IN WATTS

IT BEGAN, AS is so often the case when racial confrontations spin out of control, with a routine traffic stop. California Highway Patrol officer Lee Minikus, notified by a Black motorist that a Buick was being driven erratically up Avalon Avenue on the edge of the Watts neighborhood of Los Angeles, gunned his motorcycle and pulled the Buick over. The driver was Marquette Frye, twenty-one, who had just picked up his brother Ronald, twenty-two, from a friend's house and was heading to their mother's house, a block away from the traffic stop. The car belonged to their mother. Marquette had had a couple of drinks—just enough to make his driving unsteady and his general mien less than wholly inhibited. He was Black and the patrolman white. It was seven o'clock on August 11, 1965, a sweltering evening in the dog days of summer.

Frye, out of the car and vamping for bystanders, failed the patrolman's sobriety test. He admitted that he was not carrying his driver's license. When Minikus, now backed up by his partner, Bob Lewis, placed him under arrest and informed him that the car was to be impounded, Frye asked, in vain, to be let off with a warning. Then his mother, Rena, alerted by a neighbor, arrived on the scene. Los Angeles police officers drove up. The crowd had grown to about a hundred people, almost none of whom had witnessed the initial stop. What they saw were two Black men and a Black woman in a hostile encounter with white officers. In Watts, bitter experience told them that this was another case of police harassment.

The police sirens attracted more onlookers. A patrolman reported that one of them had spit on him, and police tried to arrest a young woman for the offense. A melee ensued. At about 7:40, the police, sensing themselves enveloped in a hostile crowd, began to retreat. Their vehicles and those of motorists trapped in traffic jams on Avalon and other streets were pelted with rocks, bottles—any projectiles near at hand.

The Watts rebellion had begun. For six days, until Governor Pat Brown lifted a curfew that had covered some forty-six square miles—far beyond the boundaries of the neighborhood that gave the rebellion its name—the Black community displayed its rage at a history of prejudice and discrimination.

Watts was not the first big city "race riot" of the 1960s nor the last. It had been preceded by disturbances in Philadelphia and New York's Harlem in 1964. Others in Atlanta, Boston, Buffalo, Chicago, Cincinnati, Detroit, Milwaukee, Newark, and again in New York would follow in the next three years. But those all would be measured against Watts, the one that truly woke America to the consequences of two hundred years of social and economic oppression and decades of complacent inaction in the face of deepening poverty and social pathology. Watts marked "a turning point in Negro-white relations in the United States," symbolizing "the end of the era of Negro passivity," observed Robert Conot, a leading chronicler of the event. "In Los Angeles the Negro was going on record that he would no longer turn the other cheek . . . Frustrated and goaded, he would strike back."

WATTS WAS A swampy tract of land that had evolved over decades into the de facto Black ghetto of Los Angeles, largely because it was shunned by people who had the option to settle anywhere else in the vast basin. In 1965 it was ringed by what contemporaries almost invariably described as "lily-white" communities that maintained a deceptively placid coexistence with the adjacent ghetto. As it happened, even at its height, the Watts riot never reached into those neighborhoods—the rioters' targets were chiefly white-owned businesses in their own neighborhood that had reputations for overcharging and demeaning their customers.

Watts developed from a Mexican land grant known as Rancho Tajauta.* After the original grantee died in the 1870s, his heirs sold it off to speculators who pared it down further into twenty-five-foot lots and resold them for a dollar down and a dollar a week. Many buyers were laborers recruited by

---

* The name is sometimes rendered by historians as Rancho Tajuata or Rancho Tajuato.

Henry Huntington to build his Pacific Electric rail line, which ran between
Los Angeles and the coast at Long Beach and San Pedro. Huntington himself
bought a few parcels at the line's midway point for a depot and named the
stop Watts Station after one of the sellers, Julia A. Watts. The label would
stick.

The neighborhood was known more familiarly by its residents as
Mudtown—not a racial slur but a reference to the marshiness caused by
the terrain's high water table. (Into the 1930s, the residents could trawl for
crayfish and catfish in its slimy pools.) As it was described by the Harlem Renaissance writer Arna Bontemps, who grew up there, Mudtown at the turn
of the century was not much more than "three or four dusty wagon paths"
littered with broken carts and wagons. Chickens and turkeys strutted about
the yards amid mules and cows. Some residents were forty-niners or their
descendants, but most had migrated later from the Deep South—"Mudtown
was like a tiny section of the deep south literally transplanted," Bontemps
wrote. The residents lived quietly in shacks, some of them shaded by the walnut trees that had bloomed over the land before the subdividers came.

Watts and the adjacent neighborhoods along Central Avenue soon housed
a vibrant and ethnically diverse population of Blacks, Mexicans, and Japanese that was often measured favorably against the urban ghettos of the
East and Midwest. W. E. B. Du Bois, visiting in 1913 to raise money for a
local church, described LA's rapidly growing Black community admiringly
as "without doubt the most beautifully housed group of colored people in
the United States. They are full of push and energy and are used to working
together." The city's somewhat mythical image as a hospitable destination
for Black migrants from the South exercised a certain allure. The Black population in the city of Los Angeles rose from 2,131 in 1900 to 7,599 ten years
later, more than doubled to 15,579 in 1920, and reached 63,774 in 1940,
though it never exceeded about 4 percent of the total population, reflecting
how fast the city was growing in the same time span.

"When people from Texas or Louisiana came out and wrote back South,
it made people in the South believe that this was heaven," recalled Augustus
F. Hawkins, who arrived with his family in the 1920s and would eventually
represent Watts in Congress. "There was some idea that it was a land of
golden opportunities—orange groves and beautiful beaches—and life was all
a matter of milk and honey." Journalists such as Jefferson L. Edmonds, editor
of the *Liberator*, a Los Angeles Black newspaper, perpetuated this idea: Black

immigrants from the South came "in search of better things and were not disappointed," he wrote. "The hospitable white people received them kindly, employed them at good wages, treated them as men and women. . . . Feeling perfectly safe, the colored population planted themselves." Edmonds's words echoed those of Chinese newcomers of decades earlier who thought themselves similarly welcomed; things would not turn out appreciably better for Black immigrants than they had for the Chinese.

White residents basked complacently in the conviction that the Black community was content with being relegated to a cordoned-off niche in the burgeoning Southern California economy. In February 1909, on the one-hundredth anniversary of Abraham Lincoln's birth, the *Los Angeles Times* published a well-meaning but spectacularly condescending eight-page section describing the social achievements of the Black population—their "remarkable progress" in school, their "refined and cultured" women, the property ownership of "flourishing" business leaders. The *Times* commissioned an essay by the eminent Black educator Booker T. Washington, who counseled that "the patient and persistent effort of individual negroes to improve their own condition . . . [is] bound to win for them the recognition from their white neighbors which they deserve."

In summing up, a *Times* editorial writer concluded that "if the negroes of Los Angeles and Southern California are taken as examples of the race, it would seem from their own showing of indisputable facts that the 'negro problem' is a thing that has no existence."

It was true that California was more accommodating to Black newcomers than other states to which they had immigrated after the Civil War and into the twentieth century. Racial violence was rarer. The state had repealed discriminatory laws such as the ban on Black testimony against whites in court and had, at least nominally, abolished segregation in the schools.

The city's Black community had reached a level of cohesiveness and stability exceeding that of such other metropolises as New York and Chicago. A pioneering African American church, the First African Methodist Episcopal, had been founded in 1872 under the leadership of Bridget "Biddy" Mason, who had been brought to California from Mississippi as an enslaved person in 1850.

Mason's life story, which spanned California's development from the granting of statehood through the first Los Angeles land booms, is remarkable enough to warrant special scrutiny. In 1855, when her owner decided to leave California for the slave state of Texas, Black activists filed a habeas corpus petition for Biddy, her sister Hannah, and their children, asserting that under the state constitution, enslaved people brought to California were free and could not be bound again by transporting them to a slave state. The case arose in the brief interval between the expiration of California's fugitive slave act in 1855 and the Dred Scott decision in 1857, under which Mason and her family would have been treated as their owner's property and forcibly removed to Texas as he wished.

Under slavery, Mason had not been permitted to learn to read or write, but she had been trained in animal husbandry, nursing, and midwifery, among other domestic duties. As a free person, she established a practice as a nurse and midwife, delivering "hundreds of babies, children of Los Angeles' leading families as well as children of the impoverished." By 1866, she had accumulated enough of a nest egg—$250—to purchase a homestead in Los Angeles, launching herself on a new phase as a real estate entrepreneur in yet another example of California's hospitality to personal reinvention. Riding along with the city's rapid growth, she built a brick-and-wood commercial building in 1884 with a place for her to live on the ground floor amid spaces rented to shops and a restaurant and bakery. By then she owned enough land to offer some to her grandsons, one of whom had already established a career in politics and real estate, for the construction of a livery stable. By the time of her death in 1891 at the age of seventy-four, she had become celebrated for her piety and philanthropy; an oft-repeated story recounted her paying for an open order at a grocery to provision families made homeless by floods in the early 1880s. She was then the richest Black woman in Los Angeles, the founder of a real estate and philanthropic dynasty that would leave its mark on the city for generations. In 1990 the city established a downtown park in her name with a wall display depicting the milestones of a life trajectory that brought her from slavery to civic renown.

THE *LOS ANGELES TIMES* was not wrong to celebrate the achievements of the city's Black community, though it was hopelessly blinkered in declaring that the "negro problem," by its definition, was nonexistent. When its laudatory section was published in 1909, nine other Black churches served the community along with the First AME Church. Black organizations such as the Los Angeles Men's Forum and the Sojourner Truth Club, which built a hostel as a "safe refuge" for Black women—both founded in the first years of the twentieth century—enhanced the community's cultural and social solidarity while providing a base from which to exercise political activism. Three Black-owned newspapers—the *Liberator*, the *Los Angeles New Age*, and the *California Eagle* (its publisher the redoubtable Charlotta A. Bass)— brought the community a unified identity. Its growing political heft led to the election in 1918 of Frederick M. Roberts as the first Black state assembly-man in state history. A Republican, Roberts represented a district known to local residents as the "Black Belt of Los Angeles," although the area was still majority white. Black voters interpreted Roberts's victory as a sign that the community had moved into a position to help guide policy and not merely submit to the indulgence of the white political establishment. By compar-ison with Black communities in other cities, Los Angeles residents seemed remarkably prosperous; the 1910 census revealed that more than one-third of Black Angelenos owned their own homes. That was the largest percentage by far of any major city, easily outstripping that of New York (2.4 percent), Chicago (6.4 percent), and Baltimore (5.2 percent). Real estate agents pro-moted Watts with ads in Black newspapers urging readers to "Buy Lots now in Watts: where values are sure to double . . . Terms $10.00 cash and $5.00 per month."

The lifeblood of the Black community in Los Angeles was Central Ave-nue, more specifically the stretch of "the Avenue" that comprised the thirty blocks from Twelfth Street to Forty-First. Here were prospering Black busi-nesses as well as the theaters, cafés, and nightclubs that attracted white and Black patrons alike to hear the artists who gave the community its cultural style. At its southernmost end stood the glittering Somerville Hotel, which was widely viewed as not only the best Black-owned hotel in the country but one of the best hotels in the United States, period. "The symbol of Black achievement" in Los Angeles, the hotel had been erected in 1928 by John Somerville, a dentist, who meant it to be a refuge for Black visitors to the city who were refused accommodations in white-owned hotels. Its grand opening was timed to coincide with the national convention of the NAACP, held that year in Los Angeles. Du Bois and other Black leaders visiting the city for the convention "ate in the same dining room, slept in adjoining rooms, lounged in the same lobby with . . . distinguished white people of Los Angeles," Somerville recalled proudly. "Yet there were no disturbances along the color line."

The hotel's opening brought more outside capital into the district.

Somerville's personal fortune, however, did not survive the 1929 crash. That year he sold the hotel to new owners, who changed the name to the Dunbar Hotel. Yet it remained the hotel of choice for distinguished Black visitors, with a register that "read like a 'who's who' of Black America: Jack Johnson, Ethel Waters, Bill 'Bojangles' Robinson and thousands of others." Los Angeles became Harlem's only rival as a magnet for Black artists and intellectuals, attracting luminaries such as the poet, novelist, and playwright Langston Hughes and the pioneering Black composer William Grant Still, who wrote his first opera, *Blue Steel,* after moving permanently to Los Angeles. In 1936, Still became the first Black composer to conduct a major American symphony orchestra, the Los Angeles Philharmonic (for a performance of his own music at the Hollywood Bowl). Hughes became associated with the Los Angeles Negro unit of the New Deal's Federal Theater Project, though he never managed to break into Hollywood in any significant way, which he attributed to the movie industry's racism and its determination to perpetrate what he called "every ugly and ridiculous stereotype of the deep South's conception of Negro character."

The truth was that anti-Black prejudice was endemic in Los Angeles, if perhaps better concealed than in other cities. Du Bois, notwithstanding his admiration for the way African Americans lived in Los Angeles, was not blind to the underlying truth: "Los Angeles is not paradise," he wrote in the *Crisis*, which he had co-founded as the NAACP's official magazine. "The color line is there and sharply drawn. . . . The hotels do not welcome colored people; the restaurants are not for all that are hungry."

Jim Crow laws, which fostered and enforced racial segregation, were alive and well in Los Angeles and became cinched ever tighter through the 1920s. One especially detested manifestation of pro forma discrimination was the "Shenk rule," promulgated by city attorney John Shenk in 1912. The rule arose after Black businessman Caleb Holden stopped at a bar for a beer with a white friend. The bartender charged the white customer a nickel for his beer and Holden a dollar. When Holden called for the establishment's license to be revoked, Mayor George Alexander referred the matter to Shenk, who decided that it was "neither extortion or a violation of the [state] Civil Rights Act to charge a negro more for an article than a white man." White-owned cafés, restaurants, and other businesses took advantage of this open invitation for discrimination, fending off Black patrons by openly overcharging them.

Shenk would pay for his ill-considered ruling a year later, when he lost a race for mayor despite the support of white progressives. Although the role of Black voters in his defeat was never conclusively established, Black newspapers, chiefly the *Liberator* and the *Eagle*, had vociferously rallied their readers against him—and against later municipal candidates associated with mercantile discrimination. When Vincent Morgan, a member of the police commission that oversaw licenses for restaurants and cafés and that consistently ignored Black demands to enforce the civil rights laws, lost his 1914 race for district attorney in part due to Black opposition, the *Eagle* boasted: "The colored voters would not eat crow, Thank You."

Black Angelenos were powerless to resist some instruments of segregation, such as deed covenants banning residential parcels from being sold to or occupied by "alien races" or "non-Caucasians." These provisions began to appear in real estate contracts as early as the 1890s but became increasingly common through the 1920s; they applied equally to Mexican, Chinese, Japanese, and Jewish buyers but in practice it was the Black population that felt their bite most acutely. In 1925, Los Angeles authorities decreed that "colored groups" could use municipal bathhouses and pools only one afternoon a week, on the day just before the pools were given their weekly cleanings.

Courts tiptoed gingerly around the discriminatory effect of racial covenants and Jim Crow restrictions. In 1919, the California Supreme Court issued a particularly cynical gloss on the covenants, ruling that while restrictions on the transfer of land were "repugnant" restraints on real estate and therefore void, racial restrictions on the *occupancy* of a property were valid. In other words, Black families could buy property in a segregated white neighborhood but could not live on it. In 1926, local courts upheld the pool restrictions. That same year, the US Supreme Court refused to invalidate a whites-only covenant on a home in Washington, DC.

Not until 1948 would the Supreme Court revisit the issue, finally ruling that racially restrictive covenants were unenforceable by law. By then it was too late to reverse the covenants' impact on land use in Los Angeles. Black neighborhoods such as Watts and South Central LA were confined within what one commentator described as "invisible walls of steel," adding that "the whites surrounded us and made it impossible for us to go beyond these walls."

In the 1920s, the Ku Klux Klan emerged as a force for white supremacy in Southern California civic affairs. Speaking from the group's traditional base in the deep South, a Klan official boasted to the *Times* of having recruited Los Angeles city officials to form as many as seven branches. He did not mention names, but the organization's local influence soon became obvious. Its combination of anti-Catholic and white supremacist rhetoric found a receptive audience among disaffected white Angelenos; one of its most vocal promoters was the radio evangelist Robert P. "Fighting Bob" Shuler, whose sermons were broadcast from 1920 to 1933 (when the federal government revoked his radio license) from his Trinity Methodist Church on Flower Street, only blocks from the busiest stretch of Central Avenue. Few Los Angeles institutions or ethnic groups, from the public library and the schools to "the Jews," the Catholic Church, and leading public citizens, escaped the sting of Shuler's bilious broadcasts, uttered with "almost hysterical zeal"—except the Klan, which he lauded for "standing for American idealism" and for its racist rhetoric, "as sweet music as my ears have ever heard."

The Klan campaigned openly against Black landownership, notably in the case of Bruce's Beach, a seafront resort and fishing pier built in Manhattan Beach in 1912 by Willa and Charles Bruce, a Black couple who had relocated from New Mexico. As the Bruces' facilities grew more popular among Black residents, they provoked increasing hostility from whites.

Things came to a head after the Klan interested itself in the conflict.

Klan members placed threatening calls to the Bruces around the clock. "Blacks who ventured off the Bruces' roped-off beach were harassed and insulted by hooded white men who slashed or let the air out of their tires," the *Times* reported in a historical retrospective. The local press accused the Klan of fomenting a "race war" by its burning and dynamiting of homes of Black residents. The Bruces refused to sell, so in 1924 the city seized their property by eminent domain, ostensibly to build a beach park. After that, police commonly arrested Black beachgoers for trespassing while whites were permitted to swim and sunbathe without harassment. After a court battle lasting years, the Bruces were awarded a paltry $14,500 for their properties. They moved to Los Angeles, but the episode remained a moral stain on Manhattan Beach until 2022, when Los Angeles County returned the property to the Bruces' descendants, who deeded it back to the county for twenty million dollars.

The Klan was also making its voice heard in Watts, where it campaigned to annex to Los Angeles what was then an independent city. The annexation might have been inevitable in any event, for that was the only way for Watts to secure permanent access to the LA water system. The Klan's real goal, however, was to obstruct the installation of a Black-controlled municipal government in Watts, because that would give Black voters a significant voice in Los Angeles County policymaking. The annexation was approved in a special election in 1926 after what Charlotta Bass's *Eagle* reported was a Klan campaign of intimidation aimed at Black voters. ("The white people of Watts are tired of being run by people who are not 100% Americans," California Klan leader G. W. Price had written to the annexation committee. "So it will be only necessary to corral [i.e., discourage] the Negro vote.") Of the 21,000 residents of Watts, only about 2,500, most of them white citizens, were registered to vote. Of those, about 1,900 cast ballots, favoring annexation by a two-to-one margin.

The annexation, compounded by the Great Depression and wartime demographics, launched Watts on a downward economic spiral. As Depression-era joblessness sent thousands of Black workers on the road to California in search of work, the Black population of Los Angeles County ballooned from 18,738 in 1920 to 75,209 in 1940. The newcomers were sequestered in Watts and the few other increasingly congested districts where Blacks were permitted to reside. The wave of Black immigrants intensified in 1942, when the Southern Pacific offered southern Blacks free rail passage to Los Angeles to work on its tracks. Instead of railroad work, many of the newcomers gravitated toward wartime shipyards, where wages were higher. Over the next few years, Black workers continued to arrive at the rate of about ten thousand a month. In the 1950 census, the Black population of Los Angeles County numbered nearly 218,000, or more than 5 percent of the county's population; in the highly segregated city itself, the 170,880 Black residents accounted for 8.7 percent of the population. Many remained unemployed due to discrimination by unions and employers until labor shortages in the wartime defense industry began to break down the color bar, albeit never entirely. At state employment offices 90 percent of employers were still specifying "whites only" in 1949. "White supremacy may be scientifically dead," declared John Somerville, "but its ghost still walks the streets of Los Angeles."

Meanwhile, the housing crisis became more dire. Los Angeles mayor Fletcher Bowron urged the federal government to step in, since the government's recruitment of workers for defense factories had exacerbated overcrowding in the ghetto. Interracial tensions sporadically erupted in violence, not only between Blacks and whites but also between Black and Chicano

(Americans of Mexican descent) residents. Federal housing projects perpetuated segregation because of the tendency to locate the projects in Watts, including Hacienda Village, a 184-unit development built in 1942 and designed by the pioneering Black architect Paul R. Williams in partnership with architects Richard Neutra and Welton Becket.

The use of racial covenants to preserve "lily-white" neighborhoods actually expanded the racial and ethnic diversity of Watts and its adjacent ghetto communities. Blacks and Chicanos lived for a time in relative harmony, joined in shared awareness of their enforced position low on LA's socioeconomic ladder.

Their common experience of prejudice and discrimination was manifested in their unified response to attacks by white servicemen on Chicano youths in Los Angeles from June 3 to June 8, 1943, in what was known as the "Zoot Suit riots." The attacks were triggered in part by articles in the white press, notably the *Times*, blaming Chicanos for gang violence. The *Times* described the youths' signature zoot suit—a long coat with exaggerated shoulders and loose trousers pegged at the ankles—as "a badge of delinquency." Its coverage was virtually an invitation to ethnic violence.

The June riots erupted after a group of about a dozen sailors alleged that they had been mugged by a gang of Chicano boys while walking along a rundown stretch of North Main Street in the central city ghetto. Police were unable to turn up any assailants. The following night, June 4, about two hundred sailors from the Naval Reserve Armory in Chavez Ravine (later the site of Dodger Stadium) hired a fleet of taxicabs and cruised into the same neighborhood. They proceeded to waylay and beat up four lone pedestrians wearing the emblematic zoot suits before returning to base, where the Shore Patrol took seventeen into custody and sent the rest to the barracks. No one was charged in the assaults, however.

The following night, scores of sailors joined by soldiers and Marines repeated their foray into the Chicano districts, harassing residents and administering beatings as police watched from a distance. The rioting reached a peak on Monday and Tuesday, June 7 and 8, when thousands of servicemen wreaked sadistic havoc on the neighborhood, dragging residents out of movie theaters and off streetcars, pummeling them and stripping them of their clothing. Their indiscriminate assaults spread panic through the area. To the extent the police acted, it was to arrest Blacks and Chicanos on suspicion of fomenting the disorder. Only after the military authorities declared all of downtown Los Angeles off-limits to service personnel did the assaults stagger to an end. Before then, however, the mobs had been goaded on by the white press, which almost invariably described the victims as the assailants and wrote admiringly of the servicemen for their efforts to chastise Chicano delinquents. "The zoot suiters . . . learned a great moral lesson from servicemen, mostly sailors, who took over their instruction three days ago," the *Times* celebrated on June 7, just as the rioting was about to spin out of control. In the aftermath, the city council even pondered a proposal to make the wearing of zoot suits a criminal offense.

The Black press, however, recognized the familiar signs of white oppression in the authorities' indulgence toward the attackers and the demonization of the victims. In the NAACP journal the *Crisis*, Black novelist Chester B. Himes described the riots as "the birth of the storm troopers in Los Angeles. . . . Los Angeles was at last being made safe for white people—to do as they damned well pleased." Charlotta Bass's *Eagle* fearlessly printed accounts of the mayhem illustrated with photos of bloodied Black and Chicano men and published her open letter to Mayor Fletcher Bowron describing the episode as "a white heat of lynch fury." She wrote: "Nothing in my experience has been so vicious, deliberate, or disruptive as the campaign of our city's metropolitan papers against" Mexican Americans. Bass wrote later of having gone "into dark alleys" during the riots to rescue "scared and badly beaten Negro and Mexican American boys, some of them children, from the clubs of city police."

BY WAR'S END, Watts had changed from a community about evenly divided among Blacks, whites, and Hispanics to one that was four-fifths Black. Incoming residents were crowded into decrepit, absentee-owned housing. Public services both reflected and furthered the community's ghettoization. The faculty and student bodies of its grade schools were integrated, noted sociologist Lloyd H. Fisher in 1945, but its only high school was devoted exclusively to vocational courses while white students were "actively encouraged to go elsewhere to school." That prompted the community college in neighboring Compton, then an all-white city, to reject applicants from the Watts high school. "In this way," a civic organization reported, "the high school has been an instrument for increasing social distance between groups in the community, and exacerbating tension between Watts and the surrounding communities."

By 1947, Los Angeles city planners had all but written off Watts as irremediably blighted, describing it as "an obsolescent area within which all of the social and physical weaknesses of urban living are to be found." The neighborhood was crisscrossed by unpaved streets and dotted with vacant lots and tumbledown houses. The overall impression was of neglect and insensitivity to the residents' need for even rudimentary amenities and civic services.

Neglect is often prelude to more neglect. At the dawn of the 1960s, more than a third of Watts residents were living in cramped public housing quarters. The Harbor Freeway, built between 1952 and 1957, divided the community into a poorer section on its east side and a more middle-class community to its west. The whole area, however, remained hemmed in by exclusionary white neighborhoods. The massive postwar boom in residential construction in Southern California passed Watts by.

Disaffection continued to build. A 1964 survey of Watts residents by UCLA sociologists found that none considered themselves to have equality with whites. The most stinging rebuke to the dream of equality was delivered by California voters in 1964 with the passage at the ballot box of Proposition 14, a constitutional amendment overturning a one-year-old law that had prohibited discrimination in the sale or rental of housing statewide.* Governor Pat Brown had condemned the ballot measure as a "cudgel of bigotry," but it passed by a two-to-one margin. Equality seemed more than ever a distant dream.

Relations between the Los Angeles Police Department and Black neighborhoods had deteriorated under the leadership of Chief William H. Parker, who had been viewed upon his appointment in August 1950 as an agent for professionalizing a police force that had degenerated into a hive of brutality and petty corruption. At least at first, Parker fulfilled that promise. He instituted strict character standards for recruits, introduced the latest science and technology into the department's crime-solving and prevention efforts, and reorganized the force along paramilitary lines in what was lauded at the time as a progressive and efficient approach to "command and control."

Parker's innovations, however, made the police presence more impersonal by discarding an individualized approach to law enforcement where

---

* The state supreme court invalidated Proposition 14 in 1966 as a violation of the Fourteenth Amendment to the US Constitution.

it mattered most—on the streets. He junked the traditional foot patrols by officers who had thereby come to know the neighborhoods at pavement level and to appreciate the concerns of the residents they met day to day on their beats. Parker replaced them with round-the-clock surveillance by officers ensconced in radio cars. Because most officers were white despite Parker's efforts to integrate the department, this change resulted in more confrontations in Black precincts between residents and officers who were strangers to one another. The residents came to see themselves as targets of indiscriminate and unwarranted official mistreatment. Accusations of police harassment and brutality soared.

Watts was a tinderbox in 1965. All it needed was a spark. The most pertinent question raised after the riot was not why it had happened but why the explosion had taken so long.

THE FIRST NIGHT of the riot, August 11, instantly caught the attention of Los Angeles residents. The *Los Angeles Times* bannered the disorder across its front page the next morning: "1,000 Riot in L.A./Police and Motorists Attacked/Routine Arrest of 3 Sparks Watts Melee/8 Blocks Sealed Off."

The narrative advanced by political leaders and police brass on that first day would remain in place for the rest of the week: that the disturbances of August 11 were the handiwork of small groups of opportunistic troublemakers goaded by the doctrine of civil disobedience pushed by civil rights activists. "You cannot tell the people to disobey the law and not expect them to have a disrespect for the law," Parker said at a press conference. "You cannot keep telling them that they are being abused and mistreated without expecting them to react." A deputy police chief dismissed the riot as "just a night to throw rocks at the police," prefiguring Parker's subsequent staggeringly racist explanation that the unrest had started "when one person threw a rock, and like monkeys in a zoo, others started throwing rocks."

The next day—the day after the Frye arrests—dawned calmly. Civil rights leaders, clergy, and other trusted figures circulated through the neighborhood to counsel order. John Buggs, a county human relations officer, arranged for a community meeting that afternoon at the clubhouse of Athens Park, eleven blocks from the scene of the traffic stop. Politicians and representatives of the NAACP and other civil rights organizations filled the chairs, but the room bristled with television cameras. The meeting turned into a forum for the airing of long-simmering community grievances—about anti-poverty programs whose budgeted funds mysteriously disappeared, police who seldom appeared on the streets except to brutalize innocent residents, and a political leadership that was missing in action. But there were also pleas for calm, notably from Rena Frye. "I'm here to ask you, please, to help me and to help others in this community to calm the situation down so that we will not have a riot tonight!" she said. But her plea did not lead newscasts that evening; the cameras had focused instead on an unidentified Black youth's menacing declaration into the microphone that rioters would be venturing into nearby white communities—"They're going to do the white man in tonight." The threat unnerved Chief Parker, who alerted the California National Guard that its troops might need to deploy in Watts.

The rioting resumed that night, some of it provoked by the presence of police, with Molotov cocktails added to the rioters' arsenal and tear gas to that of the police. The next day, Friday, the rioting began in daytime. As night fell, fires blazed along the retail strip of 103rd Street. On Saturday, authorities finally started to gain control by deploying guardsmen in a "massive show of force" and imposing an eight p.m. curfew amid mass arrests. On Monday, Governor Brown lifted the curfew. The *Times* on Tuesday bannered the result on the front page. It read "Brown Declares: Riot Is Over."

THE POST-RIOT ARRAIGNMENTS in the downtown Hall of Justice, starting on Monday, August 16, and continuing through the week, documented the abnormal relationship between the police and the Black community as well as the manifold pathologies of ghetto life. The arrestees numbered 3,952, comprising 3,438 adults and 514 minors; of the adults, 92 percent were Black. Fully two-thirds of the adults had previous criminal records, mostly for petty misdemeanors such as loitering that carried jail sentences of ninety days or less. Of the minors, half had already been arrested at least once. The prevalence of criminal records among the juveniles for what would have been routinely dismissed in any other community as nuisance charges reflected, in the words of an urban historian, "not so much . . . criminality as the high incidence of arrests in the ghetto."

Statistics compiled by probation officers attested to the depth of social dysfunction in the Black community. Among the juveniles arrested, three out of four came from broken homes. The families of more than 70 percent had incomes below the city median, with one-third of those families living below the poverty line. More than one in six of the youths had already dropped out of school, and only about 12 percent of those still in school achieved academic success equivalent to the average among middle-class white students. There had been no relief from the economic and educational inadequacies that had shown up in the Black neighborhoods as early as the 1940s.

The raw arrest figures prompted Chief Parker to portray the riot as a manifestation of a preexisting criminal environment in Watts and the neighboring Black neighborhoods. The commission that Governor Brown empaneled to investigate the causes of the riot under the chairmanship of John A. McCone, a former director of the Central Intelligence Agency, largely gave Parker and the police department a pass for their maladroit approach to law enforcement in Black neighborhoods. Although the commission acknowledged in its report, issued barely three months after the riot, that evidence existed of "a deep and long-standing schism between a substantial portion of the Negro community and the Police Department," it depicted Parker as the target of unwarranted criticism: "Most Negroes . . . carefully analyze for possible anti-Negro meaning almost every action he takes and every statement he makes. . . . Despite the depth of the feeling against Chief Parker expressed to us by so many witnesses, he is recognized, even by many of his most vocal critics, as a capable Chief who directs an efficient police force that serves well this entire community."

The McCone Commission report stands to this day as a monument to narrow-minded blame-shifting in the face of a cataclysm rooted in years of racial injustice. That result was virtually preordained given the commission's makeup: six whites, including McCone, a prominent attorney, two university administrators, an insurance company chairman, and the president of the League of Women Voters. There were only two Blacks on the panel, a city judge and a Presbyterian minister.

The commission parroted the viewpoint of Parker and Mayor Sam Yorty, a former New Deal Democrat who had moved steadily rightward during his journey from the state assembly and Congress to the mayoralty, that accusations of "police brutality" were fabricated by "Communists, dupes, and demagogues irrespective of the facts" (as Yorty put it). It endorsed Parker's view that the riot grew out of "the widespread support of civil disobedience as a tool for social and economic progress," adding its own gloss that "the angry exhortations [by national civil rights leaders] and the resulting disobedience to law . . . appear to have contributed importantly to the feeling of rage that made the Los Angeles riots possible."

The commission praised Parker for his initiatives in integrating patrol cars and for having promoted a single Black lieutenant to a command rank over white officers. But it failed to come to grips with the numerous reasons for the Black community's profound antipathy toward the police. In this and many other respects, the commission lost sight of the underlying causes of what was then the worst outbreak of civil disorder in California history.

What was remarkable was how much else the commission got wrong about what it called a "spasm" that "terrified the entire county and its 6,000,000 citizens"—nearly a week of rioting that left 34 persons dead and 1,032 injured while causing as much as $40 million in property damage. After hiring more than seventy consultants and other employees and presenting seventy-nine witnesses at public hearings, the commissioners minimized the event by concluding that only about 2 percent of the county's more than 650,000 Black residents were "involved in the disorder."

The report was replete with contradictions. It asserted that the rioters were "caught up in an insensate rage of destruction" but acknowledged that they "concentrated primarily on food markets and other retailers," many of them white-owned and long the subject of complaints about overcharging. "We note with interest," the panel wrote, "that no residences were deliberately burned, [and] that damage to schools, libraries, churches and public buildings was minimal"—hardly evidence of "insensate destruction."

The commissioners seemed perplexed that the residents of Watts failed to appreciate their salubrious environment. "While the Negro districts of Los Angeles are not urban gems," the report stated, "neither are they slums." When Commissioner Warren Christopher, a corporate attorney, observed to a witness, "I wouldn't say that this is a garden spot of South Los Angeles, but I see street after street of small well-kept homes," the witness crisply informed him that one of every three houses in the district was dilapidated or derelict and that, in any case, what made a slum was not merely its physical condition but the social, economic, and psychological condition of its residents—and by that standard, Watts and its adjacent communities were slums indeed.

The McCone Commission paid only lip service to the legitimate grievances of the ghetto residents. It bowed sanctimoniously to the need for better job opportunities, the eradication of employment discrimination, and improved education. But it provided no road map for achieving these goals. Its admonitions that Blacks must pull themselves up by their bootstraps to take advantage of improved opportunities and that they and their leaders should moderate the tone of their protests elicited a sharp dissent from Reverend James Edward Jones, one of the two Black commissioners. "I do not believe it is the function of this Commission to put a lid on protest registered by those sweltering in ghettos," he wrote.

The McCone Commission exemplified the wrong way to interpret a social upheaval. The National Advisory Commission on Civil Disorders would learn this lesson, if imperfectly. Established by President Lyndon Johnson in 1967 under the chairmanship of Illinois governor Otto Kerner following two more years of urban unrest, the Kerner Commission was itself overwhelmingly Caucasian, with nine white and two Black members. But it acknowledged what the McCone panel had overlooked—that the Watts riot had destroyed any confidence that "race relations were improving" in America and that a new mood had emerged in Black ghettos nationwide. It did not excuse the police for actions that led them to "symbolize white power, white racism, and white repression. . . . The fact is that many police do reflect and express these white attitudes." It also acknowledged the futility of all the official expressions of concern about race relations that had followed surges of protest in the past. The Black scholar Kenneth B. Clark, one of its first witnesses, delivered a thunderous dismissal of white hand-wringing. Recounting his reading of official reports following a Chicago race riot in 1919, Harlem riots in 1935 and 1943, and the McCone report of 1965, he lumped them all together as "a kind of Alice in Wonderland—with the same moving picture reshown over and over again, the same analysis, the same recommendations, and the same inaction."

Clark's condemnation suggested that racial disturbances in Los Angeles were destined to recur. In 1992 the city exploded again. This time the fuse was lit when a state jury acquitted four LA police officers who had brutally beaten Rodney King, a Black motorist who had led them in inebriated condition on a high-speed chase, of assault. The riots started within hours of the verdicts being announced and lasted six days, with 63 lives lost, nearly 2,400 people injured, and property damage estimated at one billion dollars. Mobs targeted Korean groceries that were accused of profiteering from Black consumers, but the underlying incitements had not materially changed from

1965—grinding poverty in the minority enclave of South Los Angeles and the continuation of the police department's paramilitary law enforcement style under the leadership of Chief Daryl Gates, who had assumed command in 1978. (Parker had died in office in 1966.) The city deployed the National Guard, the army, and the Marines to quell the riots. But they were a reminder of Clark's warning that the same analysis and the same recommendations, unaccompanied by action, would do nothing to alleviate California's profound racial inequalities.

24

THE CRISIS OF GROWTH

WEDGED INTO A frame of tubular steel, his leg braces locked to hold him upright, Franklin D. Roosevelt stood at a lectern overlooking the Colorado River and declared: "This morning I came, I saw, and I was conquered, as everyone will be who sees for the first time this great achievement." He was referring to the landmark structure then known as Boulder Dam. Roosevelt had come to the riverside on this scorching day, September 30, 1935, to dedicate the newly finished dam in the name of the Democratic New Deal—never mind that ground had been broken during the term of his predecessor, Republican Herbert Hoover.* Roosevelt pledged to a nationwide radio audience that the dam would bring future residents of the West "a just, safe and permanent system of water rights."

It was not to be.

Although the dam spans a steeply walled canyon on the border between Nevada and Arizona, it had been a Californian enterprise from the very beginning. Farmers in the Imperial Valley had conceived the project after their rich croplands were devastated by a raging flood in 1905, when canal builders cut into the Colorado's banks to provide irrigation but were unable to keep the torrential outflow from swamping the valley.

---

* Two years earlier, Roosevelt's interior secretary, the liberal Republican Harold Ickes, had changed the project's name from Hoover Dam, which had been bestowed by Hoover's own interior secretary, Ray Lyman Wilbur. The original name would be permanently restored in 1947, when Republicans took control of Congress for the first time since 1932.

Before the dam could be raised, California and the six other Colorado basin states—Arizona, Nevada, Colorado, Utah, New Mexico, and Wyoming—had to agree on how to share the water that would collect in the dam's reservoir. Their interstate compact was reached through negotiations concluded in 1922 under the supervision of Hoover, then the secretary of commerce. Congress did not give the project the green light until 1931, as the Great Depression took hold and after William Mulholland, the city engineer of Los Angeles, committed the city to buying every drop of water made available from its reservoir. More important, he committed Los Angeles to buying every kilowatt of electricity the dam's turbines could generate in order to pump the water over mountains and across the desert to Southern California. Mulholland told the lawmakers that the water was needed to relieve a desperate drought in Los Angeles, but he was merely resurrecting the subterfuge he had employed to persuade the city's voters to finance the building of the Owens Valley canal; the city did not need the Colorado's water in 1931 but thirsted for it to accommodate its anticipated future growth.

Hoover Dam built the West but also confined it in a straitjacket. Endowed with its bounty of water and power, the population of the seven basin states grew nearly sixfold from 1931 through the turn of the century. Yet the western states would discover that what the dam bestowed, nature could take back. Protracted droughts beginning in 1999 reduced the Colorado River's flow to well below its level in 1906, when government engineers had recorded crucial measures of its capacity. The principle driving western growth had been that "water supplies will always be available to satisfy ever-expanding population," the National Research Council observed in 2007. As the twenty-first century approached, that was plainly untrue. In fact, it never had been true; Hoover's aides had deliberately overestimated the Colorado's capacity in 1922 to guarantee the basin states that they all would have access to as much water as they would ever need—if they only signed the interstate treaty.

The "water evangelists" of that era forecast unconstrained growth in an artificially watered West, but it was a delusion. Their expectations had been challenged by John Wesley Powell, the explorer who discovered the Grand Canyon, at an irrigation conference in 1893. "I tell you, gentlemen," the grizzled one-armed pioneer declared, "you are piling up a heritage of conflict and litigation over water rights, for there is not sufficient water to supply the land." He was driven from the hall by catcalls and boos.

Nature would prove Powell's words prophetic and confound the expectations of Franklin Roosevelt—indeed, of anyone who repeated his assurances
of perpetual abundance. In 2003, George W. Bush's interior secretary, Gale
Norton, came to the river to sign twenty-four agreements reapportioning
water rights among Indian tribes, local irrigation districts, western cities,
and the government of Mexico. Her goal was to settle the conflicts and litigation over the Colorado that Powell had foreseen, made all the more intense
by the emerging symptoms of global warming. "With these agreements,"
she proclaimed, "conflict on the river is stilled."

She was as wrong as Roosevelt had been. By 2023, further agreements
were needed, for water shortages had worsened. Now it was up to Arizona,
Nevada, and California, the states with the highest water demand, to agree
on mutual reductions in water use. As always, the stakes were highest for
California, which had the smallest acreage within the Colorado basin but
by far the highest consumption. Knowing that yet more cutbacks would be
needed in only a few years, the states struggled to reach an agreement balancing water use among its stakeholders. In the meantime, growers would have
to leave croplands fallow and homeowners tear out their decorative lawns and
replace their washing machines and dishwashers with less thirsty models.
The "soft landing" in water availability that had been promised by politicians and engineers as recently as 2003 was no longer possible.

THE DIMINISHING AVAILABILITY of water was only one of the constraints
suggesting, at the turn of the new century, that Californians' postwar aspirations to create a social, economic, and cultural paradise on earth had hit a
wall.

Some limitations arose from their long love affair with cars. The automobile's penetration into the California urban environment progressed slowly
at first. In 1920, the Los Angeles City Council tried to protect its extensive
streetcar and trolley system—including the storied Red Cars of Henry Huntington's Pacific Electric Railway—by banning automobile parking in the
central city. The ban was soon rescinded under pressure from residents who
preferred their private vehicles to the increasingly congested, slow, and expensive streetcars. By 1924, some 310,000 automobiles were flooding downtown Los Angeles every day—more than the total number of cars registered
in New York State.

The city largely gave up on its streetcar systems and widened and realigned its downtown streets to ease automobile congestion. The Red Cars, having lost three-quarters of their passengers by 1935, continued drifting toward extinction until April 1961, when the last train on the line completed its final run.

The reconstruction of downtown was only the beginning. In 1937, the Automobile Club of Southern California mapped out a comprehensive plan for a freeway system extending from the mountains to the beaches, "a network of traffic routes for the exclusive use of motor vehicles over which there shall be no crossing at grade and along which there shall be no interference from land use activities." The concept of the California freeway was born.

It would not fully flower, however, until after World War II. Prior to then, only one freeway had been built—an eight-mile parkway connecting Pasadena with downtown Los Angeles, completed in 1940. Hemmed in by lush vegetation, the twisting, narrow Pasadena Freeway bears no resemblance to its successors, four-, six-, eight-, even fourteen-lane expanses of pavement laid out nearly straight or in gently sweeping curves with densely packed industrial and commercial properties and residential tracts crammed almost to their very shoulders.

Those latter routes were the product of the state's Collier-Burns Act of 1947, which aimed to finance the construction of 12,500 miles of freeways by a gasoline tax of seven cents per gallon. The Federal Highway Act of 1956 provided more funding—its model, as President Dwight D. Eisenhower said at the time, being California's system of smoothly paved, expertly engineered freeways.

What the freeway builders seldom took into consideration were the social implications of ramming freeways through existing neighborhoods— "wiping out large sections of housing, razing historic landmarks, and destroying neighborhood cohesion." The neighborhood that suffered the most was heavily Latino East Los Angeles, which was populated by "legitimate property owners in a well-established community," but who lacked a political voice, urban historian Gilbert Estrada observed. As a result, he wrote, "Eastsiders could not halt the freeways."

Evictions of its residents for freeway construction began in 1944. That year, bulldozers cleared the way for the first stretches of the Santa Ana Freeway, providing the residents of rapidly developing Orange County with an easy commute to jobs in downtown Los Angeles. The route was laid out to avoid disturbing the many industrial plants in the area, but the designers were less concerned about demolishing homes, since they judged these to be "substandard dwellings." In 1949, California Highway Division employees described East Los Angeles disdainfully as a neighborhood "infiltrated by minority groups mostly [of] Latin derivation" who planners considered to be imposing a fiscal and social burden on the city.

To the extent the designers acknowledged the toll their vast construction enterprise took on housing stock, their concern seldom moved beyond lip service. "It would not be good public policy . . . ruthlessly to evict tenants who are living in houses on right of way that is needed for freeway construction," a state highway engineer wrote in "California Highways and Public Works," his departmental newsletter, "because to carry out wholesale evictions in order to get a freeway project started would make still worse the critical housing shortage." But just as hundreds of homes were being demolished or relocated, the engineers congratulated themselves for moving the evicted families into "federally owned house trailers" or allowing them to remain in the homes while they were being moved to new locations and for six months thereafter.

The demolitions continued for more than two decades, until what had been East Los Angeles was imprisoned within a concrete moat composed of the Hollywood Freeway, opened in 1948; the San Bernardino Freeway (1953); the Golden State Freeway (1955); the Long Beach Freeway (1961); and the Pomona Freeway (1965). In no other part of California were the freeways and their interchanges packed so tightly together.

Nor was freeway construction the only threat to Chicano communities. The same era saw the groundbreaking for a stadium for the relocating Brooklyn Dodgers in 1959 in Chavez Ravine, on the northwestern edge of downtown, which required dispossessing hundreds of mostly Latino residents.

Physical and fiscal realities ultimately halted the frenzy of freeway construction in Southern California. The Century Freeway, which runs nineteen miles between Los Angeles International Airport and the city's eastern suburbs, opened in 1993 after thirty years of planning and construction. It stands today as the most expensive urban freeway ever built (at more than two billion dollars) and the most litigated. It also boasts some of the most impressive road engineering in the country, including a five-level interchange connecting to the north–south Harbor Freeway linking downtown Los Angeles and its port. But it also is destined to be the last freeway built in Los Angeles. There is no more land to pave over, and even if there were, there is no more money.

THE MANIFOLD CONSTRAINTS obstructing California's social and economic ambitions were acknowledged in word and action by the distinctly ascetic new governor of California, Edmund G. "Jerry" Brown Jr., after his election in 1974. The son of the progressive governor Edmund G. "Pat" Brown, who served from 1959 through 1966, Jerry Brown renounced the costlier trappings of office, adopting a spartan lifestyle echoing the fiscal challenge of the government he now led. He refused to move into the $1.3 million governor's mansion that had been built for Ronald Reagan in the Sacramento suburb of Carmichael. Brown derided the mansion as the "Taj Mahal" and instead rented a downtown Sacramento apartment where he slept on a mattress on the floor. (The state sold the mansion in 1984 for $1.5 million—a loss, accounting for inflation; no governor had ever lived in it.) Brown also refused the state's chauffeur-driven Cadillac limousine, preferring a late-model Plymouth, but he typically walked to work anyway.

In his second annual message to the legislature, a crisp 1,700-word speech delivered on January 7, 1976, Brown outlined the realities forcing California into a painful retrenchment. "We are entering an era of limits," he said.

> The oil boycott has shown that our economic machine is dependent on the resources of others. We began the last decade with great expectations about ending poverty and providing equal opportunity to everyone. Glib statements were made about protecting the environment. Yet we now come face to face with sluggish economic growth, increasing social instability, widespread unemployment and unprecedented environmental challenges. Something has to give. The country is rich, but not as rich as we have been led to believe. The choice to do one thing may preclude another.

The choices Brown placed before Californians encompassed many progressive initiatives put in place by his predecessors, including his father. "Freeways, childcare, schools, income assistance, pensions, health programs, prisons, environmental protection—all must compete with one another and be subject to the careful scrutiny of the common purpose we all serve," he said.

Brown was well ahead of many other politicians in warning not only of the fiscal limits on what local and state governments could provide but the limitations imposed by natural circumstances and the will of the voters. Scarcely more than two years after his 1976 speech, he was forced to come to terms with the latter constraint in ways he had not anticipated. In June 1978, California voters passed Proposition 13, which rolled back property taxes and pared down the legislature's authority to raise any taxes at all. The "tax revolt" represented by the initiative may have been the most influential export in the state's history. Within six months of its passage, tax-capping measures were placed on the ballot in seventeen states and enacted in twelve. Eventually, twenty-five states legislated tax cuts and tax limits. Promises to cut taxes became nearly a universal feature of the American political landscape, to the detriment of public services ranging from education to police and fire protection.

Proposition 13 was the product of a historic run-up in home prices in California during the 1970s. Combined with annual reassessments of residential properties, the inflationary spiral produced property tax bills that many homeowners could not afford. With legislators consistently failing to craft a remedy, Proposition 13 landed on the ballot. It passed by a two-to-one margin.

The proposition was portrayed as offering relief to overburdened homeowners, but that was misleading, if not flagrantly deceptive. Its chief promoter was Howard Jarvis, whose rough-hewn, jowly visage became ubiquitous in the pages of newspapers and on TV screens, where he was typically portrayed as a salt-of-the-earth gadfly. In fact he was a lobbyist for apartment owners, who would be among the initiative's top beneficiaries. The proposition barred reassessments except upon the sale of a property; what was little understood by voters was that commercial and industrial property owners were effectively immunized against reassessments, because transfers of those properties could be structured in ways that did not meet the legal definition of a change of ownership. They might not technically change hands for decades, if at all, with the result that massively profitable landholdings such as Disneyland, the presumed value of which had increased many times over, were assessed at their 1970s values while the assessments on neighboring homes rose relentlessly in a robust homebuying market. Proposition 13 decisively shifted the property tax burden from commercial and industrial owners to homeowners, making a mockery of the promise that it would free homeowners from their financial burdens. At the time of its passage, single-family residences accounted for about 40 percent of coastal California's assessed valuation, and commercial and industrial properties for nearly 50 percent; four decades later, the ratio had reversed, with housing accounting for nearly 60 percent of total assessed valuation, and commercial and industrial real estate less than 30 percent.

Proposition 13 wrought a lasting change in California's fiscal structure and politics. The property tax traditionally had been the most stable public revenue source and the only tax levied by local governments, providing their constituents with a keen awareness of the relationship between the money they were charged and the municipal services they received. The initiative's suffocating cap on property assessments destroyed that linkage. The state government was called upon to fill the holes suddenly opened in local budgets, shifting the center of gravity in municipal finance from city and county halls to Sacramento. School districts and town boards, reduced to supplicants to the central government, seemed to lose their ability to serve their voters' interests.

The resulting voter skepticism about the public sector's ability and even willingness to solve problems that were once squarely within its reach would energize the candidacies of small-government ideologues who had taken their cues from Ronald Reagan, who had preceded Jerry Brown as governor and moved up to the White House in 1981. The central tenet of Reagan's ideology, that government obstructed rather than fulfilled voters' freedom while enriching the political class at the expense of homeowners, was heavily reflected in the Proposition 13 pitch. Starving the public sector of funds made the inadequacy of public services a self-fulfilling prophecy. "The most important thing in this country is not the school system, nor the police department, nor the fire department," Jarvis had declared. "The right to have property in this country, the right to have a home in this country, that's important."

Generally speaking, the tax relief purportedly offered by Proposition 13 was a chimera. Property taxes were capped but income tax rates more than doubled for the highest earners. They became regular targets for increases, to the point where California's top marginal income tax rates eventually ranked as the highest in the nation. Sales taxes, which burdened middle-class and lower-income households the most, rose by nearly half. California residents found themselves being dunned for fees for services formerly financed by property taxes, such as art and music classes in the schools, the issuance of building permits, water, and garbage collection. Californians still desired all the services and amenities they had become accustomed to receiving as part of the "California dream," only now their costs would not be bundled into the property tax but broken out more painfully in separate bills.

One consequence of the fiscal instability created by Proposition 13 was political instability. The most notable manifestation of that phenomenon was the recall election of 2003, in which Democratic governor Gray Davis was ousted and replaced by actor Arnold Schwarzenegger. Several factors contributed to Davis's defeat. One was an economic slump that produced a record state budget deficit of nearly forty billion dollars; this was the consequence of the dot-com crash of 1999–2000, which stripped Silicon Valley entrepreneurs of their stock-based income and thus sharply reduced revenues from the capital gains tax. The pallid Davis, who had to announce the deficit only days before taking the oath for his second term, tried to make up for the shortfall by tripling the state's annual vehicle-licensing fee. The immensely unpopular fee increase cost some families hundreds of dollars a year.

A botched restructuring of the state's electricity market was the crowning blow for the Davis administration. This scheme, which state regulators had crafted under Davis's Republican predecessor, former San Diego mayor Pete Wilson, exposed the state to the volatile wholesale electricity market and left it vulnerable to manipulation by unscrupulous traders at firms such as Enron.

Davis's second term was therefore crippled from the outset. Conservative Republicans launched the recall in March, with the election scheduled for October 7. The qualifications for candidates were so meager—only sixty-five nominating signatures and a $3,500 fee were required—that one hundred thirty-five names appeared on the ballot, a circus sideshow lineup that included an adult film star, a used-car salesman, a faded child star, and pornographer Larry Flynt. Schwarzenegger, the candidate with the highest name recognition, won the vote to replace Davis with a plurality.

As his first act upon assuming office, Schwarzenegger made good on his campaign pledge to roll back the vehicle-licensing fee, presiding over a theatrical bit of business in which a wrecking ball was dropped on an Oldsmobile spray-painted with the words "Davis Car Tax." The rollback, however, worsened the budget deficit by four billion dollars. Schwarzenegger made up the gap by borrowing, the costliest option for covering current expenses. Throughout his first term, his proposals for cutting government spending were consistently blocked by a Democratic-controlled legislature—and by the voters. Schwarzenegger placed a budget-capping initiative on the ballot for a special election in 2005. It was voted down by a decisive margin.

Schwarzenegger retained enough popularity to win a second term in 2006, but he was increasingly confronted by the limits identified so presciently by Jerry Brown thirty years before. His budget-cutting proposals invariably targeted programs for the poor and families with school-age children—perhaps inevitably, since four-fifths of the budget was written into the constitution and therefore not amenable to gubernatorial or legislative adjustment. Schwarzenegger struggled to navigate a path between his liberal populism on social issues and his business-friendly fiscal conservatism. He proposed a system of universal health care for Californians (it was defeated by opposition from California health insurers), signed laws tightening regulations on firearms, and sued the George W. Bush administration to protect California's right to set its own automobile emission standards.

As Schwarzenegger's second and final term drew to a close, California's middle and working classes were feeling squeezed as never before. He sought praise for keeping tax increases to a minimum. But residents lived under a rainfall of stealth taxes, such as steep increases in tuition and fees at the University of California and California State University, and local budget cuts that left streets pockmarked with potholes and schools stripped of art and music classes. He left office with a popularity rating about as low as Davis's. With his successor, California voters looked ahead and looked back. He was Jerry Brown, who had been the thirty-fourth governor and now would be the thirty-ninth. He inherited some problems that had remained unresolved since his previous term, such as the state government's precarious fiscal condition, and some that had come to the forefront in the interim. Chief among the latter was a housing crisis.

"SOMEWHERE ALONG THE way, California decided that adding enough new housing is a bad thing." The speaker was state senator Scott Wiener, a San Francisco Democrat who had just witnessed the Los Angeles City Council vote unanimously to oppose a bill he drafted to promote high-density residential construction near bus and rail stops. It was March 2018, and another setback in efforts to solve California's most dire economic and social problem: a severe shortage of housing that was driving young low- and middle-income families to leave the state, filling its streets, underpasses, and parks with unkempt, unsightly, and unhealthy tent cities, and undermining its efforts to reduce greenhouse-gas emissions from commuters' automobiles.

Wiener's bill had received a blaze of positive national attention as a forward-looking solution to the housing crisis. But it died from virtually unanimous opposition from a coalition of quintessentially strange bedfellows: local politicians, labor unions, liberal community activists, environmental groups such as the Sierra Club, and health-care advocates.

That California would see more harm than good in new housing proposals is almost inevitable. The sentiment emerged as the state was growing into the most populous in the nation. By the Census Bureau's reckoning, the inflection point was July 1, 1964, when California's population first topped 18 million, exceeding New York's 17.9 million. Up to then, Californians had celebrated the state's growth in full boosterism mode; Governor Pat Brown had even saluted the state's population victory (a bit prematurely) by calling a state holiday on December 31, 1962, to mark the moment.

Over the following decade, the state's postwar enthusiasm for rapid growth evolved into a slow-growth and ultimately a no-growth posture. What happened was that a torrent of newcomers had created a critical mass of residents, especially suburbanites. Once in place, they viewed a continued inflow of newcomers as a threat to the qualities that had attracted them to California to begin with, such as its natural beauty, its ample resources, its sense of living space all one's own. Single-family homes, those salubrious but inefficient uses of real estate, blanketed the coastal landscape. Their owners felt that their neighborhoods had reached an equilibrium of uncrowded schools, efficient public services, and uncongested roads, but they feared that nirvana would disappear if people kept arriving at an unchecked pace.

Proposals for new housing tracts drew complaints from incumbent residents about the prospect of overcrowded classrooms and unmanageable traffic. New housing developments brought higher assessed valuations, but after Proposition 13, the property taxes generated by the additional housing were insufficient to pay for the increased demand on services from the newcomers.

It is true that Californians' ambivalence about growth dated further back than the sixties and seventies. "They want the state to grow, yet they don't want it to grow," Carey McWilliams wrote in 1949. "Each wave of migration is regarded with fear and trembling, and the wave next before the last invariably comes up with the idea that the latest arrivals are 'inferior' to those who came at an earlier date."

Yet anti-growth sentiment in the late postwar years was far more prevalent than ever before. From 1940 to 1970, the number of housing units tripled in the coastal zone stretching from San Francisco and Oakland to San Diego. During the following three decades, the housing stock in those communities grew by only about one-third—and by only one-fifth in Los Angeles and San Francisco, where demand was greatest. The subsequent run-up in home prices was sudden and startling: In 1970, the median California home price was 30 percent higher than the US average; by 1980 it was 80 percent higher.

Low-growth advocates often blocked new housing developments by exploiting environmental protection rules implemented under the California Environmental Quality Act. The law was enacted in 1970 during the surge of ecological consciousness after the Santa Barbara oil spill, which had also brought about the National Environmental Policy Act in 1969 and the first Earth Day in 1970. CEQA required that the impact of publicly funded construction projects on air and water pollution and on the natural environment be assessed and disclosed in public reports. In 1972, the state supreme court expanded the law to cover any project that required permitting by public agencies—in other words, almost anything.

That opened the floodgates to litigation. From the environmentalists' standpoint, the ruling properly brought CEQA oversight to projects that had evaded the law's jurisdiction through legal technicalities. But in short order, CEQA cases ceased to focus on "protecting forests and other natural lands, or fighting pollution sources like factories and freeways," which had been envisioned as the law's principal goals. Instead, transit projects and "infill" housing proposals—such as apartment blocks proposed for already-developed neighborhoods—became the prime targets for lawsuits. Established environmental groups such as the Sierra Club faded to a tiny minority of CEQA plaintiffs, yielding the courthouse to litigants such as business owners targeting projects of competitors and residents seeking to block what they saw as character-changing developments in their neighborhoods. The environmental impacts subjected to CEQA scrutiny expanded widely, even absurdly; in 2005, the state supreme court accepted that the obstruction of views from private homes by four-story townhomes qualified as a CEQA-violating environmental impact.

In his final two terms as governor (2011–2019), Jerry Brown emerged as the state's most prominent critic of CEQA. But he lamented, "You can't change CEQA. . . . The unions won't let you because they use it as a hammer to get project labor agreements. The environmentalists like it because it's the people's document that you have to disclose all the impacts. . . . 'Impact,' boy, that's a big word. Everything's an impact."

CEQA did have loopholes; environmental reviews could be truncated or waived by action of the state legislature. But such gifts were typically bestowed on big commercial projects such as sports stadiums and arenas that were promoted as boons to state and local tax collections and only rarely on housing developments opposed by residents. When it came to housing, the "incumbency effect" tied local politicians to no-growth policies. The needs of existing residents would always have more weight with elected officials than the needs or aspirations of nonresidents, who by definition were on the outside looking in. It became routine to ascribe the slowdown in housing construction to the "NIMBY" phenomenon—"Not in my backyard." That trend, ever-present in developed communities nationwide, was especially powerful in coastal California, where existing development had reached the point that virtually every buildable parcel was in *someone's* backyard.

By 2010, the shortfall in residential housing seemed almost intractable. California was estimated to need 1.8 million to 3.5 million new residential units by 2025 to absorb existing demand and future population growth. Its annual construction pace of fewer than 80,000 new homes fell short of even the lower estimate by 100,000 homes a year. Between 2020 and 2023, the state lost 800,000 residents and built 800,000 new residential units. But those trends together failed to make a dent in the housing shortage, because most of the new units were single family homes or other low-density units, and most were being built not on the coast where demand was greatest but in the inland exurbs.

That points to how the housing shortage and rapidly rising rents and home prices on the coast undermined two interrelated goals of California policy—the reduction of greenhouse-gas emissions and of air pollution. As workers pushed ever farther inland in their quest for reasonably priced housing, their commutes to workplaces, which remained clustered within the coastal zone, lengthened. Californians' commutes into Los Angeles and San Francisco were among the longest and most time-consuming in the nation, with the highest percentage of "mega-commuters," those who traveled more than ninety minutes and more than fifty miles each way. Although the state had made significant progress in reducing emissions and air pollution from static sources such as oil refineries and cement plants, the transportation sector nearly made up for the reductions, accounting for nearly half of all emissions as of this writing. Californians may have led the nation in their adoption of non-emitting electric cars, but those who preferred gasoline-fueled vehicles were gravitating toward ever-heavier SUVs and pickup trucks and were driving more, with total vehicle miles rising from about 310 billion miles in 2000 to more than 340 billion in 2018.

California seemed to have reached a crossroads. Its progressive values were again in the ascendance. As red states in the Midwest and Southeast constructed a dystopian landscape of LGBTQ discrimination, shrinking abortion rights, and heightened restrictions on voting, California's political leaders positioned the state as a haven for diversity, for reproductive rights, a place where nothing stood in the way of voters wishing for their voices to be heard. Yet the doubts were inescapable: Would California succumb to the same challenges—climatological, social, political, economic—that polarized the rest of the country and even the world? Or would it lead the way by looking within itself to the solutions?

EPILOGUE

KEEPING THE CALIFORNIA DREAM ALIVE

THE FIRST DECADES of the twenty-first century were not kind to California. Multiyear droughts struck the state in 2007, 2012, and 2020, aggravating the water crisis that had been building since the 1970s. A shortage of affordable housing within reasonable commuting distance to workplaces intensified, fueling a seemingly relentless run-up in home prices. The cost of public services continued to rise—the University of California's Board of Regents raised tuition five times from 2000 through 2021 and thereafter instituted an annual increase tied to inflation. This for a university education that had been effectively free to state residents until the 1960s.

Nine of the ten worst wildfires and seventeen of the twenty worst in the state's history (as measured by acres burned), erupted from 2003 to 2020. The very worst in terms of lives lost swept across the Northern California foothills in November 2018. This was dubbed the "Camp Fire" after Camp Creek Road in Butte County, north of Sacramento, where it originated. The fire took eighty-five lives, obliterated the bucolic town of Paradise, and took firefighters seventeen days to bring under control. It ranked as the deadliest fire in US history until the Maui wildfire of August 2023, in which ninety-eight people perished.

Alongside this ecological maelstrom, California's population declined during the COVID-19 pandemic, when a shift to working from home allowed thousands of Californians to cut the geographical ties to their workplaces. Before the end of 2022, however, San Francisco and Los Angeles, which had suffered steep population losses, had cut their rates of decline almost to zero and appeared poised to begin recovering.

But the pandemic came on top of a longer-term decline in the state's population ranking. After the 2020 census, California lost a House seat for the first time in its history. This was not because the state's population had shrunk—it had grown by 2.2 million since the 2010 census—but because states such as Texas and Florida had grown faster, in part due to outmigration from California. The state's remaining delegation of fifty-two members remained appreciably larger than that of the runner-up, Texas, with thirty-eight seats, but the details of the population change were unsettling—outmigration to other states, once concentrated in middle- and low-income families driven away by the cost of living, had spread to wealthier households. Immigration had slowed, and the birth rate had flattened out. The state's demographers tried to assure the public that California's diversified economy would save it from turning into a new "Rust Belt." California's economy remained the largest in the nation by a wide margin, with a gross domestic product of $3.6 trillion in 2022, easily outstripping that of second-place Texas ($2.4 trillion). But whether it could maintain its status indefinitely came into question.

IT IS UNSURPRISING that these developments would revive journalistic skepticism about California values, which had laid the foundation of the state's "exceptionalism" (to quote Carey McWilliams) for more than a century. The Atlantic titled a July 2021 article "The California Dream Is Dying" and followed it less than a year later with "How San Francisco Became a Failed City." The first article argued that the anti-growth movement had undermined the state's traditional embrace of diversity and economic equality; the second rather less cogently blamed the state's maladies on the Bay Area's supposed addiction to left-wing ideologies.

One assertion these articles shared was that overregulation had "paralyzed" the state's economy, stifling the creation and survivability of small businesses with "safety reviews, environmental reviews, historical reviews," as the second piece put it. Yet they overlooked the successes of California-style regulation. Over the previous five decades, California's legislators and voters had responded to the fouling of their water and air with some of the most stringent pollution regulations in the land. Targeted businesses understandably viewed this as a burden. But the regulations yielded measurable improvements in air and water quality. Smog remains an ever-present problem in Southern California partially because of its weather patterns, which trap polluting emissions low to the ground. (Juan Rodriguez Cabrillo, after all, had dubbed San Pedro Bay, now subsumed into the port of Los Angeles, the "Bay of Smoke"—in 1542!) But the attacks of smog so thick that the towering San Gabriel Mountains were rendered invisible even to residents living in their foothills, which had been common through the 1980s, had dwindled to a few days each year in high summer. California's methods of controlling pollution have become models for dozens of other states. In that respect it has been a national leader.

Still, increasingly common and severe droughts compounded by human misjudgments trigger the unprecedented and deadly wildfires that now define summer in twenty-first-century California. Humans' reliance on fossil fuels for energy has turned an essential ecological process into a supercharged destructive force. Global warming brings to California hotter and drier summers and winters, drought periods punctuated by wet years that bring down torrential precipitation in time spans so brief that much of it cannot be corralled into man-made reservoirs for long-term storage or in the Sierra snowpack, a vast natural reservoir.

Among the human misjudgments are the construction of residences in the wildlands, higher into the foothills and deeper into forested areas. This has fostered fire-suppression policies aimed at protecting residents and their houses, not allowing nature to burn off flammable detritus on the forest floor. Authorities have blamed nine of the twenty most destructive fires in state history, including the Camp Fire, on power lines that electrical utilities built to serve rural ratepayers without ensuring that the lines remain safely out of contact with flammable vegetation. The fires' impact has extended well beyond the wildlands; it became common during the ever-longer fire seasons for a thick, choking bourbon-colored pall, driven by onshore winds, to descend on cities and suburbs even on the distant coast, fostering the impression that the entire state is burning.

NOTWITHSTANDING THE SIZE of the state's economy, the state government's fiscal health suffered from its own boom-and-bust cycles, exacerbated by the income tax–heavy revenue structure bequeathed by Proposition 13 and by Arnold Schwarzenegger's decision to close the budget deficit by borrowing. The task of placing the state on a solid financial footing fell to his successor, Jerry Brown.

"We're in for a bit of a bumpy ride because of the spending by the state," he said in unveiling an austere state budget in May 2012. Brown, who had been the youngest California governor in more than a century when he began his first term in 1975, was now the oldest governor in the state's history. He approached his task with all the verve at age seventy-four that he had displayed at thirty-six. The state budget deficit had been driven up to nearly sixteen billion dollars from nine billion at the beginning of the year, thanks largely to the lingering effects of the 2008 recession. "This is real," he said as he proposed pay cuts for state employees and cutbacks in programs for the disabled and other social services—along with a seven-year tax increase to be placed before the voters.

To widespread surprise, the tax increase—a quarter-point hike in the state sales tax and higher top rates for taxpayers earning more than $250,000—passed by a margin of 55 percent to 45 percent. Even more surprising, a ballot measure to extend the income tax increases for a further twelve years, through 2030, passed in 2016 by an even more lopsided margin. Brown, who had shouldered the tax-cutting burden of Proposition 13 in his first term, began the process of rolling back the tax revolt in his final term. Due to the tax increase—and California's ability to exploit a recovering national economy—the state budget showed a surplus of thirty billion dollars when Brown left office for the last time, in January 2019.

Californians' determination to solve problems, many of them of their own making, has remained robust, if not invariably successful. The shortfall of affordable housing has continued to worsen. The gap between rich and poor is among the widest in the nation, exceeded only in New York, Massachusetts, Connecticut, and the District of Columbia. Some 20 percent of all net worth is concentrated in thirty wealthy zip codes housing only 2 percent of the state's residents. That statistic indicates that California's attraction for the well-educated and well-heeled remains strong. But when adjusted to take into account the price of housing and its effect on the cost of living, the state's poverty rate—the percentage of its residents living at or below the federal poverty line—was the highest in the nation in 2023 at 13.3 percent, albeit lower than it had been before the pandemic (16.4 percent in 2019).

Unlike many other states, California places no legal or administrative obstacles in the way of eligible voters wishing to exercise their franchise.

This gives the state's political leaders an unobstructed view of voters' goals and desires, which they have interpreted as favoring progressive policies on immigration, minority and gender rights, and business regulation, among many other issues. California has remained open to diverse communities to a degree unseen in many other states. It has raised minimum wages for employees in industries such as fast food and health care. Except in some rural and exurban pockets, discrimination against LGBTQ+ residents is rare. Reproductive health-care rights are enshrined in the state constitution. After Republican-controlled states began outlawing abortion in the wake of the Supreme Court's June 24, 2022, ruling overturning its *Roe v. Wade* decision of 1973, California established itself as a haven for reproductive-health rights, even creating a website for out-of-state residents listing California medical providers and advocacy organizations that can furnish financial assistance for lower-income patients.

Gavin Newsom, who took office as governor in 2019 after eight years as mayor of San Francisco and eight more as Jerry Brown's lieutenant governor, mapped out a series of initiatives reflecting the state's self-image as a beacon of progressivism. He proposed an amendment to the US Constitution banning the civilian purchase of assault weapons and mandating background checks and waiting periods for the purchase of any firearm. He positioned himself as a "climate change crusader" by instituting a ban on the sale of new gasoline-powered cars and trucks to take place in 2035, bringing together major automobile manufacturers to give public support to the state's exacting emissions policies, and placing the fight against global warming high on the agenda of a meeting in Beijing with Chinese president Xi Jinping in October 2023.

These policies fit neatly with the preferences of a majority of California voters and with the state's historical commitment to new technologies—in this case, electric vehicles. The unanswered question remains whether the same policies can be exported to the rest of the country, as have been so many California values and initiatives—some socially salubrious, some pernicious—over the years.

IN THE PRE-STATEHOOD period and for decades after its admission to the union, California's geographic isolation forced its residents to forge their own political and economic paths, producing a "spirit of great independence," perhaps leavened somewhat by "a self-reliance bordering on truculence," in

McWilliams's words. Californians' inventiveness, along with the state's size, are what have made it such an influential laboratory for experimentation in science, technology, and public policy. California has been the birthplace of many transformative social movements, as detailed in this book. Perhaps more to the point, it is where the ramifications of those transformations often appear first.

The outside world has not always heeded the lessons offered by California's experiences. This is well illustrated by the case of affirmative action, that perennially divisive effort to address deeply ingrained racial and ethnic discrimination by American institutions. The US Supreme Court outlawed affirmative action in university admissions policies in 2023, but California went through that wrenching change a quarter of a century earlier.

Affirmative action became part of the admissions process at the University of California in 1988, when its Board of Regents became determined to create a student body encompassing "the broad diversity of cultural, racial, geographic, and socioeconomic backgrounds characteristic of California" by applying a host of "non-academic" standards to applications. In 1995, the experiment was ended by politically conservative regents, a majority of whom had been appointed by Republican governors. The change eliminated "race, religion, gender, color, ethnicity or national origin" as criteria in admission decisions. Republicans subsequently placed a constitutional amendment on the 1996 ballot widening the ban on "quotas, preferences, and set-asides" so it applied to all state and local agencies. The measure, Proposition 209, passed 55 percent to 45 percent, with the greatest support coming from males, whites, non-college graduates, more affluent voters, and registered Republicans. The record showed that affirmative action had brought larger numbers of underprivileged but promising students into the higher-education system, enriching California society. The state only suffered from its repeal.

"The impact was immediate and widespread," UC president Michael V. Drake and the chancellors of its ten campuses advised the Supreme Court in a 2022 friend-of-the-court brief. "On every UC campus, the proportion of freshman applications, admittees, and enrollees from underrepresented minority groups declined precipitously." The effect was most noticeable at the university's two most elite campuses—Berkeley, where the proportion of African American students in the freshman class fell from 6.32 percent in 1995 to 3.37 percent in 1998, and UCLA, where the ratio dropped from

7.13 percent to 3.42 percent in the same period. Hispanic student enroll-ment fell from 15.57 percent of the incoming class to 7.28 percent in that period at Berkeley, and from 21.58 percent to 10.45 percent at UCLA.

The university struggled to rebuild those ratios, woeful as they had been even with affirmative action in place. It established outreach programs aimed at high-school students from low-income families and those in economi-cally disadvantaged districts at a cost of more than a half-billion dollars. It eliminated the reliance on standardized tests, which were seen as favoring applicants from socially and economically advantaged school systems. But nothing has made the demographics of the university's student population comparable to the demographics of California public-school students gener-ally or, indeed, brought them back to pre–Proposition 209 levels.

The effects have been felt on every campus, the administrators said, man-ifested in feelings of racial isolation experienced by students from minority groups in their interactions with other students in classrooms, dorms, and extracurricular programs. Contrary to the contention by the plaintiffs in the affirmative action cases before the Supreme Court that the benefits of diver-sity are "amorphous and unmeasurable," the UC administrators said, they are "concrete and precise"—and their loss broadly corrosive. They saw affir-mative action as a testament to the state's commitment to diversity of op-portunity for all. "If the student body of a State's flagship university—whose mission is to educate the State's future leaders—is severely out of step with the larger applicant pool, people might conclude that the pathway to leader-ship is not truly open to all, thereby undermining future leaders' 'legitimacy in the eyes of the citizenry,'" the administrators wrote.

The court majority could have taken UC's experience as a lesson. It did not.

As its record on diversity in higher education shows, California has of-ten struggled to solve its own problems. De facto segregation persists, even worsened by a geographic stratification rooted in economic inequality: Black families are excluded from communities with the best school systems be-cause they cannot afford to live there—and are getting pushed further away by the rising cost of housing.

The crisis in the availability of water, that resource so fundamental to California's economic growth in the twentieth century, persists partially be-cause stakeholders—growers, urban residents, industry, and advocates for the environment—are all equally insistent on the justness of their positions and partially because the state's web of water rights has its roots in legal claims established so long ago that they are hard to unwind today. For all that, the fundamental problem of California water is still a geographical one that both fosters and reflects cultural and economic conflicts: Two-thirds of its population and a large share of water-dependent growers are in the central and southernmost regions of the state, and two-thirds of its domestic water supplies are in the north. Proposals for infrastructure projects to move water from the north to the south have invariably brought simmering regional animosities to a full boil.

That was what happened in 1982, when a proposal by Jerry Brown for a "peripheral canal" to siphon water from the Sacramento River and funnel it southward was overwhelmingly defeated by Northern California votes. Paul Conrad, the editorial cartoonist of the *Los Angeles Times*, depicted the result with a pungent drawing of a hulking, cigar-smoking figure labeled "Northern California" standing on a state map and urinating southward. In a larger sense, it has long been clear that California's water shortages cannot be addressed without the cooperation of neighboring states that share the right to draw from the Colorado River. As large and resource-rich as it is, California cannot sustain itself purely on in-state resources such as water and energy production, even labor. The truth is that California, despite its residents' desire to stand apart from the rest of the country in so many ways, has never been entirely isolated from the world outside its borders.

Yet the state's unique character gives it the ability to play a leading role in social change. California's history is American history in microcosm, composed of successive waves of immigrants who in coming to the state preserved their ethnic character, maintaining ties to their homelands while helping to build a diverse and distinctive culture, economy, and politics in their new home. The goal of forging a common culture is still a work in progress. The path has not always been smooth, for the newcomers often have been met with discrimination and violence. But according to a 2023 survey, "nearly four in five Californians believe immigrants are a benefit to the state because of their hard work and job skill." An even larger percentage believe undocumented immigrants should be granted a way to stay in the United States legally, including a path to citizenship.

Can California solve its problems? *Solve* is perhaps too ambitious a goal, but the determination to seek solutions remains the ultimate California value.

The first line of the 1894 poem "The Coming American," by Sam Walter

Foss, is etched into a frieze above the main entrance of the Jesse M. Unruh State Office Building in Sacramento: "Bring me men to match my mountains." Leaving aside the male centrism that reflects its archaic nineteenth-century origins, the poem can be taken as a fervent celebration of California's adventurous and ambitious spirit.

Yet an even more inspiring view of California's role as a bellwether of change and social evolution in the nation and the world, its people's willingness to test new ideas and spread them around the globe, was uttered by Mark Twain in a speech in San Francisco's Congress Hall on December 10, 1866. Taking his leave of the state he had made his home for two years, he said California "stands in the center of the grand highway of the nations; she stands midway between the Old World and the New, and both shall pay her tribute. . . . Multitudes of stout hearts and willing hands are preparing to flock hither; to throng her hamlets and villages; to till her fruitful soil . . . to build up an empire on these distant shores that shall shame the bravest dreams of her visionaries. . . . Half the world stands ready to lay its contributions at her feet! Has any other state so brilliant a future?"

ACKNOWLEDGMENTS

ANY WRITERS AIMING to examine the history of California are indebted to a great degree on the labors of two twentieth-century authors who preceded them: Carey McWilliams and Kevin Starr.

The breadth of McWilliams's topics as an independent journalist, activist, muckraker, and historian is truly astonishing. They included Southern California as a region unto itself, California agriculture and the treatment of its army of migrant farmworkers, prejudice against the state's Japanese residents and Japanese Americans, and biographies of two writers with significant ties to the state, Ambrose Bierce and Louis Adamic. His one-volume history *California: The Great Exception* (1949) chronicled the state's development since its first appearance in European written records and looked ahead to its future prospects.

As historian, educator, and ultimately as California's state librarian, Starr devoted his professional life to an expansive and digressive history of the state and its people, published in eight volumes beginning in 1973 and known collectively as *California and the American Dream*.

The works of both authors were the inspirations and indispensable starting points for this new history of California, examining its past, present, and future from a twenty-first-century vantage point. Their books and articles provided me with invaluable insights into the high points and low points of the state's more than five-hundred-year reign as an object of obsessive fascination on a global scale, while pointing me to source material of compelling richness.

Several institutions provided me with access to archival materials and other primary sources crucial for my research. I owe particular thanks to the staff of the Jack Langson Library of the University of California, Irvine, which—as has been the case with several of my previous books—was my bibliographic home away from home during the research stage of *Golden State*. The Bancroft Library of the University of California, Berkeley, is a vital repository of historical writings, first-person recollections of early California, and other important artifacts—as one would expect, given that it was founded with the university's acquisition of the personal library of historian Hubert Howe Bancroft, a collection of reference works that Bancroft began assembling in 1859. I was privileged to be granted access to material from the collection of the Huntington Library in San Marino, California, one of the world's premier research institutions.

I was fortunate in pursuing this project to benefit from the wise counsel of my editor, Ivy Givens of HarperCollins, whose feel for the threads of the California story from which I fashioned my narrative made her a full partner in shaping the final product. Sandra Dijkstra, my agent, perceived the richness of this story with her customary acuteness and helped drive it forward with the enthusiasm, advocacy, and confidence on which I have long come to rely, along with the assistance of her very able staff.

Finally but most importantly, this book could not have been researched and written without the love, forbearance, and support of my wife, Deborah. As always, my sons Andrew and David provided the optimism for the future that made this effort worthwhile.

NOTES

PROLOGUE: CALIFORNIA, LAND OF CONTRADICTIONS

1 *"The best way"*: Hiltzik, *Dealers of Lightning*, 122.

3 *"It is yet"*: Henry George, "The Kearney Agitation in California," *Popular Science Monthly* (August 1880).

3 *"They who came"*: Didion, *Where I Was From*, 16.

4 *"ten gold suns"*: Vachel Lindsay, *The Golden Whales of California and Other Rhymes in the American Language* (New York: Macmillan, 1920), 5.

4 *"spiritual gold"*: Lindsay, *The Golden Whales*, xx.

4 *"There has always been"*: McWilliams, *California*, 4.

4 *"The skeptics who"*: McWilliams, *California*, 4.

4 *anticipating the dream's*: See, for example, Conor Friedersdorf, "The California Dream Is Dying," *Atlantic*, July 2021.

5 *"rottenness and its corruption"*: Helper, *The Land of Gold*, vi.

5 *"The rush to California"*: Thoreau, "Life Without Principle," *The Atlantic*, October 1863.

5 *"The fig-tree"*: Greeley, *An Overland Journey*, 116.

5 *"No more merchants"*: Greeley, *An Overland Journey*, 132.

7 *the* California effect: Vogel, *Trading Up*, 6.

9 *Bill Clinton became*: Mark Z. Barabak, "How California, Land of Nixon and Reagan, Turned Blue and Changed American Politics," *Los Angeles Times*, June 4, 2023.

10 *"a country full"*: Royce, *California*, 4.

10 *"Nowhere else"*: Royce, *California*, 2.

10 *"In general"*: Schoenherr, *A Natural History of California*, 480.

12 *an area less*: Schoenherr, *A Natural History of California*, 266.

12   *three million cattle:* Schoenherr, *A Natural History of California,* 467.

14   *"uneasy truce":* Reisner, *Cadillac Desert,* 4.

14   *One of the largest:* Schoenherr, *A Natural History of California,* 52.

I. A TERRESTRIAL PARADISE

19   *"the gilded man":* A. F. Bandelier, *The Gilded Man (El Dorado) and Other Pictures of the Spanish Occupancy of America* (New York: D. Appleton and Company, 1893), 10.

20   *the climate is:* Bancroft, *History of California,* vol. 1, 65.

20   *"in none of the various":* Edward Everett Hale, "The Name of California," *Proceedings of the American Antiquarian Society* (April 30, 1862).

20   *Speculation about a Greek:* Bancroft, *History of California,* vol. 1, 66.

20   *The most enduring:* Hale, "The Name of California."

21   *"Know ye that":* George Davidson, "The Origin and the Meaning of the Word California," *Transactions and Proceedings of the Geographical Society of the Pacific* (1910).

22   *"meek, gentle, quiet":* Vizcaíno to King Felipe III of Spain, May 23, 1603, in Beebe and Senkewicz, *Lands of Promise and Despair,* 45.

23   *"as if they were stones":* The report was by Father Antonio de la Ascensión, a Carmelite monk who accompanied Vizcaíno on the 1602 voyage as cartographer; see Bolton, *Fray Juan Crespi,* 112.

24   *Cabrillo was a Portuguese:* Wagner, *Juan Rodríguez Cabrillo,* 10.

24   *It is widely:* Wagner, *Juan Rodríguez Cabrillo,* 5.

25   *They brought along:* The allegation that the boys were kidnapped is in Madley, *An American Genocide,* 26.

25   *"two small vessels":* Wagner, *Juan Rodríguez Cabrillo,* 29.

25   *"chief of the pirates":* Harry Kelsey, "Did Francis Drake Really Visit California?," *Western Historical Quarterly* (November 1990).

26   *exposed in 1979:* H. V. Michel and F. Asaro, "Chemical Study of the Plate of Brass," *Archaeometry* 21 (February 1979).

27   *in bad odor:* Bolton, *Fray Juan Crespi,* 44–45.

27   *He would leave:* Wagner, *Juan Rodríguez Cabrillo,* 30–31.

27   *"the best port":* Caughey, *California,* 81.

29   *The experience of forcing:* Chapman, *A History of California,* 207–15.

29   *twenty-five soldiers:* Richman, *California Under Spain and Mexico,* 75.

29   *All but two:* Chapman, *A History of California,* 225.

30   *"a small company":* Portolá, according to a recollection by Juan Manuel de Viniegra, in Chapman, *A History of California,* 225.

30   *"unknown lands":* Diary of Miguel Costansó, in Beebe and Senkewicz, *Lands of Promise and Despair,* 116–17.

30   *"no object to greet"*: Chapman, *A History of California*, 225.

30   *The expedition seldom:* The route and progress of the expedition is in Bancroft, *History of California*, vol. 1, 143–46.

30   *"tall trees of reddish-colored"*: Richman, *California Under Spain and Mexico*, 82.

31   *"You come from Rome"*: Chapman, *A History of California*, 227.

31   *Portolá calculated:* Richman, *California Under Spain and Mexico*, 84.

31   *"we got very particular"*: Chapman, *A History of California*, 227.

32   *"renders the Indians'"*: Beilharz, *Felipe de Neve*, 52.

32   *"In the matter"*: Serra, *Writings*, vol. 3, 411–13.

32   *the Indian population:* Cook, *The Conflict*, 4.

32   *"From the first"*: Cook, *The Conflict*, 13.

33   *"ate together"*: Cook, *The Conflict*, 31.

33   *"putrid and contagious"*: Cook, *The Conflict*, 23.

33   *"vicious license"*: Cook, *The Conflict*, 25.

33   *Indians resented:* Cook, *The Conflict*, 116.

33   *Indians who fled:* Madley, *An American Genocide*, 32.

34   *Cook estimated:* Cook, *The Conflict*, 61.

34   *More than 450:* Cook, *The Conflict*, 60.

2. THE AMERICANS ARRIVE

35   *On that day:* Adele Ogden, *The California Sea Otter Trade, 1784–1848* (Berkeley: University of California Press, 1941), 33.

35   *Despite Spanish laws:* Robert Glass Cleland, "The Early Sentiment for the Annexation of California I," *Southwestern Historical Quarterly* (July 1914).

36   *"only the show"*: Robert Shaler, "Journal of a Voyage Between China and the Northwest Coast of America," *American Register*, 1804.

37   *The story has been mined:* Treatments have included Bret Harte's narrative poem of 1800 *Concepcion de Arguello* and a rock opera, *Juno and Avos*, set to a libretto by the Russian poet Andrei Voznesensky in 1983.

37   *"wholly without defense"*: Cleland, "Early Sentiment I."

37   *"as a principle"*: For Monroe's address on December 2, 1823, see https://www.presidency.ucsb.edu/documents/seventh-annual-message-1.

37   *"Those who traverse"*: Reuben Gold Thwaites, *Early Western Travels 1748–1846*, vol. 18 (Cleveland: Arthur H. Clark, 1905), 306.

37   *"are equally calculated"*: Thwaites, *Early Western Travels*.

38   *"a country embracing"*: Dana, *Two Years Before the Mast*, 216.

38   *"an idle, thriftless"*: Dana, *Two Years Before the Mast*, 162.

38   *"a Frenchman named"*: John Bidwell, "The First Emigrant Train to California," in Royce, *John Bidwell*, 13.

39   *"men of a turbulent"*: Bancroft, *History of California,* vol. 4, 3.

39   *"I was insulted"*: Alfred Robinson, *Life in California* (San Francisco: William Doxey, 1897), 191.

40   *The other three:* Robert W. Merry, *A Country of Vast Designs: James K. Polk, the Mexican War, and the Conquest of the American Continent* (New York: Simon & Schuster, 2009), 131.

40   *Four paths:* Cleland, "The Early Sentiment for the Annexation of California II," *Southwestern Historical Quarterly* (October 1914).

40   *forty million dollars:* James K. Polk, *The Diary of James K. Polk: During His Presidency 1845 to 1849* (Chicago: Chicago Historical Society, 1910), entry for September 16, 1845. Polk told his cabinet that "one great object" of a mission to the Mexican government entrusted to Representative John Slidell of Louisiana was to purchase upper California and New Mexico "for a pecuniary consideration" and named the price.

41   *"a total absence"*: This and Simpson's recollections are quoted in Cleland, "Early Sentiment II," 132.

41   *"To me they presented"*: Alfred Robinson, *Life in California,* 212–13.

41   *he was ousted:* Bancroft, in *History of California,* vol. 4, 455–57, is not alone in concluding that the bad behavior of Micheltorena's troops was exaggerated by Californio rebels, who saw his ouster as a crucial step in wresting control of their territory from the government.

41   *If war turned out:* Jesse S. Reeves, *American Diplomacy under Tyler and Polk* (Baltimore: The Johns Hopkins Press, 1907), 288–89.

41   *four hundred or so:* Merry, *A Country of Vast Designs,* 301.

42   *"destined ere long"*: *Niles' National Register,* May 17, 1845.

42   *"the fulfillment of our manifest"*: John L. O'Sullivan, "Annexation," *United States Magazine and Democratic Review* (July 1845).

42   *"We only want"*: Smith to Calhoun, December 30, 1845, in *Correspondence of John C. Calhoun,* vol. 2, part 2 (Washington, DC: Government Printing Office, 1900).

43   *This had produced:* Reeves, 104–6.

44   *"designs upon California"*: Buchanan's letter to Slidell, November 10, 1845, in *The Works of James Buchanan,* vol. 6 (Philadelphia: J. B. Lippincott Company, 1909), 304.

3. THE BEAR FLAG REVOLT

45   *"A more peaceful"*: Bancroft, *History of California,* vol. 5, 111.

46   *"Neither would have"*: Bancroft, *History of California* vol. 4, 518.

46   *"There will soon"*: *Niles' National Register,* June 7, 1845, 211.

47   *"The times were"*: Frémont, *Memoirs*, 345.

47   *"into the woods"*: Frémont, *Memoirs*, 344.

47   *"All this gave"*: Frémont, *Memoirs*, 485.

47   *"a pale intellectual"*: Alfred S. Waugh, *Travels in Search of the Elephant* (St. Louis: Missouri Historical Society, 1951), 15.

47   *a book-length refutation*: Ide, *Who Conquered California?*

47   *The most acrid description*: The bulk of Bancroft's treatment of Frémont appears in volume 5 of his *History of California*, from which the following terms are taken.

48   *Contemplating the narrow*: Frémont, *Memoirs*, 512.

49   *their standard practice*: Harlan Hague, "'The Jumping Off Place of the World': California and the Transformation of Thomas O. Larkin," *California History* (December 1991).

49   *"We have neither"*: "Paisano," *New York Herald*, June 12, 1845. For a further discussion of Larkin's newspaper correspondence, see Hague and Langum, *Thomas O. Larkin*, 108–11.

49   *a secret letter*: Larkin Papers, vol. 4, 45–46.

49   *"a secret mission"*: Polk, *The Diary of James K. Polk*, October 30, 1845.

50   *"I was engaged"*: Frémont, *Memoirs*, 454.

50   *"immediately retire beyond"*: José Castro to Frémont, March 3, 1869, in Mary Lee Spence and Donald Jackson (eds.), *The Expeditions of John Charles Frémont, vol. 2* (Urbana: University of Illinois Press, 1973), 74–75. (Henceforth, *Expeditions*.)

50   *"General Castro's breach"*: Frémont, *Memoirs*, 459.

50   *"your encamping"*: Larkin to Frémont, March 8, 1846, in *Expeditions*, vol. 2, 79.

50   *"If we are unjustly attacked"*: Frémont to Larkin, March 9, 1846, in *Expeditions*, vol. 2, 81.

51   *"The information through"*: Frémont, *Memoirs*, 488–89.

51   *"War with Mexico"*: Frémont, *Memoirs*, 490.

51   *Whether he hesitated*: Among his biographers, Chaffin, in *Pathfinder*, 322, calls Frémont a "nervous prevaricator" and cites the absence of legal authority for his participation in the Bear Flag Revolt; Inskeep, *Imperfect Union*, 144, cites "indecision," conjecturing that Frémont, notwithstanding his braggadocio, did not think he could prevail against Castro's forces (153); and Bancroft (*History of California*, vol. 5, 90–91) implies that as an act of personal ambition, he was waiting to see how the revolt turned out before claiming to be involved— indeed, claiming leadership.

51   *"not at liberty"*: Ide, *Who Conquered California?*, 34.

52   *"all foreigners"*: Ide, *Who Conquered California?*, 26.

52   *"after having provoked"*: Ide, *Who Conquered California?*, 25.

52   *Bancroft's conclusion*: Ide, *Who Conquered California?*, 85.

52 *"not wearing a uniform"*: Mariano Guadalupe Vallejo, *Recuerdos: Historical and Personal Remembrances Relating to Alta California, 1769–1849,* trans. Rose Marie Beebe (Norman: University of Oklahoma Press, 2023), 1248.

52 *"a large group"*: Rosalia Vallejo Leese, "History of the Bear Party," June 1874, manuscript, Bancroft Library, University of California.

52 *"The sun was"*: Ide, *Who Conquered California?,* 42.

53 *These allowed:* The articles of capitulation are in Bancroft, *History of California,* vol. 5, 113–14, note 24.

53 *Responsibility for its design:* Ide, *Who Conquered California?,* 48.

54 *"I decided"*: Frémont, *Memoirs,* 520.

54 *"There were Americans"*: Fred Blackburn Rogers, *William Brown Ide, Bear Flagger* (San Francisco: John Howell Books, 1962), 53.

54 *"our squadron"*: Polk to Congress, December 8, 1846; see https://millercenter .org/the-presidency/presidential-speeches/december-8-1846-second-annual -message-congress.

54 *A notable defeat: Expeditions,* xxxiv.

55 *Eighteen American men:* Lisbeth Haas, "War in California, 1846–1848," *California History* (July 1997).

55 *This pact:* The Cahuenga Articles of Capitulation are in *Expeditions,* 253–54.

55 *In truculent written:* See Kearny to Stockton and Stockton to Kearny, both January 16, 1847, *Expeditions,* 263–64.

55 *In the meantime:* The only mark Frémont left on California as governor may have been his purchase of Alcatraz Island as a possible fortress from which to monitor bay traffic. Frémont agreed to a price of $5,000 to be paid to Francis Temple, whose family claimed the property by virtue of a Mexican grant. Frémont's superiors, however, considered the purchase to be wildly outside his authority, refused to pay, and listed the deal among the charges against him in his court-martial. Frémont subsequently put up the $5,000 himself and claimed Alcatraz as his property. The government ignored him and developed fortifications on the island on its own. Frémont's heirs finally ceased pursuing the claim in the 1890s.

56 *"The present system"*: *California Star,* February 13, 1847.

57 *Historians debate:* Pitt, *Decline of the Californios,* 79–82.

57 *"Large portions"*: Ruckel to Mason, December 28, 1857, in Bancroft, *History of California,* vol. 6, 268, note 31. See also Pitt, *Decline of the Californios,* 41.

57 *The merchants originally:* Roger D. McGrath, "A Violent Birth: Disorder, Crime, and Law Enforcement, 1849–1890," *California History* (January 2003).

57 *During the next:* Bancroft, *Popular Tribunals,* vol. 1, 101.

4. THE SORDID CRY OF GOLD

59 *"Now lock"*: John A. Sutter and James W. Marshall, "The Discovery of Gold in California," *Hutchings' California Magazine* (November 1857). The article comprises separate reminiscences by Sutter and Marshall.

60 *"I believe this"*: Bancroft, *History of California,* vol. 6, quoting reminiscences he obtained from Sutter.

60 *"I declared this"*: Sutter and Marshall, "The Discovery."

60 *"I have found"*: Sutter and Marshall, "The Discovery."

61 *He had studied:* Gay, *James W. Marshall,* 147.

61 *"Gold mining is"*: "Dame Shirley," letter 15, April 10, 1852, *Pioneer* (May 1855).

61 *The average daily:* Paul, *California Gold,* 120.

61 *It is true:* Wage rates of the era are in "History of Wages in the United States from Colonial Times to 1928," US Department of Labor, 1934.

62 *Altogether, $670 million:* Thomas Senior Berry, "Gold! But How Much?," *California Historical Quarterly* (Fall 1976). Berry's estimate is based on prices established during the Gold Rush period by the US Mint.

62 *"When everybody is digging"*: The author can find no verified source for the quote or its numerous variants in Twain's works.

62 *54 K Street:* Lavender, *The Great Persuader,* 49.

62 *"saw that night"*: Bancroft, *History of California,* vol. 6, 39.

62 *It was inscribed:* Dana, *Two Years Before the Mast,* 302.

63 *"made a discovery"*: Bancroft, *History of California,* vol. 6, 43.

63 *"I have something"*: Bancroft, *History of California,* vol. 6, 43.

63 *"A few fools"*: Bancroft, *History of California,* vol. 6, 54.

63 *"it was in the line"*: E. C. Kemble, "Confirming the Gold Discovery," *Century Illustrated Monthly Magazine* (February 1891).

64 *"anywhere you're a mind"*: Kemble, "Confirming the Gold Discovery."

64 *"the reputed wealth"*: *California Star,* May 20, 1848.

64 *"we saw a few"*: *California Star,* April 1, 1848.

64 *"Brannan took his hat off"*: "Extracts from the Diary of Henry W. Bigler," *Utah Historical Quarterly* (July 1932), 150.

64 *"Yesterday and to-day"*: J. Tyrwhitt Brooks, *Four Months Among the Gold-Finders* (Paris: A. and W. Galignani, 1849), https://tile.loc.gov/storage-services//service/gdc/calbk/125.pdf.

64 *"The whole country"*: *Californian,* May 24, 1848.

65 *"A man would pay"*: Bancroft, *History of California,* vol. 6, 93.

65 *"his negro waiter"*: Brooks, *Four Months Among the Gold-Finders.*

65 *"our servants have run"*: Colton, *Three Years in California,* 248.

65   *"For the present"*: Jones to J. Y. Mason, November 2, 1848, published in Joseph Warren Revere, *A Tour of Duty in California* (New York: C. S. Francis & Co., 1849), 253–55.

66   *"reduced to a mere skeleton"*: Rich to General N. Towson, October 23, 1848, in Revere, 256.

66   *"all, or nearly all"*: Mason to Brigadier General Roger Jones, August 17, 1848. This is Mason's official report, which helped trigger the forty-niners' frenzy and was largely written by Sherman.

66   *a "toll" or "rent"*: Bagley, *Scoundrel's Tale*, 270, quoting journals of Azariah Smith and John Borrowman.

68   *Some ten thousand of them:* deBuys, *Salt Dreams*, 34.

68   *"tall, strong and alert"*: John Woodhouse Audubon, *Audubon's Western Journal: 1849–1850* (Cleveland: Arthur H. Clark, 1906), 34–37.

69   *"There was not"*: Audubon, *Audubon's Western Journal*, 166–67.

69   *"Truly here was a scene"*: *Audubon's Western Journal*, 167.

69   *"Dead mules by scores"*: Bieber, *Southern Trails*, 229–30.

69   *water "detestable"*: Bieber, *Southern Trails*, 234.

69   *"One man of the party"*: John S. Robb in Bieber, *Southern Trails*, 218.

70   *"broke out in"*: A. B. Stout, "First Steamship Pioneers," *Association of First Steamship Pioneers*, 84.

70   *it was greeted:* Bancroft, *History of California*, vol. 6, 133–34.

71   *By 1861:* Gerald D. Nash, "A Veritable Revolution," *California History* (December 1998).

71   *"Gold Rush widows"*: Malcolm J. Rohrbough, "The California Gold Rush as a National Experience," *California History* (April 1998).

71   *"I never want"*: Rohrbough, "The California Gold Rush."

71   *"There never yet"*: *New York Daily Tribune*, January 4, 1849.

72   *"Why don't you dig"*: Young, *Discourses of Brigham Young*, 458.

72   *they were partially:* Kenneth Owens, "Far from Zion: The Frayed Ties Between California's Gold Rush Saints and LDS President Brigham Young," *California History* (January 2012).

72   *"Bro{ther} Brigham has long"*: Young to Brannan, April 5, 1849, in Bagley, *Scoundrel's Tale*, 286.

72   *A cholera outbreak:* Bancroft, *History of California*, vol. 6, 231.

72   *"Let the citizens"*: William Taylor, *Seven Years' Street Preaching in San Francisco, California* (New York: Carlton and Porter, 1856), 114.

72   *"terribly dusty"*: Marryat, *Mountains and Molehills*, 203–4.

73   *On June 10: Alta California*, June 11, 1851. Brannan denied all involvement in a notice he placed in the *Alta California* of June 13.

5. THE THIRTY-FIRST STAR

75 *"Suffice it to say"*: Helper, *The Land of Gold*, 36–37.

76 "We are in fact": Burnett, *Recollections and Opinions*, 320.

76 *"Every man carried"*: Crosby, *Reminiscences of California*, 42.

76 *"he was powerless"*: Crosby, *Reminiscences of California*, 33.

77 *The forty-eight elected*: J. Ross Browne, "Report of the Debates in the Convention of California, on the Formation of the State Constitution, in September and October, 1849," https://digitalcommons.csumb.edu/hornbeck_usa_3_d/18/, 478–79 (hereafter cited as "Debates").

77 *"carried an enormous"*: Crosby, *Reminiscences of California*, 46.

77 *"I don't believe"*: Crosby, *Reminiscences of California*, 38–39.

77 *"Money amounts to"*: Browne to Lucy, August 22, 1849, in Browne, *Letters*, 125–26.

78 *"neither slavery nor"*: "Debates," 44.

78 *"All here are diggers"*: Colton, *Three Years in California*, 374.

78 *Their political adversaries*: Smith, *Freedom's Frontier*, 8.

78 *"It would appear"*: "Debates," 49.

79 *"every prominent and valuable"*: "Debates," 170.

80 *"special cases"*: "Debates," 341.

80 *property of married women*: John F. Burns, "Taming the Elephant: An Introduction to California's Statehood and Constitutional Era," *California History* (January 2003).

80 *"the God of nature"*: "Debates," 259.

80 *"we can prove"*: "Debates," 18.

80 *"the most creative"*: Judson A. Grenier, "'Officialdom': California State Government, 1849–1879," *California History* (January 2003).

81 *"Boys, let's go"*: Crosby, *Reminiscences of California*, 58–59.

81 *"There was no order"*: Kelly, *An Excursion to California*, 309.

81 *"rump parliament"*: Mary Joan Elliott, "The 1851 Journal of M.V.B. Fowler," *Southern California Quarterly* (September 1968).

81 *"an infamous, ignorant"*: Lawrence Clark Powell, *Philosopher Pickett* (Berkeley: University of California Press, 1942), 49.

81 *"there was nothing"*: Bancroft, *History of California*, vol. 6, 311, note 5.

81 *"they had to begin"*: Burnett, *Recollections and Opinions*, 361.

82 *"Act for the Government"*: Statutes of California, chapter 133, 1850.

82 *Taylor confided*: Polk, March 5, 1849, *The Diary of James K. Polk*, 376.

82 *"the only safeguard"*: "Memoirs of Hon. William M. Gwin," *California Historical Society Quarterly* (March 1940), 16.

83 *"California will become"*: *Congressional Globe*, Thirty-First Congress, first session, 451–55.

83 *Webster replied: Congressional Globe,* Thirty-First Congress, first session 476–84.

83 *"She made a constitution": Congressional Globe,* Thirty-First Congress, first session, 260–69.

84 *"Here was a community":* Bancroft, *History of California,* vol. 6, 350, note 50.

84 *"a glorious day": Mississippian,* January 14, 1853, in Jason Gillmer, "Litigating Slavery's Reach: A Story of Race, Rights, and the Law During the California Gold Rush," *Loyola of Los Angeles Law Review* (March 19, 2021).

84 *The California measure:* Gillmer, "Litigating Slavery's Reach."

85 *"a place where":* Gillmer, "Litigating Slavery's Reach."

85 *"The ability and willingness":* Ray R. Albin, "The Perkins Case: The Ordeal of Three Slaves in Gold Rush California," *California History* (December 1988).

85 *"could be counted":* Cole, *Memoirs,* 113.

86 *Among Cole's arguments:* Gillmer, "Litigating Slavery's Reach."

86 *neither the state: In re Perkins,* 2 Cal. 438 (1852).

87 *"the adoption of a free":* Cole, *Memoirs,* 96.

87 *"I am satisfied": In re Perkins.*

87 *Some sources reported:* Albin, "The Perkins Case."

87 *the 1858 case of Archy: Ex parte Archy,* 9 Cal. 147.

6. THE AGE OF GENOCIDE

89 *"During the night": Northern Californian,* February 29, 1860.

90 *Over the following:* Madley, *An American Genocide,* 283.

90 *"exterminating the Indians": Daily Alta California,* February 29, 1860.

90 *The names of:* Madley, 610, note 127.

90 *Their diets included:* Madley, 18–21.

90 *"It is now impossible":* Stevenson to Thomas J. Henley, December 31, 1853, in Heizer, *The Destruction of California Indians,* 13–16.

91 *"Let a tribe":* Powers, *Tribes of California,* 404–5.

91 *"there were not many":* Madley, *An American Genocide,* 30.

91 *By the 1880:* 1880 Census, Volume 1: Statistics of the Population of the United States, 379.

92 *He received a delegation:* Frémont, *Memoirs,* 473.

92 *"drive them back":* Camp, *Kit Carson,* 17.

92 *Upon spotting:* Madley, *An American Genocide,* 45–46.

92 *"The number killed":* Camp, *Kit Carson,* 17.

92 *"This was a rude":* Frémont, *Memoirs,* 517.

92 *"had accomplished what":* Camp, *Kit Carson,* 17.

92 *"the daring and predatory": New York Herald,* December 1, 1846.

93 *a cannon:* Madley, *An American Genocide,* 78.

93 *"We do not know"*: Bancroft, *History of California,* vol. 7, 474.

93 *Ethnographers would come*: Madley, *An American Genocide,* 23.

93 *"the California Indians"*: Ellison, *California and the Nation,* 79.

93 *"occasionally took a bullock"*: Statement of Thomas Knight, in Heizer, *The Destruction of California Indians,* 246–47.

94 *"carrie out all"*: William Ralganal Benson, "The Stone and Kelsey 'Massacre' on the Shores of Clear Lake in 1849: The Indian Viewpoint," *California Historical Society Quarterly* (September 1932).

94 *"a battle-hardened"*: Madley, *An American Genocide,* 115.

94 *"waste no time"*: Madley, *An American Genocide,* 128.

94 *"a perfect slaughter"*: Captain Nathaniel Lyon to Major E.R.S. Canby, May 22, 1850, in Heizer, *The Destruction of California Indians,* 244–46.

94 *"two good suits"*: For provisions of the Bidwell bill, see Madley, *An American Genocide,* 157.

95 *"An Act for the Government"*: Heizer, *The Destruction of California Indians,* 220–24.

95 *"put in jail"*: Browne, *The Indians of California,* 2–3.

95 *Amendments enacted in 1860*: Madley, *An American Genocide,* 286–87.

95 *"I am informed"*: *Congressional Globe,* May 26, 1860, 2366.

96 *The settlers, he said*: *Congressional Globe,* May 26, 1860, 2367.

96 *"it was an act"*: Hanson to William P. Dole, U.S. Commissioner of Indian Affairs, December 31, 1861, in *Report of the Commissioner of Indian Affairs for the Year 1862,* 313–16.

97 *"but one alternative"*: The letter is in *Daily Alta California,* January 14, 1851.

97 *"cheaper to feed"*: McKee, Barbour, and Wozencraft, in Annual Report of the Commissioner of Indian Affairs for 1850, 224. (Emphasis in the original.)

97 *By January 1852*: William H. Ellison, "The Federal Indian Policy in California, 1846–1860," *Mississippi Valley Historical Review* (June 1922).

97 *"indispensable servants"*: *Journal of the Senate 1852,* 597–601.

97 *The assembly document*: *California State Assembly Journal 1852,* 202–5.

98 *They would not be*: Madley, *An American Genocide,* 168.

98 *"While we are discussing"*: Henry Rowe Schoolcraft, *Archives of Aboriginal Knowledge,* vol. 3 (Philadelphia: J. B. Lippincott, 1860), 210. See also Madley, *An American Genocide,* 168–70.

98 *"Driven from their fishing"*: Beale to Lea, November 22, 1852, Senate Ex. Docs., 33rd Congress, Special Session, Doc. 4, 377–80. (Emphasis in the original.)

98 *appropriating $250,000*: Ellison, "Federal Indian Policy." See also Madley, *An American Genocide,* 170–71.

99 *"We are aggrieved"*: Tehama County citizens to Secretary of the Interior, 1859, in Heizer, *The Destruction of California Indians,* 137–39.

99   *"An honest Indian Agent"*: Browne, *Adventures in the Apache Country*, 484.

99   *"little more than"*: Browne to Charles E. Mix, Commissioner of Indian Affairs, October 8, 1858, in Heizer, *The Destruction of California Indians,* 116.

99   *"Sad experience taught"*: Browne, *The Indians of California*, 67–68.

100   *In part, this was because:* Madley, *An American Genocide,* 515.

100   *But convict leasing:* Madley, *An American Genocide,* 333.

100   *Governor Gavin Newsom:* Executive Order N-15-19, June 18, 2019.

101   *voted to remove:* "Hastings Legacy Review Committee Report," July 29, 2020, https://www.uchastings.edu/wp-content/uploads/2020/12/HLRC-Recommendations.pdf.

101   *"Wherever they attempted"*: Browne, *The Indians of California*, 70–73.

7. "THE CHINESE MUST GO": SAN FRANCISCO AFTER THE GOLD RUSH

105   *"by rowdies"*: Muscatine, *Old San Francisco,* 403.

106   *"few or none"*: Hittell, *A History of the City*, 460.

106   *city records:* Hittell, *A History of the City*, 462.

106   *six to ten thousand:* Soulé et al., *The Annals of San Francisco,* 410.

106   *Under King's editorship:* Hittell, *A History of the City*, 470.

107   *"public respectability"*: The description is from Royce, *California*, 434.

107   *"dark of complexion"*: Coblentz, *Villains and Vigilantes,* 114–15.

107   *"for the sole purpose"*: Coblentz, *Villains and Vigilantes,* 135–36.

107   *"exciting, dramatic"*: David A. Williams, *David C. Broderick: A Political Portrait* (San Marino, CA: Huntington Library, 1969), 12.

107   *"If the jury"*: Hittell, *A History of the City*, 473.

107   *"richly figured"*: *Daily Alta*, December 2, 1855.

108   *"The money of the gambler"*: *Daily Evening Bulletin,* January 17, 1856.

108   *"had made a business"*: Royce, *California*, 433.

108   *"honest, brave"*: William T. Coleman, "San Francisco Vigilance Committees," *Century Illustrated Monthly* (November 1891).

108   *The new body:* Hittell, *A History of the City*, 567.

108   *"no thief, burglar"*: Bancroft, *Popular Tribunals*, vol. 2, 112.

108   *"the best organized"*: Don Warner, "Anti-Corruption Crusade or 'Businessman's Revolution'?: An Inquiry into the 1856 Vigilance Committee," *California Legal History* (2011).

109   *"throw aside and abjure"*: Percy V. Long, "Consolidated City and County Government of San Francisco," *American Political Science Review* (February 1912).

109   *"There are two thousand"*: Frank F. Fargo, *A True and Minute History of the Assassination of James King of Wm.* (San Francisco: Whitton, Towne & Co., 1856), 18.

110   *"Business Man's"*: Royce, *California*, 461.

110 *"double improved"*: Hittell, *A History of the City*, 461.

110 *"a state of insurrection"*: Johnson's proclamation is in Bancroft, *Popular Tribunals*, vol. 2, 297–98.

110 *when the army refused*: Sherman, *Memoirs*, 130–31.

111 *"black list"*: A running count is in Hittell, *A History of the City*, 460, but it is unclear whether Hittell had a full count.

111 *"the atmosphere morally"*: Coleman, "San Francisco Vigilance Committees."

111 *Of the city's thirty-five thousand*: Starr, *California*, 106.

112 *Women accounted for*: Commonwealth Club of California, "The Population of California" (1946), 192.

112 *"home and hearth"*: David A. Johnson, "Vigilance and the Law: The Moral Authority of Popular Justice in the Far West," *American Quarterly*, Winter 1981.

112 *"The people of the Flowery Land"*: Appendix to the Opening Statement and Brief on the Chinese Question, Joint Committee of the Senate and House of Representatives (1877).

113 *"one of the most worthy"*: Charles J. McClain Jr., "The Chinese Struggle for Civil Rights in Nineteenth-Century America: The First Phase, 1850–1870," *California Law Review* (July 1984).

113 *"A large business"*: J.D. Borthwick, *Three Years in California* (Edinburgh: William Blackwood and Sons, 1857), 79.

113 *only three Chinese*: Coolidge, *Chinese Immigration*, 498.

113 *Bigler called on*: McClain, "The Chinese Struggle."

113 *"In order to enhance"*: *Journal of the Senate of the State of California*, April 23, 1852.

113 *"subjected to many"*: Daniel Cleveland to J. Ross Browne, July 27, 1868, in *Papers Relating to Foreign Affairs, Accompanying the Annual Message of the President to the Third Session of the Fortieth Congress*. Cleveland was a San Francisco lawyer who had made a study of the Chinese experience in California; Browne was then the US minister (effectively ambassador) to Peking.

114 *"soon see them"*: *People v. Hall*, 4 Cal. 399 (1854).

114 *"employing China or Cooly"*: *Alta California*, September 14, 1859.

114 *"Asia, with her"*: Sandmeyer, *The Anti-Chinese Movement*, 43–44.

114 *Chinese immigration*: Sandmeyer, *The Anti-Chinese Movement*, 16.

114 *"Without them"*: Leland Stanford, "Central Pacific Railroad Statement Made to the President of the United States, and Secretary of the Interior, on the Progress of the Work," October 10, 1865.

114 *California remained the epicenter*: Sandmeyer, *The Anti-Chinese Movement*, 21.

115 *"was accepted as proof"*: Sandmeyer, *The Anti-Chinese Movement*, 20.

115 *"The completion of the railroad"*: Henry George, "What the Railroad Will Bring Us," *Overland Monthly* (October 1868).

115 *"cursed the railroad"*: Samuel Bowles, *Springfield Republican*, February 12, 1870, in Cross, *A History of the Labor Movement,* 63.

116 *protecting "white labor"*: San Francisco *Chronicle*, September 14, 1870.

116 *An anti-Chinese mass meeting*: Cross, *A History of the Labor Movement,* 66.

116 *In an 1879 opinion: How Ah Know v. Nunan*, 12 F. Cas. 252 (CCD Cal. 1879).

116 *"the anti-Chinese party"*: George, "The Kearney Agitation in California."

117 *"in some respects"*: *Bulletin*, December 22, 1874.

117 *Evidence soon emerged*: Starr, *California,* 122–23.

118 *"There is more"*: *Bulletin*, November 16, 1875.

118 *"quiet, orderly"*: Cross, *A History of the Labor Movement,* 89.

118 *"To Chinatown"*: George, "The Kearney Agitation in California."

118 *"the venom with which"*: George, "The Kearney Agitation in California."

119 *"a little judicious"*: Cross, *A History of the Labor Movement,* 95.

119 *"If I give an order"*: *Bulletin*, November 1, 1877.

119 *"the Chinese question"*: Dennis Kearney, *Speeches of Dennis Kearney, Labor Champion* (New York: Jesse Haney and Co., 1878), 27.

119 *As critics had predicted*: See *In re Tiburcio Parrott*, 1 F. 481 (1880).

120 *Chinese arrivals*: Sandmeyer, *The Anti-Chinese Movement,* 16.

120 *In 1880 the party elected*: McWilliams, *California,* 176.

121 *"another breed"*: Daniels, *The Politics of Prejudice,* 20.

8. THE OCTOPUS

122 *Dignitaries huddled*: Daggett, *Chapters on the History,* 65. See also Tutorow, *The Governor,* 220.

122 *"with no delay"*: Tutorow, *The Governor,* 220.

123 *"a bunch of local"*: Charles Frederick Carter, *When Railroads Were New* (New York: Henry Holt and Company, 1910), 238.

123 *"It is difficult"*: Carl I. Wheat, "A Sketch of the Life of Theodore D. Judah," *California Historical Society Quarterly* (September 1925).

123 *"heard his story"*: Wheat, "A Sketch."

123 *"Everything he did"*: Wheat, "A Sketch."

124 *"There was no"*: Strong testimony, *Pacific Railway Commission,* vol. 5, 2839 (hereafter cited as *PRC*).

124 *"Less than a dozen"*: Cole, *Memoirs,* 148.

124 *Other than Cole*: Lewis, *The Big Four,* 14.

124 *He sailed*: Lewis, *The Big Four,* 161.

125 *"the ambition"*: Lewis, *The Big Four,* 112.

125 *Stanford hailed*: Lewis, *The Big Four,* 116.

125 *"I had always"*: Bancroft, *History of California,* vol. 7, 546.

125 *"thin as a fence post"*: Lewis, *The Big Four,* 90.

125 *"When Hopkins wanted"*: Lewis, *The Big Four,* 91.

126 *"none of them"*: Bancroft, *California,* vol. 7, 545.

126 *Huntington told:* PRC, vol. 7, 3774. The lower estimate comes from Bancroft, *History of California,* vol. 7, 545, note 7. Tutorow, *The Governor,* 193, places the assessed value of the Big Four's properties at only $118,000.

126 *"We agreed"*: Cole, *Memoirs.*

126 *By the time:* For municipal and state contributions, see Daggett, *Chapters on the History,* 26.

127 *Judah submitted:* The revised cost estimates are in Lavender, *The Great Persuader,* 99.

127 *"We looked down"*: PRC, vol. 6, 2618.

127 *"Over slumbering California"*: *Alta California,* December 15, 1866.

128 *"for on that curtain"*: George, *The Life of Henry George,* 100. As his son reported, Henry George related the anecdote to an audience at a San Francisco speaking engagement in February 1890.

128 *"no one who walks"*: George, "What the Railroad Will Bring Us."

129 *"with customary energy"*: Cross, *A History of the Labor Movement,* 62.

129 *"Chicago was there"*: Cross, *A History of the Labor Movement,* 62.

129 *In effect, the railroad:* Drabelle, *The Great American Railroad War,* 24.

129 *Contract and Finance was eventually:* Harry J. Carman and Charles H. Mueller, "The Contract and Finance Company and the Central Pacific Railroad," *Journal of American History* (December 1927).

129 *Under questioning:* Lavender, *The Great Persuader,* 293.

130 *the resulting behemoth:* Daggett, *Chapters on the History,* 140.

130 *"one has only"*: Ayers, *Gold and Sunshine,* 280–81.

130 *"It looked as if"*: Ayers, *Gold and Sunshine,* 282.

9. THE SHADOW OF MUSSEL SLOUGH

131 *"Big Four-and-One-Half"*: Ramirez, *The Octopus Speaks,* 5.

131 *The so-called Colton:* Ramirez, *The Octopus Speaks,* 6ff.

131 *"the worst body"*: Huntington to Colton, April 9, 1878, in Ramirez, *The Octopus Speaks,* 490.

132 *"a slippery fellow"*: Huntington to Colton, October 19, 1879, in Ramirez, *The Octopus Speaks,* 5.

132 *"The boys are"*: Huntington to Colton, January 12, 1878, in Ramirez, *The Octopus Speaks,* 452.

132   *"From San Francisco to Ogden"*: Daggett, *Chapters on the History*, 182.

133   *In 1883:* Gerald D. Nash, "The California Railroad Commission, 1876–1911," *Southern California Quarterly* (December 1962).

133   *"he seemed anxious"*: Nash, "The California Railroad Commission."

133   *"sudden acquisition of wealth"*: Daggett, *Chapters on the History*, 198.

133   *Historians continue:* Among the treatments of Mussel Slough on the historical bookshelf, all of which and more have been consulted by the present author, are Brown, *The Mussel Slough Tragedy*; McWilliams, *California*, 95; Deverell, *Railroad Crossing*, 56–57; Lewis, *The Big Four*, 280–87; and Orsi, *Sunset Limited*, 92–103.

133   *its sixty thousand acres:* Rice et al., *The Elusive Eden*, 236.

134   *Although the railroad:* The land transfer issue is described by Orsi, *Sunset Limited*, 77–78.

134   *"from $2.50"*: Brown, *Mussel Slough Tragedy*, 34.

134   *In practice:* An analysis of land records is in Barbara M. Bristow, "Mussel Slough Tragedy: Railroad Struggle or Land Gamble," master's thesis, Fresno State College (1971).

134   *"murder the red-eyed"*: Orsi, *Sunset Limited*, 469, note 22.

134   *"strike the first blow"*: Rice et al., *The Elusive Eden*, 240.

134   *In a series:* Rice et al., *The Elusive Eden*, 246.

134   *They were assembled:* Orsi, *Sunset Limited*, 96–97.

135   *The most credible:* Brown, *Mussel Slough Tragedy* 64ff.

135   *Eventually he was:* Brown, *Mussel Slough Tragedy* 111.

135   *Settlers trying:* Brown, *Mussel Slough Tragedy* 78–79.

135   *Charles Crocker led:* Lewis, *The Big Four*, 286.

136   *"What chief executive"*: Bassett, "Dear Pard," quoted in Daggett, *Chapters on the History*, 216.

136   *The three governors:* Rice et al., *The Elusive Eden*, 344.

136   *Herrin paid:* Bean, 150. See also McAfee, *California's Railroad Era*, 223.

136   *When the journalist:* Older, *My Own Story*, 17.

136   *"The entire State"*: Older, *My Own Story*, 14.

137   *"the chief consideration"*: Deverell, *Railroad Crossing*, 132.

137   *"men who have"*: Daggett, *Chapters on the History*, 402.

137   *"Mr. Huntington is not"*: McWilliams, *Bierce*, 239.

138   *"My price is"*: This version is from Alex Beam, "Ambrose Bierce, Mon Amour," *Boston Globe*, June 24, 2008. Numerous alternate versions exist, including one in McWilliams, *Bierce*, 240. According to Bierce's own version, published under his own name in 1899, the exchange occurred between Huntington and a Bierce intermediary (Drabelle, *The Great American Railroad War*, 152).

138   *"San Francisco Wild"*: *San Francisco Examiner*, January 12, 1897.

138   *access to which*: Tejani, *A Machine to Move*, 297–300.

138   *"seal its grip"*: Tejani, *A Machine to Move*, 297–300.

139   *"shall in good faith"*: Tutorow, *The Governor*, 810.

139   *"studied malice"*: Tutorow, *The Governor*, 812.

139   *"he appeared to have"*: Bertha Berner, *Incidents in the Life of Mrs. Leland Stanford* (Ann Arbor, MI: Edwards Brothers, 1934), 76.

10. THE FIRST WATER WAR

140   *"The West begins"*: Bernard DeVoto, "The West: A Plundered Province," *Harper's Monthly* (August 1934).

141   *both had accumulated*: Igler, *Industrial Cowboys*, 16.

141   *Miller tended to shun*: Igler, *Industrial Cowboys*, 17.

141   *In this way*: Treadwell, *The Cattle King*, 55.

141   *"a farce and a sham"*: Greeley, *Recollections of a Busy Life*, 231.

142   *According to an enduring*: The story of the horse-drawn boat appears in McWilliams, *California*, 96. Treadwell, however, in *The Cattle King*, 293, disputes it, describing it as a rumor referring to someone else.

142   *"They have established"*: "Final Report: Commission on Industrial Relations," vol. 6, 5456.

142   *"There was not sufficient"*: Torchiana, *California Gringos*, 157–58.

142   *"There is not another"*: Powers, *Afoot and Alone*, 314.

143   *"have taken every means"*: "Final Report: Commission on Industrial Relations," vol. 6, 5454.

143   *160 miles*: George, *Our Land*, 72.

143   *"sleep every night"*: See McWilliams, *California*, 98. The quote was challenged by Treadwell, who dismissed it as journalists' exaggeration (Treadwell, *The Cattle King*, 152). As has already been noted, however, Treadwell's biography might not be reliable in discussing circumstances that place his subject in a bad light.

143   *"induce emigration"*: *Journal of the Senate of the State of California* (January 5, 1853), 22.

143   *the largest 122 farms*: Gerald D. Nash, "The California State Land Office 1858–1898," *Huntington Library Quarterly* (August 1964).

143   *"the lords of California"*: George, *Our Land*, 72.

144   *There was no state*: George, *Our Land*, 37.

144   *"The railroad was"*: Treadwell, *The Cattle King*, 201.

144   *"Assessors could not"*: Treadwell, *The Cattle King*, 201.

145   *"the whole country"*: Miller to Lux, March 23, 1877, in David Igler, "Industrial

Cowboys: Corporate Ranging in Late Nineteenth Century California," *Agricultural History* (Spring 1995).

145   Lux v. Haggin: 69 Cal. 255 (1886).

145   *Notwithstanding his exotic:* Phelps, *Contemporary Biography,* 325–28.

146   *"a ring of mercenary":* San Francisco *Argonaut,* quoted in Pisani, *From the Family Farm,* 194.

146   *Acting as land agent:* Donald J. Pisani, "Land Monopoly in Nineteenth-Century California," *Agricultural History* (Autumn 1991).

146   *three times as much:* Pisani, "Land Monopoly."

146   *"My object has not":* Haggin, "The Desert Lands of Kern County, California," quoted in Hundley, *The Great Thirst,* 95. A similar quote appeared under Haggin's name in the *Bakersfield Californian,* May 20, 1880; see Pisani, "Land Monopoly."

146   *He cut off:* Pisani, *From the Family Farm,* 200.

147   *"green and slimy":* Wallace M. Morgan, *History of Kern County, California* (Los Angeles: Historic Record Company, 1914), 88.

147   *They tried to strike:* Hundley, *The Great Thirst,* 96.

147   *"deliverance through irrigation":* Worster, *Rivers of Empire,* 99.

148   *"The thirsty ground":* John Muir, *San Francisco Evening Bulletin,* October 29, 1874.

148   *"there is more:"* Treadwell, *The Cattle King,* 93–94.

148   *"all that stands":* San Francisco *Chronicle,* January 17, 1887, quoted in Pisani, "Land Monopoly."

148   *one and a half million acres:* Hundley, *The Great Thirst,* 102.

148   *All but a handful:* Rice et al., *The Elusive Eden,* 288. See also Hundley, *The Great Thirst,* 103.

149   *"golden age":* Rice et al., *The Elusive Eden,* 288.

149   *those two perennially:* M. Catherine Miller, "Water Rights and the Bankruptcy of Judicial Action: The Case of *Herminghaus v. Southern California Edison,*" *Pacific Historical Review* (February 1989).

149   *riparian landowners' rights:* Herminghaus v. Southern California Edison, 200 Cal. 81 (1926).

149   *"reasonably required":* California Constitution, article 10, section 2. The language, still in place as of this writing, is drawn directly from the 1928 constitutional amendment.

11. "CITY OF THE DAMNED"

150   *Hopper's ears were:* James Hopper, "Our San Francisco," *Everybody's Magazine* (June 1906).

151   *It had begun:* US Geological Survey, "The Northern California Earthquake,

April 19, 1906," https://earthquake.usgs.gov/earthquakes/events/1906calif/virtualtour/earthquake.php.

151 *a recurrent image:* See, for example, Lawrence J. Treat to Eleanor Treat, "I can best liken my sensations to those of a rat being shaken by a bull terrier," and Ivan S. Rankin's recollection, "I waked up feeling something shaking me like a dog does a rat in its jaws," both in 1906 Earthquake and Fire Collection, Bancroft Library, University of California (hereafter cited as EFC).

151 *buried by debris:* Philip L. Fradkin, *The Great Earthquake and Firestorms of 1906* (Berkeley: University of California Press, 2005), 70.

152 *as much as $1 billion:* "San Francisco Conflagration Report of the Committee of 5 to the Thirty-Five Companies," December 31, 1906.

152 *average annual wage:* Gilson Willets, et al., *Workers of the Nation, vol. II* (New York: P. F. Collier and Son, 1903), 1047.

152 *the Baltimore fire:* Sherry H. Olson, *Baltimore: The Building of an American City* (Baltimore: Johns Hopkins University Press, 1980), 247.

152 *"better residential section":* "San Francisco Conflagration Report."

152 *Among the destroyed:* Fradkin, *The Great Earthquake*, 187.

152 *"tore about":* Recollections of Caruso's reaction are from Fradkin, 90–91, quoting the *Argonaut*, November 6 through November 20, 1926.

152 *"Within an hour":* Jack London, "The Story of an Eye-Witness," *Collier's* (May 5, 1906).

153 *"that awful shock":* Baxter to parents, April 23, 1906, EFC.

153 *Dolly Brown, a secretary:* Brown to Henry Anderson, April 21, 1906, EFC.

154 *"everything is gone":* "Account by Margaret Brindley," EFC.

154 *"filled with people":* Letter, Charles Ross to A. M. Von Metzke, April 26, 1906, EFC.

154 *"entangled in the debris":* Fradkin, *The Great Earthquake*, 56.

154 *"dropped the fronts":* Captain Kelly (undated), EFC.

154 *"enjoyed my first":* Twain, *Roughing It*, 316–17.

155 *"one of the wickedest":* "Providence and the San Francisco Disaster," *Current Literature* (June 1906).

155 *"may have been":* "Providence and the San Francisco Disaster."

155 *"It required a convulsion":* John P. Young, *Journalism in California* (San Francisco: Chronicle Publishing Company, 1915), 171.

156 *"wholesale looting":* Fradkin, *The Great Earthquake*, 292–93.

156 *a free four-page:* Young, *Journalism in California*, 171–74. See also Fradkin, *The Great Earthquake*, 89.

156 *"Many acts of vandalism":* *Call-Chronicle-Examiner*, April 19, 1906. The newspapers' cooperation lasted one day. The *Examiner* secured exclusive access to

the *Tribune*'s printing presses, and the *Chronicle* reached an agreement with the *Oakland Herald* that enabled it to publish on April 20. The *Call* reappeared on April 21.

157 *the use of powder:* Report of Captain Le Vert Coleman of the Artillery Corps, in Greeley, *Recollections of a Busy Life.*

157 *"planned systematically":* "After Earthquake and Fire," *Mining and Scientific Press*, 85.

157 *"We appeared to be":* Leroy Armstrong and J. O. Denny, *Financial California* (San Francisco: Coast Banker Publishing, 1916), 134.

157 *"Are we not damaging":* *San Francisco Call*, May 20, 1906.

158 *"It soon became clear":* Steinbrugge, *Earthquake Hazard,* 39.

158 *599 killed:* Gladys Hansen, "The San Francisco Numbers Game," *California Geology* (December 1987). Hansen's figures, which updated the estimate of 478 that prevailed for decades, were subsequently updated to roughly 3,000; see John M. Glionna, "On Trail of 1906 Quake's Victims," *Los Angeles Times*, February 7, 2005. That is itself regarded as an undercount, however, because it overlooked an untold number of deaths among Chinese residents and members of other ethnic groups.

159 *Special freight trains:* Kennan, *E. H. Harriman,* 69–70.

159 *The Harriman system:* Kennan, *E. H. Harriman,* 72–73.

160 *"It was a cruel":* Charles S. Aiken, "San Francisco's Upraising," *Sunset* (October 1906).

12. THE PROGRESSIVE REVOLUTION

161 *"a friend, not":* *Sacramento Bee*, August 19, 1910, quoted in Lower, *A Bloc of One,* 18.

161 *"Little more than boys":* Steffens, *Autobiography*, vol. 1, 49.

161 *In two documented:* For the attack on Ryan, see Irving McKee, "The Background and Early Career of Hiram Warren Johnson, 1866–1910," *Pacific Historical Review* (February 1850); for the second, see *San Francisco Call*, August 7, 1907.

162 *"struggle that led":* Older, *My Own Story,* 33.

162 *"took toll everywhere":* George Kennan, "The Fight for Reform in San Francisco," *McClure's* (July 1910).

163 *"eat the paint":* Franklin Hichborn, *The "System": As Uncovered by the San Francisco Graft Prosecution* (San Francisco: Press of the James H. Barry Company, 1915), 24, note 18.

163 *The assailant:* "Report on the Causes of Municipal Corruption in San Francisco," January 5, 1910, 41.

163 *"History contains no":* *San Francisco Call*, December 18, 1908.

163 *When he died:* Bean, *Boss Reuf's San Francisco*, 316.

164 *Through timely:* Tom Sitton, "California's Practical Idealist, John Randolph Haynes," *California History* (March 1988).

164 *Haynes's campaign:* Sitton, "California's Practical Idealist."

164 *the state supreme:* Olin, *California's Prodigal Sons*, 5.

165 *County bosses in thrall:* Olin, *California's Prodigal Sons*, 191, note 8.

165 *"The railroad was":* Caughey, *California*, 447.

165 *"overturning the Southern":* Older, *My Own Story*, 33.

165 *"shattered beyond repair":* Orsi, *Sunset Limited*, 18.

165 *"kick the Southern":* Olin, *California's Prodigal Sons*, 26.

166 *"The first notes":* Current Literature (August 1, 1912).

166 *"Like Father Like Son":* Los Angeles Times, July 27, 1910.

166 *The Ohio-born Otis:* Gottlieb and Wolt, *Thinking Big*, 17–21.

166 *"we have been":* Mowry, *The California Progressives*, 126.

167 *"almost a frenzy":* Los Angeles Times, August 6, 1910.

167 *Late in the campaign:* Mowry, *The California Progressives*, 135.

167 *"Forgoing any form":* Lower, *A Bloc of One*, 28.

168 *"to take serious":* Chester Rowell quoted in Lower, *A Bloc of One*, 29.

168 *Proposition 4 of 1911:* "Rights of Suffrage (Permitting Women to Vote)," Prop. No. 4, 1911 General Election, https://sfpl.org/pdf/libraries/main/sfhistory /suffrageballot.pdf.

168 *The exception was:* John M. Allswang, *The Initiative and Referendum in California, 1898–1998* (Stanford: Stanford University Press, 2000), 10.

169 *During Johnson's first:* Mary Ann Mason, "Neither Friends nor Foes: Organized Labor and the California Progressives," in Deverell and Sitton, *California Progressivism*, 58.

169 *some 450 initiatives:* For totals through 1998, see Allswang, *The Initiative and Referendum*, 252–69.

169 *"superstitious belief":* Herbert Croly, *Progressive Democracy* (New York: Macmillan, 1914), 269.

169 *"with little concern":* Croly, *Progressive Democracy*, 269.

170 *The claim was:* See, for example, George Kennan, "The Japanese in the San Francisco Schools," *Outlook* (June 1907).

171 *"violent extremists":* Roosevelt to California governor James Gillett, March 9, 1907, cited in Thomas A. Bailey, *Theodore Roosevelt and the Japanese-American Crises* (Gloucester, MA: Peter Smith, 1964), 171.

171 *"most discreditable":* Roosevelt's address is at https://www.presidency.ucsb.edu /documents/sixth-annual-message-4.

171 *resident workers' wives:* Daniels, *The Politics of Prejudice*, 44.

171   *Five anti-Japanese measures:* Hichborn, *Story of the Session of the California Legislature of 1909*, 203.

172   *"The Japanese does not":* Chester H. Rowell, "Orientophobia," *Collier's*, February 6, 1909.

172   *only about 19,000:* U.S. Census for 1910, California supplement, https://www2.census.gov/library/publications/decennial/1910/abstract/supplement-ca.pdf.

172   *During the 1911:* Daniels, *The Politics of Prejudice*, 50.

173   *"national policy of exclusion":* Herbert P. Le Pore, "Prelude to Prejudice: Hiram Johnson, Woodrow Wilson, and the California Alien Land Law Controversy of 1913," *Southern California Quarterly* (Spring 1979).

174   *"to protect Japanese":* Daniels, *The Politics of Prejudice*, 61.

174   *"Is Japan offended":* Hichborn, *Story of the Session of the California Legislature of 1913*, 257.

174   *"the Japanese or any other":* Johnson to Bryan, April 23, 1913, in Daniels, *The Politics of Prejudice*, 62.

174   *"We have shown":* Johnson to Roosevelt, June 21, 1913, in Olin, *California's Prodigal Sons*, 88.

13. JOHN MUIR AND THE BATTLE FOR CONSERVATION

175   *On the first:* Muir, *The Yosemite*, 4.

175   *"miles in height":* Muir, *The Yosemite*, 5.

176   *"wonderfully exact counterpart":* John Muir, "The Endangered Valley," *Century Illustrated Monthly* (January 1909).

176   *The valley floor:* Jones, *John Muir*, 87.

177   *"The Significance of the Frontier":* Turner's paper was originally published in the *Annual Report of the American Historical Association* (1893), 197.

177   *"Climb the mountains":* Muir, *Our National Parks*, 56.

177   *"wilderness health":* Wolfe, *Son of the Wilderness*, 227.

177   *"mostly ugly":* Muir, *The Mountains of California*, 93.

178   *Yosemite escaped:* Mark David Spence, *Dispossessing the Wilderness: Indian Removal and the Making of the National Parks* (New York: Oxford University Press, 1999), 131.

178   *"the best tree-lover's":* Muir to Kent, February 6, 1908, in Roderick Nash, "John Muir, William Kent, and the Conservation Schism," *Pacific Historical Review* (November 1967).

178   *Muir brought:* Jones, *John Muir*, 7.

178   *"ignorance, stupidity":* Richard J. Orsi, "'Wilderness Saint' and 'Robber Baron,'" *Pacific Historian* (1985).

179   *"the first confrontation":* Hundley, *The Great Thirst*, 178.

180 *"miraculous qualities"*: Taylor, *Hetch Hetchy*, 10.

180 *a dollar a bucket*: Taylor, *Hetch Hetchy*, 10

180 *"An element as vital"*: Taylor, *Hetch Hetchy*, 18.

181 *In February:* The supervisor's resolution is reprinted in Taylor, *Hetch Hetchy*, 60.

181 *"a scheme to sell"*: *San Francisco Bulletin*, September 29, 1906.

182 *"to dam and submerge"*: Muir to Roosevelt, September 9, 1907, John Muir correspondence, Bancroft Library, University of California.

182 *"the great natural beauties"*: Roosevelt to Muir, September 16, 1907, Theodore Roosevelt Papers, Library of Congress.

182 *"mistaken zealots"*: Marsden Manson, "San Francisco's Side of the Hetch Hetchy Reservoir Matter," *Twentieth Century Magazine* (June 1910).

182 *"short-haired women"*: Manson to G. W. Woodruff, April 6, 1910, quoted in Hundley, *The Great Thirst*, 181.

182 *"Everything in the Hetch"*: Muir to R. U. Johnson, October 27, 1909, in Kendrick A. Clements, "Politics and the Park: San Francisco's Fight for Hetch Hetchy, 1908–1913," *Pacific Historical Review* (May 1979).

182 *the railroad had steered:* Clements, "Politics and the Park."

183 *"In every case"*: Pinchot, *The Fight for Conservation,* 44.

183 *"not much interested"*: M. Nelson McGeary, *Gifford Pinchot, Forester-Politician* (Princeton: Princeton University Press, 1960), 87.

183 *This was a winning:* Clements, "Politics and the Park."

183 *"Dam Hetch Hetchy"*: Muir, *The Yosemite*, 262.

183 *"The ideal conservation"*: Congressional Record, Sixty-Third Congress, session 1 (August 30, 1913), 3963.

184 *"I hope you"*: Kent to Anderson, July 2, 1913, in Nash, "John Muir."

184 *"It's hard to bear"*: Muir to Vernon Kellogg, December 27, 1913, quoted in Jones, *John Muir*, 168.

184 *Today the valley provides:* Tom Philp, "The Lost Yosemite: It's Time to Imagine Hetch Hetchy Restored," *Sacramento Bee*, August 22, 2004.

184 *"birthright"*: Tom Philp, "San Francisco's Paradox—a Green Agenda Everywhere—Except Yosemite," *Sacramento Bee*, August 30, 2004.

184 *"Mention Hetch Hetchy"*: "Restore Hetch Hetchy," *Sierra Club Yahi Group* newsletter VII, no. III (Fall 2002): 4, https://www.sierraclub.org/sites/default/files/sce-authors/u808/fall2002.pdf.

14. CONJURING LOS ANGELES

189 *"Los Angeles"*: Mayo, *Los Angeles,* 319.

190 *"conjured into existence"*: McWilliams, *Southern California Country*, 134.

190 *"healthy, robust"*: Marion Parks, trans., "Instructions for the Recruital of Soldiers

and Settlers for California," *Annual Publication of the Historical Society of Southern California* 15, no. 1 (1931).

191 *The adults were:* Bancroft, *History of California,* vol. 1, 345, note 24. Bancroft casts doubt on the Chinese background of the settler named Antonio Miranda, but historians have been unable to settle on the truth.

191 *"active and exacting":* Beebe and Senkewicz, *Lands of Promise and Despair* 223–25.

191 *"no newspaper":* Cleland and Putnam, *Isaias W. Hellman,* 3.

191 *"So unlike":* Lindley and Widney, *California of the South,* 1.

192 *"The English tongue":* Ayers, *Gold and Sunshine,* 255–56.

192 *the six thousand voting residents:* Caughey, *California,* 336.

192 *"often startled":* Cleland, *A History of California,* 308.

192 *An early boom:* Remi A. Nadeau, *City Makers: The Men Who Transformed Los Angeles from Village to Metropolis During the First Great Boom, 1868–76* (Garden City, NY: Doubleday & Co., 1948), 15–16.

193 *"haven for thugs":* Paul M. De Falla, "Lantern in the Western Sky, Part 1," *Historical Society of Southern California Quarterly* (March 1960). Most of the details of the massacre of October 24 are drawn from De Falla's account. See also Robert W. Blew, "Vigilantism in Los Angeles, 1835–1874," *Southern California Quarterly* (Spring 1972).

193 *The homicide rate:* Eric Monkkonen, "Western Homicide: The Case of Los Angeles, 1830–1870," *Pacific Historical Review* (November 2005). See also Scott Zesch, "Chinese Los Angeles in 1870–1871: The Makings of a Massacre," *Southern California Quarterly* (Summer 2008).

193 *"policed in theory":* Paul M. De Falla, "Lantern in the Western Sky, Part 2," *Historical Society of Southern California Quarterly* (June 1960).

193 *"rotten from head":* Los Angeles Star, May 9, 1872.

193 *"a man could sell":* Los Angeles Star, May 9, 1872.

194 *the 1863 state law:* Statutes of California, chapter 70, 1863.

194 *a force of special:* Coolidge, *Chinese Immigration,* 260.

194 *"relentlessly castigated":* Zesch, "Chinese Los Angeles."

195 *thirty-seven indictments:* Zesch, "Chinese Los Angeles." Other sources are less specific, as the record of indictments has been lost; estimates range from 30 to 150.

195 *"no evil":* Los Angeles Star, October 30, 1871, quoted in Zesch, "Chinese Los Angeles."

195 *"The diseases of children":* Charles Dudley Warner, *Our Italy* (New York: Harper & Brothers, 1891), 39.

196 *"Fevers and diseases":* Ben C. Truman, *Homes and Happiness in the Golden State of California* (San Francisco: H.S. Crocker & Co., 1885), 51.

196 *"You will not find"*: Nordhoff, *California: For Health,* 114–15.

196 *"meant no more"*: Nadeau, *City Makers,* 23.

196 *"bouncing over the mountains"*: Harris Newmark, *Sixty Years in Southern California, 1853–1913* (Boston: Houghton Mifflin, 1930), 496.

197 *"little country towns"*: Daggett, *Chapters on the History,* 127.

197 *"Railway companies are"*: Los Angeles Evening Express, May 24, 1872, quoted in *An Illustrated History of Los Angeles County* (Los Angeles: Lewis Publishing, 1889), 136.

197 *The Southern Pacific's demand*: Daggett, *Chapters on the History,* 129.

197 *the city staged*: Gottlieb and Wolt, *Thinking Big,* 12.

198 *"full-fledged metropolis"*: Timothy Tzeng, "Eastern Promises: The Role of Eastern Capital in the Development of Los Angeles, 1900–1920," *California History* (January 2011).

198 *"I have caught"*: Sunset, January 1901.

198 *some 120,000 passengers*: McWilliams, *Southern California Country,* 118.

198 *"suddenly changed"*: Willard, *History of Los Angeles,* 336.

198 *"Everybody that could find"*: H. Ellington Brook, *An Illustrated History,* 348.

199 *"golden opportunity"*: Willard, *History of Los Angeles,* 340.

199 *"A miniature city"*: Brook, *An Illustrated History,* 349.

199 *brass bands and free lunches*: Guinn, *A History of California,* 263.

199 *"Buy land in Los Angeles"*: Joseph Netz, "The Great Los Angeles Real Estate Boom of 1887," *Annual Publication of the Historical Society of Southern California, 1915–1916.*

199 *"gambling was open"*: Smith, *Freedom's Frontier,* 153–54.

199 *Townsites that had been mapped*: McWilliams, *Southern California Country,* 121.

200 *The 1880s frenzy*: For completed infrastructure, see McWilliams, *Southern California Country,* 122.

200 *"California on Wheels"*: Willard, *A History of the Chamber of Commerce,* 152.

200 *"the best advertised"*: McWilliams, *Southern California Country,* 129.

200 *"white-bearded"*: Hine, *California Utopianism,* 27.

201 *"Venice of America"*: Dumke, *The Boom of the Eighties,* 213.

201 *"odds and ends"*: McWilliams, *Southern California Country,* 72.

201 *"climatically insulated"*: Jackson, *Glimpses of California,* 214.

202 *"the largest internal"*: McWilliams, *Southern California Country,* 135.

202 *"Healing is a tremendous"*: Louis Adamic, "Los Angeles! There She Blows!," *Outlook* (August 13, 1930).

203 *Otis would boast*: See Otis testimony, "Final Report: Commission on Industrial Relations," vol. 6, 5487 (September 8, 1914).

203 *"bitterness of attack"*: Cross, *A History of the Labor Movement,* 276.

203 *Wages in Los Angeles:* McWilliams, *Southern California Country*, 277.

203 *they were invalids:* Cross, *A History of the Labor Movement*, 271.

204 *Within weeks:* McWilliams, *Southern California Country*, 280.

204 *Shortly after one:* For the explosion and its aftermath, see Gottlieb and Wolt, *Thinking Big*, 84–88.

204 *On Labor Day:* Errol Wayne Stevens, "Two Radicals and Their Los Angeles: Harrison Gray Otis and Job Harriman," *California History* (January 2009).

204 *"They seek an":* Harriman testimony, "Final Report: *Commission on Industrial Relations*, 5805 (September 14, 1916).

205 *" an orgie of evil":* Los Angeles Times, October 31, 1911.

205 *"a cruel, brutal":* Darrow, 180.

206 *eleventh richest person:* Gottlieb & Wolt, p. 125.

206 *"war of extermination":* Los Angeles Times, Oct. 2, 1919.

15. GHOSTS OF THE OWENS VALLEY

207 *Crews from navy:* The details of the celebration are from Mulholland, *William Mulholland*, 244. Catherine Mulholland (1923–2011) was a granddaughter of William Mulholland; her biography of her forebear is admirably fair-minded.

208 *"one of the costliest":* Mayo, 245–46.

209 *"we never could":* Mulholland, *William Mulholland*, 112.

209 *Eaton was that:* Hoffman, *Vision or Villainy*, 31.

210 *The Dublin-born:* The biographical details come from Mulholland, 10ff.

210 *"clearing brush":* Mulholland, *William Mulholland*, 23.

210 *its thirty-year franchise:* Ostrom, *Water and Politics*, 45–46.

210 *"liquid embezzlement":* Hoffman, *Vision or Villainy*, 36.

211 *"I laughed":* Mulholland recounted the exchange at the ceremony marking the final land acquisition for the Owens Valley aqueduct; see *Los Angeles Times*, July 29, 1905.

211 *"enough bicarbonate":* Hoffman, 12.

211 *Eaton quietly bought: First Annual Report of the Chief Engineer of the Los Angeles Aqueduct to the Board of Public Works* (1907), 17–18.

211 *At the General:* Hoffman, *Vision or Villainy*, 79–80.

213 *"The last spike":* Los Angeles Times, July 29, 1905.

213 *Eaton found himself:* William L. Kahrl, "The Politics of California Water: Owens Valley and the Los Angeles Aqueduct, 1900–1927," *California Historical Quarterly*, Spring 1976.

213 *"I shall never":* Mulholland, 123.

213 *"interest and cooperation":* Los Angeles Times, July 29, 1905.

213 *But he resigned:* Hoffman, *Vision or Villainy,* 137.

213 *Paiute-Shoshone Indians:* Madley, *An American Genocide,* 309–10.

213 *the most savage:* J.M. Guinn, "Some Early History of Owens River Valley," *Annual Publication of the Historical Society of Southern California* (1917).

213 *"horse thief Indians":* Guinn, "Some Early History."

214 *Along the way:* Mulholland, *William Mulholland,* 129.

214 *"The total population":* Lippincott to Frederick Lungren, September 19, 1905, reprinted in Abraham Hoffman, "Joseph Barlow Lippincott and the Owens Valley Controversy: Time for Revision," *Southern California Quarterly* (Fall 1972).

214 *"It is a hundred":* Roosevelt to Hitchcock, September 27, 1906. The full text of the letter is in *Los Angeles Times,* September 28, 1906.

215 *"Goethals of the West":* Remi A. Nadeau, *The Water Seekers* (Garden City, NY: Doubleday & Company, 1950), 60.

215 *"as unlikely as":* Erie, *Beyond Chinatown,* 36.

215 *"the best piece":* Mulholland, *William Mulholland,* 149.

215 *The 233-mile aqueduct:* "The Completion of the Los Angeles Aqueduct," *Scientific American* (November 8, 1913).

215 *"water famine":* Hundley, *The Great Thirst,* 153.

215 *"if Los Angeles runs out":* Hundley, *The Great Thirst,* 153.

216 *"would be practicing":* *Los Angeles Times,* April 15, 1913.

216 *"the greater Los Angeles":* Ostrom, *Water and Politics,* 155.

216 *Real estate developers:* Hoffman, *Vision or Villainy,* 126.

216 *In 1909:* W. W. Robinson, *The Story of San Fernando Valley* (Los Angeles: Title Insurance and Trust Company, 1961), 37.

216 *But once the valley:* The $1,000 valuation came from State Engineer W. F. McClure's 1924 report on the Owens Valley conflict ordered by Governor Friend Richardson; McClure had lived and worked in the valley, however, and his report was regarded in the city as unduly favorable to valley residents.

216 *"The cable that":* *Los Angeles Times,* July 29, 1905.

217 *"ever since tantalized":* Hoffman, *Vision or Villainy,* 126.

217 *The valley's farmers set:* See Gary D. Libecap, "Chinatown: Transaction Costs in Water Rights Exchanges: The Owens Valley Transfer to Los Angeles," ICER Working Papers Series 16 (2005).

217 *"a hotbed":* Ostrom, *Water and Politics,* 130.

218 *"California's Little Civil War":* *Literary Digest,* December 6, 1924.

218 *"The only weapon":* Mark Watterson to Mary Austin, December 18, 1924, in Hoffman, *Vision or Villainy,* 190.

219 *"honest, earnest, hard-working":* *Los Angeles Times,* November 18, 1924.

16. THE UTOPIANS

220 *A baton was raised:* This description of McPherson's revival meetings is drawn from Sarah Comstock, "Aimee Semple McPherson: Prima Donna of Revivalism," *Harper's Monthly* (December 1927); H. L. Mencken, "Sister Aimée," *Baltimore Evening Sun*, December 13, 1926; and others.

220 *"Brothers and sisters":* Quinn, *The Original Sin,* 128.

221 *"a brass band":* Mayo, *Los Angeles,* 273.

221 *"In bleakest Vermont":* Mayo, *Los Angeles,* 275.

221 *"scattering religious tracts":* McWilliams, *Southern California Country,* 259.

222 *John Updike:* Updike, "Famous Aimee," *New Yorker,* April 23, 2007.

222 *"her followers":* McWilliams, *Southern California Country,* 262.

222 *"the time-honored":* Mencken, "Sister Aimée."

222 *"the most magnetic":* Quinn, *The Original Sin,* 127.

223 *The legacy she left:* Matthew Avery Sutton, *Aimee Semple McPherson and the Resurrection of Christian America* (Cambridge: Harvard University Press, 2009), 271.

223 *nearly one-third:* Rice et al., *The Elusive Eden,* 341.

224 *"United States in microcosm":* Burnette G. Haskell, "Kaweah: How the Colony Died," *Out West* (September 1902).

224 *"The pigs ate":* Hine, *California's Utopian Colonies,* 99.

224 *"the jumping-off place":* Edmund Wilson, "The Jumping-Off Place," *New Republic* (December 23, 1931).

225 *"out in the golden":* Didion, *Slouching Towards Bethlehem,* 28.

225 *By August 1917:* Hine, *California's Utopian Colonies,* 118ff.

225 *"an inquisition":* Ernest S. Wooster, "They Shared Equally," *Sunset* (July 1924).

225 *"Swarms of self-appointed 'saviors'":* George Creel, *Rebel at Large: Recollections of Fifty Crowded Years* (New York: G. P. Putnam's Sons, 1947), 280.

226 *"This old gentleman":* Sinclair, *I, Candidate for Governor,* 7.

226 *After sending Republicans:* Charles E. Larsen, "The Epic Campaign of 1934," *Pacific Historical Review* (May 1958).

227 *"I say, positively":* Sinclair, *I, Governor,* 7.

227 *"socially-minded clergymen":* Carey McWilliams, "Upton Sinclair and his E.P.I.C.," *New Republic* (August 22, 1934).

227 *"as if by default":* McWilliams, "Upton Sinclair."

227 *"very much 'on the spot'":* Sinclair, *I, Candidate for Governor,* 76.

227 *"He wanted the":* Rexford G. Tugwell diary (undat.), Franklin D. Roosevelt Presidential Library and Museum.

228 *"I found that he had read":* Sinclair, *I, Candidate for Governor,* 84.

228 *"They had a staff":* Sinclair, *I, Candidate for Governor,* 144.

228 *"It is difficult"*: Sinclair, *I, Candidate for Governor*, 109.

228 *Merriam also made*: Jackson K. Putnam, "The Progressive Legacy in California," in Deverell and Sitton, *California Progressivism*, 255.

229 *"palliate lunacy"*: *Los Angeles Times*, November 30, 1934.

229 *"haggard, very old women"*: Richard L. Neuberger and Kelley Loe, "The Old People's Campaign," *Harper's Monthly* (March 1936).

229 *The movement's birth*: *Long Beach Press-Telegram*, September 30, 1933.

230 *"gentle general of a growing army"*: *New York Times*, December 29, 1935.

230 *"soul-wracking"*: Townsend, *New Horizons*, 132.

230 *"The easiest tax in the world"*: Townsend, *New Horizons*, 139.

231 *"in the realm"*: Hearings, Economic Security Act, House Committee on Ways and Means (January 23, 1935), 203.

231 *"read somewhere"*: Lippmann, "Dr. Townsend's Trillions," *Los Angeles Times*, January 10, 1935.

231 *"whatever the exaggerations"*: *New Republic*, December 19, 1934.

231 *"Congress can't stand"*: Perkins, *The Roosevelt I Knew*, 294.

17. EXECUTIVE ORDER 9066

232 *California's popular Republican*: Warren's testimony can be found at part 29, February 21, 1942, *Hearings Before the Select Committee Investigating National Defense Migration* (hereafter cited as Tolan). His written statement and accompanying documents are at 10973–11009, oral testimony at 11009–11023. Quotes are all taken from the official record.

232 *a friend and neighbor*: Jim Newton, *Justice for All: Earl Warren and the Nation He Made* (New York: Riverhead Books, 2006), 135.

233 *"they, and they alone"*: Daniels, *Concentration Camp*, 71.

233 *More than 120,000*: "Evacuated People: A Quantitative Description," War Relocation Authority, US Department of the Interior, 11. The precise figures in the report published in 1946 are 120,313 total evictees and 109,030 from California. (Some unofficial estimates place the number of evictees at more than 125,000.) By the War Relocation Authority's reckoning, the incarceration period ran from May 8, 1942, when the authority opened the Colorado River Relocation Center in Yuma County, Arizona, to March 20, 1942, when its Tule Lake Center in Modoc County, California, was closed.

233 *Warren's defenders*: Newton, *Justice for All*, 134–35.

233 *"It is known"*: Daniels, *Concentration Camps*, 60.

234 *"If there is"*: Bowron's speech was entered into the *Congressional Record* for February 9, 1942. See *Congressional Record Appendix* for that date, A457–458.

234 *entirely unwarranted*: For the absence of any indications of shore-to-ship signaling,

see *Personal Justice Denied*, Report of the Commission on Wartime Relocation and Internment of Civilians (December 1982), 7.

234 *"at once insecure"*: Newton, *Justice for All*, 127.

234 *"in a category different"*: Grodzins, *Americans Betrayed*, 93.

234 *He took a similar*: Grodzins, *Americans Betrayed*, 93.

234 *On February 2*: The meeting was described by Percy C. Heckendorf, then the district attorney of Santa Barbara County, in the Earl Warren Oral History Project: Japanese-American Relocation Reviewed, Online Archive of California (hereafter cited as Warren OH).

235 *"The Fifth Column"*: Lippmann's column appeared in the *Los Angeles Times* on February 12, 1942.

235 *"armchair Strategists"*: Biddle to FDR, February 17, 1942, at Franklin D. Roosevelt Library, Hyde Park, N.Y.: https://www.fdrlibrary.org/documents /356632/390886/cti.001internment.pdf.

235 *Federal agriculture officials*: Daniels, *Concentration Camps*, 48.

236 *Nearly five thousand*: Carey McWilliams, "What About our Japanese-Americans?" Public Affairs Committee, May 1944.

236 *"reclaim and improve"*: Masakazu Iwata, "Japanese Immigrants in California Agriculture," *Agricultural History* (January 1962).

236 *"would probably require"*: Rowe to Grace Tully, February 2, 1942, Franklin D. Roosevelt Library, Hyde Park, New York, https://www.fdrlibrary.org/documents /356632/390886/cti.001internment.pdf.

236 *"are in agreement"*: Daniels, *Concentration Camps*, 55.

236 *"not being instigated"*: Telephone conversation, DeWitt with Bendetsen, January 28, 1942, in Kent Roberts Greenfield, ed., *Command Decisions* (Washington, DC: Center of Military History, 1987), 133.

236 *Rowe would later*: Warren OH. In his part of this omnibus oral history, Rowe also expressed regret at having participated in a Justice Department policy to steer clear of responsibility for the Japanese relocation by ceding the matter entirely to the War Department.

237 *"a disturbing situation"*: Tolan, 10973.

237 *"scraps of property"*: Newton, *Justice for All*, 131.

237 *"there is more potential"*: Tolan, 11014.

237 *citing census records*: Tolan, 11014.

237 *"Many of our"*: Tolan, 11011.

238 *"There are many"*: Tolan, 11015.

238 *"They don't want"*: Tolan, 11054.

238 *"Suddenly the whole"*: Tsukamoto in Tateishi, *And Justice for All*, 6.

238 *He was an FBI*: Uchida, *Desert Exile*, 46.

239 *Donald Nakahata:* Nakahata in Tateishi, *And Justice for All,* 33–34.

239 *"a dangerous element":* DeWitt to House Naval Affairs Subcommittee, April 13, 1943, cited in McWilliams, "What About our Japanese-Americans?"

239 *This narrow spit: Personal Justice Denied,* 108.

239 *Panic swept:* Bill Hosokawa, in Daniels, *Concentration Camps,* 86.

240 *"Unscrupulous vultures":* Yoshihiko Fujikawa in *Personal Justice Denied,* 108.

240 *"The secondhand dealers":* Houston and Houston, *Farewell to Manzanar,* 13–14.

240 *"Then a nurse":* Tateishi in Tateishi, *And Justice for All,* 24.

241 *"places where nobody":* Daniels, *Concentration Camps,* 96.

241 *Upon reporting:* These and the following recollections of Tanforan are from Uchida, *Desert Exile,* 70–71.

241 *"a seldom interrupted":* Leonard J. Arrington, "The Price of Prejudice," faculty honor lecture no. 25, Utah State University, 1962.

241 *dysentery outbreaks: Personal Justice Denied,* 165.

242 *"Businesses lost their": Personal Justice Denied,* 117.

242 *about $37 million:* Conrat and Conrat, *Executive Order 9066,* 23. See also https://www.archives.gov/research/japanese-americans/redress.

242 *more than 65,000:* Daniels, *Concentration Camps,* 114.

242 *In a series:* Hirabayashi v. U.S., 320 U.S. 81; Korematsu v. United States, 323 U.S. 214; Ex parte Endo, 323 U.S. 283.

243 *"timid and evasive":* Eugene V. Rostow, "The Japanese-American Cases—A Disaster," *Yale Law Journal* (June 1945).

243 *Liberal justice Frank Murphy:* Sidney Fine, "Mr. Justice Murphy and the Hirabayashi Case," *Pacific Historical Review* (May 1964).

243 *"a matter of": Korematsu v. United States,* 227.

243 *"True, exclusion": Korematsu v. United States,* 218.

243 "Korematsu *was gravely":* Trump v. Hawaii, 585 US _ (slip opinion).

243 *Warren sometimes expressed:* Newton, *Justice for All,* 138.

244 *One notable incident: Pacific Citizen,* April 25, 1969.

244 *"I have since":* Earl Warren, *The Memoirs of Earl Warren* (Garden City: Doubleday and Company, 1977), 149. There is evidence that someone, possibly Warren's son, may have edited the memoir's text to add "deeply" before the word "regretted" in this passage; see Newton, *Justice for All,* 141.

18. THE SELLING OF RICHARD NIXON

245 *a few years earlier:* Paul Bullock, "'Rabbits and Radicals,' Richard Nixon's 1946 Campaign Against Jerry Voorhis," *Southern California Quarterly* (Fall 1973).

246 *"that is saleable":* Bullock, "'Rabbits and Radicals.'"

246 *"All of us simply":* Bullock, "'Rabbits and Radicals.'"

247 *a cautious Voorhis:* Voorhis, *The Strange Case,* 14.

247 *"Voorhis would never know":* Bullock, "'Rabbits and Radicals.'"

247 *"unfair accusations":* Voorhis, *The Strange Case,* 13.

247 *"the quality of life":* Nixon, *RN,* 41.

248 *"the first victim":* Voorhis, *The Strange Case,* 9.

248 *"a letterhead":* Hill, *Dancing Bear,* 111.

248 *"a motley":* M. J. Heale, "Red Scare Politics: California's Campaign Against Un-American Activities, 1940–1970," *Journal of American Studies* (April 1986).

248 *"Flagrant self-seeking":* Rogin and Shover, *Political Change,* 157.

249 *"a host of spies":* McWilliams, *Southern California Country,* 291.

249 *"break up meetings":* McWilliams, *Southern California Country,* 291.

249 *deployed three hundred police:* "Violations of Free Speech and Rights of Labor," Report of the U.S. Senate Committee on Education and Labor (LaFollette Committee), 131.

249 *"pasty-faced":* Cherny, *Harry Bridges,* 59.

249 *a watershed event:* Cherny, *Harry Bridges,* 84.

249 *"armed with riot":* Cherny, *Harry Bridges,* 84.

250 *"the secret boss":* Samish and Thomas, *The Secret Boss,* 8.

250 *"I played piano":* Samish and Thomas, *The Secret Boss,* 129.

250 *"labor, welfare, educational":* Heale, "Red Scare Politics."

250 *invention of the cyclotron:* For Lawrence's background and accomplishments, see Hiltzik, *Big Science.*

251 *Combs was able:* Edward L. Barrett Jr., *The Tenney Committee: Legislative Investigation of Subversive Activities in California* (Ithaca, NY: Cornell University Press, 1951), 33.

251 *"I am not a member":* Gardner, *The California Oath Controversy,* 25.

251 *one out of ten:* Gordon Pates, "California—The Oath Epidemic," *Reporter,* December 26, 1950.

252 *"Until the Hiss":* Nixon, *RN,* 47.

252 *"tall, elegant, handsome":* Nixon, *RN,* 54.

252 *"one of the most disheveled-looking":* Nixon, *RN,* 52–53.

252 *"a mouth full":* Allen Weinstein, *Perjury: The Hiss-Chambers Case* (New York: Random House, 1997), 203.

253 *"His manner was":* Nixon, *Six Crises,* 6.

254 *"a junior member":* Nixon, *RN,* 72.

254 *"the worth of":* Nixon, *RN,* 72.

255 *Having eked out:* Ingrid Winther Scobie, "Helen Gahagan Douglas: Broadway Star as California Politician," *California History* (December 1987).

255 *She collected:* Scobie, "Helen Gahagan Douglas."

256 *"no name-calling":* Ingrid Winther Scobie, "Helen Gahagan Douglas and Her 1950 Senate Race with Richard M. Nixon," *Southern California Quarterly* (Spring 1976).

256 *"Dirty tricks":* Los Angeles Times, April 9, 1990.

256 *"the most conspicuous":* Los Angeles Times, October 31, 1950.

257 *"Mrs. Douglas":* Nixon, *RN*, 78.

257 *"The purpose":* Los Angeles Times, April 9, 1990.

19. TOMORROWLAND

258 *"Here is the world's":* Bruce Bliven, "Roses in January; Morons in June," *New Republic* (December 18, 1935).

258 *"handled more seaport tonnage":* Richard G. Lillard, "Problems and Promise in Tomorrowland," *California History* (April 1981).

258 *"40 percent more":* Lillard, "Problems and Promise."

259 *By the turn:* Los Angeles Almanac, https://www.laalmanac.com/transport/tro1 .php.

260 *"about as much":* Charles K. Field, "On the Wings of To-Day," *Sunset* (March 1910).

260 *"he soared":* Los Angeles Times, January 11, 1910.

260 *The air show:* Field, "On the Wings of To-Day."

260 *"one of the greatest":* Los Angeles Times, January 16, 1910.

261 *In 1925:* Scott, *Technopolis*, 57.

261 *Yet within another dozen:* Cunningham, *The Aircraft Industry*, 105.

261 *Among the earliest:* Schoneberger, *California Wings*, 23.

261 *They fronted Douglas:* Gottlieb and Wolt, *Thinking Big*, 156.

262 *"faster and plushier":* Frank J. Taylor, *High Horizons: The United Air Lines Story* (New York: McGraw-Hill, 1951), 76.

262 *a letter arrived:* Rae, *Climb to Greatness*, 68.

262 *"an amiable cow":* Ernest K. Gann, *Fate Is the Hunter* (New York: Simon & Schuster, 1961), 28.

263 *The DC-3 then accounted:* Rae, *Climb to Greatness*, 71.

263 *William Selig:* Gabler, *An Empire of Their Own*, 105.

263 *By the time:* Gabler, *An Empire of Their Own*, 105.

263 *"Westerns in the desert":* Balio, *The American Film Industry*, 108.

264 *"Apples, avocados, pineapples":* Gabler, *An Empire of Their Own*, 105.

264 *Efforts to add sound:* See Douglas Gomery, "The Coming of Sound: Technological Change in the American Film Industry," in Balio, *The American Film Industry*, 229ff.

265   *the main impetus:* Cameron, *Sound and the Cinema,* viii.

265   *AT&T was installing:* Balio, *The American Film Industry,* 249.

266   *With the surge:* See *U.S. v. Paramount Pictures, Inc., et al.,* 334 U.S. 131.

266   *"improvised factories":* Lillard, "Problems and Promise."

267   *the federal government had spent:* Hiltzik, *Big Science,* 311–12.

267   *The guiding spirit:* Saxenian, *Regional Advantage,* 20.

267   *"underprivileged institution":* Saxenian, *Regional Advantage,* 21.

268   *"might not be fully":* Luger and Goldstein, *Technology in the Garden,* 124.

268   *In 1955, the industrial:* Saxenian, *Regional Advantage,* 24.

268   *"the Moses of Silicon Valley":* Michael A. Hiltzik, "The Twisted Legacy of William Shockley," *Los Angeles Times,* December 2, 2001.

269   *"Silicon Valley U.S.A.":* *Electronic News,* January 11, 18, and 25, 1971.

270   *among the four hundred:* Saxenian, *Regional Advantage,* 30.

270   *"office of the future":* Hiltzik, *Dealers of Lightning,* 51.

271   *He was granted:* Hiltzik, *Dealers of Lightning,* 329ff.

272   *California companies attracted:* Statistics are drawn from National Venture Capital Association, 2022 Yearbook, 29.

20. RONALD REAGAN AND THE LEGACY OF PAT BROWN

275   *In a pretaped:* Cannon, *Governor Reagan,* 141.

275   *"a small minority":* Ronald Reagan's "Morality Gap" Speech (1966), Bay Area Television Archive news footage, https://diva.sfsu.edu/collections/sfbatv/bundles /229317 . An edited version of the speech appears in Ronald Reagan, *The Creative Society: Some Comments on Problems Facing America* (New York: The Devin-Adair Company, 1968), 125–27.

276   *"a rallying point":* The report was the "Thirteenth Report Supplement of the Senate Factfinding Subcommittee on Un-American Activities," May 6, 1966, which was entirely devoted to accusations of Communist influence and sexual misconduct at Berkeley.

276   *1960 Master Plan:* "A Master Plan for Higher Education in California, 1960–1975," California State Department of Education, 1960.

277   *"a state rushing":* Douglass, *The California Idea,* 11.

277   *"The California of the new":* George, "What the Railroad Will Bring Us."

277   *"coming glory":* David Jordan, "The University and the Common Man," address to Stanford students, 1903.

277   *In the 1920s:* Douglass, *The California Idea,* 1.

277   *"To a degree":* Douglass, *The California Idea,* 1.

277   *"a higher education system":* Douglass, *The California Idea,* 8.

277   *the nation's largest:* Douglass, *The California Idea,* 8.

278 *"cultivates both mechanics"*: Douglass, *The California Idea,* 105.

278 *"We faced this enormous"*: "The California Master Plan for Higher Education," July 2002, https://regents.universityofcalifornia.edu/regmeet/july02/302attach1 .pdf.

278 *about 45 percent*: Marginson, *The Dream Is Over,* 17.

278 *"educational ladder"*: Douglass, *The California Idea,* 9.

279 *"the United States came closer"*: Marginson, *The Dream Is Over,* 15.

279 *"not just legitimate"*: Marginson, *The Dream Is Over,* 17.

279 *Berkeley activists held:* Senate supplement, 78.

279 *"Students were alienated"*: Rorabaugh, *Berkeley at War,* 10.

280 *"You won't have Nixon"*: *New York Times*, November 11, 1962.

280 *In any case: Los Angeles Times*, September 20, 1966.

280 *The members of the old guard:* Robert A. Goldberg, "The Western Hero in Politics," in *The Political Culture of the New West*, ed. Jeff Roche (Lawrence: University Press of Kansas, 2008), 15.

281 *"the classic western"*: Goldberg, "The Western Hero," 14.

281 *"Americans like the cowboy"*: The interview in which Kissinger made this statement was conducted by Italian journalist Oriana Fallaci. Originally published in an Italian periodical and republished 1972 in the *New Republic*, it can be found in Oriana Fallaci, *Interview with History*, trans. John Shepley (Boston: Houghton Mifflin, 1976), 29. Kissinger was actually describing *himself* as the lone cowboy.

281 *"in jeans"*: Perlstein, *Before the Storm,* 260.

281 *"Reagan was a"*: Cannon, *Governor Reagan,* 140.

282 *"A Time for Choosing"*: "A Time for Choosing Speech, October 27, 1964," Ronald Reagan Presidential Library & Museum, https://www.reaganlibrary.gov /reagans/ronald-reagan/time-choosing-speech-october-27-1964.

282 *"the right to participate"*: Michelle Reeves, "'Obey the Rules or Get Out': Ronald Reagan's 1966 Gubernatorial Campaign and the 'Trouble in Berkeley,'" *Southern California Quarterly* (Fall 2010).

282 *"The University was apparently"*: Savio et al., *The Free Speech Movement,* 15.

283 *"There is a time"*: Rorabaugh, *Berkeley at War,* 31.

283 *"the largest mass arrest"*: Rorabaugh, *Berkeley at War,* 33.

283 *"buzz word"*: Frederick G. Dutton OH, Oral History Center, Bancroft Library, University of California.

283 *Reagan beat Brown:* Cannon, *Governor Reagan,* 160.

283 *"personal political arena": Los Angeles Times*, September 11, 1967.

284 *"surefire applause line"*: Cannon, *Governor Reagan,* 285.

284 *"someone who dresses"*: Cannon, *Governor Reagan,* 285.

284 *"No one is compelled"*: *Los Angeles Times*, December 3, 1966.

284 *"there are political"*: Gerard J. De Groot, "Ronald Reagan and Student Unrest in California, 1966–1970," *Pacific Historical Review* (February 1996).

284 *"a concerted plan"*: Reagan press conference, December 17, 1968, https://www.reaganlibrary.gov/public/digitallibrary/gubernatorial/pressunit/p02/40-840-7408622-p02-007-2017.pdf.

284 *"Reagan chose to exploit"*: McGill, *The Year of the Monkey*, 158.

284 *Their movement had begun*: Elaine Lewinnek, "Social Studies Controversies in 1960s Los Angeles: *Land of the Free*, Public Memory, and the Rise of the New Right," *Pacific Historical Review* (February 2015).

284 *seventeen recall campaigns*: *Los Angeles Times*, March 23, 1961.

285 *"pro–United Nations"*: *Los Angeles Times*, March 31, 1966.

285 *"a romanticized, top-down"*: Lewinnek, "Social Studies Controversies."

285 *At a meeting*: For video, see https://americanarchive.org/catalog/cpb-aacip-55-bk16m33g2c.

286 *"He wasn't restrained"*: *Los Angeles Times*, January 7, 1973.

286 *"the foundation upon"*: De Groot, "Ronald Reagan and Student Unrest."

286 *"the patient, almost Madisonian"*: Garin Burbank, "Governor Reagan and California Welfare Reform: The Grand Compromise of 1971," *California History* (Fall 1991).

286 *"Reagan had his head"*: John L. Burton OH, Oral History Center, Bancroft Library, University of California.

287 *"Look, governor"*: Burbank, "Governor Reagan and California Welfare Reform." Reagan would recall the encounter differently.

21. LA CAUSA

288 *The family had*: Pawel, *The Crusades*, 159.

289 *more than quadrupled*: Pawel, *The Crusades*, 191.

289 *"immoral" and "blackmail"*: Pawel, *The Crusades*, 187.

289 *"It is tragic"*: *New York Times*, July 30, 1970.

289 *"This experiment"*: Pawel, *The Crusades*, 208.

289 *"This event justifies"*: *New York Times*, July 30, 1970.

290 *"homeless, starving, destitute"*: McWilliams, *Factories in the Field*, 9.

290 *"deserts have been changed"*: McWilliams, *Factories in the Field*, 5.

290 *"huge plows"*: Gerald D. Nash, "Stages of California's Economic Growth, 1870–1970," *California Historical Quarterly* (Winter 1972).

290 *"granary of the world"*: Nash, "Stages of California's Economic Growth."

290 *Hugh Glenn*: Nash, "Stages of California's Economic Growth."

291 *"White men and women"*: *Los Angeles Times*, August 14, 1893.

291 *Riots in Fresno:* McWilliams, *Factories in the Field,* 75.

291 *"Indispensable as the Chinese are":* McWilliams, *Factories in the Field,* 64.

291 *more than a half a million:* McWilliams, *Factories in the Field,* 77.

291 *one estimate:* McWilliams, *Factories in the Field,* 88.

291 *"We reach from the Imperial":* "Seasonal Agricultural Laborers from Mexico," Hearing before the Committee on Immigration and Naturalization, House of Representatives (January 28, 1926), 7.

292 *"There are thousands":* McWilliams, *Factories in the Field,* 195.

292 *"quietly," to avoid:* McWilliams, *Factories in the Field,* 105.

292 *more than 70 percent:* McWilliams, *Factories in the Field,* 111–12.

293 *average of 58,000:* McWilliams, *Factories in the Field,* 125.

293 *"cheap, plentiful, and docile":* Carey McWilliams, "Repatriados," *American Mercury* (March 1933).

294 *"Indio to Edom":* Woody Guthrie, *Bound for Glory* (New York: E. P. Dutton, 1968), 294.

294 *"filth, squalor":* McWilliams, *Factories in the Field,* 225.

294 *The Southern Pacific agreed:* McWilliams, "Repatriados."

295 *an anti-union statute:* McWilliams, *California,* 148.

295 *"general deportation":* McWilliams, *Factories in the Field,* 130.

295 *The average daily wage:* Bernstein, *The Turbulent Years,* 148.

295 *Seven-year-old Roy:* Bernstein, *The Turbulent Years,* 148.

296 *"strike-breakers, vigilantes":* Lew Levinson, "California Casualty List," *Nation,* August 29, 1934.

296 *An accounting:* Levinson, "California Casualty List."

296 *empowered to recruit:* Hurt, *American Agriculture,* 308.

297 *This was the world:* Pawel, *The Crusades,* 8–9.

298 *As the expiration date:* Los Angeles Times, July 26, 1973.

298 *the UFW lost:* Pawel, *The Crusades,* 456.

298 *only seven thousand members:* Los Angeles Times, August 20, 2022.

299 *Premiere Raspberries in Watsonville:* Watsonville Pajaronian, March 26, 2020.

299 *A survey established:* "Farmworker Health in California," Community and Labor Center, University of California, Merced, 2022.

22. DISASTER AT PLATFORM A

300 *farmland on its banks:* Steinhart and Steinhart, *Blowout,* 2.

301 *At 10:45 that morning:* This recounting of the drilling is based on Easton, *Black Tide,* 7–15.

301 *When the sun rose:* Easton, *Black Tide,* 31.

302 *"lay on the blue":* Macdonald, *Sleeping Beauty,* 3.

302 *By the first week:* Dye, *Blowout at Platform A,* 12.

302 *"amorphous concern":* Spezio, *Slick Policy,* 145.

302 *The expectation:* White, *Formative Years,* 3.

302 *"large marshes":* Bolton, *Fray Juan Crespi,* 149.

303 *"covered with a thick":* Vancouver, *A Voyage of Discovery,* vol. 4, 325.

303 *As a lubricant:* White, *Formative Years,* 16.

303 *"many dealers":* *Commercial Herald,* quoted in White, *Formative Years,* 78.

303 *"practically no commercial supply":* See Harvey S. Perloff, et al., *Regions, Resources, and Economic Growth,* (Baltimore: The Johns Hopkins Press, 1960), 183.

303 *California production surged:* Gerald T. White, "California's Other Mineral," *Pacific Historical Review* (May 1970).

303 *Every year between 1894 and 1918:* Williamson et al., *The American Petroleum Industry,* 27.

303 *"As gold was":* White, "California's Other Mineral."

303 *He and a partner:* McWilliams, *Southern California Country,* 130ff.

304 *"as breezy as a circus":* McWilliams, *Southern California Country,* 243.

304 *"the squarest and surest":* *Los Angeles Times,* June 18, 1922.

304 *"See the Oil":* Steinhart and Steinhart, *Blowout,* 27.

305 *ninety-eight million:* Steinhart and Steinhart, *Blowout,* 47.

305 *When the Mobil:* *Los Angeles Times,* December 3, 1967.

306 *"America today stands":* Udall, *The Quiet Crisis,* viii.

306 *"agonized" over the decision:* Transcript, Stewart L. Udall Oral History Interview 3, 4/18/69, Lyndon Baines Johnson Oral History Collection, University of Texas (hereafter cited as Udall OH).

307 *he approved the auction:* Spezio, *Slick Policy,* 43–44.

307 *"the conservation Bay of Pigs":* Udall OH.

307 *The oil continued:* Easton, *Black Tide,* 110.

307 *On the day:* Easton, *Black Tide,* 50.

308 *Tent-shaped plastic:* Steinhart and Steinhart, *Blowout,* 75.

308 *A presidential panel:* Steinhart and Steinhart, *Blowout,* 69.

308 *In the first days:* Spezio, *Slick Policy,* 139.

308 *"Santa Barbara Is Alive":* Dye, *Blowout at Platform A,* 72.

308 *On the morning of February 5:* Dye, *Blowout at Platform A,* 65.

309 *"shutting down the whole":* Dye, *Blowout at Platform A,* 69.

310 *Bud Bottoms:* Easton, *Black Tide,* 32.

310 *"See, Mr. President":* MacDonald oral history at https://www.aip.org/history-programs/niels-bohr-library/oral-histories/32156.

311 *"a great instinct":* Easton, *Black Tide,* 244.

312 *tanker Exxon Valdez:* See NOAA's Damage Assessment, Remediation, and

Restoration Program on the *Exxon Valdez*, https://darrp.noaa.gov/oil-spills
/exxon-valdez.

23. SIX DAYS IN WATTS

313   *California Highway Patrol officer:* This description of the events of August 11,
      1965, is drawn chiefly from Conot, *Rivers of Blood*, 6ff, and "Violence in the
      City—an End or a Beginning?," Governor's Commission on the Los Angeles
      Riots (hereafter cited as McCone), 10–21.

314   *"a turning point":* Conot, *Rivers of Blood*, ix.

314   *After the original grantee:* Bullock, *Watts*, 11.

315   *"three or four dusty":* Bontemps, *God Sends Sunday.* 117.

315   *"without doubt the most":* *Crisis* (August 1913).

315   *The Black population:* Rice et al., *The Elusive Eden,* 519.

315   *"When people from Texas":* Augustus F. Hawkins oral history, Center for Oral
      History Research, Charles E. Young Research Library, UCLA.

316   *"in search of better":* Quoted in Sides, *L.A. City Limits,* 11.

316   *"remarkable progress":* *Los Angeles Times*, February 12, 1909.

316   *Bridget "Biddy" Mason*: For Mason's life story, see Dolores Hayden, "Biddy
      Mason's Los Angeles, 1856–1891," *California History* (Fall 1989).

317   *"hundreds of babies":* Hayden, "Biddy Mason's Los Angeles," 221.

317   *an oft-repeated:* *Los Angeles Times*, February 12, 1909.

317   *nine other Black churches:* Sides, *L.A. City Limits,* 16.

317   *"safe refuge":* Lonnie G. Bunch, "A Past Not Necessarily Prologue: The Afro-
      American in Los Angeles," in Klein and Schiesl, *20th Century Los Angeles,* 101.

318   *"Black Belt":* Douglas Flamming, "African-Americans and the Politics of Race
      in Progressive-Era Los Angeles," in Deverell and Sitton, *California Progressiv-
      ism,* 221.

318   *the 1910 census:* "Black Population 1790–1915," US Census Bureau, 473.

318   *"Buy Lots now":* Bunch, "A Past Not Necessarily Prologue," 103.

318   *"ate in the same":* Somerville, *Man of Color,* 127.

319   *"read like a 'who's who'":* Bunch, "A Past Not Necessarily Prologue," 112.

319   *"every ugly and ridiculous":* Arnold Rampersad, *The Life of Langston Hughes*, vol.
      1 (New York: Oxford University Press, 1986), 368.

319   *"Los Angeles is not":* Quoted in Bunch, "A Past Not Necessarily Prologue," 105.

319   *"neither extortion or a violation":* Bunch, "A Past Not Necessarily Prologue," 106.

320   *"The colored voters":* *Eagle*, August 28, 1914, quoted in Flamming, "African-
      Americans," 216.

320   *"alien races":* Sides, *L.A. City Limits,* 18.

320   *"colored groups":* Bunch, "A Past Not Necessarily Prologue," 114.

320 *restrictions on the transfer:* Los Angeles Investment Co. v. Gary, 181 Cal. 680 (1919). The California Supreme Court cited the *Gary* decision as precedent when it again ruled that excluding the occupancy of property by non-whites was valid in *Wayt v. Patee,* 205 Cal. 46 (1928).

320 *That same year: Corrigan v. Buckley,* 271 U.S. 323.

320 *Not until 1948: Shelley v. Kraemer,* 334 U.S. 1 (1948).

320 *"invisible walls of steel":* J. Max Bond, "The Negro in Los Angeles," PhD dissertation, University of Southern California, 1936, quoted in Sides, *L.A. City Limits,* 17.

320 *a Klan official boasted: Los Angeles Times,* July 20, 1921.

321 *"almost hysterical zeal": Los Angeles Times,* June 1, 1930. The *Times'* listing of Shuler's targets in that article took up almost a full page.

321 *"as sweet music":* Gordon, *The Second Coming,* 90.

321 *"Blacks who ventured": Los Angeles Times,* July 21, 2002.

321 *"race war":* History Advisory Board Report, Bruce's Beach Task Force, City of Manhattan Beach, 37.

321 *police commonly arrested:* History Advisory Board Report, 12.

322 *"The white people":* Bass, *Forty Years,* 55–56.

322 *Of the 21,000: Los Angeles Times,* April 3, 1926. Contemporary reports stated that the Klan opposed annexation, but that appears to have been a formality while the organization agitated for annexation behind the scenes through intimidation and violence. See Bass, *Forty Years,* 55–56; Conot, *Rivers of Blood,* 203; and Bunch, "A Past Not Necessarily Prologue," 115.

322 *The wave of Black immigrants:* Nash, "Stages of California's Economic Growth," 92.

322 *"White supremacy may be":* Somerville, *Man of Color,* 149.

322 *Interracial tensions:* Somerville, *Man of Color,* 95.

323 *The use of racial:* Sides, *L.A. City Limits,* 18.

323 *their unified response:* Gustavo Arellano, "How Black L.A. Defended Mexican Americans," *Los Angeles Times,* June 2, 2023.

323 *"a badge of delinquency": Los Angeles Times,* June 2, 1943.

323 *The June riots erupted:* McWilliams, *North from Mexico,* pages 221 and following.

324 *"The zoot suiters": Los Angeles Times,* June 7, 1943.

324 *the city council even pondered: Los Angeles Times,* June 11, 1943.

324 *"the birth of the storm troopers":* Chester B. Himes, "Zoot Riots Are Race Riots," *Crisis* (July 1943).

324 *"a white heat":* Arellano, "How Black L.A. Defended."

324 *"into dark alleys":* Bass, *Forty Years,* 115.

324   *By war's end:* Lloyd H. Fisher, "The Problem of Violence: Observations on Race Conflict in Los Angeles," American Council on Race Relations (1945), 7.

324   *"actively encouraged":* Fisher, "The Problem of Violence," 13.

325   *Parker fulfilled:* Martin J. Schiesl, "Behind the Badge: The Police and Social Discontent in Los Angeles Since 1950," in Klein and Schiesl, *20th Century Los Angeles,* 153ff.

326   *"1,000 Riot":* Los Angeles Times, August 12, 1965.

326   *"You cannot tell":* Conot, *Rivers of Blood,* 103.

326   *"when one person":* Conot, *Rivers of Blood,* 349.

327   *"I'm here to ask":* Conot, *Rivers of Blood,* 151.

327   *"massive show of force":* McCone, 20.

327   *The arrestees numbered:* McCone, 24. See also Conot, *Rivers of Blood,* 379.

327   *"not so much":* Robert M. Fogelson, "White on Black: A Critique of the McCone Commission Report," *Political Science Quarterly* (September 1967).

327   *Among the juveniles:* Conot, *Rivers of Blood,* 380.

328   *"a deep and long-standing":* McCone, 27.

328   *"Communists, dupes":* Conot, *Rivers of Blood,* 429.

328   *"the angry exhortations":* McCone, 85.

329   *"spasm":* McCone, 1.

329   *"caught up in":* McCone, 1, 23–24.

329   *"While the Negro":* McCone, 3.

329   *"I wouldn't say":* Fogelson, *The Fragmented Metropolis.*

330   *"I do not believe":* McCone, 87.

330   *"symbolize white power":* Report of the National Advisory Commission on Civil Disorders, 93.

330   *"a kind of Alice in Wonderland":* Report of the National Advisory Commission, 13.

24. THE CRISIS OF GROWTH

333   *"water supplies will always":* "Colorado River Basin Water Management," National Research Council, 52.

333   *"I tell you, gentlemen":* Hiltzik, *Colossus,* 399.

334   *banning automobile parking:* Scott L. Bottles, *Los Angeles and the Automobile: The Making of the Modern City.* (Berkeley: University of California Press, 1987), 15.

334   *310,000 automobiles:* Starr, *California,* 185.

335   *"a network of traffic":* "Traffic Survey, Los Angeles Metropolitan Area, Nineteen Hundred Thirty-Seven," Engineering Department, Automobile Club of Southern California, 30.

335   *Collier-Burns Act:* Rice et al., *The Elusive Eden,* 491.

335 *"wiping out"*: Rice et al., *The Elusive Eden*, 493.

335 *"legitimate property owners"*: Gilbert Estrada, "If You Build It, They Will Move: The Los Angeles Freeway System and the Displacement of Mexican East Los Angeles, 1944–1972," *Southern California Quarterly* (October 2005).

336 *"substandard dwellings"*: California Division of Highways, "California Highways and Public Works" (March–April 1946).

336 *"infiltrated by minority"*: Estrada, "If You Build It."

336 *"federally owned house trailers"*: "California Highways and Public Works" (July–August 1948).

338 *Within six months:* Schwadron, *California and the American Tax Revolt,* 180.

339 *"The most important thing"*: New York Times, October 16, 2016.

340 *This scheme:* Christopher Weare, "The California Electricity Crisis: Causes and Policy Options," Public Policy Institute of California, 2003.

341 *"Somewhere along"*: Los Angeles Times, March 29, 2018.

342 *But it died: Los Angeles Times,* April 17, 2018.

342 *By the Census Bureau's: New York Times,* September 1, 1964.

342 *"They want the state"*: McWilliams, *California*, 20.

343 *From 1940 to 1970:* Mac Taylor, "California's High Housing Costs: Causes and Consequences," California Legislative Analyst's Office, March 17, 2015.

343 *the state supreme court: Friends of Mammoth v. Board of Supervisors*, 8 Cal.3d 247 (1972).

343 *From the environmentalists' standpoint:* Antonio Rossmann, "The 25-Year Legacy of *Friends of Mammoth*," *Environs* (February 1998).

343 *"protecting forests"*: Jennifer Hernandez, "California Environmental Quality Act Lawsuits and California's Housing Crisis," *Hastings Environmental Law Journal* (Winter 2018).

343 *"You can't change CEQA"*: Jim Newton, "Gov. Jerry Brown: The Long Struggle for the Good Cause," *UCLA Blue Print* (Spring 2016).

344 *California was estimated: Los Angeles Times,* March 29, 2018.

344 *Between 2020 and 2023:* Hans Johnson, "Large Cities Lose Population Even as They Add New Housing," Public Policy Institute of California, August 9, 2023.

EPILOGUE: KEEPING THE CALIFORNIA DREAM ALIVE

346 *Nine of the ten:* See https://www.fire.ca.gov/incidents.

347 *cut their rates of decline:* William H. Frey, "Big Cities Are Showing Signs of Recovery After Historic Population Losses, New Census Data Shows," Brookings Institution, June 22, 2023.

347 *state's "exceptionalism"*: McWilliams, *California*, 344.

347 The Atlantic *titled:* Friedersdorf, "The California Dream," and Nellie Bowles, "How San Francisco Became a Failed City," *Atlantic*, June 2022.

349 *The gap between rich and poor:* "Income Inequality in California," Public Policy Institute of California, March 2023, https://www.ppic.org/publication /income-inequality-in-california/.

349 *the state's poverty rate:* "Poverty in California," Public Policy Institute of California, October 2023, https://www.ppic.org/wp-content/uploads/JTF_Poverty JTF.pdf.

350 *"climate change crusader":* Jeremy B. White, "How Gavin Newsom Became a Climate Change Crusader," *Politico*, October 23, 2023.

351 *"the broad diversity":* Regents Policy 2102: Policy on Undergraduate Admissions (adopted May 20, 1988).

351 *"race, religion, gender":* "UC Regents, in Historic Vote, Wipe Out Affirmative Action," *Los Angeles Times*, July 21, 1995.

351 *passed 55 percent:* Ballotpedia, California Proposition 209, Affirmative Action Initiative (1996), https://ballotpedia.org/California_Proposition_209,_ Affirmative_Action_Initiative_(1996).

351 *"The impact was immediate":* Brief for the President and Chancellors of the University of California, Students for Fair Admission v. President and Fellows of Harvard University, August 1, 2022.

353 *Paul Conrad:* The editorial cartoon was published in the *Los Angeles Times* on June 11, 1982.

353 *"nearly four in five":* "Immigrants in California," Public Policy Institute of California, January 2023, https://www.ppic.org/publication/immigrants-in -california/.

SELECTED BIBLIOGRAPHY

Ayers, James J. *Gold and Sunshine: Reminiscences of Early California.* Boston: Gorham Press, 1922.

Bagley, Will, ed. *Scoundrel's Tale: The Samuel Brannan Papers.* Spokane: Arthur H. Clark, 1999.

Balio, Tino, ed. *The American Film Industry.* Madison: University of Wisconsin Press, 1985.

Bancroft, Hubert Howe. *History of California.* Vol. 1. San Francisco: A. L. Bancroft, 1884.

———. *History of California.* Vol. 2. San Francisco: A. L. Bancroft, 1885.

———. *History of California.* Vol. 3. San Francisco: A. L. Bancroft, 1885.

———. *History of California.* Vol. 4. San Francisco: A. L. Bancroft, 1886.

———. *History of California.* Vol. 5. San Francisco: A. L. Bancroft, 1886.

———. *History of California.* Vol. 6. San Francisco: A. L. Bancroft, 1888.

———. *History of California.* Vol. 7. San Francisco: A. L. Bancroft, 1890.

———. *Popular Tribunals.* 2 vols. San Francisco: History Company, 1887.

Bass, Charlotta A. *Forty Years: Memoirs from the Pages of a Newspaper.* Los Angeles: California Eagle Press, 1960.

Bean, Walton. *Boss Ruef's San Francisco.* Berkeley: University of California Press, 1967.

Beebe, Rose Marie, and Robert M. Senkewicz, eds. *Lands of Promise and Despair: Chronicles of Early California, 1535–1846.* Berkeley: Heyday Books, 2001.

Beilharz, Edwin A. *Felipe de Neve, First Governor of California.* San Francisco: California Historical Society, 1971.

Bernstein, Irving. *The Turbulent Years: A History of the American Worker, 1933–1940.* Chicago: Haymarket Books, 2010.

Bieber, Ralph P., ed. *Southern Trails to California in 1849.* Glendale, CA: Arthur H. Clark, 1937.

Bolton, Herbert Eugene, ed. *Fray Juan Crespi: Missionary Explorer on the Pacific Coast, 1769–1774.* Berkeley: University of California Press, 1927.

———. *Spanish Exploration in the Southwest, 1542–1706.* New York: Charles Scribner's Sons, 1908.

Bontemps, Arna. *God Sends Sunday.* New York: Harcourt, Brace, 1931.

Brown, J. L. *The Mussel Slough Tragedy.* Self-published, 1958.

Browne, J. Ross. *Adventures in the Apache Country.* New York: Harper and Brothers, 1869.

———. *Crusoe's Island: A Ramble in the Footsteps of Alexander Selkirk.* New York: Harper and Brothers, 1871.

———. *The Indians of California.* San Francisco: Colt Press, 1944.

Browne, Lina Fergusson, ed. *J. Ross Browne: His Letters, Journals and Writings.* Albuquerque: University of New Mexico Press, 1969.

Bryce, James. *The American Commonwealth,* Vol. 2. Indianapolis: Liberty Fund, 1995.

Bullock, Paul, ed. *Watts: The Aftermath: An Inside View of the Ghetto by the People of Watts.* New York: Grove Press, 1969.

Burnett, Peter H. *Recollections and Opinions of an Old Pioneer.* New York: D. Appleton, 1880.

Cameron, Evan William, ed. *Sound and the Cinema: The Coming of Sound to American Film.* Pleasantville, NY: Redgrave Publishing, 1980.

Camp, Charles L. *Kit Carson in California.* San Francisco: California Historical Society, 1922.

Cannon, Lou. *Governor Reagan: His Rise to Power.* New York: Public Affairs, 2003.

Carosso, Vincent P. *The California Wine Industry: A Study of the Formative Years.* Berkeley: University of California Press, 1951.

Caughey, John Walton. *California.* New York: Prentice-Hall, 1940.

Ceplair, Larry, and Steven Englund. *The Inquisition in Hollywood: Politics in the Film Community, 1930–1960.* Berkeley: University of California Press, 1979.

Chaffin, Tom. *Pathfinder: John Charles Frémont and the Course of American Empire.* New York: Hill and Wang, 2002.

Chapman, Charles E. *A History of California: The Spanish Period.* New York: Macmillan, 1926.

Cherny, Robert W. *Harry Bridges: Labor Radical, Labor Legend.* Urbana: University of Illinois Press, 2023.

Cleland, Robert Glass. *A History of California: The American Period.* New York: Macmillan, 1922.

Cleland, Robert Glass, and Frank B. Putnam. *Isaias W. Hellman and the Farmers and Merchants Bank.* San Marino, CA: Huntington Library, 1980.

Coblentz, Stanton A. *Villains and Vigilantes: The Story of James King of William and Pioneer Justice in California.* New York: Wilson-Erickson, 1936.

Cole, Cornelius. *Memoirs.* New York: McLoughlin Brothers, 1908.

Colton, Walter. *Three Years in California.* New York: A. S. Barnes, 1850.

Conot, Robert. *Rivers of Blood, Years of Darkness.* New York: William Morrow, 1968.

Conrat, Maisie, and Richard Conrat. *Executive Order 9066: The Internment of 110,000 Japanese Americans.* Los Angeles: California Historical Society, 1972.

Cook, Sherburne Friend. *The Conflict Between the California Indian and White Civilization.* Vol. 1. Berkeley: University of California Press, 1943.

Coolidge, Mary Roberts. *Chinese Immigration.* New York: Henry Holt, 1909.

Crosby, Elisha Oscar. *Reminiscences of California and Guatemala from 1849 to 1864.* San Marino, CA: Huntington Library, 1945.

Cross, Ira B. *A History of the Labor Movement in California.* Berkeley: University of California Press, 1935.

Cunningham, William Glenn. *The Aircraft Industry: A Study in Industrial Location.* Los Angeles: Lorrin L. Morrison Publishing, 1951.

Daggett, Stuart. *Chapters on the History of the Southern Pacific.* New York: Ronald Press Company, 1922.

Dana, Richard Henry, Jr. *Two Years Before the Mast.* Boston: Houghton Mifflin, 1923.

Daniel, Cletus E. *Bitter Harvest: A History of California Farmworkers, 1870–1941.* Ithaca, NY: Cornell University Press, 1981.

Daniels, Roger. *The Politics of Prejudice: The Anti-Japanese Movement in California and the Struggle for Japanese Exclusion.* Berkeley: University of California Press, 1962.

———. *Concentration Camps USA: Japanese Americans and World War II.* New York: Holt, Rinehart and Winston, 1972.

Daniels, Roger, and Spencer C. Olin. *Racism in California: A Reader in the History of Oppression.* New York: Macmillan, 1972.

Daniels, Roger, Sandra C. Taylor, and Harry H. L. Kitano, eds. *Japanese Americans: From Relocation to Redress.* Seattle: University of Washington Press, 1991.

Darrow, Clarence. *The Story of My Life.* New York: Charles Scribner's Sons, 1932.

Deverell, William. *Railroad Crossing: Californians and the Railroad, 1850–1910.* Berkeley: University of California Press, 1994.

Deverell, William, and Tom Sitton. *California Progressivism Revisited.* Berkeley: University of California Press, 1994.

Didion, Joan. *Slouching Towards Bethlehem.* New York: Farrar, Straus and Giroux, 1990.

———. *Where I Was From.* New York: Alfred A. Knopf, 2003.

Douglass, John Aubrey. *The California Idea and American Higher Education: 1850 to the 1960 Master Plan.* Stanford, CA: Stanford University Press, 2000.

Drabelle, Dennis. *The Great American Railroad War: How Ambrose Bierce and Frank Norris Took On the Notorious Central Pacific Railroad.* New York: St. Martin's Press, 2012.

Dumke, Glenn S. *The Boom of the Eighties in Southern California.* San Marino, CA: Huntington Library, 1963.

Dye, Lee. *Blowout at Platform A: The Crisis That Awakened a Nation.* Garden City, NY: Doubleday, 1971.

Easton, Robert. *Black Tide: The Santa Barbara Oil Spill and Its Consequences.* New York: Delacorte, 1972.

Eaves, Lucile. *A History of California Labor Legislation.* Berkeley: University Press, 1910.

Ellison, Joseph. *California and the Nation, 1850–1869.* Berkeley: University of California Press, 1927.

Erie, Steven P. *Beyond Chinatown: The Metropolitan Water District, Growth, and the Environment in Southern California.* Stanford, CA: Stanford University Press, 2006.

Fogelson, Robert M. *The Fragmented Metropolis: Los Angeles, 1850–1930.* Berkeley: University of California Press, 1967.

Foster, G. G., ed. *The Gold Regions of California.* New York: DeWitt and Davenport, 1848.

Fox, Stephen R. *John Muir and His Legacy: The American Conservation Movement.* Boston: Little, Brown, 1981.

Frémont, John Charles. *Memoirs of My Life.* Chicago: Belford, Clarke, 1887.

Friedricks, William B. *Henry E. Huntington and the Creation of Southern California.* Columbus: Ohio State University Press, 1992.

Gabler, Neal. *An Empire of Their Own: How the Jews Invented Hollywood.* New York: Crown, 1988.

Gardner, David P. *The California Oath Controversy.* Berkeley: University of California Press, 1967.

Gay, Theresa. *James W. Marshall: The Discoverer of California Gold.* Georgetown, CA: Talisman Press, 1967.

George, Henry. *Our Land and Land Policy.* Garden City, NY: Doubleday, Page, 1911.

George, Henry, Jr. *The Life of Henry George.* Garden City, NY: Doubleday, Page, 1911.

Girdner, Audrie, and Anne Loftis. *The Great Betrayal: The Evacuation of the Japanese-Americans During World War II.* New York: Macmillan, 1969.

Goines, David Lance. *The Free Speech Movement: Coming of Age in the 1960s.* Berkeley: Ten Speed Press, 1993.

Gordon, Linda. *The Second Coming of the KKK: The Ku Klux Klan of the 1920s and the American Political Tradition.* New York: Liveright Publishing, 2017.

Gottlieb, Robert, and Irene Wolt. *Thinking Big: The Story of the Los Angeles Times, Its Publishers, and Their Influence on Southern California.* New York: G. P. Putnam's Sons, 1977.

Greeley, Horace. *An Overland Journey, New York to San Francisco, the Summer of 1859.* New York: C. M. Saxton, Barker, 1860.

———. *Recollections of a Busy Life.* New York: J. B. Ford, 1869.

Grodzins, Morton. *Americans Betrayed: Politics and the Japanese Evacuation.* Chicago: University of Chicago Press, 1949.

Guinn, James Miller. *A History of California and an Extended History of Los Angeles and Environs.* Los Angeles: Historic Record Company, 1915.

Hague, Harlan, and David J. Langum. *Thomas O. Larkin: A Life of Patriotism and Profit in Old California.* Norman: University of Oklahoma Press, 1990.

Harte, Bret. *Condensed Novels: And Other Papers.* New York: G. W. Carleton, 1867.

———. *The Writings of Bret Harte.* Vol. 14. Boston: Houghton Mifflin, 1896.

Heizer, Robert F., ed. *The Destruction of California Indians.* Santa Barbara: Peregrine Smith, 1974.

Helper, Hinton R. *The Land of Gold: Reality Versus Fiction.* Baltimore: Henry Taylor, 1855.

Hichborn, Franklin. *Story of the Session of the California Legislature of 1909.* San Francisco: James H. Barry, 1909.

———. *Story of the Session of the California Legislature of 1913.* San Francisco: James H. Barry, 1913.

———. *"The System" as Uncovered by the San Francisco Graft Prosecution.* San Francisco: James H. Barry, 1915.

Hill, Gladwin. *Dancing Bear: An Inside Look at California Politics.* Cleveland: World Publishing, 1968.

Hiltzik, Michael. *Big Science: Ernest Lawrence and the Invention That Launched the Military-Industrial Complex.* New York: Simon and Schuster, 2015.

———. *Colossus: The Turbulent, Thrilling Saga of the Building of Hoover Dam.* New York: Free Press, 2010.

———. *Dealers of Lightning: Xerox PARC and the Dawn of the Computer Age.* New York: Harper Business, 1999.

Hine, Robert V. *California Utopianism: Contemplations of Eden.* San Francisco: Boyd and Fraser, 1981.

———. *California's Utopian Colonies.* Berkeley: University of California Press, 1983.

Hittell, John S. *A History of the City of San Francisco and Incidentally of the State of California.* San Francisco: A. L. Bancroft, 1878.

Hittell, Theodore H. *History of California*. San Francisco: N. J. Stone, 1898.

Hoffman, Abraham. *Vision or Villainy: Origins of the Owens Valley–Los Angeles Water Controversy*. College Station: Texas A and M University Press, 1981.

Houston, Jeanne Wakatsuki, and James D. Houston. *Farewell to Manzanar*. Boston: Houghton Mifflin, 1973.

Hundley, Norris, Jr. *The Great Thirst: Californians and Water: A History*. Berkeley: University of California Press, 2001.

Hurt, R. Douglas. *American Agriculture: A Brief History*. Ames: Iowa State University Press, 1994.

Ide, Simeon. *The Conquest of California, A Biography of William B. Ide*. Oakland: Biobooks, 1944.

Ide, William Brown. *Who Conquered California?* Claremont, NH: Simeon Ide, 1880.

Igler, David. *Industrial Cowboys: Miller and Lux and the Transformation of the Far West, 1850–1920*. Berkeley: University of California Press, 2001.

Inskeep, Steve. *Imperfect Union: How Jessie and John Frémont Mapped the West, Invented Celebrity, and Helped Cause the Civil War*. New York: Penguin, 2020.

Jackson, Helen Hunt. *Ramona: A Story*. Boston: Roberts Brothers, 1896.

———. *Glimpses of California and the Missions*. Boston: Little, Brown, 1919.

Johnson, Robert Underwood. *Remembered Yesterdays*. Boston: Little, Brown, 1923.

Jones, Holway R. *John Muir and the Sierra Club: The Battle for Yosemite*. San Francisco: Sierra Club, 1965.

Kelly, William. *An Excursion to California*. Vol. 2. London: Chapman and Hall, 1851.

Kemble, Edward C. *A History of California Newspapers, 1846–1858*. Edited by Helen Harding Bretnor. Los Gatos, CA: Talisman Press, 1962.

Kennan, George. *E. H. Harriman: A Biography*. Vol. 2. Boston: Houghton Mifflin, 1922.

———. *The Salton Sea: An Account of Harriman's Fight with the Colorado River*. New York: Macmillan, 1917.

Klein, Norman M., and Martin J. Schiesl, eds. *20th Century Los Angeles: Power, Promotion, and Social Conflict*. Claremont, CA: Regina Books, 1990.

Lavender, David. *The Great Persuader*. Garden City, NY: Doubleday, 1970.

Lewis, Oscar. *The Big Four*. New York: Alfred A. Knopf, 1938.

Lewis, Oscar, ed. *This Was San Francisco*. New York: David McKay Company, 1962.

Lew-Williams, Beth. *The Chinese Must Go: Violence, Exclusion, and the Making of the Alien in America*. Cambridge, MA: Harvard University Press, 2018.

Lillard, Richard G. *Eden in Jeopardy: Man's Prodigal Meddling with His Environment: The Southern California Experience*. New York: Alfred A. Knopf, 1966.

Lindley, Walter, and J. P. Widney. *California of the South: Its Physical Geography, Climate, Resources, Routes of Travel, and Health-Resorts*. New York: D. Appleton, 1888.

Lotchin, Roger W. *Fortress California 1910–1961: From Warfare to Welfare*. New York: Oxford University Press, 1992.

———. *San Francisco, 1846–1856: From Hamlet to City*. Urbana: University of Illinois Press, 1997.

Lower, Richard Coke. *A Bloc of One: The Political Career of Hiram W. Johnson*. Stanford, CA: Stanford University Press, 1993.

Luger, Michael I., and Harvey A. Goldstein. *Technology in the Garden: Research Parks and Regional Economic Development*. Chapel Hill: University of North Carolina Press, 1991.

Macdonald, Ross. *Sleeping Beauty*. New York: Vintage, 1973.

Madley, Benjamin. *An American Genocide: The United States and the California Indian Catastrophe, 1846–1873*. New Haven, CT: Yale University Press, 2016.

Marginson, Simon. *The Dream Is Over: The Crisis of Clark Kerr's California Idea of Higher Education*. Berkeley: University of California Press, 2016.

Marryat, Frank. *Mountains and Molehills, or Recollections of a Burnt Journal*. New York: Harper and Brothers, 1855.

Maynard, Crosby. *Flight Plan for Tomorrow: The Douglas Story*. Santa Monica: Douglas Aircraft Company, 1966.

Mayo, Morrow. *Los Angeles*. New York: Alfred A. Knopf, 1933.

McAfee, Ward. *California's Railroad Era 1850–1911*. San Marino: Golden West Books, 1973.

McGill, William J. *The Year of the Monkey: Revolt on Campus 1968–69*. New York: McGraw-Hill, 1982.

McGlashan, C. F. *History of the Donner Party: A Tragedy of the Sierra*. Sacramento: H. S. Crocker, 1902.

McWilliams, Carey. *Ambrose Bierce: A Biography*. New York: Albert and Charles Boni, 1929.

———. *California: The Great Exception*. Berkeley: University of California Press, 1949.

———. *Factories in the Field*. Berkeley: University of California Press, 1935.

———. *Louis Adamic and Shadow-America*. Los Angeles: Arthur Whipple, 1935.

———. *North from Mexico*. 1948. New edition updated by Matt S. Meier. New York: Praeger, 1990.

———. *Southern California Country: An Island on the Land*. New York: Meredith Press, 1946.

Morrison, Michael A. *Slavery and the American West: The Eclipse of Manifest Destiny and the Coming of the Civil War*. Chapel Hill: University of North Carolina Press, 1997.

Mowry, George E. *The California Progressives*. Berkeley: University of California Press, 1951.

Muir, John. *Edward Henry Harriman.* Garden City, NY: Doubleday, Page, 1912.

———. *The Mountains of California.* New York: Century Company, 1911.

———. *Our National Parks.* Boston: Houghton Mifflin, 1901.

———. *The Yosemite.* New York: Century Company, 1912.

Mulholland, Catherine. *William Mulholland and the Rise of Los Angeles.* Berkeley: University of California Press, 2000.

Muscatine, Doris. *Old San Francisco: The Biography of a City from Early Days to the Earthquake.* New York: G. P. Putnam's Sons, 1975.

Nash, Gerald D. *The American West Transformed: The Impact of the Second World War.* Lincoln: University of Nebraska Press, 1990.

Nixon, Richard M. *RN: The Memoirs of Richard Nixon.* New York: Grosset and Dunlap, 1978.

———. *Six Crises.* Garden City, NY: Doubleday, 1962.

Nordhoff, Charles. *California: For Health, Pleasure, and Residence.* New York: Harper and Brothers, 1874.

Norris, Frank. *The Octopus: A Story of California.* Garden City, NY: Doubleday, 1901.

Older, Fremont. *My Own Story.* New York: Macmillan, 1926.

Olin, Spencer C., Jr. *California Politics 1846–1920: The Emerging Corporate State.* San Francisco: Boyd and Fraser, 1981.

———. *California's Prodigal Sons: Hiram Johnson and the Progressives, 1911–1917.* Berkeley: University of California Press, 1968.

Orsi, Richard J. *Sunset Limited: The Southern Pacific Railroad and the Development of the American West, 1850–1930.* Berkeley: University of California Press, 2005.

O'Shaughnessy, M. M. *Hetch Hetchy: Its Origin and History.* San Francisco: Recorder Printing and Publishing Company, 1934.

Ostrom, Vincent. *Water and Politics: A Study of Water Policies and Administration in the Development of Los Angeles.* Los Angeles: Haynes Foundation, 1953.

Paul, Rodman W. *California Gold: The Beginning of Mining in the Far West.* Lincoln: University of Nebraska Press, 1947.

Pawel, Miriam. *The Crusades of Cesar Chavez.* New York: Bloomsbury Press, 2014.

Perkins, Frances. *The Roosevelt I Knew.* New York: Viking, 1946.

Perlstein, Rick. *Before the Storm: Barry Goldwater and the Unmaking of the American Consensus.* New York: Nation Books, 2001.

Phelps, Alonzo M. *Contemporary Biography of California's Representative Men.* San Francisco: A. L. Bancroft, 1881.

Pinchot, Gifford. *The Fight for Conservation.* New York: Doubleday, Page, 1910.

Pisani, Donald J. *From the Family Farm to Agribusiness: The Irrigation Crusade in California and the West, 1850–1931.* Berkeley: University of California Press, 1984.

Pitt, Leonard. *Decline of the Californios: A Social History of the Spanish-Speaking Californians, 1846–1890*. Berkeley: University of California Press, 1999.

Powers, Stephen. *Afoot and Alone: A Walk from Sea to Sea by the Southern Route*. Hartford, CT: Columbian Book Company, 1884.

———. *Tribes of California*. Washington, DC: Government Printing Office, 1877.

Putnam, Ruth. *California: The Name*. Berkeley: University of California Press, 1917.

Quinn, Anthony. *The Original Sin: A Self-Portrait*. Boston: Little, Brown, 1972.

Rae, John B. *Climb to Greatness: The American Aircraft Industry, 1920–1960*. Cambridge, MA: MIT Press, 1968.

Ramirez, Salvador A., ed. *The Octopus Speaks: The Colton Letters*. Carlsbad, CA: Tentacled Press, 1982.

Ramsaye, Terry. *A Million and One Nights: A History of the Motion Picture*. New York: Simon and Schuster, 1926.

Reagan, Ronald. *The Creative Society: Some Comments on Problems Facing America*. New York: Devin-Adair, 1968.

Reisner, Marc. *Cadillac Desert: The American West and Its Disappearing Water*. New York: Penguin Books, 1986.

Rice, Richard B., William A. Bullough, and Richard J. Orsi. *The Elusive Eden: A New History of California*. New York: McGraw-Hill, 1996.

Richman, Irving Berdine. *California Under Spain and Mexico, 1535–1847*. Boston: Houghton Mifflin, 1911.

Robinson, Alfred. *Life in California, Being a Residence of Several Years in That Territory*. San Francisco: William Doxey, 1897.

Robinson, Greg. *By Order of the President: FDR and the Internment of Japanese Americans*. Cambridge, MA: Harvard University Press, 2006.

Rogin, Michael P., and John L. Shover. *Political Change in California: Critical Elections and Social Movements, 1890–1966*. Westport, CT: Greenwood Publishing, 1970.

Rohrbough, Malcolm J. *Days of Gold: The California Gold Rush and the American Nation*. Berkeley: University of California Press, 1997.

Roney, Frank, and Ira B. Cross, eds. *Frank Roney, Irish Rebel and California Labor Leader: An Autobiography*. Berkeley: University of California Press, 1931.

Rorabaugh, W. J. *Berkeley at War: The 1960s*. New York: Oxford University Press, 1989.

Royce, C. C. *John Bidwell: Pioneer, Statesman, Philanthropist*. Chico, CA: 1906.

Royce, Josiah. *California, from the Conquest in 1846 to the Second Vigilance Committee in San Francisco: A Study of American Character*. Boston: Houghton Mifflin, 1886.

———. *The Feud of Oakfield Creek: A Novel of California Life*. Boston: Houghton, Mifflin and Company, 1887.

Samish, Arthur H., and Bob Thomas. *The Secret Boss of California: The Life and High Times of Art Samish.* New York: Crown, 1971.

Sandmeyer, Elmer Clarence. *The Anti-Chinese Movement in California.* Urbana: University of Illinois Press, 1939.

Savio, Mario, Eugene Walker, and Raya Sunayevskaya. *The Free Speech Movement and the Negro Revolution.* Detroit: News and Letters, 1965.

Saxenian, AnnaLee. *Regional Advantage: Culture and Competition in Silicon Valley and Route 128.* Cambridge, MA: Harvard University Press, 1994.

Saxton, Alexander. *The Indispensable Enemy: Labor and the Anti-Chinese Movement in California.* Oakland: University of California Press, 1971.

Schoenherr, Allan A. *A Natural History of California.* Oakland: University of California Press, 2017.

Schoneberger, William, with Paul Sonnenburg. *California Wings: A History of Aviation in the Golden State.* Woodland Hills, CA: Windsor, 1984.

Schulberg, Budd, ed. *From the Ashes: Voices of Watts.* New York: New American Library, 1967.

Schwadron, Terry, ed. *California and the American Tax Revolt: Proposition 13 Five Years Later.* Berkeley: University of California Press, 1984.

Scott, Allen J. *Technopolis: High-Technology Industry and Regional Development in Southern California.* Berkeley: University of California Press, 1993.

Sherman, William Tecumseh. *Memoirs of Gen. William T. Sherman.* New York: D. Appleton, 1891.

Sherwood, Mary Elizabeth Wilson. *An Epistle to Posterity: Being Rambling Recollections of Many Years of My Life.* New York: Harper and Brothers, 1897.

Sides, Josh. *L.A. City Limits: African American Los Angeles from the Great Depression to the Present.* Berkeley: University of California Press, 2003.

Siler, Julia Flynn. *The House of Mondavi: The Rise and Fall of an American Wine Dynasty.* New York: Gotham Books, 2007.

Sinclair, Upton. *I, Candidate for Governor: And How I Got Licked.* New York: Farrar and Rinehart, 1935.

———. *I, Governor of California, and How I Ended Poverty: A True Story of the Future.* Los Angeles: Upton Sinclair, 1933.

Smith, Stacey L. *Freedom's Frontier: California and the Struggle Over Unfree Labor, Emancipation, and Reconstruction.* Chapel Hill: University of North Carolina Press, 2003.

Somerville, J. Alexander. *Man of Color: An Autobiography.* Los Angeles: Lorrin L. Morrison, 1949.

Soulé, Frank, John H. Gihon, and James Nisbet. *The Annals of San Francisco.* New York: D. Appleton, 1854.

Spezio, Teresa Sabol. *Slick Policy: Environmental and Science Policy in the Aftermath of the Santa Barbara Oil Spill.* Pittsburgh: University of Pittsburgh Press, 2018.

Spicer, Edward H., Asael T. Hansen, Katherine Luomala, and Marvin K. Opler. *Impounded People: Japanese-Americans in the Relocation Centers.* Tucson: University of Arizona Press, 1969.

Starr, Kevin. *California: A History.* New York: Modern Library, 2005.

Steffens, Lincoln. *The Autobiography of Lincoln Steffens.* Vol. 1, *A Boy on Horseback/Seeing New York First.* New York: Harcourt, Brace and World, 1931.

————. *The Autobiography of Lincoln Steffens.* Vol. 2, *Muckraking/Revolution/Seeing America Last.* New York: Harcourt, Brace and World, 1931.

Steinbrugge, Karl V. *Earthquake Hazard in the San Francisco Bay Area: A Continuing Problem in Public Policy.* Berkeley: Institute of Governmental Studies, 1968.

Steinhart, Carol E., and John S. Steinhart. *Blowout: A Case Study of the Santa Barbara Oil Spill.* North Scituate, MA: Duxbury Press, 1972.

Stewart, George R. *Ordeal by Hunger: The Story of the Donner Party.* Lincoln: University of Nebraska Press, 1936.

Stimson, Grace Heilman. *Rise of the Labor Movement in Los Angeles.* Berkeley: University of California Press, 1955.

Taber, George M. *Judgment of Paris: California vs. France and the Historic 1976 Wine Tasting That Revolutionized Wine.* New York: Scribner, 2005.

Tateishi, John. *And Justice for All: An Oral History of the Japanese American Detention Camps.* New York: Random House, 1984.

Taylor, Bayard. *Eldorado; or, Adventures in the Path of Empire.* New York: G. P. Putnam's Sons, 1871.

Taylor, Ray W. *Hetch Hetchy: The Story of San Francisco's Struggle to Provide a Water Supply for Her Future Needs.* San Francisco: Ricardo J. Orozco, 1926.

Tejani, James. *A Machine to Move Ocean and Earth: The Making of the Port of Los Angeles—and America.* New York: W. W. Norton, 2024.

Torchiana, H. A. Van Coenen. *California Gringos.* San Francisco: Paul Elder, 1930.

Townsend, Francis Everett. *New Horizons (An Autobiography).* Edited by Jesse George Murray. Chicago: J. L. Stewart, 1943.

Treadwell, Edward F. *The Cattle King: A Dramatized Biography.* New York: Macmillan, 1931.

Trollope, Anthony. *A Letter from Anthony Trollope Describing a Visit to California in 1875.* San Francisco: Colt Press, 1946.

Tutorow, Norman E. *The Governor: The Life and Legacy of Leland Stanford, a California Colossus.* 2 vols. Spokane: Arthur H. Clark, 2004.

Twain, Mark. *Roughing It.* New York: Signet Classics, 1962.

Tygiel, Jules. *The Great Los Angeles Swindle: Oil, Stocks, and Scandal During the Roaring Twenties.* New York: Oxford University Press, 1994.

Uchida, Yoshiko. *Desert Exile: The Uprooting of a Japanese American Family.* Seattle: University of Washington Press, 1982.

Udall, Stewart L. *The Quiet Crisis.* New York: Holt, Rinehart, and Winston, 1963.

Vancouver, George. *A Voyage of Discovery to the North Pacific Ocean and Around the World.* London: John Stockdale, 1801.

Van Dyke, T. S. *Millionaires of a Day: An Inside History of the Great Southern California "Boom."* New York: Fords, Howard and Hulbert, 1890.

Vogel, David. *Trading Up: Consumer and Environmental Regulation in a Global Economy.* Cambridge, MA: Harvard University Press, 1995.

Von Langsdorff, Georg Heinrich. *Voyages and Travels in Various Parts of the World, Part II.* London: Henry Colburn, 1814.

Voorhis, Jerry. *The Strange Case of Richard Milhous Nixon.* New York: Popular Library, 1973.

Wagner, Henry R. *Juan Rodríguez Cabrillo, Discoverer of the Coast of California.* San Francisco: California Historical Society, 1941.

Warner, Charles Dudley. *Our Italy.* New York: Harper and Brothers, 1891.

Warren, Earl. *The Memoirs of Chief Justice Earl Warren.* Garden City, NY: Doubleday, 1977.

White, Gerald T. *Formative Years in the Far West: A History of Standard Oil of California and Predecessors Through 1919.* New York: Appleton-Century-Crofts, 1962.

Willard, Charles Dwight. *A History of the Chamber of Commerce of Los Angeles, California.* Los Angeles: Kingsley-Barnes and Neuner, 1899.

————. *History of Los Angeles City.* Los Angeles: Kingsley-Barnes and Neuner, 1901.

Williams, Mary Floyd. *History of the San Francisco Committee of Vigilance of 1851.* Berkeley: University of California Press, 1922.

Williamson, Harold F., Ralph L. Andreano, Arnold R. Daum, and Gilbert C. Close. *The American Petroleum Industry: The Age of Energy 1899–1959.* Evanston, IL: Northwestern University Press, 1963.

Wolfe, Linnie Marsh. *Son of the Wilderness: The Life of John Muir.* New York: Alfred A. Knopf, 1945.

Worster, Donald. *Rivers of Empire: Water, Aridity, and the Growth of the American West.* New York: Oxford University Press, 1986.

Young, Brigham. *Discourses of Brigham Young.* Salt Lake City: Deseret Book Company, 1925.

INDEX

ABOUT

MARINER BOOKS

MARINER BOOKS traces its beginnings to 1832 when William Ticknor cofounded the Old Corner Bookstore in Boston, from which he would run the legendary firm Ticknor and Fields, publisher of Ralph Waldo Emerson, Harriet Beecher Stowe, Nathaniel Hawthorne, and Henry David Thoreau. Following Ticknor's death, Henry Oscar Houghton acquired Ticknor and Fields and, in 1880, formed Houghton Mifflin, which later merged with venerable Harcourt Publishing to form Houghton Mifflin Harcourt. HarperCollins purchased HMH's trade publishing business in 2021 and reestablished their storied lists and editorial team under the name Mariner Books.

Uniting the legacies of Houghton Mifflin, Harcourt Brace, and Ticknor and Fields, Mariner Books continues one of the great traditions in American bookselling. Our imprints have introduced an incomparable roster of enduring classics, including Hawthorne's *The Scarlet Letter*, Thoreau's *Walden*, Willa Cather's *O Pioneers!*, Virginia Woolf's *To the Lighthouse*, W.E.B. Du Bois's *Black Reconstruction*, J.R.R. Tolkien's *The Lord of the Rings*, Carson McCullers's *The Heart Is a Lonely Hunter*, Ann Petry's *The Narrows*, George Orwell's *Animal Farm* and *Nineteen Eighty-Four*, Rachel Carson's *Silent Spring*, Margaret Walker's *Jubilee*, Italo Calvino's *Invisible Cities*, Alice Walker's *The Color Purple*, Margaret Atwood's *The Handmaid's Tale*, Tim O'Brien's *The Things They Carried*, Philip Roth's *The Plot Against America*, Jhumpa Lahiri's *Interpreter of Maladies*, and many others. Today Mariner Books remains proudly committed to the craft of fine publishing established nearly two centuries ago at the Old Corner Bookstore.